POLITICAL AUTHORITY
AND PARTY SECRETARIES
IN POLAND 1975–1986

Soviet and East European Studies: 63

Editorial Board

Ronald Hill (*General editor*), Judy Batt, Michael Kaser,
Paul Lewis, Margot Light, Alastair McAuley,
James Riordan, Stephen White

Soviet and East European Studies

Series list continues on p. 341.

POLITICAL AUTHORITY AND PARTY SECRETARIES IN POLAND 1975–1986

PAUL G. LEWIS

The Open University

CAMBRIDGE UNIVERSITY PRESS

Cambridge
New York   New Rochelle   Melbourne   Sydney

Published by the Press Syndicate of the University of Cambridge
The Pitt Building, Trumpington Street, Cambridge CB2 1RP
32 East 57th Street, New York, NY 10022, USA
10 Stamford Road, Oakleigh, Melbourne 3166, Australia

© Cambridge University Press 1989

First published 1989

Printed in Great Britain at Redwood Burn Limited, Trowbridge, Wiltshire

British Library cataloguing in publication data

Lewis, Paul G. (Paul Geoffrey), *1945–*
Political authority and party secretaries
in Poland 1975–1986. – (Soviet and
East European studies).
1. Poland. Politics
I. Title   II. Series
320.9438

Library of Congress cataloging in publication data

Lewis, Paul G., 1945–
   Political authority and party secretaries in Poland 1975–1986 /
Paul G. Lewis.
      p.   cm. — (Soviet and East European studies)
Bibliography.
Includes index.
ISBN 0–521–36369–1
1. Polska Zjednoczona Partia Robotnicza.   2. Communism – Poland.
3. Power (Social sciences)   4. Poland – Politics and
government – 1945–   I. Title.   II. Series.
JN6769.A52L48   1989
324.2438'075'09 – dc19   88–23436 CIP

ISBN 0 521 36369 1

For Chantal, Nicholas and Simon

Such people were devoid of any authority, not because they had been
unlawfully deprived of it, but because they were no longer capable of
wielding it. They were hollow shells with their insides eaten out.

Stanisław Witkiewicz, Insatiability

No one can have faith in a party that will not believe in itself.

Stanisław Kania at the IV Plenum of
the PZPR CC, October 1981

Contents

Tables

Preface

Recent Polish politics is often characterised as having well-publicised spells of popular unrest, unexpected leadership change and heightened political drama, separated by longer periods of relative political stability, uncertain economic development and the generally normal operation of what we understand as the 'communist system'. This impression is not in itself misleading, but it does not promise much for a better understanding of the processes that have governed developments in communist Poland and it is unlikely to offer a solid basis for political analysis. For one thing, the periods of relatively pacific, 'normal' politics are those which have seen the growth of forces and have generated the pressures that have brought about the periods of accelerated change and heightened political drama. A more detached view of Polish politics, and one which seeks to contribute some form of political analysis or explanation, must combine the two kinds of political activity in its analysis and base itself on a broader view of political processes.

Further, the contrastive view underestimates the significant continuities that have spanned the different political periods, and the similarities in both the tasks that have faced strategic groups in communist Poland over the longer period and the nature of their responses to them. This has particular relevance to recent developments, when the structural continuities that ran through the Gierek regime, the Solidarity period and the military administration have frequently been ignored to the detriment of a full understanding of the political dynamics of recent Polish history. This study therefore directs attention to issues of political authority and the role of key elements in the apparatus of the Polish United Workers' Party (PZPR) from 1975 to 1986. It concentrates on the characteristics and activities of the secretaries heading the provincial party committees and on the role, structural location and performance of the committees over that period.

It is a major part of this argument that the staff and political organisation of the provincial committees form a critical portion of the party apparatus, which itself acts as the major determinant of the nature of party work, the degree of party leadership and its effectiveness in terms of the overall operation of the system. The account begins with the major institutional reorganisation introduced by Gierek in 1975 in consequence of which, it is argued, the role of the provincial committees and their secretaries was reduced and their position further weakened by the adoption of inappropriate party policies concerning the provincial organ. The level of staff turnover that accompanied the institutional reorganisation meant that extensive information on the characteristics of the secretaries became available. It suggests additional reasons for the ineffectiveness of party operations at provincial level, itself a major contribution to the failure of the Gierek leadership and the partial collapse of the regime in 1980.

The weakening of the provincial committees and the position of their secretaries coincided with a critical decline in the party's authority, a certain political retreat and the redefinition of its leading role. Indeed, it is argued that to a great extent the party's authority and its capacity effectively to perform a leading role is determined by the status and performance of the provincial committees and their officers. The changes in this area that followed Gierek's 1975 reform therefore had a critical effect on the party's authority and leadership capacity. It is important, nevertheless, to distinguish this from any threat to communist power and the erosion of the power base of communist rule in Poland. There were, in fact, few signs of the latter during the mid-1980 crisis and awareness of this fact within the party hierarchy – not least in the provincial apparatus – contributed to the wide-spread official reluctance to depart from existing patterns of political behaviour.

In the period immediately following the fall of Gierek there was little inclination throughout the country to develop new modes of party leadership in keeping with the policy of political renewal newly adopted by the central leadership. The conversion of the central authorities to a less dogmatic form of political leadership and some measure of reform had a relatively small effect on the party hierarchy and the approach taken to both local party members and the newly formed Solidarity union. This contributed to the more aggressive actions taken by the union and to the growing sense of conflict in political life. It is quite possible that the imperviousness of the party establishment to change was of little consequence for the central leadership and that its espousal of political renewal was largely a tactical move. Nevertheless, in keeping with the commitment to a political (that is, non-coercive) solution to the crisis, further concessions were made by the leadership in the face of dissatisfaction within the party rank and file about the little progress made in the area of inner-party democracy.

It was only after the Bydgoszcz crisis and apparent moves made by a hard-line faction – backed, it appeared, by much of the provincial apparatus – to seize the leadership and change the political course that a firmer commitment was made by the ruling group to renewal and more concrete steps taken within the party to achieve it. These included the calling of an Extraordinary Congress, promised at an early stage but its organisation much delayed, and the election of new party organs and leaders throughout the hierarchy. Change among provincial secretaries was extensive, and the differences in the characteristics of the secretaries elected under conditions of unprecedented inner-party democracy from those appointed under more normal procedures of central party control suggested how the reconstitution of the party leadership might serve to reestablish its authority. Extensive changes were also made in the central party organs. But the apparatus of full-time party employees was less affected by these changes. The continuing prominence of their role in political life, in association with that of the top party–state leadership whose approach and actions retained major ambiguities, made more difficult the resolution of the authority deficit that the extensive changes which had taken place within the party organisation suggested might occur.

Within the party leadership conflict continued and the political solution to the ongoing crisis, which the Kania leadership had remained committed to, became an increasingly unlikely prospect. The evidence suggests that influential parts of the communist establishment, including major sections of the party apparatus and the provincial organisations, placed a higher priority on maintaining the existing power base of the communist system and perpetuating conventional methods of party–state rule than on continuing with a policy involving some measure of political accommodation. To the extent that the redefinition of the party's leading role and the establishment of its political authority on a broader social base might have meant some qualification of its control over those power resources, it was clear that many of those in leading positions preferred to preserve their contested monopoly and identify themselves with the realities of communist power rather than with the promise of party leadership and the exercise of political authority.

These pressures moved the leadership steadily in the direction of the State of War and the reaffirmation of the considerable power resources that resided within the Polish party–state. Central party discipline was reimposed throughout the organisation. Even amongst those not identified with the party reform movement or associated with revisionist tendencies, this development was not welcomed without reservation. On the Central Committee some provincial secretaries were among the first to point out that not all the problems of the party were solvable by force and that the party should not neglect the process of establishing its authority by other means. These observations tend to confirm the close association of the provincial secretaries with this aspect of party rule and their sensitivity to the implications of party leadership.

Such qualms persisted and gained more publicity as the suspension of the State of War came under consideration, with both the effectiveness of party work and the low level of support for its activities continuing to cause much disquiet. The view that the apparatus had been responsible for many of the problems that contributed to the party's earlier loss of authority and its inability to regain it received some substantiation as military representatives intensified their efforts in the field of cadres policy and kept the apparatus under close scrutiny. Efforts to enhance party authority by gaining more support from the working class and involving it more closely in party activities bore little fruit, and the quality of party cadres has continued to be regarded as one of the main means by which the party might recover its political position and establish some new basis of political authority.

The account contained in this book ends with the party's X Congress convened in the summer of 1986 and the provincial conferences held throughout the country shortly afterwards. By this time, the position of the party and its leadership had been consolidated to some extent, but the party had certainly not established its 'leading role' or made good the authority deficit that had undermined its status in earlier years. The part it played in the political system continued to be a reduced one and there were signs that Poland's leaders were looking increasingly to other areas for the means to consolidate their rule. Although it lies outside the period covered in this study, it should be noted that a major new factor was introduced in this situation by the policies developed by Mikhail Gorbachev, particularly by the acceleration of *perestroika* announced at the Plenary Session of the Central Committee of the Communist Party of the Soviet Union (its ruling body) in January 1987. While its importance for the future development of the East European systems and their parties is evident, subsequent events have not yet made clear what the nature of its influence is likely to be. It is worth noting, though, that Gorbachev's proposals for the democratisation of the party and the reform of the CPSU's cadre policy indicate the international relevance of Poland's attempt at political renewal in 1980–81 which may, indeed, carry certain lessons for the leaders of other communist states.

Initial research on the Gierek reforms of 1975 began in 1979 and the study that has led to the production of this book has, like political life in Poland, passed through several phases since then. Many people have contributed to this process and I have benefited greatly from discussion of papers given in Britain, Australia and the United States, as well as the different meeting-places of the European Consortium for Political Research. Particular thanks for detailed criticism and encouragement are due to Ron Hill and Peter Frank, Michael Waller and Wiesława Surażska have also helped with their comments. The research committees of the Open University and its Faculty of Social Sciences have contributed with a number of grants over the years and have generally continued to be supportive of research during a period when teaching and research within British higher education have been placed under great strain, a state of affairs which unfortunately shows no sign of coming to an end.

Abbreviations

CKKP	Centralna Komisja Kontroli Partyjnej (Central Party Control Commission)
CKR	Centralna Komisja Rewizyjna (Central Auditing Commission)
CPSU	Communist Party of the Soviet Union
DiP	Doświadczenie i Przyszłość (Experience and the Future – discussion group)
KOR	Komitet Obrony Robotniczej (Workers' Defence Committee)
KPP	Komunistyczna Partia Polski (Polish Communist Party)
KW	Komitet Wojewódzki (Provincial Committee)
KZ	Komitet Zakładowy (Factory Committee)
MKS	Międzyzakładowy Komitet Strajkowy (Inter-factory Strike Committee)
MO	Milicja Obywatelska (Civil Militia)
MPA	Main Political Administration (of the army)
NIK	Najwyższa Izba Kontroli (Supreme Control Chamber)
NSZZ	Niezależny Samorządny Związek Zawodowy (Independent Self-Governing Trade Union)
PPR	Polska Partia Robotnicza (Polish Workers' Party)
PPS	Polska Partia Socjalistyczna (Polish Socialist Party)
PRON	Patriotyczny Ruch Odrodzenia Narodowego (Patriotic Movement for National Rebirth)
PZPR	Polska Zjednoczona Partia Robotnicza (Polish United Workers' Party)
ROMO	Rezerwa Ochotnicza Milicji Obywatelskiej (Voluntary Reserve of Civil Militia)
ROPP	Rejonowe Ośrodki Pracy Partyjnej (Regional Centres of Party Work)
RSFSR	Russian Soviet Federal Socialist Republic

WKKP   Wojewódzkie Komisje Kontroli Partyjnej (Provincial Party
        Control Commissions)
WKO   Wojewódzki Komitet Obrony (Provincial Defence
        Committee)
ZOMO   Zmotoryzowane Odwody Milicji Obywatelskiej
        (Motorised Units of Civil Militia)

1 Communist power and party authority in Poland

Polish experience and communist authority

The political history of modern Poland has been marked by a number of features that appear to distinguish its experience from that of its communist neighbours. It did not suffer the worst rigours of Stalinism in the fifties and has retained both a thriving Catholic Church and a high level of private land ownership in the agricultural sector; its political leadership has shown considerable instability and has proved to be susceptible to shifts in the popular mood and manifestations of public opposition; its economy, while capable of short bursts of growth, has not been able to sustain a balanced form of long-term development and has suffered the worst crisis yet seen in the European communist states. All this has often been ascribed to the unpopularity of the post-war regime and the consequent rejection of the Soviet-imposed political order – in short, to the weakness of communist power in Poland.

Although by no means wholly untrue, this view has had to be revised in the light of the pronouncement of a State of War in December 1981 and the reinforcement of the political order by means which were indeed unorthodox but which were by no means uncommunist in either inspiration or subsequent orientation. The sources of state power, it appeared, had been sapped neither by the conflicts of the Solidarity period nor by the confusion and disagreements that had served further to undermine the leading role of the PZPR (in English, Polish United Workers' Party). The pronouncement of the State of War and installation of a militarised regime demonstrated the difference between the power of the associated party–state apparatuses and the authority claimed to be inherent in party leadership. The distinction was only slightly blurred by the assumption of the party first secretary-ship by General Jaruzelski (already Minister of Defence and Prime

Minister) less than two months before the military initiative. It will be my argument, then, that the peculiarities of Polish political life have been associated less with the insufficiency of political power in communist Poland and more with the inability of the party leadership to acquire and exercise political authority.

Until the recent Polish developments, this distinction has not been clear and there was little incentive to emphasise the difference between party-state power (including that exercised through the military hierarchy and the police and security apparatuses) and the authoritative nature of party leadership, which is able to achieve its ends through inspiration, exhortation and generally non-coercive means. The dual nature of power in communist party-state systems, characterised by Politburo control over party organisation, government structure and military hierarchy, has served both to secure relatively effective communist rule and to demonstrate party leadership as the general embodiment of political authority. The pervasive importance of party membership and party office holding, centralised control of *nomenklatura* appointments, and the overlapping roles of party and state institutions similarly have helped to make such a sharp distinction impossible to draw and, in any case, tend to reduce its political significance.

To this extent party authority has been regarded as a relatively unproblematic aspect of political leadership and communist rule. It has either been seen as emanating from the fact of 'actually existing' Soviet hegemony over Eastern Europe and the inevitable dominance of the local communist party, or it has been considered to flow from the consolidation of the East European communist systems and the gradual accretion of some normative basis for communist rule. As Rose has put it, 'The longer a regime can remain in power, the more the turnover of generations works to its advantage', the East European countries in the late sixties, he considered, providing 'interesting tests of this hypothesis'.[1] Prevalent theoretical conceptions of political legitimacy and the apparent stability of the Soviet and associated systems have, notes Pakulski, 'led to increasingly frequent suggestions that it involves legitimate authority.'[2] Meyer, too, lists a number of factors serving to strengthen the authority of communist systems.[3] Major features of Marxist-Leninist ideology and conventional communist practice have acted to sustain the credibility of such observations.

According to the orthodox formulations of Marxism-Leninism the party claims powers of general leadership and reflects the belief in overall party supremacy. This has been the case regardless of the capacity of the party to exercise exclusive leadership and irrespective of the extent to which the claim has received social acceptance. The party was barely mentioned in the 1936 Soviet Constitution, although the mention it did receive was sufficient to assert its unqualified supremacy over all organisations of the 'working people, both public and state' (Article 126). In terms of political practice the leadership of the party is meant to be of a general rather than detailed kind, and while understood to be in charge of matters, the party and its personnel are not intended to become involved in routine administration and management. But it has been a persistent tendency for communist parties and their officers to become enmeshed in such kinds of activity, for the understandable reason that administrative and managerial structures rarely if ever work precisely as party leaders would wish. The principle of dual subordination, whereby the office holder within the communist state system is accountable to a formal superior for the specific performance of his duties and to a party body or official for the general success and tenor of his performance, is therefore a source of some confusion. The contradictory nature of the party's role is summed up in Tarkowski's statement that 'the party has the *right to interfere* in the activities of economic and administrative organisations' (emphasis added).[4] The persistence of this interference and the evident disquiet of party leaders that their staff get unnecessarily involved in administrative detail has led some analysts to conclude that the ambiguities implicit in such relations as those between party and state institutions constitute a major political problem.[5]

But this ambiguity can also be a source of political strength and a force working to sustain the authority of the party rather than to undermine it. The lack of clear, hard and fast rules determining behaviour and the fuzziness of the criteria adopted by party supervisors seem 'to provide a major constituent of the kind of "rationality" peculiar to' what Bauman calls 'partynomial rule'.[6] It is, according to Moore, one of the peculiarities of the communist system that there 'apparently exists a vested interest in confusion, and particularly confusion in the allocation of authority.'[7] A further benefit of this confusion has been the coalescence of the power of the party–state apparatuses with the authority of the party and the status accorded to it by virtue of its formal leading role. It helps to disguise the coercive basis of party–state power and underwrites party authority with the real power implicit in the operation of the diverse apparatuses of communist rule. At the same time, particularly in the contemporary period, there are forces which seek to dispel this confusion and resolve the ambiguity. One of the risks they carry is that clearer definition of the nature of the authority associated with party leadership shows the tenuousness of its base. Attempts to clarify authority may also prove, therefore, to be a destabilising factor.

Problems of communist authority

One factor that has served to redirect attention to problems of communist party authority, now somewhat distant in time but still a major background condition, is the restricted role of the security organs imposed after the death of Stalin and the search for new forms of political rule. An obvious consequence of this was the leadership's reduced reliance on coercion and the attempt to formulate a more positive mode of party leadership. In the Soviet Union at least, the full consequences of this change have taken some time to work themselves out. Thus it was in the Brezhnev years, wrote one observer, that there emerged an 'open disregard for law, coupled with an apparent decline in the fear of authority', although a major impetus to the process was the post-Stalin 'deterrorisation'.[8] With the political conflicts that broke out in several East European countries in the early post-Stalin period it was evident that the problems of communist authority and party leadership were more acute. In contrast to some commentators Gitelman, in 1970, detected 'an "authority crisis" confronting some Eastern European polities at present, and others in the foreseeable future'.[9] Involved in the crisis were a complex of factors: the declining rate of economic growth, increasing social differentiation, generation change, general lack of political development.

Such problems are also evident in Soviet society, although they have taken longer to take a more acute form. Nevertheless, problems of economic development were becoming more pronounced in the 1970s and increasing doubts were expressed about the effectiveness of party leadership. In 1981 at the XXVI CPSU Congress, Brezhnev himself agreed and affirmed that 'many shortcomings in economic activity are due to a lack of a smooth-working system of control and to armchair leadership'.[10] Subsequent action, particularly that taken by Andropov and Gorbachev, has demonstrated that the Soviet leadership has become more, rather than less preoccupied with the inadequacies of party authority and its lack of effectiveness. Apart from the more specific factors noted above, there are more general reasons why communist leaders should be paying more attention to their authority. As Nelson has put it, 'Without leadership authority, the power to rule will erode as the implementation of a ruler's policies will be difficult or impossible except through the inefficient and costly application of force.'[11] The irony is, however, that leaders' attempts to legitimate their rule by establishing diverse bases of popular support may raise questions about their claimed right to rule and act to undermine their authority. Nowhere was this clearer than in Poland where a range of strategies was pursued with consequences that were frankly disastrous.

But despite the growing importance of authority in communist systems, academic interest in its nature and prospects for development has been relatively limited. One exception has been Breslauer's study of Soviet politics in terms of Khrushchev and Brezhnev's strategies of authority-building. He sees the Soviet leader acting in two ways in the attempt to acquire authority: 'As problem-solver he attempts to forge policy programs that promise to further the goals of the post-Stalin era. As politician he attempts to create a sense of national élan, so as to increase the political establishment's confidence in his leadership ability'. Ineffective authority-building strategies are not necessarily politically fatal, but they do damage the leader to the extent that he fails 'to persuade influentials within the political establishment of his problem-solving competence and political indispensability.'[12] This conception of authority-building has certain limitations. It is concerned largely with elite politics and deals with the establishment of authority within the ruling group, a process of perhaps greater importance in the Soviet Union than in Eastern Europe where broader social groups have played a greater role in politics. It is, too, concerned essentially with the authority of individuals rather than that of the party and its capacity to exercise political leadership, the theme that has occupied our attention so far.

In the context of the elite politics discussed by Breslauer, authority-building denotes the process by which leaders seek to legitimise their policy programmes and demonstrate their competence or indispensability as leaders. In line with our discussion above it has emerged as a process of considerable importance in the post-Stalin period, when extensive use of the police apparatus is no longer used to keep the elite in order. The situation is somewhat more complicated when the broader social context is viewed. This is made clear in Rigby's description of an authority system as a 'particular pattern of legitimacy combined with a particular structure of power, the two being as closely intertwined as norm and expediency tend to be on all levels of social behaviour'.[13] The institutional character of the East European systems also exerts an influence here: 'the all-pervasive presence of the state makes for a range of pressures and constraints which cannot be classified as either coercion or consent'.[14] The bureaucratised nature of communist systems has prompted extensive reference to Weber's discussion of different forms of authority. The bulk of Weber's writings, though, were set down immediately prior to the formation of the first communist state and, while eminently suggestive in their allusion to different forms of rule, it is clear that none of his pure forms of authority capture the essence of political relations in communist societies. Instead of the meritocratic, technical criteria for recruitment and promotion characteristic of the bureaucratic type, communist procedures tend to emphasise political and ideological qualifications.[15] The typical structure of traditional authority, that of patrimonial rule 'involving a ruler and a personal administrative staff', in many ways recalls communist practice. Certainly during the Stalin period it could be argued that the source of the authority of the party official was not his office but 'the fact that his continuing to occupy the office . . . was a public mark of the Leader's favour'.[16] But practice here has changed since Stalin's death, and it is hardly possible to argue for a predominantly traditional basis to communist authority.

Bauman's solution to this problem is to develop a fourth notion of legitimation derived from neglected, earlier periods of Weber's work – that of partynomial authority, which is 'intimately attached to *Wertrationalität* (value-rationality).[17] But in terms of the more general social context this conception, too, meets several difficulties. It involves, for one thing, at least some acknowledgement by significant portions of the population of the validity of the party's claim to leadership in terms of future achievement and the construction of communism, and some legitimation on this basis. It is difficult to believe that this kind of belief is present to any significant extent or that it acts as a genuine basis for authority in contemporary Eastern Europe. It is the problems encountered in the attempt to link party leadership with any social values that have created major difficulties for the construction of party authority in Eastern Europe. Increasingly, party leadership is being justified in terms of instrumentality and negative argument rather than on the basis of any existing values or positive reasoning. But, in the understanding of many theorists, it is the latter features which characterise any solidly constituted political authority. '*Auctoritas*', states Friedrich, 'supplements a mere act of will by adding reasons to it', and Watt also emphasises that 'Reasons of some kind are associated with authority of every kind, though they may not always be good reasons.

To obey a command, we must have some reason for doing so, and this is true even when we turn out to have been obeying an impostor.'[18]

It is compliance involving consent and some rationally based agreement between rulers and ruled that characterise authority relations, and it is this that enabled Arendt to decribe authority as producing 'an obedience in which men retain their freedom'.[19] It is this kind of obedience that has often been lacking in Eastern Europe as has most obviously been demonstrated by the military interventions in East Germany, Hungary, Czechoslovakia and Poland. That is not to say that reasons for obedience and other grounds for compliance have been altogether lacking, but rather that they have not been strong enough to sustain the level or form of compliance required by East European rulers. Such reasons in Eastern Europe have been either relatively weak or have proved unconvincing in the light of experience. In their absence arguments based on the unyielding character of communist power have had to be used and the resilience of communist rule has had to be relied on to generate its own form of authority. To some extent this has not been unsuccessful. Referring to the building of the Berlin Wall and the lack of United States intervention in the Hungarian revolution, Meyer has claimed that 'the authority of communist regimes grew considerably after all hopes for an alternative that might have existed in the minds of some citizens had been dashed'.[20] Moore notes, on psychological grounds, that 'People are evidently inclined to grant legitimacy to anything that is or seems inevitable no matter how painful it may be. Otherwise the pain might be intolerable.'[21] Staniszkis, too, has described Poland's political life as a 'system legitimated mostly by a lack of alternatives'.[22]

But while such political facts have acted as potent inducements to quiescence and obedience they are not far removed from the exercise of power itself and are not really the same thing as acceptance of the reasons that underlie the establishment of a more genuine form of authority. For this reason, claims to technical competence and effectiveness, particularly with respect to economic development, have been prominent amongst East European leaders in the post-Stalin period. Apart from the obvious benefits of a materially satisfied population, party-imposed rewards and punishments, in Nelson's words, 'become rational when a regime exhibits competence'.[23] Competence, further, makes inequalities associated with the structure of power more acceptable within society: 'effectiveness, especially in services to the public, legitimates authority, and ineffectiveness makes the privileges of authority galling'.[24] This has had the effect of placing a strong political charge on economic performance and on those responsible for its administration – a factor by no means absent elsewhere. In a situation of weakly established political authority, though, this has given rise to numerous instabilities. Peabody's recognition, that 'In a system of well-established authority, men of great ability are less in demand', has proved to be highly relevant to Eastern Europe.[25] Kadar's skill has appeared to be a major factor in restoring the political order in Hungary and achieving some form of legitimacy, while Gierek's maladministration of the economy made a considerable contribution to his political demise and the public collapse of party authority in Poland.

State and authority in Poland

Recent developments in Polish political life have pushed to the fore conceptions of authority which make scant distinction between the imposition of state power and the exercise of political authority. It is, indeed, only sensible to recognise the close relationship between the two qualities in political context, and we have argued above that there is a deep-rooted and particularly close (if indistinct) relationship between the two in communist political systems. Nevertheless, particular attention has been paid to this link in some recent party writings in Poland. For example, it was opponents of socialism who maintained that 'strong authority should no longer exist under socialism'. It is officially recognised that 'coercion is characteristic of the authority of power, as is the conviction about the inevitability of power itself.' Moreover, 'power does not only not lose but even gains in authority when, under specific conditions, it acts using coercive means' – in a case, for example, when it liquidates an attack on the socialist system.[26] Such a view is not in itself particularly notable. It is interesting, however, to find it expressed in Jaruzelski's Poland which has had by force of circumstances to abandon the conventional conception of socialist authority flowing from an ill-defined notion of party leadership.

But throughout the period of communist rule in Poland, the idea of party authority has never been very distant from that of state power and the *raison d'état* that has been associated with the post-war settlement in Eastern Europe. Only for limited periods has it been realistically linked with ideas of consent and popular support, or with policies consistently applied to create such support. The weakness of such a basis for the exercise of party authority grew more pronounced through the years and during the successive leadership crises. At times it grew to be virtually indistinguishable from the threat of Soviet military intervention and, eventually, the contradiction involved in the attempt to base domestic party authority on external military power became overwhelming. As Stanisław Kania noted at the IV Plenum of the Central Committee in October 1981 (the meeting at which he was replaced as party leader by General Jaruzelski) 'the concept of *raison d'état*, although so vital to our political thought . . . can only signify inevitability, while we are really concerned with the great positive opportunity for a socialist Poland in a socialist community'.[27] Members of the leadership had not been slow to appeal to this well-established principle from the onset of the August crisis: Central Committee member Ryszard Wojna had threatened a further partition of Poland if free trade unions were recognised, while Mieczysław Rakowski (in less lurid tones) delivered a speech in the *Sejm* (parliament) which was reproduced in the paper he edited under the title, 'The Supreme Value – Our State'.[28]

The chequered history of the Polish state, and different views on the nature of its authority, thus served to play a major part in the set of ideas called on to establish and sustain the authority of the party in communist Poland. An important feature of the version of Polish history presented as part of this picture was the instability of the state and the consequent need for a strong state apparatus, under party leadership, in the contemporary period. There was some basis for this view. Founded towards the end of the first millennium, the Polish state gained in strength through to the twelfth century. Surviving the threats posed by the Teutonic Order and Tatar invasions, it became particularly prosperous in the fourteenth and fifteenth centuries, laying the basis for the impressive cultural and social development of the Renaissance period. But already part of this development had been achieved at the cost of monarchical concessions to the gentry and aristocracy. This, while proving no threat to state security for many decades and creating a climate of civil liberty and tolerance, was to prove fatal to the survival of state power in later centuries.

During the fourteenth and fifteenth centuries, in order to secure military aid and constitutional concessions, the Polish crown began to grant certain immunities from taxation, an early form of habeas corpus and an agreement to legislate in key areas only with the agreement of the nobles. With the growing grain boom in the Baltic area, economic factors combined with political privilege to encourage an untrammelled class development of the gentry. As a result of this conjuncture, Anderson argues, 'the early and abundant good fortune of the *szlachta* in a sense paralysed their capacity for constructive centralization in a later age.' As internal and external problems grew they defended their early gains with increasing disregard for national welfare. In the mid seventeenth century they achieved the notorious *liberum veto* whereby a single negative vote in the aristocratic parliament could counter any new legislation and 'paralyse the state'.[29] In a worsening international situation, Poland became increasingly unable to resist the influence and encroachments of its neighbours. In a series of partitions, Russia, Prussia and Austria succeeded in dismembering the country. As a result of the third partition in 1795 the Polish state ceased to exist and was not to reappear for a century and a quarter.

It was clearly the failure to develop a centralised modern state that played a large part in the sequence of developments that led to the disappearance of Poland as a territorial entity. Many of the libertarian and associated impulses within the gentry that had contributed to the demise of the Polish state were repeatedly harnessed in patriotic movements against the occupying forces of the foreign states. Patriotism and the rise of a modern Polish nationalism were thus restricted to actions against state organisation, whilst the growth of a national awareness amongst the peasantry and, towards the end of the nineteenth century, the growing working class took place in the absence of any state institutions that could claim to represent those ideals: 'the more patriotically inclined a Pole was, the greater was his hostility to the government and law of Austria, Prussia, and Russia. No matter what mental or real purposes a man may have had, there was a danger that by acting in accordance with law, "within the system", he was helping to keep Poland unfree.'[30] Thus Polish nationalism embodied a strong anti-state element and, it is often claimed, a generalised suspicion of state power and authority. Moreover, in terms of political techniques and the skills of government, Poles had no chance at all for sixty (in the case of the Austrian territories) or a hundred years (in that of the Russian) to participate in central parliamentary bodies. On this basis a certain Polish proclivity towards anarchy has been detected, and it is clear that there have not been favourable conditions for the development of habits of obedience to political authority.

Despite the undoubted strength of Polish nationalism it was due to a largely fortuitous combination of circumstances, the virtually simultaneous collapse of the three East–Central European empires towards the end of the First World War, that a Polish state reappeared in the twentieth century. But even with the reestablishment of the Polish state national sentiment could run counter to the consolidation of its authority: the first president of the independent state was assassinated within days of his election because the votes of non-ethnic Poles had been decisive in his election to that office. As approximately one third of the citizens of the inter-war republic were not of Polish nationality, conditions were not unfavourable for the development of such conflicts, and this was hardly conducive to the consolidation of political authority. But 'Polish anarchy' should not be exaggerated. During the Second World War an underground state was formed and run with an astonishing degree of effectiveness and success, given the unfavourable conditions of the Nazi occupation. In such a situation, the capacity of Poles for civic organisation and behaviour in accordance with the dictates of state authority proved inferior to none.

Party authority and national autonomy

Following the Second World War the problems of consolidating the new Polish state and establishing communist party authority were compounded by the parentage of both by the Soviet Union. The modern Polish state, territorially different from its pre-war predecessor due to its westward shift as part of the post-war settlement, clearly owed a great deal to the fact that the war ended with much of Eastern Europe occupied by Soviet military forces. Soviet sponsorship of the modern Polish state, though, came up against the deep-rooted conflicts that had existed between Poles and Russians. The Polish and Russian states had been in competition since the sixteenth century and the terminal decline of the former state in the eighteenth century had been closely related to the growth of Russian power, Russia in fact making the greatest territorial gains from the partitions of Poland. Russo-Polish antipathy was also fed by religious differences; the fact that the religions of the two most repressive and culturally aggressive partition powers (Russia and Prussia) were, respectively, Orthodoxy and Protestantism made it remarkably easy for the indigenous population to identify Roman Catholicism with Polish nationality. In assimilating such attitudes to its role the Church was following traditions established in the twelfth century when national integration had been threatened by internal divisions and early German tribal expansionism. In the absence of a nationally accepted monarch it had been the Church primate who had acted as head of state and maintained national unity.

The position was clearly not improved after the First World War when the newly independent Polish state now found itself faced with a

Russian communist order, whose adherence to Marxism-Leninism showed a commitment to principles fundamentally at odds with those of Catholicism. Indeed, as Ascherson points out, the religious factor remained of such importance that one major element in modern state-building was not accomplished before the war: 'it was to the Communists that it fell, after 1945, to build the first lay state in Polish history, nearly a hundred years behind most of the Catholic nations of the West'.[31] Thus, after the First World War, the prospects for Russo-Polish relations were hardly less bleak than in the eighteenth century. Open conflict was resumed with the Soviet invasion of Poland in 1920 and relations remained antagonistic until the Soviet reannexation of Eastern Poland in 1939, seventeen days after the German invasion from the west.

Not surprisingly, such conditions did not favour the development of a strong communist party or the influence of the communist movement within Polish society. Moreover, the party was made illegal in early 1919, a few weeks after the proclamation of independence, and remained so throughout the period of the inter-war republic. Neither was the adoption of a policy against the establishment of an independent (bourgeois) Poland, formulated by Rosa Luxemburg, destined to win popular support once independence had been regained. The Soviet invasion of Poland in 1920, particularly when it did not remain limited to the recuperation of Polish-occupied Ukrainian territories, also weakened the position of the communist party. Further blows were offered by virtue of its involvement in internal Soviet politics and the support extended to Trotsky against the triumvirate of Stalin, Zinoviev and Kamenev in 1923. Its position was not helped by the adoption of the Moscow line in supporting the Pilsudski *coup d'état* of 1926, which introduced an authoritarian regime verging on fascism. Because of its own strategic miscalculations and its close involvement with internal Soviet politics, quite apart from the problems created by its acting as a clandestine organisation, the party did not extend its influence in Polish political life.

But the weakness of the party within the pre-war state should not be overestimated. While limited in terms of general influence, it could count on certain areas of support. At the time of independence, claimed Isaac Deutscher (himself a member of the Polish Communist Party, KPP, until 1932), the 'influence of the Polish CP over the working classes in the main industrial centers was certainly not smaller than that of the reformist and "patriotic" PPS (socialist party)'.[32] In the mid-thirties, writes one modern historian, according to the assessment made by the Ministry of Internal Affairs and provincial governors, the party 'was a genuine opponent to be taken seriously. It was, after all, the strongest of the illegal communist parties in Europe, commanding support among all social classes.'[33] The growing authoritarianism of the regime in the late thirties caused considerable political opposition. Nevertheless, the close Soviet connection proved fatal to the KPP. In 1938 the Polish party was dissolved by Moscow and, according to Deutscher, the passivity with which the decision was accepted was due to the 'moral corrosion to which Stalinism had for so many years exposed Polish Communism'.[34] Political misjudgments, Comintern errors and the unfortunate involvement in Stalin's machinations against Trotsky had all combined to weaken the position of the pre-war party also in relations with the Soviet leadership and eventually led to its annihilation. The Molotov–Ribbentrop pact of 1939 finally destroyed any remaining chances of maintaining a Soviet-oriented political movement in Poland.

The Nazi invasion of the Soviet Union in 1941, however, could not fail to change the picture. Poles and Soviet citizens formed part of the joint forces fighting against the Axis, although it soon became clear that Polish interests and demands would be readily sacrificed by the Allies to those of Poland's more powerful neighbour. The experiences of Poles during the Second World War strongly influenced their views of the post-war situation. Unlike Hungary, Romania and Bulgaria, Poland did not choose any form of alliance with Nazi Germany, whilst it had been the first nation to engage with German troops in 1939. Its resistance forces were large and well-organised although almost wholly non-communist. The experience of the war left the Poles with no feelings of complicity in the Nazi domination of the continent and with a record of anti-Nazi resistance far stronger than that, for example, of Czechoslovakia. They also felt aggrieved by the war-time actions of the Soviet Union, which included the murder of a substantial part of the Polish officer corps at Katyn and Soviet acquiescence in the Nazi quelling of the Warsaw uprising in 1944.

As a result of the Allied victory over Germany, the Soviet Union gained significant territorial and political advantages which could not fail to be partially at the expense of the Polish state. 'Poland' was physically shifted some two hundred kilometres to the west and its political system was left under the close influence of the Soviet Union. Poles could hardly feel that they were fully sharing in the fruits of the Allied victory. The Yalta agreement and, more significantly, the fact that the Soviet armed forces extended their influence as far as the Elbe meant that the Soviet leadership was now empowered to determine the political fate of Poland. There is, in fact, considerable evidence that a Soviet-dominated Poland was Stalin's major priority from quite early on in the war and that he had briefed himself extremely well in order to achieve this aim.[35] In view of the historic development of Russo-Polish relations, as well as the particular experiences of Poland during the war, the newly resurrected communist, or workers', party (PPR) which was to play the leading political role in the new regime was not one that was likely to have much authority in the eyes of the Polish population. If, as Cochran argues, authority is best understood 'to depend upon community and right' and the 'genesis of authority in the shared values of a community suggests authority's connection with tradition', we can clearly see why the Polish party was so weak in this respect.[36] The recent war had strengthened the shared values of the Polish national community, while centuries of Russo-Polish antagonism had demonstrated the distinctiveness of the Polish national tradition. The imposition of a strong Soviet influence could not be accommodated in terms of authority with the aspirations of the Polish national community and its desire for autonomy.

Lacking popular support and with little social acceptance of the legitimacy of communist rule, the establishment of a party-dominated state in Poland necessarily involved considerable political manipulation and coercion. There were developments that contributed to the acceptance of the regime following war-time occupation – the fact of peace itself and the expulsion of practically all Germans from Polish territory, the rapid and rather successful economic recovery, the implementation of a comprehensive land reform. All this, however, took place between 1944 and 1948, before the eradication of political opposition and the establishment of the full-blown party–state. But it appeared that the rapid imposition of communist rule in Poland was a clear priority of Stalin's from the outset, unlike the cases of Czechoslovakia and Hungary where he had intended the establishment of the communist state to be part of a gradual process.[37] Further, in Czechoslovakia the Moscow-based communist group had aimed to set themselves at the head of a mass movement on their return to the country and believed that they 'could win popular confidence under the banner of national independence'.[38] Such aspirations were barely conceivable in Poland, although Gomułka and many of his colleagues did believe in the possibility of a 'Polish road to socialism' which could have proved more acceptable to the Poles. It is, doubtful however, that this conception ever fitted in with Stalin's plans.

The neutralisation of Polish forces was an immediate task of Soviet forces as they moved across the country. Soldiers of the Home Army resistance (*Armia Krajowa*), who had cooperated with the Soviet Army in liberating such cities as Vilno and Lvov, were immediately disarmed and many arrested or deported to the Soviet Union. Members of the (non-communist) Council of National Unity were invited to Moscow for talks in the spring of 1945. There they were arrested and sentenced, many (including the commander of the Home Army) dying in captivity.[39] According to one account, an effective military rule was established which lasted for the first ten years of the existence of the People's Republic.[40] The extent to which the imposition of communist rule was resisted by force or military means and can therefore be described as a civil war is open to some doubt. As a further aspect of the *raison d'état* argument, much was made of the conflict and the casualties it entailed during 1981 and particularly, by the Jaruzelski leadership, around the period of the introduction of the State of War. A total of some thirty thousand deaths was generally referred to as having occurred in this action between 1944 and 1948. Precise numbers have been difficult to establish, but it is clear that casualties were initially underestimated (in order to minimise the degree of opposition to communist rule) and then overestimated (to demonstrate the costs and danger involved in resisting party–state power). A more likely scale of losses would be around twenty thousand, which is itself high enough to reflect the fact that 'with the possible exception of wartime Yugoslavia, no East European country experienced this kind of internecine warfare'.[41] Some views, however, are more inclined to the argument that this was attributable not so much to the waging of a civil war as to the imposition of a system of terror and repression.[42]

A particularly important part in the process of consolidating power was played by the security apparatus and the military counter-intelligence department; although ostensibly a national agency Poles themselves made up only 15% of the staff of the latter.[43] The Polish reputation for ungovernability and historic problems in sustaining a stable state structure were also played on during this time. The notorious Kielce pogrom of 1946 appears to have occurred under the patronage of the security organs in an attempt to strengthen belief in the need for a strong communist power within the state.[44] It has been described by Ascherson as the 'last "classic" pogrom in European history', although he later expressed his dissatisfaction with that account of the political situation surrounding the event.[45] Developments following 1944 thus suggest that communist power was rigorously imposed by a variety of means and that the minimal level of party authority was not a major impediment to the Soviet-sponsored political transformation. This is not to say that the weakness of party authority did not leave its mark on Polish political practice and the form of rule adopted by the communist leadership.

The ruling group attempted to mitigate the lack of legitimacy of the communist state by restraining the totalitarian drive that gained intensity in Eastern Europe in the early fifties: there were no showtrials or executions of disgraced communist leaders despite apparent pressure in that direction from Moscow.[46] Poland's agriculture remained largely uncollectivised and a 'peasant party' was retained which had somewhat greater autonomy than equivalent organisations in Bulgaria, the GDR or Czechoslovakia. Treatment of the Polish Church was relatively restrained, although the Polish primate, Cardinal Wyszynski, was interned from 1953. But while Polish society was terrorised to a lesser extent than other East European countries, this was hardly in itself a source of satisfaction to the Polish population and did not generate support for the party and its rulers. The authority of the party remained low and was put under further strain following the death of Stalin.

Gomułka: from popular support to political weakness

From 1953 in Poland, as elsewhere in Eastern Europe, certain measures were taken to reduce the weight of party dictatorship and buttress its authority by seeking sources of popular support. The powers of the secret police were reduced, the attempt to collectivise agriculture by force virtually abandoned, and the Church was permitted a little more freedom. But by 1956 elite uncertainty and popular unrest were growing. In June 1956 workers demonstrated on the streets of Poznań and troops were called out to restore order. Over seventy people were killed in the ensuing conflict. After Poznań it was clear to all in the leadership that significant changes in party rule would have to take place if the party were to maintain its position and extensive conflict were to be avoided. The solution centred on the person of Władysław Gomułka who, though disgraced and jailed for treason following his removal from the leadership in 1948 had, unlike some other East European leaders, escaped execution. The possibility of his playing a positive role in the crisis after his release was recognised in April 1956. Suggestions that he return to active political life were first made in June, shortly before the events in Poznań.

Proposals that he rejoin the leadership were originally made in July by what has generally been called the Natolin or Stalinist faction, in conjunction with a number of markedly illiberal proposals – including closer ties with the Soviet Union, stricter press censorship and a limitation on the number of Jews in leading public posts. The inclusion of Gomułka was rejected as excessively provocative to Soviet interests, though, by those who saw some need for a more extensive reform of the political system. Eventually, in early October, both Ochab (the first secretary of the party endorsed earlier in the year by Khrushchev for his solidly anti-Gomułka views) and the Prime Minister, Cyrankiewicz, accepted the need to include Gomułka in the leadership. They, too, had become convinced that a sharp break with the past – or at least the appearance of one – was necessary if the regime was to survive and the authority of the party and its leadership to be enhanced. Due to his unique personal history Gomułka was able to act as the expression of diverse and conflicting claims and enabled the leadership to cope with the strains of the early post-Stalin period, even if his return as leader did not involve any real attempt to reconcile those claims or produce a lasting resolution of the crisis.

Gomułka himself did not identify closely with either of the contending groups. He disliked the Soviet leanings and 'apparent political incompetence' of the Natolin group.[47] The group convinced of the need for more thorough-going change (Puławy') were in fact largely representative of the old Stalinist elite who had earlier been implicated in the disgrace of Gomułka for his right-wing, nationalist deviation. Relatively isolated within the leadership, though, Gomułka received enormous popular support for his views on what Poles hoped would be a more nationally oriented, democratic form of socialism. This level of support facilitated his reinstallation as first secretary and impressed the need to accept the leadership changes on the Soviet ruling group. But it soon became clear that the Polish leadership did not intend to pursue the kind of political reforms sought by many Poles, including those in the party rank and file. A sharp attack on party 'revisionists' was launched and many of the changes made in late 1956 were reversed in a matter of months.[48] Gomułka soon made a series of leadership appointments from the ranks of Natolin supporters. The regime survived and appeared to be strengthened, but party authority was not really placed on a firmer base.

The nationalist credentials of Gomułka's version of communism did not have much greater impact than his temporary coalescence with reformist forces. The withdrawal of Soviet troops, one of the apparent gains of the 'Polish October', was soon followed by the conclusion of a new agreement concerning the stationing of Soviet forces on Polish territory. According to Zambrowski, an influential CC secretary in the early fifties, Gomułka's perception of the political realities of the situation reinforced his conviction that personal popularity was not a sufficient basis for communist rule in Poland. Certainly, his trajectory from enforced political retirement to sudden and rapturous popularity in October 1956 involved extensive public misperceptions regarding his degree of nationalism, commitment to party reform or liberalisation, and general departure from communist orthodoxy. He was surely correct in deciding that it would be unwise to set much store on personal popularity in that situation, and thus remained convinced that it would be the power apparatus, particularly the security organs and the army, that was of prime importance for his political position.[49] This accords with his reported view, from the same period, that in Poland 'the party is too weak to govern democratically'.[50]

Gomułka's return to power brought about little change in the overall position of the party and had few institutional repercussions. A quantitative study of the rate of turnover in CC membership (the extent to which those elected on to the Committee retained their position up to and during the next Congress) shows a 'most interesting, and somewhat unexpected' stability between 1954 and 1959, a finding that contrasts with the marked changes in personnel at the top of the hierarchy.[51] Poland, in fact, showed the lowest rate of turnover amongst CC members in Eastern Europe until 1968, a fact that seems to corroborate Ascherson's view that while the impact of Stalinism on Poland was more muted than elsewhere in Eastern Europe, its influence was more pernicious as no effective deStalinisation took place.[52] The upsurge of support for Gomułka that took place during the Polish October was not used to bring about any lasting change in the nature of party rule and did not, therefore, significantly alter the nature of party authority.

Some changes did occur as a result of the deStalinising policies of the 1953–56 period. The role of the security organs was reduced and they were placed under firmer party control. A more tolerant attitude was taken towards the Church, the peasantry and, for a time, some manifestations of industrial democracy. Soviet economic demands were reduced and economic performance picked up considerably in the late fifties. But much of the progress was short-lived and the changes were not sufficient to alter the overall Polish perception of communist rule, that it was an unsatisfactory and ill-disguised form of Soviet domination. In the absence of alternative sources of authority, party rule could only be justified in terms of the realities of power in Eastern Europe and of *raison d'état*. Being cast in terms of existing power arrangements, such arguments were hardly capable of augmenting or expanding communist power in Poland and were not able to substitute for it by establishing a political *authority*. But, in contrast to the nineteenth century or the Nazi occupation, communist rule was at least claimed to be able to guarantee the existence of a Polish state, regardless of the actual nature of that state. For much of the period of Gomułka's rule this argument gained some support from the fact that West Germany had refused to agree with the Polish leadership on the post-war borders of the two countries. In December 1970, a little more than two weeks before the workers' revolt, Gomułka signed the treaty which guaranteed Poland's post-war frontier. Sensible move though this was, it greatly weakened the idea of a revanchist Germany whose designs on Polish territory necessitated close alliance and friendship with the Soviet Union. The strong negative factor of an aggressive Germany, which had helped considerably to underpin party authority, had perforce to be compensated for by a stronger emphasis on the fraternal internationalist outlook of the Soviet Union, a far less convincing image for the Poles.

Gomułka's period of rule was therefore one of overall disappointment for the Poles and one which did nothing to enhance the authority of the party and its rule. The hopes of party reform and political change that had accompanied his return to power in 1956 were rapidly dissipated, general conservatism and the pursuit of short-sighted policies in the economy brought poor results which resulted in Polish workers receiving the lowest wage increases throughout Eastern Europe in the sixties, the value of the Soviet 'guarantee' of Polish statehood came in the end to have little meaning at all. It was not surprising, therefore, that in the late sixties Gitelman found the Polish regime to be 'among the least authoritative in Eastern Europe', its competitor in this negative race being the recently crushed and invaded Czechoslovakia.[53] Gomułka's successor, Edward Gierek, found it necessary to adopt a radically different approach.

From Gierek's 'new style' to authority crisis

Faced with this task Gierek adopted a brisk, efficient-looking style that contrasted with Gomułka's dour, puritanical outlook of the late sixties.[54] The change was well received in the West, where optimistic predictions of the effects of Gierek's rule appeared even towards the end of the seventies.[55] Other observers were more circumspect and showed greater awareness of the costs of his approach.[56] At an early stage he took steps to enhance leadership authority by presenting a new public image. Together with the relaxed, confident style was the attempt to promote the image of the party leadership as the natural power-holders in Poland: 'one of the most striking features of Gierek's policy has been his persistent effort to legitimize the position of the party as a product of native radical tradition and a permanent feature of the Polish political landscape'.[57] This was associated with greater publicity for traditional themes from Polish history (selected, of course, with due care) and such decisions as that to rebuild the Royal Castle in Warsaw. Concerted attempts were made to improve relations with the Church. Efforts were also taken with the mass media: Gierek presented himself as one who could and would establish a rapport with the people, and particularly the working class. Television programmes were livened up and an impromptu question and answer programme with public figures was transmitted for a certain period. Formal censorship was supposed to have been withdrawn from some publications, although self-censorship eliminated any political dangers this might have involved.

Particularly important was the new approach to the economy and it was in this area that most was expected of the new leadership. It gained momentum in 1972 and, according to Brus, soon became the 'main source of political legitimacy of the new leadership'.[58] Decisions were quickly taken in 1971 to improve relations with private agricultural producers, and plans for a radical overhaul of the system of economic management and administration were announced. A programme for the rapid modernisation and expansion of Polish industry was drawn up. The economy was to be run with a far greater degree of competence and dynamism. The new approach involved more trade and stronger links with the developed capitalist countries, stressing in the initial stage the import of advanced technology and with increasing use being made of foreign credit facilities. In this sphere particularly, Gierek presented an image of efficiency and modernity which promoted the elevation of living standards in Poland closer to those of the developed industrial nations. Here there were undoubted gains. Official statistics show a 42% rise in the average real wage paid to employees in the socialised economy between 1970 and 1975.[59] After this date, though, the rate of increase fell off sharply and moved into absolute decline before the end of the decade. In retrospect it is easy to see the proclaimed efficiency of the Gierek approach very much as an illusion with little substance.

A major cause of the collapse of Gierek's economic strategy was the rejection in early 1972 of a plan for 'comprehensive reform to be introduced simultaneously in all basic elements'. The comprehensiveness of any reform was crucial, as partial measures were ineffective and counter-productive. More important to Gierek, according to Brus, was the intention of 'giving the population the *impression* that a new era was beginning politically' (emphasis added).[60] A major problem was the shaky basis of Gierek's power as party leader. The ruling group was left 'without the will or the ability to impose unpopular economic reforms'.[61] The consequence was that the leadership was 'concerned more with mediation between different groups within the governing elite than with developing its own distinct strategy of economic growth'.[62] The foundations of Poland's economic growth in the early seventies were, then, very insecure. The expansion of industrial output and plant, and the rise in people's living standards, were closely linked with the level of Poland's international debt. The onset of the energy crisis and the international economic recession of the mid-seventies were a considerable blow to the Polish project, both because of the resulting inflation and rise in interest rates and because it had been hoped to start repaying Poland's debts by increasing exports to the West. But the external situation cannot really explain the mess the Polish economy fell into. Apart from the refusal to countenance significant economic reform there were other domestic failings. Many foreign imports were ill-considered and not cost-effective in the first place; much of the industrial development was not planned or centrally coordinated; inflation was a major feature of the Polish economy from the early seventies, and the international debt exceeded reasonable levels as early as 1973 or 1974. If rapid economic development was undertaken as a genuine attempt to enhance party authority by demonstrating the economic skills of the leadership and its ability to create a modern consumer society, then all it did – as became fatally evident after 1975 – was to lay bare its irresponsibility and lack of economic competence. Gierek was not successful in developing the economy and his strategy failed to enhance leadership authority, while that of the party was fatally weakened.

As well as general economic reform, there had also been no moves to improve market stability by increasing the prices of foodstuffs: Gomułka's price rises had been withdrawn in early 1971 and the whole issue quietly shelved until 1976. In June of that year price rises were announced as brusquely as they had been in 1970 with very similar results, notably in Radom and the Ursus industrial centre. This time they were swiftly withdrawn and the leadership was left to nurse its defeat. Later that year an emergency 'economic manoeuvre' was introduced to cut back on investment in order to achieve a reduction in the foreign debt, rein in the increase in domestic demand and help secure stability on the market. It was to enable investment resources to be transferred to favour production directly for the market, increase the supply of foodstuffs and help provide more housing – all areas crucially important for the satisfaction of popular demands. In this, too, party leadership was inadequate to secure the economic aims: state bodies were not amenable to party influence and many important decisions were determined by local units beyond central control.[63] The authority of the party and its leadership was not sufficient to exert discipline over the economic administration and was increasingly sapped by repeated failure. The leadership showed a surprising inability to put the principles of democratic centralism into operation; particularly serious was the rampant material exploitation of elite status and the corruption of the *nomenklatura* principle.[64] This further contributed to the tendencies to disintegration within the elite and the collapse of Gierek's ruling group.[65]

Yet structural change and a sharper definition of institutional powers and functions had taken a leading place in the rhetoric of Gierek's new approach. Considerable attention had been paid to the nature of party leadership and major steps taken to strengthen the power of central party organs. In ideological terms Gierek identified the ambiguity discussed above concerning the role of the party and the nature of party leadership. He argued for the stricter demarcation of the functions of party and state, and for an end to the doubling of their activities: 'the party should lead and the government should govern'. But, as argued above, though rather messy and imprecise, the dual subordination of government officials sustained the practice of party leadership and contributed to some realistic notion of party authority. Gierek, however, launched a series of organisational changes which appeared to have an effect opposite to that intended. With respect to the network of People's Councils the executive arm was separated from the legislative–representative elements in the government structure and strengthened by being placed under the direction of officials occupying the newly created post of chief administrator. The formally representative bodies were then placed under the charge of the local party first secretary in order to facilitate their function as agencies of 'social control'.[66] In fact the opposite result was achieved and, as a result of the changes, Polish administrators were probably less accountable to representatives of the community than those in any other East European country.[67]

In a second reform the existing twenty-two provincial units, consisting of the five largest cities together with the major units of territorial administration, were abolished and their place taken by forty-nine smaller provincial units. While, naturally, the changes were described as democratic and claimed to have a decentralising effect, the thrust of Gierek's policy here too was a decidedly centralising one. He intended particularly to increase central party control over the national organisation. The large old provincial party committees had played an important part in political skirmishes within the party – Gierek himself had been first secretary of the Katowice provincial committee since 1957 and had used his position to further his career very successfully during the Gomułka period – and the composition of the Central Committee elected at the 1968 Congress had marked a decisive shift of power to the provinces.[68] The establishment of effective central control over the middle ranks of the party apparatus had been a particular problem for Gomułka and it was to avoid this problem that Gierek's initiative was largely aimed.[69] As well as reducing the power of individual provincial party committees the reorganisation gave considerable scope for effecting a change in party personnel and getting rid of unwanted officials. Apart from those of dubious talents this was also an opportunity to dispose of former Gomułkaite antagonists.[70] But while making central control more effective it also brought about a general diminution of local party authority and reduced its influence over government and industry.[71]

In some ways Gierek's reorganisation could be seen as placing the Polish party–state in a considerably stronger position in relation to Polish society than had previously been the case.[72] During this period, too, the organisation and position of the police was strengthened; while this appears to have been a general tendency within Eastern Europe during the seventies it has been suggested that in Poland they constituted a 'new independent political force' which reflected the changing position of the political elite as a whole in its relation with society.[73] On balance the period saw an enhancement of party–state power over Polish society, but the implications for the position of the party leadership and its authority were more negative. The attempt to redefine the functions of party and state and reformulate the conception of party leadership had mixed consequences. As ex-minister Bieńkowski pointed out, there was really no way in which the Polish party could be seen as a 'leading' or 'directing' force in the strict sense of the terms, and its political role had been limited since 1956 to that of a governmental force (prior to that it did not really have an autonomous role at all).[74]

While the influence of local party organs had been curtailed in the economic sphere, this by no means reflected any significant reduction in party interference overall. Judgments on the failure of the economy towards the end of the decade were unanimous that its causes lay with the political system and that the party domination of economic processes played a major part in this.[75] It was argued in the DiP (Experience and the Future – discussion group) report that it was essential to separate the party organisationally from the administrative and economic apparatus: it should be a 'corner-stone of the contemporary Polish system' that party leadership should be exercised only by constitutional means, through its members' participation in representative bodies rather than by methods of direct organisational control.[76] By these means the party as an institution could prevent itself being blamed for all economic shortcomings and for the numerous problems which it never had the capacity to deal with.

The role of the central party organs had in fact developed in quite the other direction under Gierek, despite his emphatic redefinition of party leadership at the beginning of the decade. The Politburo not only took over the policy-making functions but also became the sole decision-making body for the economy: 'The distribution of roles to be played in the political system by the party's top executive body and the top-level state executive body – so strongly declared at the beginning of the 1970s – soon practically disappeared.'[77] The consequences of this for the authority of the party were clearly evident for one Polish political scientist: involvement in the operational decision-making process, 'as past experience has proved, weakens the policy-making capacity of the party . . . When the Communist Party loses initiative in this field, it is then losing its sense of vision and its capacity to shape attractive programs that would mobilize people and motivate their economic and other public activities'.[78] The evaporation of the party's capacity to perform a leading role was so evident by 1980 that pointed comments were appearing in the party press (with, of course, appropriate references to Lenin): the party had the choice of dominating the state apparatus or submitting to the influences generated by it and thus becoming subject to bureaucratisation. That danger could not be avoided if the party substituted itself for the government and failed to exercise the due level of control.[79]

By this stage, it was clear that Gierek's new style of political rule had failed on several counts, and that his drive to enhance party leadership and thus raise its authority had had the opposite effect. It is reasonable to claim that in 1976, following the Radom and Ursus demonstrations and the leadership retreat, the regime entered a period of outright authority crisis. For a few years relations between the leadership and the mass of the ruled were in a state of unstable equilibrium: 'the great majority of our society neither revolts against the authorities nor does it cooperate with them'.[80] Reykowski, a leading Polish psychologist and Academician, later spelt out the elements involved in the collapse of political authority: the worsening economic situation deprived the leadership of the capacity to reward social groups and society felt it could only lose further in the future; while the leadership could still curb the activities of intellectuals it had lost this capacity with regard to the workers who now realised they could exert effective pressure against the leadership; wide-spread belief in leadership incompetence and doubts concerning their level of intelligence; lack of belief in the justice of the legal structure caused by the authorities' disregard for the law themselves. The only aspect of authority that retained any force was the 'conviction in the inevitability of the existing form of power', and the apparent fact that most believed that 'such a state corresponded to Polish interests'.[81]

The authority of the party and its leadership was therefore reduced to the barest elements of *raison d'état* – although Reykowski's statement clearly overstates the degree of effectiveness of this argument within Polish society. Even the principle of *raison d'état* had become seriously attentuated under Gierek. Wolicki has pointed out that in the immediate post-1956 period the principle for Gomułka had been one that 'had determined the limits of the communists' national role, but not its essence'; this he contrasted with the Gierek conception, where it came to be seen as the sole point of intellectual contact between society and the leadership.[82] In this sense, *raison d'état* simply came to reflect the conflict between the interests and orientations of society and that of the leadership under Gierek. This reflected the attenuation of the principle in providing any kind of basis for party authority. This was not just the fault of the Polish regime. The stricter conception and application of the Brezhnev doctrine also played a part in the seventies. As a result of the combination of domestic and international pressures, the pro-Soviet sentiments of the Polish leadership received stronger expression and reached 'levels of servility unknown since Stalinism. The effect on the population was probably the reverse of what was intended'.[83] Thus, following the failure of the attempt to reestablish leadership and party authority by demonstrating competence, even the base-line notion of party authority as emanating from the inevitability of communist rule in Poland (although, as we have suggested, this was hardly a valid basis for authority but rather a simple expression of power and brute force) also became distorted and carried less conviction.

Political authority and provincial secretaries

Competence and the effectiveness of political rule and party leadership have, as we have noted above, been closely associated by many theorists with the process whereby political authority is established. Conversely, the lack of competence and ineffective rule served to destroy the authority of the Gierek regime in Poland. The notion of 'party authority' is a general one, however, and particular elements in the party organisation may be understood to play an especially important role in the establishment or otherwise of political authority. In view of the centralised character of communist systems, the top leadership will of course play one of the leading roles. But the demonstration of competence and establishment of effectiveness will depend not only on the decisions taken by central leadership but also on how and the degree to which such decisions are implemented. To the extent that authority is concerned with effectiveness, it may be argued that communist party authority is determined not so much by the rhetoric of and decisions taken by central leadership, as by the nature and activity of intermediate party officials, notably the secretaries heading provincial party committees and their apparatus. In analysing the fate of party authority under Gierek and subsequent political developments, we will pay particular attention to the nature of the provincial party apparatus and its leading officials.

Some mention of the structural changes made in the party organisation has already been made in this chapter. The nature of these changes and their effects have been discussed elsewhere.[84] In succeeding chapters therefore, we will examine the qualifications and experience of the staff heading the provincial committees. As some analysis of equivalent staff in other communist systems has already been conducted, this will enable us to place Polish developments in comparative perspective and identify the particular characteristics of the Polish situation. We shall then outline the role allotted to the provincial party organisation following the changes made by Gierek in the middle of the seventies and establish the consequences of their operation for the fate of party authority in Poland.

With the collapse of the Gierek regime and the evident failure of party leadership, the reconstituted party authorities sought to reclaim control and assert their primacy by establishing new bases of authority. Their efforts centred on a conception of party 'renewal' (*odnowa*) which involved the recasting of party activity and the reformulation of party leadership. It brought under critical scrutiny the status and power of leading party officials and the role of the party apparatus which created the ground for extensive political conflict within the party organisation as it brought into question the interests and orientation of those who had formed the core of the established party–state system, but who had brought the principle and practice of party leadership to a state of virtual collapse. To this extent provincial party secretaries continued to play a central political role in the post-August developments, as it was both in the regional party organisations and within the Central Committee that these conflicts were fought. For most of this time, until the Extraordinary Party Congress of July 1981, regional party staff and apparatus workers played an important part within the Central Committee and were well placed to defend their position.

Insofar as established party officials attempted to safeguard their position and protect the existing bases of party–state power, they undermined the efforts of the Kania leadership to establish new forms of party authority in order to resolve the Polish political crisis. Their position was closely associated with the interests and preferences of the Soviet authorities, although it is naturally very difficult to establish the precise nature of that relationship. Both, however, were clearly suspicious of certain elements of Kania's strategy for reestablishing party authority and of their implications for the established principles of communist political practice. Some resolution of these conflicts as well as the uncertainties surrounding the prospects for party–state power in Poland was found in the pronouncement of the State of War and the militarisation of the political system. This, however, was clearly unhelpful to the attempt to restore party authority and left a number of questions concerning the nature and capacity of party leadership unresolved. It also left uncertain the precise role of the party organisation and the status of the provincial party secretary. State power and party authority have thus remained divorced in communist Poland and their changing fortunes have, as we hope to demonstrate, been closely associated with the changing position of the provincial party secretaries since the major changes introduced by Gierek in the mid-seventies.

2 Provincial party secretaries: Polish officials in comparative perspective

Provincial party organs and political authority

The close connection between the effectiveness of political rule and the competence of rulers, and the establishment of authority in communist systems directs attention to the mechanisms of political rule and, in particular, to the role of the intermediate party organs, situated midway between the central party–state leadership and the grass-roots party members. The central leadership is, of course, dependent on the party apparatus and state bureaucracy to implement its decisions. One of the major political problems encountered by Gierek, further to conflicts within the central party–state apparatus and the confusion in party leadership and party–state relations, was the failure to implement nationally agreed policies such as the economic manoeuvre throughout the country. Contributing to this failure were the changes in party–state organisation introduced by Gierek which reduced the capacity of the sub-national party organisation to exercise control over economic and social bodies. In particular, I have argued, it was the autonomy and coherence of party organisation that was adversely affected by these changes.[1] The declining effectiveness of party action was most clearly apparent in connection with the provincial party committee (*Komitet Wojewódzki*) and its staff. By increasing the number of these committees from twenty-two to forty-nine Gierek enhanced his power and that of the central party leadership in relation to that of their respective secretaries. But the diminished power of the individual committee had a significant effect on its capacity to supervise and control economic processes, as the tendency in economic organisation was towards the creation of larger units which were not restricted to the territory of the single province. Aspects of party control and the effectiveness of its supposed leading role at this level further affected party authority and weakened its overall position within the political system.

The political role of the intermediate party organ was singled out for attention in the seventies by the prominent journalist Mieczysław Rakowski, who later joined Jaruzelski's government. In an article entitled 'The important link' he indicated both its particularly important political role and its exposed nature – secretaries at this level were not able to shrug off local complaints with the excuse that 'it's not our business', although they might well be fully aware how difficult it was to modify some unrealistic directive that had been transmitted from above.[2] The importance of the provincial organ may be gauged from the fact that the provincial first secretary was the only non-central party appointment within the *nomenklatura* of the Politburo, while the provincial first secretaries and regional military commanders were the only non-central appointments reserved for the specific responsibility of the top party body.[3] Rakowski's view is similar to that taken in the Soviet Union and elaborated on by Western observers of Soviet politics. Frank quotes Brezhnev himself who, referring to republic and regional first secretaries, stated in 1976 that it was on them that rested 'the chief responsibility for putting party policy into effect in the localities'.[4] If the party was to be an effective agency to rule the success or failure of cadres at this level would be decisive.

This view is also prominent in the leading Western works on Soviet politics. Rigby stresses the close relation of cadres placed at this level with the top leadership: the secretaries of republic and regional party committees are 'the most important reserve from which members of the supreme leadership are coopted.'[5] In the seventies well over half the central Soviet party leadership had served as *obkom* first secretary and in every case that had been the last post held by them before they moved into the central apparatus of the party.[6] Their role in articulating party authority and determining the concrete nature of party leadership has also been recognised: 'the party asserts its capacity to make "correct" decisions, to adopt "correct" policies. The representative of party authority at local level . . . can thus speak with all the authority conferred by this tradition. A further result of the tradition is that at any level the party secretary enjoys far more authority than anyone else.'[7] Hough, on the other hand, has drawn the influential parallel between the secretary and the Napoleonic prefect – 'an authoritative figure who cuts across the departmental lines of command', while the local party organs act as the 'representatives and embodiment of the Party at each territorial level'.[8]

To the extent that political authority, particularly in communist systems, has a close relationship with the effectiveness of rule, it is such pivotal components that play a major role in determining the level of that effectiveness. This particularly concerns the intermediate organs at regional or provincial level and the status of those representing the provincial committees. There is a considerable body of literature on developments with the Soviet *obkom* and republican committees, the relevant bodies within the Soviet system. Analyses of the Soviet secretaries have close links with consideration of processes concerning the maintenance and enhancement of party authority. It has been well recognised that the traditions of party authority and the pre-eminence of the provincial committees are not self-sustaining. The party's claim to be taking the correct decisions and adopting appropriate policies must have a reasonable degree of plausibility, and the party must demonstrate its ability to keep the system going in practical terms. Amongst other things, the local committees and their personnel need to acquire the skills and resources appropriate to the kind of society created by the Soviet leadership and to the requirements of its further development. Party officials must keep up with the changing needs of economic management if they are to be perceived as still being in control and the 'party apparatus must assiduously resist any developments that decrease its decision-making authority'; one of the leading questions here has been 'how the party organization can obtain the expertise it needs in order to provide leadership in an industrial society'.[9]

Analysis of the means by which the CPSU acquired this expertise played an important part in the new ways of thinking about Soviet political processes which gained in influence as dissatisfaction with the earlier totalitarian model became more wide-spread. The changing character of the party leadership was noted by observers like Fischer, who remarked on the 'rising proportion of top party executives whose past career lies within the economy and in it combines two kinds of jobs'.[10] Attention was paid to the methods by which new skills and expertise were acquired by the party, and an important distinction was made between trained officials who were recruited (joining the party apparatus having just acquired specialist qualifications) and those who were coopted (joining the apparatus after becoming established in a non-party career).[11] At Central Committee level the party was found to have extended the pool of skills at its disposal by both methods, although the political consequences of the choice of method were felt to be different. Cooptation not only brought technical skills into the political elite but it 'also allowed active participation of the specialised elites in the political elite. The net result is to increase the legitimacy of the political elite in the eyes of these specialized elites.'[12] The party was seen therefore, not only to raise its level of competence by these means, but also to increase its authority by extending its social base.

Changes in Soviet provincial secretaries

Analysis of Soviet provincial secretaries has shown a more complicated picture with the existence of diverse tendencies in the selection and appointment of party secretaries having mixed implications for the maintenance and enhancement of party authority. An initial contribution by Hodnett to the study of the *obkom* secretaries referred to the 'less than impeccable' credentials of those appointed in 1962 to perform the economic tasks assigned by Khrushchev and the 'relative lack of economic administrative experience of the group' of *obkom* secretaries as a whole. It was felt in general that, despite recent changes in the composition of this group, 'no transformation has occurred in its basic characteristics – age, degree of education, non-political experience, or route to political power'.[13] Writing six years later, however, and reviewing materials published between 1958 and 1969, Frank concluded that 'what is clear from these accounts is that the "typical" first secretary has changed significantly in the period covered by these studies'. Hough detected a process of specialisation in the career patterns of *obkom* first secretaries during the 1960s, and separate career paths for those with industrial and technical, agricultural and pedagogical training acting as first secretary between 1950 and 1966 were identified by Stewart.[14] More recently, Harasymiw has dated a shift in emphasis in the selection of leading cadres from political characteristics to specialised knowledge from the mid-1950s.[15]

Further detail on these matters is provided by Blackwell, who noted a secular trend towards the recruitment of those with technical education, although this was qualified by a similar rise in the number of those with pedagogical education and by the fact that the increase was not consistent in all periods. Thus a growing emphasis on economic expertise appeared after 1957. After the fall of Khrushchev, however, this emphasis appeared more in combination with a stress on political education (that is recruits having both technical qualifications and higher party school training).[16] *Obkom* secretaries were being appointed at a later age, and this was also true of appointment at other levels of career development before that of the *obkom* leadership was reached. 'Strong, but only partial, support' was found for the argument that the ageing was due to the degree of career specialisation and a major trend towards longer political apprenticeship (that is, more time being spent in other political work prior to appointment as *obkom* first secretary) was identified. This increase in the apparent requirement for greater political experience was thought to demonstrate the 'increasing rigidity of élite recruitment in the Soviet system' and Blackwell argued that the trends he detected worked 'against the development of creative and innovative leadership essential to problem-solving'.[17]

Other indications of a greater stability in the secretarial cadre were detected. Hough noted a marked slow-down in the rate of turnover in *obkom* secretaries between 1966 and 1971 (or even between 1961 and 1971) in comparison with the 1956–61 period as well as the emergence of a pattern of appointment that drew predominantly on the existing pool of local officials. The latter point was interpreted to mean that the autonomy of leading regional officials was growing in relation to the centre and that 'some increase in authority for all republics as they became more industrialized was occurring'.[18] The growing tendency towards local recruitment of first secretaries was also noted by Moses, but he was more reluctant to draw any definite conclusion about its significance.[19] In connection with the observation that the rate of turnover of *obkom* secretaries had slowed down Hough noted that the first secretaries were now roughly the same age as United States state governors and cast doubt on any suggestion that the rate of change in the Soviet political system was 'so slow in comparison with societal requirements that the system must be called immobilized'.[20] This judgment was clearly at odds with the 'increasing rigidity in elite recruitment' detected by Blackwell.

Later findings from the Brezhnev period appeared to confirm the empirical trends identified both by Hough and Blackwell, although the implications of these trends continued to be subject to conflicting interpretations. The tendency to recruit first secretaries from the local apparatus continued, and by 1976, 69% were of local origin.[21] This practice had in fact been described by Brezhnev at the XXIV CPSU Congress in 1971 as a 'consistent policy' of the Central Committee, and Miller suggests that the tendency had been established well before the Brezhnev period.[22] The average age of the provincial first secretary continued to rise, but the effect of this should not be exaggerated – the average age of the first secretary rose from fifty-two in 1965 to fifty-six in 1976. Compared with other areas of Soviet political life the provincial leadership was still quite youthful and it could be concluded that, whilst blocked elsewhere (notably in the Council of Ministers), Brezhnev had succeeded in introducing 'large doses of new blood' in the regions.[23] The changes in the secretaries' educational background also continued: they were increasingly likely to have professional qualifications and not just party political training. Industrial and agricultural expertise were the dominant specialisms, and teacher training remained the only other professional qualification. In terms of career history, though, industrial experience was gaining precedence over that in agriculture. The importance of experience in party office noted by Blackwell continued through the Brezhnev period, and there was a 'clear tendency for obkom first secretaries to be chosen from among those officials who have worked their way up from the lower echelons of the party hierarchy.'[24]

But between 1965 and 1976 the proportion of first secretaries whose careers had included technical or managerial experience declined from 78% to 70%, despite the rising average age of secretaries and the possibility of broader career experience this would have seemed to offer. For Rigby, however, these observations did not promote the somewhat exaggerated judgments passed by Blackwell. Because of the large number of secretaries with different forms of professional training and having some form of specialised work experience 'their capacity to intervene in the name of the party in these fields probably has not been impaired.'[25] Bialer, too, did not think this issue an important one as those engaged in party and managerial careers within the party apparatus could no longer be so clearly distinguished as when the party had been primarily a mobilising institution: 'The party secretary is becoming more and more a manager at a different level of decision making.'[26] But the problems arising from the composition of the provincial secretarial cadre should not be ignored. Following the upheavals of the late Khrushchev years the rate of change in *obkom* secretary posts had slowed markedly – thirty-two had been changed between 1966 and 1971 but only nineteen between 1971 and 1976, while a further fifteen of the seventy-one RSFSR (Russian Soviet Federal Socialist Republic) secretaries were changed during the five years preceding Brezhnev's death in 1982.[27] In 1978 Rigby did not comment on the slowing rate of turnover; two years later Bialer stated that 'It is not a natural situation to find that over a quarter of the first provincial secretaries have reached or are approaching the age of 65.'[28] Frank, too, observed that 'By 1982, the party apparatus, especially at the regional level, had become elderly, set in its ways, smug, parochial, and very often corrupt to boot.'[29]

On the other hand, the rate of change in *obkom* secretary positions was gaining pace before Brezhnev's death, particularly during the post-XXVI Congress period, and there were signs that the log-jam was beginning to break up. This process was accelerated by Andropov and has been pushed forward by Gorbachev. In his first year as party leader nearly a third of the provincial first secretaries were changed.[30] It is clear, then, that Brezhnev's successors felt some dissatisfaction with what they perceived as the excessive stability that had come to characterise the provincial party leadership. But developments among the provincial secretarial cadre had by no means been uniformly negative. Over the previous thirty years provincial secretaries had become older, although probably not disquietingly so until the last four or so years of Brezhnev's rule. They had become better qualified and were trained particularly in industrial subjects; they had more political experience and had spent increasing amounts of time in party posts prior to appointment to the leading *obkom* position. But the degree of party specialism should not be exaggerated. The provincial leader had always been a 'man with broad experience, accustomed to directing the affairs of some considerable segment of the apparatus and frequently having experience of the immediate territory for which he is responsible as first secretary'.[31] The latter characteristic, though, meant that the *obkom* leader often had experience of work in the state apparatus.

This feature did not disappear during the later period. Rigby's analysis of the jumping-off posts held prior to *obkom* appointment showed that amongst a total of seventy-two first secretaries, forty-nine had previously held party posts in 1965 while only slightly fewer, forty-seven, had in 1976.[32] Moses has identified fifteen posts assumed to confer *obkom* bureau membership (that is, the rank of *obkom* secretary – not just that of first secretary) and only just over half of these were clearly within the party apparatus. He also distinguished certain quasi-bureaucratic career paths that have emerged from functional specialism and suggested that a form of lateral job rotation has become institutionalised.[33] Stewart and Miller also show how *obkom* secretaries have often acted as chairman of the Soviet (that is, government) executive committees (*oblispolkom*).[34] Information on postings subsequent to work as *obkom* secretary is less frequently encountered. An indication of further sequencing of party and government appointment, however, is the fact that in the Soviet national republics the most common transition from the *obkom* first secretaryship is to the chair of the

Council of Ministers of the respective republic.[35] The development of party specialism, therefore, should not be over-emphasised. There are, nevertheless, signs that the role of party generalist is less favoured by the Gorbachev leadership and that the 'representation of the pure party official has noticeably weakened' since Brezhnev's death.[36] This was one aspect of the general judgment made by the new leadership on the cadres policy followed by Brezhnev, which was felt to have paid insufficient attention to qualities of technical and political competence on the part of provincial party leaders. The link between overall party authority and the effectiveness of the intermediate party organs has clearly been recognised by Brezhnev's successors, and efforts to improve the state of both have been one of the major features of their evolving policies.

Provincial secretaries in comparative perspective

There is, of course, far more involved in an evaluation of the effectiveness of provincial party organs than charting the changing biographical characteristics of provincial secretaries. Party authority involves considerably more than just the personal characteristics of the incumbents of even the leading party roles. There is clearly a great deal of assumption involved in deducing political trends from the rather skimpy biographical data we have at our disposal. One such line of reasoning has been reflected in the work of Hough and Bialer, who have argued for the political impact of the growing dominance amongst provincial secretaries of a different generation of party officials.[37] Their approaches are slightly different, with Hough concentrating on those of a particular chronological age (for example, those born in 1926 or after) and Bialer on different political generations (those, for example, receiving their first political position after the death of Stalin). The implication, of course, is that the later generation is more sophisticated, innovative and less hide-bound by the orthodoxies of the Stalinist establishment. As Breslauer has pointed out, though, 'such methodologies either force us to take too much for granted or beg the question'.[38] The easy assumption that younger party leaders are better educated and more appropriately qualified for modern political tasks, for example, is placed in question by Yugoslavian experience. Fewer than 10% of regional secretaries were over fifty years of age in 1980 but they were in fact less well educated than members of other sectors of the Yugoslav regional elite.[39] The question of how different background and socialisation experiences form political attitudes and incline the individual to different forms of behaviour has yet to be fully faced.

But we can take some guidance from the recent actions of communist leaderships themselves, who have shown that they do see a connection between the personal qualities of the incumbents of leading party posts and the effectiveness of party work, and that significant improvements in this respect are anticipated from personnel changes. The Soviet leadership is not the only one to have demonstrated its concern for the high age and excessive stability of its provincial cadres. The old revolutionary generation persisted in China into the eighties and exercised strong control over the provincial leadership. Of those appointed to the post of provincial party committee first secretary between 1976 and 1978, 20% were over the age of seventy and none were under sixty.[40] The strength of such gerontocratic practices eventually evoked equally strong counter-measures. During a period of six weeks in 1983, following the XII Party Congress, drastic measures were taken and as many as 38% of the provincial secretaries were replaced.[41] As in the Soviet Union, extensive change among provincial secretaries has been promoted and made possible in other countries following the accession of a new national leader and as a consequence of conflict over power and policy within the central leadership. This happened in Bulgaria with the removal of the first secretaries of many districts following the discovery in 1965 of a partisan–military conspiracy.[42] Gierek was also quick to take such measures in Poland, and changed twelve of the twenty-two provincial secretaries in the first year of his rule.[43]

Other leaders have been concerned to maintain a high rate of turnover of party cadres to forestall the formation of stable political groups at provincial level and to enhance the probability of local compliance with central directives. This was a policy pursued by Ceausescu who maintained a high level of party–state centralisation in Romania by these means during the 1970s.[44] His emphasis on the rotation of cadres was also driven by a strong concern to maintain levels of professional competence.[45] This approach has also been followed in the German Democratic Republic, where cadres policy was systematically revised in the late 1960s. As a result of this reappraisal 'The old equation: cadre = party-member has been replaced by the equation: cadre = leader/specialist', an approach that also had major consequences for appointments in the party apparatus.[46] Following the contribution of Gierek's cadres policy to the disaster that befell communist rule in Poland at the end of the seventies, and the evident dissatisfaction of the Gorbachev leadership with the Soviet record on this count during the later Brezhnev period, there has been a keener awareness throughout the communist world of the importance of cadres policy in general and of the need to improve appointment procedures within the party apparatus in particular. This has been a major element in Jaruzelski's approach to the reform of party activities in Poland, and the influence of the military on cadres policy has been particularly strong. Awareness of the current prominence of cadres policy review has also been strong in Poland, and recent discussion has noted its importance 'starting with the Soviet Union, and extending to China, Cuba and the European countries'. The importance of the principles of moral rectitude and ideological commitment have also been noted, their particular significance being recognised 'above all, in the Soviet Union' but also in the cadres policy followed by Bulgaria and Yugoslavia.[47] The reappraisal of cadres policy has been a major response to the perceived need throughout the communist world to raise the level of effectiveness of qualified personnel and enhance party authority. Appointments to the provincial party leadership and the secretaries attached to the intermediate organs of the party have been an important focus of this emphasis.

The criteria of appointment for party officials and the overall approaches adopted have been subject to variation throughout the communist world. In some countries the turnover of officials has been rapid, in others there has been an emphasis on stability. Some leaders have encouraged party officials to develop as political specialists, others have emphasised breadth of experience and the acquisition of technical or economic skills. The emphasis has, of course, changed in different countries over time. The encouragement of more qualified personnel and the development of a more highly educated party cadre has, however, been a general theme. Gierek placed great emphasis on this aspect following his accession to power in 1970. Weydenthal thus writes of his preference for 'officials with management training and experience' and describes how 'the importance of leadership administrative training has been endorsed from the highest party level for the entire organisation. The main accent was put on improving the quality of the party's professional staff', whilst 'considerable emphasis has been placed on expanding and tightening ideological preparation for party activists and staff members'.[48] To some extent this policy was successful and the party underwent significant modernisation under Gierek.[49] On the other hand, as we are already aware, the adoption of such policies was not sufficient either to increase the effectiveness of party work or to enhance, or even maintain, leadership authority. The shortcomings of cadres policy under Brezhnev have now been well aired, while the collapse of the Polish party was a sign of far greater failure. The precise reasons for the collapse of the Polish party, and the role of the provincial organs and their secretaries towards the end of the seventies, have not been fully examined. We shall examine in the rest of this chapter developments in the provincial committee secretariat following Gierek's 1975 reforms and changes in the characteristics of the provincial secretaries.

Polish party secretaries under Gierek

Those seeking to explain the decay and enfeeblement of the political system that became apparent in Poland in the summer of 1980 have often alighted on the inappropriate use of cadres as a major explanatory factor. The misappropriation of funds and the inefficient use of economic resources were one of the more obvious aspects of the Polish crisis, and most observers agree that the problem lay not so much in the malfunctioning of the economy *per se* as in the poor quality of management and faulty administration. Reviewing the catalogue of disasters, Montias concluded that the 'principle that links these errors is of course personnel policy. The incompetent Party functionaries appointed to responsible positions at every level of the economy undercut every positive move and initiative'.[50] Others stressed not so much the incompetence of functionaries as the fact that officials were placed in the wrong jobs. It was the view of Szczypiorski that 'The four sectors of power – the party, the police, the state administration, and the economic administration – had lived separate lives, consisted of different sorts of people. Gierek broke this principle. His team changed posts in a totally irrational manner . . . Trained technologists, needed in industry, became ministers, and ministers received posts in industry or in the party apparatus.'[51] The picture presented here is one of total confusion in terms of staff appointments and a somewhat absurd mismatch between individual talents and qualifications and the demands of the job.

But others, towards the end of the Gierek era, were presenting a definition of the situation that was not only different but quite the opposite in its implications. The Polish sociologist Hirszowicz, in fact, saw a decline in the interchangeability of cadres, the 'gradual disappearance of the traditional pattern of the reliable functionary transferred by the party from one important task to another . . . Public functionaries are more and more confined for their life's work to such institutions as the army, economic management, research institutes, the secret police, the health service or the party apparatus'.[52] Hirszowicz was therefore suggesting a process of advanced institutionalisation or bureaucratisation which bore a close resemblance to the changes that had been detected with respect to the Soviet *obkom* secretaries and the growing degree of political specialisation they had been characterised by under Brezhnev. It must be said, however, that the more general judgment on the roots of the Polish crisis in terms of faulty cadres policy was that exemplified in rather different ways by Montias and Szczypiorski. The faults of the Gierek administration were not generally held to be those of excessive stability and over-institutionalisation. This view gained further support in discussion at the VI Plenum of the party's Central Committee in October 1980, shortly after the fall of Gierek. Lending support to the idea of the 'carousel of cadres' or the 'jobs roundabout' it was stated that 'our party accounts for practically two-thirds of cadre changes in all socialist countries in the past ten years'.[53] The deformation here, then, was attributable to an excessive rotation of cadres – the antithesis, it might be noted, of the practices encouraged under Gomułka, who held that 'people placed in leading positions should exercise their function for a long period in order to perfect their skills and acquire experience'.[54]

The apparently generally held view that much of the Polish crisis could be attributed to excessively frequent cadre changes and a persistent habit of appointing people to the wrong job is also somewhat surprising in view of Gierek's expressed interest in cadres policy and in his concern to systematise appointments and extend *nomenklatura* practices in Poland. Later criticisms of Gierek's rule concerned precisely the prominence of *nomenklatura* procedures and excessively rigorous control over appointments. The two observations are not, of course, necessarily contradictory but they do suggest a remarkably high degree of irresponsibility and/or ineptitude on the part of the leadership. Certainly, concerted attempts were made to develop *nomenklatura* procedures in the early seventies. Ito claims that 'It was only under Gierek that the nomenklaturistic control of all political and social activities was systematized.'[55] Tarniewski refers to the attempt made under Gierek to 'subordinate the whole of social life to the party' and the role that the elaboration of the *nomenklatura* system played in this.[56] Smolar describes the process of *nomenklatura* formalisation as one of 'rationalizing, institutionalizing, and even bureaucratizing', which was 'surely intended to increase the sense of security of apparatchiks at various levels of government'.[57] This process suggests, therefore, a process of bureaucratisation and stabilisation rather than one of excessive and irrational change.

Initial examination of provincial first secretaries in post under Gierek does not suggest any excessive rotation of cadres. Those in post in May–June 1975 immediately after the reform of the territorial administration and party hierarchy had the prospect of staying in post for, on average, four years and eight months – and it must be remembered that the careers of many were cut short in 1980 and 1981 by the accelerated turnover of cadres caused by the political crisis and the rise of effective popular opposition to incumbent party officials. It would be difficult to describe this rate of change as a high one, and Polish secretaries at this time had greater prospects of stability than those studied by Armstrong in the Ukraine up until the mid-fifties, when the average tenure of the *obkom* first secretary was a little over three years.[58] Neither did the appointment of first secretaries appear to be made irrationally, as Szczypiorski had suggested. His statement that 'ministers received posts in industry or in the party apparatus' is not substantiated in our overview of the provincial secretaries. Of the fifty-nine first secretaries appointed following the 1975 reorganisation until Gierek's fall only two were made directly from ministries and one of these, appointed first secretary in 1975, had already served a training period as provincial secretary from 1965 to 1968. The second, appointed in 1980, had been deputy minister of agriculture from 1974 (and also chairman of the collective farm union from 1974 to 1977) and had held posts in the ministry from 1950. He was, however, appointed first secretary in Leszno in the west of Poland, where most of Poland's collective farms are concentrated. Whatever else it may have suggested, such an appointment could hardly be judged irrational.

In this section of the apparatus *nomenklatura* procedures appeared to work smoothly and according to apparently reasonable principles (we shall look more closely at its outcome in later sections). The dysfunctions of the *nomenklatura* system as it was extended under Gierek seemed to concern, in fact, not so much the criteria of appointment as the implicit guarantees of tenure and privilege they came to carry. These were underwritten by two Council of State decrees issued in 1972 (not, it should be noted, by parliamentary act) which provided for life-long pensions for holders of leading party–state posts – and for members of their family. Outside the central organs of the party only provincial first secretaries were covered by these provisions.[59] This degree of security and privilege was the factor that really brought the *nomenklatura* system under Gierek into such disrepute rather than the criteria of appointment per se. It made a significant contribution to the reputation of *nomenklatura* appointments for irresponsibility and for being above the law, and provoked much anger on the part of the opposition in 1980 and 1981.[60] It also encouraged the formation of a proprietorial attitude to the post occupied and the party apparatus was identified as being particularly open to this threat, as so many cadres flowed through party posts. This was recognised to give rise to the 'danger of a utilitarian approach to party functions and the threat of careerism'.[61] The experiences of the 1970s, governed by the development of the system of centralised bureaucratic appointment which 'achieved its final form only after 1971', remain a signal lesson to the party authorities, having demonstrated the dangers of irresponsibility inherent in the *nomenklatura* system and the removal of power from social control, and proving that '*Nomenklatura* should not be a guarantee, as it has been in the past, of the life-time occupation of leading posts.'[62]

Provincial secretaries in Poland, 1975–80: personal characteristics and education

In this section we look at the general characteristics of the provincial secretaries in post between 1975 and 1980 in the attempt to identify factors which may have influenced their effectiveness as local leaders and thus had some effect on the fluctuations of party authority in Poland in the late seventies. The secretaries are the 'leading party cadres' within the province. As we have noted, the post of first secretary falls within the *nomenklatura* of the Politburo and he may therefore be regarded as a member of the national political elite. Like the other secretaries, as local party leader he is formally elected by the provincial party conference composed of delegates of the local party organisations. In practice, though, his candidature will emerge from deliberations within the CC Secretariat and he will be endorsed centrally as the most appropriate cadre for the job. There is no question, under normal conditions, of his candidature being contested or rejected and the 'election' is a symbolic local acceptance of the central decision. Provincial first secretaries are usually 'elected' at meetings attended by a Politburo member and a high-ranking official from one of the Central Committee departments.

At the IX PZPR Congress in 1981 there were acknowledged to be around 11,000 political workers in the party apparatus. Of these 32%

were based on the provincial committee, which implied an average party staff in the province of sixty-seven, who worked directly under the leadership of the first secretary.[63] In line with the apparent extension of *nomenklatura* appointments under Gierek, it is highly likely that the party apparatus grew during this period. Certainly, a total of 210 provincial secretaries were reported to be in post in 1975, while at least 244 such offices were reported to have been established by 1981. In three of four provinces for which detailed records of the provincial leadership are available the number of secretaries in post rose between 1975 and 1978. In Lublin province the number of secretaries rose from four to six during this period.[64] In national terms, however, official records show that the average number of secretaries rose from four to five between 1975 and 1981. Apart from the KW (*Komitet Wojewódzki*: Provincial Committee) secretaries who formally (and hardly surprisingly) make up the provincial secretariat, the records show also that the secretariats grew also during this period to include heads of some major departments attached to the provincial committees (organisation or economic departments) and the secretary of a major local party committee, as well as the chairman of the provincial party control commission.

In consequence of the changes made in territorial structure and the party organisation in 1975, increasing the number of provincial committees from twenty-two to forty-nine, thirty-eight new provincial first secretaries were appointed. Between that reorganisation and the resignation of Gierek in September 1980 twenty-two new first secretaries were appointed to the provincial committees. These appointments will provide the basis for the initial examination of the KW secretaries. They provide us with examples of placements made under conditions of relatively normal processes of central party control, thus illuminating the characteristics of cadre policy under Gierek and the political processes that were associated with the failure of communist party authority and the inauguration of the Solidarity period. Firstly, though, we summarise the changes (reported in full elsewhere) that occurred between 1975 and 1980 in the body of KW first secretaries as a whole (that is, not just of those newly appointed). This concerns, therefore, the changing characteristics of all first secretaries in post on these two dates (the latter date is mid-1980, just before the fall of Gierek).[65]

The typical KW first secretary in 1975 was in his forties (68% aged between forty-one and fifty years of age), having joined the party in the first decade of communist rule (75% having joined between 1946 and

1956). Most (59%) had received their first apparatus posting over fifteen years previously and they had spent, on average, twelve years overall working in the party apparatus. Nearly all had a higher education qualification, frequently obtained on a part-time basis. Only a quarter had qualifications of a technical character and fewer than a third had industrial or agricultural production experience. Over half had their main non-apparatus career experience in government departments or branches of the youth movement. By 1980, on the eve of Gierek's downfall and the dramatic emergence of Solidarity, this picture had changed relatively little. The average first secretary was somewhat older (59% between forty-six and fifty-five) and had career experience even more strongly entrenched in the party apparatus. Nearly three-quarters (73%) had received their first apparatus posting over fifteen years earlier and each had spent, on average, fifteen years working in the party apparatus. The number of those with significant production experience in industry or agriculture was even lower and stood at exactly a quarter. Again, the changes among KW first secretaries do not suggest that the 'jobs roundabout' had been spinning any faster. Party secretaries had in fact shown greater specialisation in terms of political work in the party apparatus and had become less likely to have switched over from an industrial or agricultural career.

The characteristics of the newly appointed first secretaries during this period were, not surprisingly, slightly different. The average age of first secretaries on appointment was, in 1975, forty-six and, for those appointed between 1975 and 1980, forty-five. This was slightly older than the Soviet *obkom* secretaries in post in 1966 when they had first been appointed, but younger than *obkom* first secretaries in post in 1976, over half of whom were fifty-six or more.[66] Personal characteristics of the KW secretaries are presented in tables 2.1 and 2.2.

The dominant cohorts can be easily distinguished: amongst the KW first secretaries appointed in 1975 66% were born in the seven years between 1926 and 1933, and 32% of the 1975–80 group were born between 1931 and 1933 – with as many as 68% falling between the birth-dates 1926–38. Throughout the period 1975–80 only two appointments were made over the age of fifty-five. A tendency to bring in younger cadres is clearly detectable during the late Gierek period, and nearly a quarter of first secretaries appointed between 1975 and September 1980 were born in 1939 or after. The process of appointment was starting to bring about a change in the representation of those whose formative experience would have been marked by the Second World War, a particularly traumatic period in Polish history. Of those

Table 2.1 *KW secretaries (1975, 1975–80): date of birth*

| | First secretaries | | | | Other secretaries | | | |
| | 1975 | | 1975–80 | | 1975 | | 1975–80 | |
	N	%	N	%	N	%	N	%
1911–25	6	16	2	9	13	10	6	5
1926–30	16	42	4	18	18	14	13	11
1931–33	9	24	7	32	28	22	20	17
1934–38	6	16	4	18	42	33	32	27
1939–51	1	2	5	23	26	21	46	40
Total	38	100	22	100	127	100	117	100

Table 2.2 *KW secretaries (1975, 1975–80): date of joining party*

| | First secretaries | | | | Other secretaries | | | |
| | 1975 | | 1975–80 | | 1975 | | 1975–80 | |
	N	%	N	%	N	%	N	%
1944–49	14	37	3	14	14	11	4	3
1950–52	6	16	6	29	16	13	11	10
1953–55	13	34	3	14	26	20	19	16
1956–59	2	5	2	10	20	16	12	10
1960–73	3	8	7	33	51	40	71	61
Total	38	100	21	100	127	100	117	100

Sources: Biographies published on appointment in *Życie Partii* (organisational journal of the Polish United Workers' Party), appearing monthly throughout the seventies, fortnightly from September 1981, with additional information from its calender of events. Statistics in these and all subsequent tables reflect the characteristics of secretaries at the time they were appointed.

appointed in 1975, 58% would have been at least fifteen years old by the time the war ended, and thus would have had clear memories of the nature and extent of war-time devastation. Amongst those appointed after June 1975 only 27% would have reached this age by 1945 and the majority of secretaries had reached maturity in the post-war years. Nevertheless, within the group of first secretaries as a whole in

1980 43% were over fifty years of age and the representation of the war-time generation remained strong.

During the reorganisation that took place in May and June 1975 many other new officials were appointed to the provincial secretariats to join the first secretaries. In this process 122 new secretaries, other than first secretaries, were appointed to the provincial committees. As the biographies of some of the incumbent secretaries are known, they have been added to give a fuller picture of the group of secretaries in post in 1975. The resulting total of 127 makes up around 79% of the total group of KW secretaries (excluding first secretaries). Between the 1975 reorganisation and the fall of Gierek a further 117 KW secretaries were appointed, which provides us with further evidence on changes within the KW secretariat as a whole. The other secretaries, being less advanced in their careers than the first secretaries, were also slightly younger than them. While only 18% of the 1975 first secretaries were born in 1934 or after, 54% of the other secretaries were born in this period. Those born in 1939 or after are also quite numerous amongst the other secretaries, particularly those appointed after mid-1975. Correspondingly fewer were representatives of the 'war-time' generation and, of those appointed in mid-1975, only 24% would have reached fifteen before the end of the war. This representation declined further after 1975 and only 16% were of this age-group amongst the 1975–80 appointments.

In terms of the date of commencement of party membership table 2.2 shows a certain bunching in both the 1975 and 1975–80 cohorts of KW first secretaries. Those having joined in the early years of communist power (1944–49) and the years of late Stalinism (1953–55) were clearly dominant in the 1975 group. Subsequently the part played by those joining the party in the pre-Stalinist period fell markedly and a larger role was played by those who had joined in the years of early Stalinism (1950–52) and the more recent period (notably the years of Gomułka's conservative 'stabilisation', 1960–67). The dual-peak character of first secretary appointments thus persists, although with emphasis on quite different periods. In both groups the average length of party membership prior to appointment was twenty-three years, a longer period of membership than that of Soviet *obkom* secretaries in post in 1966 when they had been appointed.[67] Nevertheless, a tendency to appoint younger secretaries with shorter party tenure is evident in the late Gierek period. In terms of early party experience the years of early communist rule and of Stalinism remained, however, dominant. This was clearly so in the case of first secretaries appointed in 1975, 87% of whom had joined the PZPR prior to 1956, and still remained the case with the 1975–80 appointments, 57% of whom had joined the party before that date.

With the other secretaries, who were in any case younger than the first secretaries, the proportion of those who had joined the party before the onset of full Stalinism was far lower and became minimal with the post-1975 appointments. In the second group only 29% had even joined the party before 1956. Thus the proportion of those who had joined the party during the Stalinist period was high only amongst the first secretaries, 50% of those who had been appointed in 1975 having joined between 1950 and 1955. But even amongst the other secretaries relatively few had joined the party in the years immediately following 1956 and during the period of relatively greater reformism in Poland. Among the post-1975 appointments, for example, the concentration of early membership comes in the early and mid-sixties and the generation of those who had been attracted to the party by developments during the relatively reformist period that followed 1956 was strongly represented neither amongst first secretaries nor their more junior colleagues.

The educational qualifications of the secretaries are presented in table 2.3. One of the most striking features in the educational background of the first secretaries is the predominance of qualifications in economics, and the low number with qualifications in subjects related to industrial and agricultural activity. Comparing this with Soviet experience, it is notable that the economics qualification does not appear in Rigby's survey of Soviet first secretaries in 1976 and is shown as an unusual one in Frank's survey of 1966 secretaries.[68] Such differences make comparison hazardous, but the decline in the number of Polish first secretaries with economic and industrial qualifications after 1975 does appear striking, particularly when compared with the 64% of *obkom* first secretaries who had educational qualifications in industry and agriculture in 1976 (a total that does not include those with qualifications derived only from attendance at the Higher Party School). If the Polish first secretaries with economic qualifications are subtracted, the small number of those with exclusively industry or agriculture related qualifications is even more striking, particularly with the appointments made between 1975 and September 1980.

From this comparative perspective the significance of the Polish secretaries' qualifications hinges on the character of their 'economics' degree. If sufficiently technical in terms of its industrial and agricultural relevance it would presumably serve to offset the secretaries'

Table 2.3 *KW secretaries (1975, 1975–80): higher education qualifications*

	First secretaries				Other secretaries			
	1975		1975–80		1975		1975–80	
	N	%	N	%	N	%	N	%
Economics	22	56	8	35	32	25	42	35
Industry	5	13	1	4	15	11	12	10
Agriculture	4	10	3	13	19	15	20	16
History	2	5	2		10	8	7	6
Education	2	5	–		11	8	6	5
Law	1		3		10	8	2	
Sociology	1		2		5	4	5	
Language	1		–		3		4	
Arts	–	8	2	48	3	14	5	26
Administration	–		1		4		9	
Political Science	–		–		3		3	
Geography	–		–		4		–	
Medicine, social sciences, philosophy, psychology, journalism, unspecified.	–		1		2		4	
No higher education	1	3	–		9	7	2	2
Total	39	100	23	100	130	100	121	100

Note: Some secretaries had more than one qualification. Amongst first secretaries appointed in 1975, for example, Fiszbach (Gdańsk) combined qualifications in economics and milk processing, whilst amongst those appointed between 1975 and 1980 Gadomski (Kielce) also had two qualifications.

apparent weakness as a group in this area and suggest that they were reasonably competent to perform the tasks they were faced with as party leaders in a developed society. If, on the other hand, it reflected the prevalence of a standard form of party in-service training, the qualifications of the secretaries might be regarded as less than satisfactory. Both Hodnett and Rigby have pointed out that the value of Soviet party training in terms of technical education was very dubious, the most suspect secretaries being – in Hodnett's view – those who had received party higher education by correspondence.[69] Brown has referred to the fact that academic degrees awarded to establish party officials 'often owe more to their political standing than to their scholarly endeavors', while Zaslavsky alludes to the high number of regional party staff with PhDs – which 'usually have a fictitious character'.[70] It would appear that the Soviet party leadership agreed with this judgment, as party-trained *obkom* secretaries (particularly those for whom such training gave them their sole qualification) were becoming less numerous in the seventies and more conventional industrial and agricultural training had become more common.

The emphasis on educational qualifications and the further training of Polish party officials had, indeed, been a strong one. The inadequate educational background of apparatus workers had been an early cause for concern. In the early fifties some employees were barely able to read and write and further educational problems rose with the extensive growth of the apparatus.[71] Concerted measures were taken under Gomułka and a significant amount, it appeared, was achieved.[72] Yet the emphasis on educational improvement within the apparatus did not slacken. In July 1978 the Organisation Department of the Central Committee was instructed to draw up a five-year plan for education and the upgrading of political qualifications for all local party workers.[73] The emphasis on educational improvement was therefore strong and persistent. It is, of course, not necessarily clear that such upgrading has a direct effect on the effectiveness of party work. In a related party sphere, Mason concluded that higher levels of technical education among CC members did not lead, for example, to more pragmatic economic decision-making.[74] This, however, was not quite the same thing and one might well expect party secretaries with more technical education to be at least more capable of effective action. Further questions arise, nevertheless, in relation to the precise nature of the qualifications held by the Polish secretaries.

Our knowledge of this nature is imprecise, as published biographical information does not generally tell us where or how the educational qualification was obtained. None of the biographies of the first secretaries appointed in 1975, for example, contains any information about periods spent as full-time students, and some biographies do not begin until the appointee was in his mid-twenties. Although some secretaries obviously did follow courses of conventional full-time education, it is likely that many of them obtained their qualifications through part-time study or through party training courses. Of the twenty-two provincial first secretaries appointed in 1975, for example, nine had attended party schools for an average of 2.9 years each amongst those who claimed an economic qualification. As their professional and occupational careers began just over the age, on average, of twenty years it is most likely that such party training in conjunction with part-time study was the path through which the qualifications were gained. In a further three cases attendance at non-party institutions of higher education is suggested. Of the remaining ten cases no full-time education of any sort is indicated and, as the first secretaries began professional work at an average age of 21.5 years (in seven cases under the difficult conditions of the 1940s and early 1950s), they would seem to have had little chance of acquiring qualifications before starting full-time work. It is therefore likely that party training and in-service courses played a large part in conferring the economic qualifications. As party training does not figure in the biographies of the nine first secretaries appointed in mid-1975 with industrial or agricultural-type qualifications and as they began work, on average, at the age of twenty-four, it seems likely that these secretaries underwent conventional non-party education.

This tendency continued in appointments made through to 1980. Of the further twenty-five secretaries with some 'economic' qualification who were appointed between mid-1975 and the end of 1980, nine had received some full-time non-party education, six had passed through full-time party courses and ten appeared to have gained their qualification through part-time study. Amongst the other secretaries the proportion with higher education qualifications was also high, particularly towards the end of the seventies. The proportion of those with qualifications that could be associated with industrial and agricultural activity was, however, somewhat higher than amongst first secretaries. The proportion of other secretaries with qualifications in economics was, on the other hand, generally lower, this probably being associated with the fact that they were less likely to have received party training or undergone party schooling in preparation for promotion within the apparatus.

From our knowledge of the Polish secretaries, then, it does not seem that the low representation of those with conventional education in technical subjects of industrial and agricultural relevance was compensated for by the secretaries' experience of alternative forms of training. As the degeneration of the Polish economy during the seventies might suggest, the education received by the provincial secretaries did not prepare them at all well for managerial tasks. This view was certainly prevalent during the Solidarity period, when party educational institutions were described by workers in one factory as 'schools for cretins' where they would 'try to turn someone who couldn't even read into an editor'.[75] The continuing stress on education and the acquisition of qualifications by party cadres clearly did not give the desired results in terms of effective party work and the enhancement of party authority. Some official recognition of this was made in 1980. Writing of the party's cadre policy, CC secretary Żandarowski warned of a 'fetishisation of expertise', and of a 'simplistic judgment and evaluation of people exclusively on the basis of their qualifications and technical efficiency'.[76] This seems to affirm the relevance of our doubts concerning ing the relationship between the acquisition of formal qualifications by provincial secretaries and the enhancement of their capacity to act as party leaders contributing to the raising of party authority.

Provincial secretaries in Poland, 1975–80: career experience

Having identified the apparent weakness of KW secretaries in terms of educational background we now turn to examine the characteristics of provincial secretaries derived from their occupational experience and career patterns. To what extent was the secretaries' weakness in terms of qualification in fields related to industrial and agricultural production compensated for by direct production experience in these areas? To judge from the evidence presented in table 2.4, not at all. Only around a third of the Polish secretaries had any extensive production experience amongst those appointed in May–June 1975 and, amongst those appointed after mid-1975, even fewer had this kind of background. During the late Gierek period Polish provincial secretaries became less experienced in industrial and agricultural activities. Unlike the Soviet *obkom* secretaries, of course, the decline in the proportion of first secretaries appointed with direct production experience was not compensated for (as Rigby has argued in the Soviet case) by better educational qualifications.[77] It is difficult not to draw some intuitive link between this finding and the critical economic situation in Poland which deteriorated rapidly in the late seventies. The above observation applies to the KW first secretaries. Amongst the other secretaries the picture was slightly different. Between 1975 and 1980 those appointed had rather more direct production experience than did the first secretaries – although their number still failed to reach half the total. To a limited extent this could be seen as some compensation for what we have perceived as a weakness in the group of first secretaries and the potential effectiveness of the provincial party organisation. The higher proportion of other secretaries with industrial or agricultural backgrounds compared with the first secretaries meant a lower representation of those with back-

Table 2.4 *KW secretaries (1975, 1975–80): main non-apparatus experience*

	First secretaries				Other secretaries	
	1975		1975–80		1975–80	
	N	%	N	%	N	%
Industry	11	28	2	9	31	26
Agriculture	3	8	1	5	19	16
Government	9	24	10	45	27	23
Education	2	5	2	9	17	15
Youth organisations	9	24	5	22	21	18
Military	2	5	–	–	1	1
Parapolitical	1	2.5	1	5	–	–
No non-apparatus experience	1	2.5	1	5	1	1
Total	38	100	22	100	117	100

Note: This table shows *main* career experience outside the party apparatus. Subsidiary, though perhaps important areas of experience, may therefore be neglected in favour of work to which more time was devoted. If an equal period of time was spent in two areas of experience, the most recent has been selected. Information not available for mid-1975 appointments of other secretaries, as only abbreviated biographies were available.

grounds primarily in government and administrative activity (although obviously it is difficult to draw a clear line between the two).

Educational careers were also more common amongst the other secretaries appointed between mid-1975 and 1980, while the proportion coming from activity in youth movements was roughly the same as amongst the first secretaries. However, amongst all KW secretaries appointed in mid-1975 and afterwards, the proportion of those with experience in industry was considerably less than for local first secretaries appointed during the early seventies, prior to the reorganisation of the party structure.[78] In the late 1970s within the local party apparatus as a whole, 47% of political workers had industrial or agricultural production experience, a proportion close to that found among the other secretaries appointed between 1975 and 1980.[79] The declining proportion of first secretaries appointed having direct industrial experience during the decade of Gierek's rule is an interesting, and rather surprising finding, which is highly likely to have had some impact on the authority of local party leadership during this period.

Table 2.5 *KW secretaries (1975, 1975–80): time from first party appointment*

| | First secretaries | | | | Other secretaries | |
| | 1975 | | 1975–80 | | 1975–80 | |
Years	N	%	N	%	N	%
0–5	4	10	3	13	42	36
6–10	3	8	5	23	28	24
11–15	8	21	6	27	26	22
16–20	12	32	5	23	13	11
over 20	11	29	3	14	8	7
Total	38	100	22	100	117	100

In terms of career experience within the party apparatus we also find (table 2.5) a declining length of time spent in party work prior to appointment as first secretary. In view of the fact that we have already detected a tendency to appoint younger first secretaries between mid-1975 and 1980 it should not be surprising that the average length of time spent working in the party apparatus prior to appointment as first secretary did not lengthen. While 61% of secretaries appointed in 1975 had received their first party job sixteen or more years previously, that proportion was nearly halved (at 33%) in appointments made from then to the fall of Gierek. The average length of time from first party job to secretarial appointment was seventeen years in 1975, but only thirteen years for subsequent appointments. The average length of time spent working in the party apparatus also fell (though less markedly) from eleven to ten years.

This finding also stands in some contrast to the tendency among Soviet *obkom* first secretaries noted both by Rigby and Blackwell. They identified an increasing length of time spent in the socio-political or party apparatus before appointment as first secretary.[80] Trends in appointments within Poland therefore diverge from observations made of Soviet appointments. In Poland, the new first secretaries were being appointed at an earlier age, with fewer qualifications in industrial and technical subjects, and with less experience in industry and agriculture. They also had less experience working in the party apparatus. All in all, it is difficult to detect the improvements that Gierek was supposed to be making in the party apparatus following the 1975 party reorganisation. Dangers of excessive ageing were certainly avoided, but economic and political experience also declined. More surprisingly, the influx of a new generation (born after 1939 and having joined the party after 1960) sacrificed the advantages of experience but did not appear to have introduced the benefits of more up-to-date and appropriate qualifications. It is possible to see in the first secretaries, then, the rise of characteristics that helped to undermine leadership effectiveness and contributed to the decline of party authority. In keeping with their lower age and lower level of career advancement, the other KW secretaries had been appointed to their first job in the apparatus even more recently. Over a third had been working in the apparatus for five years or less amongst those appointed in the late seventies. Nevertheless, amongst local leaders the secretaries of the party committees were older than the average and remained the senior group in more than one way.[81]

But it would be wrong to conclude that the system of cadre appointment was as chaotic as some people have implied. Examination of those assuming the post of first secretary does not suggest that the process had become less systematic, although some of the criteria applied might have changed and become in some ways less rigorous, for example in the treatment of educational qualifications. Those without responsible party experience were very rare among new secretaries. Only two of those appointed in 1975 and one of those placed between 1975 and 1980 had no previous apparatus experience at all (equivalent to 5% of the total in both cases). The great majority had held within the party hierarchy posts which can easily be seen as the most appropriate training position for the job of provincial committee first secretary. It can be seen in table 2.6 that most of the May–June 1975 first secretary appointments had previously served as a secretary of the provincial committee and that a considerable number had also been first secretary of a party committee at a lower level.

Only four were without either experience and 89% had served in one or the other capacity. Of the four without such secretarial experience, two had been heads of national socio-political organisations (the youth movement and the construction workers' union) and two had been deputy heads of Central Committee departments. Only two, then, were without party apparatus experience. Thirty-six-year-old Stanisław Ciosek had, nevertheless, sixteen years experience in the closely allied apparatus of the youth movement. Janusz Prokopiak, on the other hand, had twenty years' experience in the construction industry before becoming chairman of the construction workers' union

Table 2.6 *KW first secretaries (1975, 1975–80): previous apparatus experience*

	1975		1975–80	
	N	%	N	%
Provincial committee secretary	30	79	15	68
First secretary of other party committee	15	39	12	55
Responsible party post, i.e. either provincial committee secretary or other first secretaryship, or both	34	89	19	86

in 1972. He had, in fact, spent precisely three weeks in the party apparatus before taking up the post of KW first secretary in Radom.[82] It is difficult to avoid the conclusion that the evident problems he had in handling the demonstrations that broke out in the town of Radom in 1976 were related to this lack of apparatus experience and his avoidance of the more normal political training posts. His inaction during much of the June 1976 drama was described in an article by H. Krall which *Polityka* was not allowed to publish. It was printed elsewhere and it emerges that, having agreed to report the workers' demand for the withdrawal of the price rises that had sparked off the revolt, he spent the rest of the time until the crowd set fire to the party headquarters alone in his office, waiting for some response from Warsaw. The CC office failed to inform him that the Prime Minister had decided to make a television broadcast and he therefore had nothing to say to the irate workers. It was in this state of isolation, he later said, that he realised he had not been 'exercising power' during those years in the construction industry and the trade union: 'I understood what power was at Radom.'[83]

Despite the differences already noted between the group appointed in mid-1975 and those selected for the first secretaryship between 1975 and 1980, the pattern of apparatus experience was remarkably similar. The only person appointed after 1975 without apparatus experience had spent thirty years in a Warsaw ministry and could well have been expected to acquire political and administrative skills adequate to the task. Amongst the others, fifteen had previously been provincial secretaries and twelve had been first secretary of another party committee at the next level down. In total, 86% of the first secretaries appointed had served in one or both of these positions. Of the three who had not, one (previously mentioned) had been for six years a deputy minister and spent the preceding twenty-four years in the same ministry. Another had held responsible posts (inspector and higher) in the CC Secretariat. The pattern of party-office holding or employment in central organisations was therefore similar to the mid-1975 group of appointments.

Apart from apparatus experience most first secretaries had spent time in non-party posts, this being particularly true of the May–June 1975 appointments. This often involved service as chairman of the Presidium of the *Województwo* or *Powiat* People's Council (or, following the 1973 reform, *wojewóda*), the post in the state hierarchy equivalent to the provincial party first secretary and similar to the Soviet post of *oblispolkom* chairman which, for *obkom* first secretaries in post in 1976, was the post most commonly held prior to *obkom* appointment.[84] Other frequent examples of non-apparatus employment included periods spent in other departments of the local and central government hierarchy, in the administration of the youth, trade union, cooperative or agricultural circle movements, in industrial or agricultural production or, more rarely, in diplomatic or military service. The distribution of the experience has already been shown in table 2.4. Thus the experience of those appointed to the leadership of the provincial party committees under Gierek, despite certain apparently unorthodox features, was systematised and party posting had generally been admixed with other official employment. Well over half those appointed in May–June 1975, for example, had been employed outside the party apparatus either in their previous post or in the one before that.

The system of career advancement and first secretary placement, therefore, appears to have been well organised and not dissimilar to Soviet processes. If, indeed, the material presented in table 2.4 is arranged to combine industrial, agricultural and governmental career experience the similarity in the career background of the secretaries appointed in mid-1975 to those posted between 1975 and 1980 becomes more obvious. The similarity in terms of youth organisation service and other non-party experience is also striking. Characteristic of cadre policy under Gierek, then, was the introduction of a younger generation of party cadres but with the lack of rigorous distinction being made between industrial, agricultural and governmental experience and equivalent disregard for the actual content of educational qualifications possessed by the new first secretaries. Some experience of state organisation and activity (governmental, industrial or agricultural) was apparently required as was the possession of some higher education qualification, but not the focus on industry and (to a lesser extent) agriculture that appears to have been a priority for Soviet decision-makers in this area. It may therefore be concluded that Polish cadre policy was somewhat lax in comparison with the Soviet, but hardly subject in this area to the kind of deformation identified by some observers. Nevertheless, there were also signs of contradictions within the provincial secretarial appointments and of an increased rate of 'rotation of cadres' with regard to some officials. We have noted that younger secretaries were being appointed between 1975 and 1980 compared with appointments in May–June 1975, and that their level of party experience was correspondingly lower. But within the group of provincial first secretaries *as a whole* the average age had risen between 1975 and 1980, and the level of experience in the party apparatus had risen. The accelerated rotation of cadres may therefore have been one tendency within the apparatus, although not a uniform one, which might well have played some part in the weakening of party authority in this area during the late Gierek period.

3 Provincial Party Committees in Poland, 1975–80

Provincial party leadership and the Gierek reform

Political authority, we have argued, has a close relationship with the effectiveness of party rule and the performance of the party's intermediate organs. Performance, in turn, is influenced by a number of factors: the structure of party organisation and its activities, which affects its capacity for action; the function of the party organ and the role it is assigned to play by the leadership within the system as a whole; and its staff, whose nature, outlook and characteristics will have a strong influence on the degree of success with which their allotted tasks are implemented. In the last chapter we paid particular attention to the question of party staff, the provincial committee secretariat, and made some assessment of their capacity for effective action in the light both of their changing characteristics and of comparative evidence. The structure of the party, the changing form of its organisation, and the role allotted to the provincial committee, the precise function it is intended to perform, are also crucial factors here and major determinants of the overall effectiveness of party activity. In this chapter we look more closely at the changing party structure and the role of the provincial committee during the second half of the Gierek period.

The position of the provincial party (KW) committees as they developed following the establishment of the new party structure on 1 June 1975 was influenced by the principles that had been laid down during the early stages of the Gierek leadership. These included a strong emphasis on the qualifications of party cadres, the development of a closer relationship with Polish society and particularly with the working class, and the evolution of a new style of party leadership. A series of articles published in the run-up to the First Party Conference (a meeting now held at the mid-point between the more important

Party Congresses) elaborated on these features and reflected the new direction of party activity that Gierek promoted. Characteristic in party cadre policy was what was described as a 'wager on youth' in association with an emphasis on the role of educational qualification which was felt to determine the climate of internal party work and resolve problems experienced earlier with apparatus employees who were otherwise 'without an occupation', that is lacking occupational qualifications and experience other than work in the party apparatus.[1] This was associated with a positive view of the 'rotation of cadres', as people were no longer trapped in the party apparatus because of lack of employment opportunities elsewhere. It was noted that those now working at intermediate levels of the apparatus had gained their qualifications in a regular manner, unlike members of the preceding generation whose education had been disrupted by the war and who had made up for their deficiencies in an irregular and often rushed manner. This was felt to foster a sense of personal security and accounted for the growing dominance of 'ambitious comrades' in the apparatus.[2]

Such people were felt to play an important role in the implementation of Gierek's strategy of socio-economic development and it was thought appropriate to switch on the 'green light for those who had the disposition and preparation to act as real leaders in their environment'.[3] Staffing policy and the character of party personnel were therefore seen as prime determinants of the effectiveness of party work. 'The scope and level of realisation of tasks by the apparatus is mainly conditioned by the composition of its personnel', stated one KW secretary.[4] As we have seen, however, the opportunities opened up for such rotation of cadres could also have less positive consequences, and the emphasis on educational qualifications might have been less beneficial than it appeared. The reorganisation of the party also introduced some new factors into this situation. The old three-tier structure, based on district (*powiat*) party committees, had permitted the acquisition, noted the KW secretary, of 'much valuable experience, of forms and methods of work tested in the activity of the district committees'. But, with the change in organisational context, the abolition of the district committees and the introduction of a two-tier system, much of this experience 'lost its relevance or required adaption under the new conditions'. The nature of the reform and the manner of its introduction had further consequences.

The reform was, firstly, carried out with surprising rapidity and with little public warning. One report states that the existing provincial committees had five weeks to allocate staff to the new units and that work did not begin until early April, the reform coming into practical effect at the end of the following month.[5] Hints of dissatisfaction with this procedure did not take long to emerge. The failure of central authorities to conduct any 'broad consultation' was noted by the first secretary of Siedlce province in 1977 and the problems experienced by the provincial party organs in consolidating the new political network lasted well into 1976.[6] In fact no real advance publicity was issued concerning the changes and consultation was extremely limited. Blanket censorship restrictions were issued to cover all speculation concerning the reasons for the reform further to those given in offical CC materials.[7] Whilst the changes themselves were the subject of some controversy after August 1980, their crude imposition and the fact that the reform 'was not the subject of consultation with society' were universally condemned.[8] The 'new' provinces – those which had not previously been the seat of a provincial centre – experienced particular difficulties and lacked cadres, experience, and an adequate material base. The balance of achievement, stated the head of the state executive in Biała Podlaska at a later date, was 'far from equal to expectations'.[9]

In this difficult and uncertain situation the organisation of the staff attached to the new provincial committees was one of the major initial concerns of those charged with putting the reform into operation. The issue was clearly a sensitive one which could complicate work within the new structure and even provoke certain political conflicts. One KW first secretary is reported as urging the greatest delicacy in settling personal matters during the implementation of the reform as a result of which, he stressed, no group of people should find themselves cast out of political work. Some problems were foreseen, though, with the continued employment of those 'with no occupational or secondary education'.[10] Weydenthal alludes to a 'massive relocation of administrative personnel' as a result of the reforms, and notes that the stress on educational background during this period was in fact a 'potent political weapon' that could be used against established officials.[11] There were certainly problems encountered in settling staff within the new political network. By the end of the first year, provincial committee workers were described as being 90% stabilised in one area, a figure that was presented as a success by comparison with a level of 65% in some other provincial institutions.[12] Some apparatus workers had failed to achieve a 'proper evolution of the forms and methods of activity' appropriate to the new situation. In consequence, 'those who did not understand these laws simply had to leave the provincial apparatus. So life itself verified the professional party cadres and, especially under the conditions of our province, it proved to be a harsh master'.[13]

High levels of staff turnover appear to have been widespread after the reform. One new KW first secretary gained the reputation for having caused a 'cadre earthquake' when he arrived.[14] Staff problems were by no means restricted to the party apparatus and, to judge from press reports, were more prevalent at some levels of the government hierarchy, particularly in the case of the rural *naczelnik* – the executive appointed to exercise state authority in rural areas. In the three and a half years that followed the establishment of Konin province its first secretary, Tadeusz Grabski (himself soon to be removed for criticism of Gierek and his policies), sacked 30% of the rural executives and 20% of the first secretaries of local party committees solely for failing to fulfil party obligations or for infringing the party statute.[15] In the first six months of 1979 alone, 32 cadre changes took place in the Gdańsk party organisation, whose staff totalled 248.[16] Despite the emphasis on cadre policy and earlier commendation of the quality of party cadres, then, their capacity for leadership and performance within the new party structure appears to have been less than satisfactory in many cases.

There can be little doubt that these developments had negative consequences for the work of the provincial committee. Piekalkiewicz's conclusion was the straightforward one that 'chaos' was one of the prime initial results of the reform.[17] Certainly echoes of the disturbance were still present nearly two years after the change. Problems in rural party activities in one locality were ascribed partly to the fact that 'the province committee and its *aktiv*, absorbed in the implementation of the reform in the organs of local authority and administration, were delayed in perceiving these matters'.[18] Other reports linked the conflict that broke out in Radom and Ursus following the announcement of price rises in 1976 with the disruption of local party work following the reforms.[19] Despite, too, the overall strengthening of the position of the centre with the subdivision of the provincial apparatus that occurred as a result of the reform, a further development during this period was a reduction in detailed central control over the apparatus.[20] Certainly this is likely to have been the case with the numerical growth of the party apparatus, which is generally accepted to have been accelerated by the reform although this was explicitly ruled out in the guidelines provided by CC secretary Babiuch when the measures were introduced.[21] We have already noted this tendency in the previous chapter with the average level of staffing of the provincial committee at something over sixty people during this period. Exact staffing levels are, however, difficult to ascertain. Those on the payroll of other organisations (trade unions, for example) could be delegated to work for the party, as one provincial first secretary later admitted.[22] An empirical work by French sociologists also described a factory party committee run by four secretaries, only two of whom were paid from KW funds. The other two were officially employed by the factory but would transfer to party work when activities intensified.[23] There does not seem to be much doubt that the party apparatus was significantly larger in fact then official figures suggested.

The role of the provincial committees in 'social dialogue'

The changing structure of the party organisation was accompanied by changing official views of the role of the provincial party organ. A major part of Gierek's early political approach had been an emphasis on 'dialogue' with society, a natural response to the growing antipathy that had developed between the Gomułka leadership and Polish society and culminated in the conflicts of 1970. An important role in this process was assigned to the party, and the establishment of a denser provincial committee network was intended to foster closer links between the party organ and local social groups. The growth in number of provincial committees from twenty-two to forty-nine gave some basis to the claim that the reform had brought the party 'closer to the people'. Six months after the reorganisation the judgment on its effects expressed by Rakowski, editor of *Polityka* and an influential political spokesman close to Gierek, was a decidedly positive one. The link between the provincial committees and lower party organs was claimed to have been 'visibly strengthened'. 'Nothing strengthens the authority of party organs', he stated, 'like keeping constant and attentive track of the popular mood, analysing every opinion, and the mutual solution of difficult problems.'[24] The meaning and actual form of the 'mutual solution' presented the provincial committee and its staff with some major problems.

Another element in Gierek's approach had been summed up in the slogan 'The party leads and the government governs', meaning that the tasks of party and government were different, and that the party was not supposed to do the government's job or to supplant it. This represented a further attempt to tackle the vexed and long-standing issues arising from party–state relations in communist systems. As developments during the final phase of the Gierek regime demonstrated, the distinction could be exploited in the attempt to provide some measure of protection for the position of the party, whose leadership could attempt to lay the blame for the shortcomings of the system at the door of the government. But what 'party leadership' really meant in this conception was never made clear, and the task given the intermediate and lower-level party organs to achieve a dialogue with society under these conditions placed them under considerable pressure. In a society where Marxism-Leninism had so clearly failed to win popular support the work of the party propagandist was clearly not an easy one, and to exercise party leadership in purely ideological and political terms presented him with a formidable challenge.

Party leaders at all levels of the organisation, for one thing, were acutely aware that their power had little association with authority either based on legal principles or derived from social approbation. That was why 'they were desperately trying to "strengthen the authority of power" and were willing to do almost everything if one turned to them, rather than the formally designated government bodies, for a decision on any matter'.[25] To this extent, as we have suggested earlier, the confusion of party–state roles could have a positive effect on party authority and could endow the claim to party leadership with greater plausibility. The practice was, however, quite contradictory to the principle adopted by Gierek of 'The party leads and the government governs', which in formal terms at least meant a stricter separation of roles. The benefits of the old practice were also well recognised by local party officials. In their meetings with the local population the matters raised were not ideological but practical: the health centre in need of repair, muddy roads, poorly supplied shops, the brick shortage. Although none of these issues were the direct responsibility of the party committee, and still less of its propaganda workers, influence could be exerted through the committee on the appropriate agency and popular needs satisfied to the advantage of the party organisation.

Said the director of one Centre for Ideological Training attached to a provincial committee, 'If the *lektor* fixes something for people he automatically gains the trust of the locality. He grows in authority because people see him as an organiser and not just someone who has come with a lecture to give. He becomes a welcome guest, and on the next occasion he may be able to start up an open dialogue with the local inhabitants.'[26] The letters received by the provincial party office were often seen as one means of establishing authority on this basis.[27] In

Włocławek province each KW employee took it in turns to spend a six-day week, for eight hours a day, to man the desk at which personal submissions were received. This was seen as an 'excellent school of contact with so-called life'. All contacts and the action taken were noted, overall supervision being exercised by the head of the Letters and Inspection Department. The KW secretariat discussed once a quarter the contents of the letters received, KW departments were informed about action taken in their sphere of responsibility once a month, and the first secretary received a report on interventions he had personally recommended once a week.[28] This approach appears to have been part of a general emphasis placed by the first secretary on encouraging social initiative and the close contact of KW staff with the population.[29] The dangers of supplanting government agencies and the administration do not seem to have been to the fore in this case. Indeed, the first secretary was aware of the provincial committee's responsibility for pursuing activities in this area and of the growing demands on its staff in view of the 'declining discipline and inconsequential behaviour of both institutions and individuals'.

This was clearly a major aspect of party activities in some provinces and the party was seen by the population to perform a definite function in this respect. Party organs below CC level received nearly a hundred thousand such letters and nearly three hundred thousand personal applications in 1977, the great majority being addressed to the provincial committee as the visible seat of power. In Nowy Sącz around 40% of these submissions received a 'positive solution'. This, wrote one commentator, 'testified to the party's authority, particularly of its higher organs. It is a sign of faith in the party as the force which shows the greatest responsiveness to human misfortune.' But, she continued, 'the flow of such letters may on the other hand be a reflection of the fact that the PZPR provincial organ is inclined to supplant the administration even in its minor responsibilities, which must also be seen as a shortcoming in KW work.'[30] The provincial committee was the subject of conflicting pressures in this area. Although an aspect of its activity perceived as positive by the public and regarded as a usual function by provincial party staff themselves, its validity was placed in doubt by Gierek's political strategy and such activity could not be pursued without some doubts on the part of the provincial apparatus itself.

In operational terms the distinctions drawn by Gierek caused problems. Provincial first secretary Ryszard Łabuś (Gorzów Wielkopolski) interpreted party leadership to mean strategic action while that of the government was tactical, 'where to locate the shop or house, what to do about the shortage of furniture'. But he admitted that the distinction was not easily made and that the temptation to act differently was a strong one: 'A committed person wants to act effectively. He is tempted to grab the phone and say: Good morning, this is the Committee speaking, do this . . . And they do it. We raise our prestige, and its basically pleasing for a person to be able to act effectively. Do you think that we're all agreed on this thing in the KW?'[31] Obviously not all were agreed on 'this thing'. Some continued with supplanting activities because they clearly regarded it as an appropriate way to act, while others did as a continuation of established traditions. One provincial secretary complained that old habits were difficult to break after the reform: party staff continued to 'supplant the administration in decision-making, encroaching on the competence of the organs of the *gmina* [rural commune] – instead of instructing and stimulating initiative'.[32] Exercising party leadership without supplanting the administration was no easy matter, particularly within the new organisational structure which brought the KW apparatus into closer contact with local society, its grievances and its experience of shortages and administrative malfunctions.

The emphasis on closer links with society meant for the provincial committee not just, at least in formal terms, a resignation from established practices of administrative supplantation but also an emphasis on the *political* role of the party official. The member of the apparatus, it was stressed, should not be 'an "employee" in the generally used sense of the word – but a political activist'. This gave particular prominence to the KW 'instructor', as the linkman between the provincial organ and town and commune committees, the main agency of transmission of the popular mood and of discussion in organisations and the social context.[33] It directed attention to the social role of the member of the provincial committee staff rather than to his position as an official within the party hierarchy. Such strategies had, it appears, been evolved in some provinces. Some of the problems involved in conducting propaganda work in the industrial context had been overcome in Gdańsk by setting up a workers' propaganda *aktiv*. It was logical that such alternatives should be explored in a province like Gdańsk where, following the events of December 1970 and early 1971, statements and lectures from KW employees on the virtues of party leadership were unlikely to be very successful. The *aktiv*, as first secretary Tadeusz Fiszbach explained, played the part of an 'intermediate link in the intraparty information system in both directions'.[34] As many of these activists had emerged politically in 1970 this institution also provided a way of incorporating authoritative figures amongst the workers and of neutralising criticism of the party as a whole. In addition, KW staff avoided having to appear as party representatives in the face of the local workers as an undifferentiated social mass, and were less subject to the temptations of claiming party leadership by performing administrative tasks.

The Gdańsk experience, however, was probably rather special – both because of the particularly difficult position in which the provincial committee found itself in 1970 and because of the noted political skills and perception of first secretary Fiszbach, characteristics that were to bring him to national prominence after August 1980. Elsewhere the gap between provincial committee and local public was probably more marked. Shortly before the 1975 reform it was noted that, in general speech, reference to party committees meant their professional apparatus. Members of the committees elected from local party organisations were generally silent and non-participant in the work of the committees.[35] Empirical inquiries showed the size of the 'local party *aktiv*' to be relatively small and suggested that their political role was similarly limited. Of some thirty thousand party members in Słupsk province 5,755 were identified as members of the *aktiv*. Of these nearly a fifth were made up of a relatively small elite group of technical and engineering staff, a further 13% of education employees, and so on. Elected members of the provincial committee were often not considered to be part of the *aktiv* at all.[36] Relatively sympathetic analysts of Soviet politics like Jerry Hough have recorded their doubts about the accuracy of Soviet claims to high numbers of party activists, and there is no reason to conclude that Polish efforts in this direction have been more successful.[37]

The directive to the provincial committees to enhance the 'dialogue' between party and society through the medium of professional and non-professional activism cannot have been easy, therefore, to implement. The political climate of the mid-seventies was certainly not a positive one for this kind of initiative, as the workers' protests and demonstrations of 1976 clearly showed. The pronounced 'ideological crisis' within the party can hardly have made a useful contribution to the implementation of this line of policy, either, as later criticism suggested. Within the apparatus 'silence became like gold, and assent to one's superiors became the surest guarantee of making a career'. Throughout the party hierarchy, processes of government and administration played the dominant role.[38] Even allowing for the benefit of hindsight and the influence of later political conflicts, it was clear that developments within the party in the late seventies were not flowing in favour of an open dialogue with society. Workers presented one problem for party officials but the situation in the countryside, with growing authoritarianism in the rural administration, also provided favourable conditions for the persistence of old habits of party high-handedness in dealings with the peasants. 'Routinised methods of direction instead of consultation' were 'not a rarity' in KW dealings with organisations in rural areas.[39] Social contact on the part of KW staff with rural inhabitants was not, it seemed, particularly frequent, a fact which hardly facilitated the extension of 'dialogue'. In descriptions of KW staff visits to rural meetings in Gdańsk province it emerged quite often that 'KW representatives were taking part in meetings of the organisation for the first time'.[40] The new, socially oriented role of the provincial committee did not enjoy favourable conditions for its development.

As we have seen, the provincial party organs and their representatives had expressed some uncertainty on their side about the part they were to act in this dialogue. They were also aware of public resistance to the process. One of the obstacles they were reported to perceive was what was described as the lack of a proper critical awareness on the part of the Polish public. On the face of it, this observation is rather surprising in view of what we know of Polish social attitudes. Criticism, however, has to be understood in a certain sense – criticism of the mode of implementation rather than of actual decisions, of detail rather than overall policy direction, of individuals rather than the regime.[41] But it is not clear that criticism of any kind was welcomed by the party authorities during the seventies. The renewed emphasis on educational appointments evident in cadre appointments also seemed to have consequences for the lack of communication between party leaders and the Polish population. Looking back from 1980 one journalist commented: 'in the seventies the word "dialogue" was fashionable, so the *aktiv* were trained in monologues. But neither week-long courses nor years spent at an institute could compensate for the lack of those activists who were often very little educated but who spoke what they believed.'[42] Changes within the party apparatus pointed in a direction quite the opposite to that of dialogue with society.

To expect open communication and freely expressed criticism within the structures and mode of operation established under Gierek showed either excessive naivety or hypocrisy. In fact, as one perceptive observer wrote just before the 1975 changes, criticism often remained muted or unofficial because the individual had little confidence it would change things and felt that he would merely be placed in a more difficult position because of it. The problem was that the complaints of weaker members of society could easily be ignored and it was only 'criticism supported by authority [which] is never disregarded'.[43] Here, in fact, was the authentic role for the party if it was not to function by supplanting agencies of government and the administration – to identify which elements of social criticism were valid and to put the authority of the party behind them in order to improve the operation of the system as a whole. This, however, was clearly less viable as a means for the party to establish or enhance its own authority, although some of the more energetic and imaginative secretaries like Fiszbach in Gdańsk did attempt some such strategy. But in general established practices of joint party–state activity and overlapping patterns of political rule and economic management discouraged such approaches and made it considerably easier for the party organs to continue along existing lines. The idea of a party authority distinct from and even in conflict with that of government and the economic administration had no real basis in communist Poland. As the above-mentioned writer emphasised, 'In many people's consciousness the conviction has been formed over the years that the leadership of the party organisation should *always* publicly support the authority of (for example) the plant management.' This left little room for the development of a dialogue with society along the lines sketched above. Indeed, as we shall see, Gierek's reforms left the provincial committees with little basis for retaining, let alone enhancing, any autonomous authority they might have had.

Provincial authority and central power

The official claim that the 1975 reforms would bring the authorities 'closer to the people' was true only, if at all, in the sense that the reorganisation of the party organisation increased the number of provincial committees and provided more numerous channels of access to the KW staff. In fact, the reform served to protect the Gierek leadership from challenges to its position from the party apparatus and its provincial base, thus enhancing central power and having nothing to do with any process of political decentralisation. This aspect of the reform had not gone unnoticed at the time of its enactment. In a pointed allusion to the image cultivated by the Gierek team one writer noted that 'the partisans of technocratic methods utilise arguments which are apparently rational and sound very progressive'. He warned, though, that the 'optimalisation' of power resources should not take place 'at the expense of democracy and social control'.[44] This is evidently what happened, and it is obviously wrong to interpret the reform as any kind of decentralisation. On the other hand, to the extent that it involved an increase in the number of provincial committees and the abolition of the next layer of administration (the *powiat*), the reform can be interpreted as a form of de-concentration, an *'administrative* device in a hierarchical system which involves the shifting of decision-making from an overloaded centre to lower levels of the hierarchy' which should increase efficiency 'without changing any of the basic power relationships'.[45] But, at the same time, other changes tended to undermine the decision-making capacity of the provincial committee.

This particularly concerned the changing form of economic administration. The tendency to concentration of economic units had made them more amenable to central direction well before the 1975 reform, and the growing power of the combine in relation to the economic association, which dated from 1970–71, had already weakened KW influence in this respect.[46] The smaller size of the individual committee and its reduced scope of influence obviously had further consequences in this area. Tendencies within the economy at this time, however, also strengthened pressures for formal central control and prevented the full realisation of the economic reform project drawn up at the beginning of the seventies. It was precisely as more elements of the reformed system were due to come into operation in 1975 that growing economic difficulties were responsible for the suspension of the further autonomisation of economic units and a return to 'routinised, indicative, distributive instruments of directing organisations'.[47] This was made easier by the fact that major features of economic reform were yet to be introduced. The traditional branch ministries had not yet been affected and both their apparatus and conventional mode of operation remained intact. Economic conditions therefore favoured further centralisation rather than autonomisation of local units and continuing decline in the economic influence of the provincial committee.

These divergent tendencies were quick to make their mark and the consequences of centralisation came in for criticism by those relatively favourable to Gierek's overall approach. Rakowski made an important contribution in an article entitled 'The Limits of Centralisation'. In this he wrote that 'There exists an aspiration to the centralisation of decisions and the direction of all social and economic life from a single leadership centre . . . The realisation of this conceptualisation in practice may, however, bring results not at all favourable to the state.'[48] His article ended on a note which referred directly to the role of local party organs: 'Our many thousands of cadres should realise the party's directives concerning the economic manoeuvre in the conviction that they have their own sphere of responsibility, that their initiative is counted on and that they are fully trusted.' The fact was, of course, that their initiative was not counted on and that the growing centralism of the late Gierek period left little place for independent action on the part of provincial committees, although increasingly, central direction itself was becoming less effective.

Supporting the view that this criticism was not only an accurate interpretation of the trend of developments but was also felt by the leadership to be a point of major weakness, Rakowski's article provoked stinging journalistic counter-criticism. He himself clearly resented not just the content but also the tenor of the counter-attack, justifying his position in a further article entitled 'The limits of centralism and decency'.[49] His view was also current in the party as a whole, and it came to the surface in the discussion at the IX Plenum of the Central Committee in October 1977 where centralism was criticised for restricting 'the initiative of lower-level authorities'.[50] The capacity of the provincial party committee to perform the role formally allotted to it and still expected of it was becoming the subject of much doubt within the post-1975 framework. At the II Party Conference in 1978 the local party *aktiv* was described as having decided views on this subject and this was reflected particularly in the speech of KW first secretary Andrzej Żabiński. It was later noted by Rakowski once more, who described the 'clear emergence over the past few years of a wave of public criticism directed towards the methods of government which have introduced extreme centralism into our state organism'.[51] This provided particular problems for the provincial committee, which after 1975 was placed in more direct contact with the local population and was expected to carry more executive responsibility. On the other hand it had little capacity for independent action and its ability to mobilise the local population was 'directly tied to the popularity or distrust' of national policies.[52] At a time when Gierek's economic strategy was running into serious problems this placed them in a difficult position.

At the XIII Plenum, held in December 1978, similar complaints were heard, but expressed with greater vehemence by provincial party leaders. Szymański (Włocławek) called for decentralisation of the decision-making process and complained that 'we still have too many unreal plans with revisions sent up and down that are incomprehensible to the workforce'; Kapitan (Toruń) called for information to be sent to the local authorities of changes in the plans of local enterprises; Buziński (Bielsko-Biała) described it as indispensable that lower levels of the state administration should 'retain their proper competence and the capacity to make certain decisions'; Balawajder (Krosno) pointed to the decentralisation possibilities inherent in the new structure and affirmed that 'local authorities do have the capacity to solve more complicated social and economic problems'.[53] It appears that it was only under the critical conditions of the 1978/1979 winter, with atrocious weather, transport breakdowns and severe energy shortages, that the central authorities, unable or unwilling to cope, relaxed their hold and permitted – or enforced – greater autonomy on the provinces. There was, then, some transfer of decision-making power down the line. But it was in effect a 'decentralisation of difficulties' which did nothing to strengthen the position of the provincial party leadership and gave them little scope for regaining authority.[54] From late 1976 the Poznań provincial committee was aware that local workers felt that the party 'was leading the country into ruin'.[55] The following year the picture was so bleak that apparently in consequence the biennial report did not even mention the content of discussions within the local organisations, while in 1978 the KW assessment warned central authorities of a further deterioration in workers' attitudes.

Provincial committees and the question of 'control'

It was significant that the period immediately following the party reorganisation was one in which a significant downward shift occurred in Poland's political and economic situation. This placed further pressure on the already sensitive position of the provincial committee. 1975 was reckoned to be the year in which the limit within which Poland's international debt could reasonably be serviced was reached; OPEC action had fed Western levels of inflation which, in view of growing dependence on imports for both production and consumption purposes, posed further problems for the Polish economy; the resulting international recession placed further obstacles in the way of the export of Polish goods, the growth of which was a major objective (and assumption) of Gierek's development policy;

agricultural production, after several years of good results, began to stagnate and shortages of consumer goods became severe on the Polish market. By 1976 Gierek had to consider one of the problems that had played a direct role in the downfall of Gomułka, that of changing food prices. Since the rescinding of the earlier price rises in February 1971 Gierek had let the matter rest. With growing agricultural problems, shortages in the shops and an increasing market imbalance, rises in food prices were suddenly announced in June 1976. As in the case of the 1975 organisational reforms, the consultation aspect of Gierek's 'dialogue' with the people was virtually neglected. Workers' demonstrations broke out in Ursus (Warsaw) and Radom. The action of the KW first secretary, Prokopiak, to this situation has already been referred to in the previous chapter. This time the price increases were swiftly withdrawn and the political situation brought under control.

The events of 1976 weakened the political position of the leadership whilst the basic economic problem remained untouched. As a partial response, an 'economic manoeuvre' was announced in December 1976 which was designed to direct increasingly scarce investment resources to priority areas, restrict the use of such funds, which had hitherto been dispensed very freely, and to generally tighten up on economic management and management practices. It soon became clear that, as in the case of the price rises, this policy measure too was encountering major implementation problems. Leadership decisions did not have the desired effect and the effectiveness of the party organisation as a mechanism for ensuring their implementation and checking on the efficacy of this process also came into question. This, however, had been one of the major emphases of the 1975 reform, particularly as it concerned the responsibilities of the KW staff: 'Provincial committees as well as the Central Committee will place still greater emphasis on both local work and inspection and control activity' was the formulation made at the CC meeting of May 1975.[56]

'Control' activities have always played a large part in the operation of communist systems and the emphasis placed on their role at this stage of Polish developments was not new, although the progressive disintegration in Polish economic and political affairs during this period did provide a more unusual context. Such activities have an extensive history not only in Soviet but also in pre-communist Russian experience.[57] Indeed, the specifically Russian origins of the concept provide some problems both of political interpretation and of translation. The Russian term, *kontrol'*, which provides the basis for such practice throughout Eastern Europe, carries a number of connotations which are certainly not reducible to the English expression, control. Hough discusses the term, and its considerable ambiguities, at some length. In the case of a factory cell, for example, he suggests that the party's right of 'control' conveys the 'impression of a primary Party organization checking, verifying, inspecting the work of the manager and enforcing his adherence to laws and plans established else-where'.[58] Schwartz refers to 'an administrative process of inspection and verification' and simply suggests the use of the English 'super-vision'.[59] This is a reasonable suggestion, although the significance of *kontrol'* activities is not so far removed from the exercise of political and economic control as has been supposed. *Kontrol'*, or in Polish, *kontrola*, particularly as exercised by party organs, is clearly an expression of party leadership and represents an attempt to enhance central party control.

The very emphasis placed by Soviet authorities on *kontrol'* as a significant and distinctive kind of activity reflects the problems they have encountered in actualising the concept. The confusion between control and managerial or executive power began at an early stage, as 'both Bolshevik doctrine and Russian conditions were erasing the previous boundary between them'.[60] The precise functions of party organs in this respect have remained a source of conflict, though to a varying degree, throughout the Soviet period and emerged as such in the 1970s with the introduction of the *ob"edinenie* reform, itself highly similar to the change occurring within the sphere of Polish economic organisation.[61] The basic source of conflict concerns the extent to which the local official acts as an agent of the higher party leadership and represents general party interests against the local manager or admin-istrator, or to which he acts as an overall, stabilising political presence (the 'prefect') and cooperates with the manager in order to help him achieve his particular goals. The two activities are not wholly contra-dictory and both reflect the overall objectives of party leadership. The particular emphases, though, are clearly different and represent a constant tension in the role and orientation of provincial officials. They are closely related to the practical problems faced when interpretation of the concrete meaning of 'control' is called for in application to specific contexts. These are conditioned by the structural setting, policy emphases and organisational possibilities characteristic of the relevant situation.

In Poland, the possibility of party 'control' at provincial level had been significantly changed by the 1975 reform. At the same time the difficulties experienced by the Gierek administration in achieving some sort of economic equilibrium and in implementing the economic manoeuvre directed the attention of party leaders to the importance of 'control' and its dubious effectiveness.[62] Condemnation of poor KW performance in the areas of coordination and control was expressed at provincial committee sessions held during the summer of 1977.[63] The subject was discussed in detail at the IX Plenary Session of the Central Committee in October 1977, which was concerned with the level of implementation of the decisions made at the V and VI sessions of the Committee at which the measures making up the economic ma- noeuvre had been announced. Twenty-four KW first secretaries sat on the Central Committee (the remaining twenty-five were alternate members) and nine of them spoke at the Plenum. A major theme was launched by Tadeusz Grabski, Konin first secretary, whose persistent criticism of Gierek's economic approach was to lead to his removal from the apparatus in 1979. He stressed the problems which faced the provincial committees caused by divergencies from central plans and directives and the instability of investment planning. Hebda (Zielona Góra) and Grochmalicki (Wałbrzych) also drew attention to this problem, the latter pointing out that 'we have yet to work out a well organised system of party control over individual investment measures'.[64] Later criticism from Gdańsk province was equally forth- right, when a KW secretary rejected administrators' excuses about the lack of financial cooperation and integration within the recently estab- lished large economic unit.[65] A Warsaw secretary also expressed the view that recent economic reorganisation had not been thought through properly and that its introduction had been rushed and was consequently ineffective.[66]

A second area of criticism concerned staff behaviour and the atti- tudes of leading personnel. This was alluded to at the IX Plenum by Warsaw committee secretary Dryll as 'The formalism emerging some- times in the course of implementing the manoeuvre shown by some elements within the economic administration'. He criticised the 'decla- rative, verbal support' expressed for the manoeuvre by those who at the same time denied that their sphere of activity should be affected.[67] Individual managers and economic administrators were clearly deter- mined to protect their own projects and individual interests and it was rapidly becoming clear that the central authorities and the party hier- archy were unable to prevent this. There were suggestions that Poland lacked the systems of control and supervision of managerial cadres that had been developed in countries like Czechoslovakia, East Ger- many and the Soviet Union.[68] The constant criticism of the quality of cadres and their anti-social attitudes certainly appeared to have some basis in this area. But it was clearly not just a matter of their personal attributes. The system of cadre appointment and of staff supervision also appeared to be at fault. Related problems were noted in the party apparatus, particularly in connection with an aspect we have already noted, namely the dubious relationship between formal qualifications and political aptitude. This point was made by, somewhat paradoxically, KW first secretary Prokopiak, shortly before the outbreak of mass demonstrations on his own territory. 'It struck me at the beginning', he stated, 'that we have a number of young educated people in their early thirties and I thought why shouldn't they take on [leadership] positions? But when I looked at them more closely it turned out that they were only able to lead "in general" and that they lacked concrete practice.'[69] In this the general views we have alluded to above on the deformation of the cadres system appear to have some substance.

The growing economic problems facing Poland in conjunction with the obstacles encountered in exerting discipline over economic administrators and the managerial cadres indicated the crucial role of the party and the demands placed on its capacity for control. 'The party', stated one of the more forthright Polish industrial journalists, 'is the only force in the country which has sufficient authority to overcome the barriers of routine, the strong defences of particularism, the fortress of technocratic and bureaucratic mentality.'[70] Whether this residual authority could be mobilised for effective action was a matter of some doubt. Not long earlier, Rakowski had optimistically claimed that the formula of party leadership was now 'correctly understood. Party organs do not supplant or replace the state and economic administration. They mark their presence in social life with increasing emphasis as a force of control, overseeing the correct implementation of the general line by all components of the state and national economic administration'.[71] This statement was made just before the II Party Conference in early 1978 largely, one suspects, with the intention of rallying the troops. Reports on the effectiveness of party work at provincial and local level painted a rather different picture.

The year following the decision concerning the 'economic manoeuvre' a number of reports on the work of the Provincial Party Control Commissions (WKKP: *Wojewódzkie Komisje Kontroli Partyjnej*) suggested a less satisfactory state of affairs. An early report showed an apparent correlation between the poor performance of economic units and an unacceptable level of activity undertaken by the party cell, particularly in conducting work that was 'insufficiently concrete'.[72] A common complaint was that too much 'tolerance' was shown at local party meetings – thus the absence of a manager or plant director, or his failure to perform some task set by the party would be treated more leniently than the equivalent transgression by a less senior member.[73] Management was, perhaps not surprisingly, suspicious of control activities and resented what was often felt to be 'unfounded criticism' which simply served to 'obstruct' the plant's work.[74] It could not be regarded as surprising that managers often felt too busy to take part in what was probably routine party work, or that they were not impressed by what was likely to be somewhat inexpert criticism. Administrative disregard for the party, however, went far beyond this.

Some of the corrupt practices about which so much was heard after the August strikes were beginning to come to light in 1977, although the party played little part in this. Following the inspection by the government inspection commission, the Supreme Control Chamber (NIK: *Najwyższa Izba Kontroli*), of one case where public-funded purchases had ended up in private apartments, it was discovered that all previous statements had been drawn up and circulated by the director. When this became known, though, no word of criticism was made by the party cell.[75] 'Blanket liberalism and tolerance of diverse bad phenomena' were widespread within the party, and while many party members found it difficult to condemn the unsatisfactory behaviour of some colleagues it was 'quite impossible' to do so when the guilty party was the chairman or a director.[76] Even when party members had, in some cases, received court sentences (a total of 225 in 1977) no action was generally taken by the party organisation.[77] The 'control' of professional superiors was clearly one of the major problems.

In a study of one factory the first secretary of the party organisation spoke of how the plant director was a member of the provincial committee and thus well positioned to exert general authority in the plant and, broadly speaking, to get his own way. Yet, formally speaking, he was obliged as a party member to work according to the jurisdiction of the plant cell – itself, of course, subject to the guidance of the provincial committee and its secretariat.[78] It is easy to see, in such a context, not just how difficult it often was for local party organisations to exercise control over management, but also how ambiguous the concept of control was within the party as a whole. The factory organisation might well be overruled by the provincial committee not so much on grounds of party practice as on the manager's status within the economic administration. The close association of party leadership in communist systems with the state administration made the formal notion of party control rather doubtful. It enhanced the dangers noted in a broader historical and comparative context that were associated with the probability that controlling agencies 'will enter into collusion with those they monitor'.[79]

Particular problems developed in Poland following the reform as the subdivision of political units, which determined the scope of party control, was accompanied by the concentration of economic production units and the increased status of their management. This represented a further stage in the restriction of party autonomy.[80] When the head of a construction association, for example, was found to have been pursuing a policy at odds with the principles underlying the economic manoeuvre, the KW executive found itself powerless to impress its critical appraisal on the managing body of the association and to impose some discipline on the culprit. It was only by going through central government that the director could be removed.[81] Similar problems could occur with some variants of party organisation following the Soviet *ob''edinenie* reform.[82] The local orientation of party officials could come in conflict in such a context with allegiance to party superiors, and 'localism' on occasion provided a basis for opposition to the reform.

With many instances of party discipline being broken and the processes of party 'control' being found wanting, attention was turned to the apparatus of internal party regulation. The activity of provincial control commissions appeared to have been stepped up. In Kielce, the WKKP chairman announced that they were dealing with more cases in 1978 than they had before the 1975 reform – even though the committee was now responsible for an area less than half the size than before 1975.[83] In 1977 and 1978 a total of 70,315 candidates and members were removed from party lists (*skresloni*), equivalent to 14% of new members during this period. This, however, represented a lower level of removal than earlier years. In 1975 and 1976 as many as 133,302 had been removed, equivalent to 35% of new members. The total removed between 1971 and 1978, nearly half a million in all, represented 38% of all new members.[84] This reduction in party ranks resulted from simple removal from party lists, not essentially a form of party punishment, applied in 'the case of passivity, failure to pay dues or resignation'.[85] Expulsion from the party was a different matter, and this fate befell, 4,536 members in 1978, the largest group (1,894) being expelled (*wydaloni*) for malpractice, theft and corruption. Amongst the total expelled were 148 plant directors. A further 5,800 received statutory party punishments.[86]

Amongst a total party membership of 2.93 million in 1978 (see table 3.1) such totals for removal and expulsion do not look strikingly high, taking into account the climate of public opinion in Poland at this time and the higher rate of membership turnover during the preceding period. Neither was it necessarily the case that even those expelled from the party were barred from holding further responsible posts. The chairman of the Central Party Control Commission (*Centralna Komisja Kontroli Partyjnej*) warned that those thus shown to be incompetent or compromised should not be subject to the 'harmful practice of being moved from one responsible position to another'.[87] This was the socially negative side of a policy which encouraged the rotation of cadres. As practised under Gierek, those who gained access to the 'jobs roundabout' had considerable security of tenure and were rarely removed for mere incompetence or criminality. KW first secretary Fiszbach was one who firmly believed in the benefits of the circulation of cadres, but he was aware of the danger of creating a well-protected power elite and argued both for the application of clear criteria of appointment and of stronger sanctions against those who abused their office.[88] As with his approach to local party work and the systemic formation of a party *aktiv*, though, Fiszbach was considerably more rigorous in his approach to party matters than were either the central party authorities or many of his colleagues in the provincial committees.

Internal party 'control' mechanisms in fact appeared to be applied more rigorously to the working-class component of the party membership and to older party members. In 1976 and 1977, 60% those expelled were workers (they made up 47% of total membership in 1977) and 'in some provinces' older party activists with more than twenty years membership had been making up from a quarter to a third of those expelled.[89] The attitude of some party leaders towards the latter category, it was suggested, was both thoughtless and inhumane. It is also likely that this action represented the new trends in party life that had developed under Gierek, with the growing dominance of younger party careerists within the provincial committees and the replacement of practical party experience by more formal education qualifications. It appears that the changing personal characteristics we have noted did have practical political consequences and represented a broader process of generational change whose political impact was far from positive for the authority of the party within Poland.

The principles of party recruitment had become very lax, though, under Gierek and there is every reason to suspect that the quality of

Table 3.1 *PZPR membership (1970–86)*

	1970a	1978a	1980b	1982a	1984a	1986a
Total membership (mil.)	2.320	2.930	3.092	2.327	2.117	2.129
women (per cent)	22.5	26.2	26.8	26.8	26.9	27.2
workers	40.3	45.7	46.1	40.2	38.5	38.0
intelligentsia	42.3	35.8	32.5	49.0	51.0	51.7
Age: 18–29 (%)	25.3	23.5	24.8	11.1	7.6	6.9
30–49	56.5	53.1		57.1	57.4	56.8
50+	18.2	23.4		31.8	35.0	36.3
Education:						
Full higher (%)	7.9	12.0	12.0	15.8	17.4	18.3
Full secondary	27.0	32.5	32.4	35.9	36.7	37.2

a = state at end of year; b = membership total at end of year, percentage composition at VIII Congress (February 1980).
Sources: Rocznik Statystyczny 1981, p. 31; *Rocznik Statystyczny* 1985, p. 31; *Maly Rocznik Statystyczny* 1986, p. 23; *Życie Partii (ZP)* 1980/2, p. 14; *ZP* 1980/3, p. 16.

new members was poor. As Kolankiewicz suggests, the weaker the party organisation felt itself, the more likely it was that 'it would seek to artificially swell its ranks, abandoning all semblance of recruitment criteria or selectivity'.[90] This laxity was particularly likely to affect working-class recruits, which the leadership was especially keen to incorporate into the party during the seventies. Nevertheless, the way in which party discipline was applied did cause considerable disquiet. In one urban district a ratio of ten severe party punishments (such as expulsion) to one mild one (such as a rebuke) was found to have been imposed, which reflected practice elsewhere and was felt to be an unconstructive approach to party discipline.[91] In Bielsko-Biała, where workers made up 67% of those removed from party lists between 1975 and 1979, a KW secretary complained that far too little care was taken in exercising this kind of discipline and referred to 'organisational carelessness and chaos'.[92] There was also, it appeared, extensive ignorance or carelessness in party organisations about the kind of party sanctions that should be applied. Removal from party lists was often regarded as the ultimate party sanction but this, wrote one journalist, was 'a typical mistake. Removal from the list is not a party punishment', but should occur rather in cases of passivity or resignation.[93]

Neither was the situation any more satisfactory in rural areas.

'Plenary KW sessions', stated first secretary Grochmalicki (Wałbrzych), 'have clearly demonstrated the weakness of party work, especially in the countryside'.[94] At the XIII Plenum of the Central Committee, held in December 1978, a number of first secretaries gave expression to their growing worries about the condition of the party organisation and the attitudes of the membership. Local party cells, said Stasiak (Sieradz), 'shrink from applying their statutory rights'. Grabski (Konin), to be removed from the party apparatus altogether the following year, expressed further criticism of the leadership and indicated his dissatisfaction with the state of the local organisation through the information that he had had to remove 20% of first secretaries since the 1975 reform.[95] Buziński (Bielsko-Biała) confessed that the 'control function is performed considerably worse than the function of inspiration'. With some understatment, he said that 'We do not always succeed in taking good political decisions, which are productive of thought and action, through to their conclusion.'[96]

In response to these general feelings about the ineffectiveness of party work and a passive and weakly motivated membership, a considerably greater emphasis on control activities emerged throughout the party organisation. In Szczecin concerted action was taken to combat 'the phenomena of high costs of production, mediocre quality of manufactured goods, declining work discipline, incorrect determination of prices and profits', as economic enterprises themselves showed little inclination to tackle such problems.[97] Out of eight provincial committee plenaries held in Włocławek in 1977, only one had had the character of a 'control' session – but in 1978 the topic had been tackled at half the sessions so far held.[98] In Sieradz the provincial committee, in association with sociologists from Łódź University, initiated a complex study of the 'whole system of party political action, local power-holders and the administration'.[99] A range of suggestions for practical improvements emerged subsequently.

It is hardly surprising that this emphasis did not bring the results hoped for, confirming Christian's view of analagous activities in the Russian Empire and Soviet Union that 'monitoring agencies are always bound to have a limited effect on the system'.[100] Many of the problems to be tackled in this campaign were rooted in the economic system, which was now in a very serious condition both because of the defects in the policies adopted and of the weaknesses in their implementation. Party strategy had been determined from the beginning of the decade, moreover, by the principle that the party organs should in any case not involve themselves directly with the affairs of the economy and its administration. Party officials had been placed in a very ambiguous position with regard to matters of production and supply which weakened their capacity for purposive action. The centralisation of the economic administration and of government agencies under Gierek further curtailed the possibilities open to the provincial committees to exercise their formal 'control' function. In practice, too, the privileged position held by managers on major party committees, their ability to influence both party decisions and their implementation, and the implications of the 'rotation of cadres' policy as pursued under Gierek all combined to undermine the exercise by the party of its 'control' powers. Neither were the characteristics of the party officials appointed under Gierek such as to enhance their effectiveness in this area.

By the end of the decade the view of the party leadership of the state of the party had become extremely bleak and, faced with worsening problems on all fronts, was becoming tinged with fatalism. The view of Zdzisław Grudzień, first secretary of Katowice, Poland's largest province, Politburo member and (perhaps most significant) close associate and ally of Gierek, is instructive in this respect. Describing the condition of the party in the province he wrote of the 'unreliable collation of reports, evaluations and information', of too much attention being paid to individual position and personal interests, of 'harmful tolerance' of misbehaviour in order to gain personal popularity, of 'inadequacies which reduced the dynamism of political and ideological activity', including the avoidance of discussion and failure to take proper note of party resolutions, and of 'weakness in the operation of intra-party control'.[101] In Gdańsk, characterised by a different approach to party work the diagnosis of the situation at a provincial party conference was equally grave but the judgment as to where the great problems lay was more pointed. In the view of Gdańsk delegates the root of the problem lay not so much in the party organisation and the failure of the provincial committee to mobilise party members as in the unresponsiveness of, in particular, the economic administration. Emphasised here was the unwillingness of many cadres, including those within the party apparatus, to follow the changing policy indicated by the economic manoeuvre. Identified at the Gdańsk conference was a 'very threatening tendency among managerial cadres to take a wait-and-see attitude, one of hiding away until better times arrive'.[102] Whatever the major source of resistance, the party was beginning to acknowledge its failure to ensure policy implementation and the inadequacy of the party 'control' process.

In early 1980 it was acknowledged that party organs which 'replaced or came under the competence of organs of state' were not well placed to play an inspirational or controlling role. It was 'well known', for example, that 'an organ controlling itself was not in a position to perform the controlling function in the full sense of the word'.[103] The chairman of the new (post-VIII Congress) Central Party Control Commission admitted that the provincial party control commissions were not really in a position to exert discipline over people in managerial positions within institutions of a supra-province character, particularly when any malpractices concerned organisations located in several different provinces.[104] It was becoming clear, then, that the provincial committee's role was less one of party leadership and 'checking' on managers than, as often had been the case in Soviet experience, 'another example of party officialdom cooperating with and generally oiling the state machine rather than meddling in its affairs'.[105] The role of the provincial leader was later summed up by KW secretary Ryszard Kurylczyk (Słupsk), who described the party's facilitating function in the following way: 'the KW secretary organises a "directorate", a weekly gathering of bosses and party organisation secretaries from the largest plants in the province. It was a market for raw materials, services, resources, in a word entrepreneurial self-help'.[106] The party secretary had become less of a political leader than an economic master of ceremonies.

Neither, it was recognised, were the personal characteristics of party staff appropriate to the political tasks they were supposed to perform. Żandarowski, member of the CC Secretariat since 1972 and head of its Organisation Department after 1970, announced that the policies pursued under Gierek had fostered among cadres a 'fetishisation of expertise, simplified judgments and evaluation of people exclusively on the basis of their qualifications and the efficiency of their activity'.[107] New methods of consultation with cadres which concerned not just technical efficiency but also 'decency and honesty' were strongly recommended.[108] It was only at this late stage that the defects of the cadres policy pursued under Gierek and the nature of its implications for the effectiveness of party work were recognised. By this time any possibility of party 'control' had clearly passed.

Authority crisis and the provincial secretaries

The maintenance of channels of ideological exchange has played an important, if ill-defined, role in the development of political crises in communist Eastern Europe. Ideology has a close relationship with political organisation, elite integration and the effective exercise of power in communist systems.[109] Gierek, as we have noted, showed little concern for ideological matters and counted on perpetuating his authority with a successful economic policy. Nevertheless, the language of ideology was important, both for intra-party communication and, particularly, for provincial organs in formulating their approach to local society and structuring their necessary contacts with the local population. With the failure of Gierek's economic strategy and the inability to enforce the measures contained within the economic manoeuvre, the weakness of the ideological face of Gierek's rule became more evident. It was not just coincidental that Gierek's economic failure was accompanied by a growing awareness of the weakness of party ideological activity while indications of elite conflict were also coming to the fore. All were signs of the onset of a general authority crisis.

Significant, too, was the date set by a Łódź party committee secretary for when propagandists and lecturers 'began to realise that their arsenal of methods and forms of work developed earlier were becoming increasingly ineffective' and began seeking a new ideological approach.[110] This was set some eighteen months before the publication of the article and referred therefore to mid-1977, some months after the announcement of the economic manoeuvre and a time at which it was becoming clear that the leadership was incapable of controlling ongoing political and economic processes. A negative appraisal of ideological work emerged also from the Koszalin committee, where concern for the pressing economic and material problems was dominant. A certain fatalism seemed to have developed within the party *aktiv* which cast doubt on the efficacy of political action. This 'harmed the party, weakened its authority, and led to the rise of opinions about the futility of party activity'.[111] An avoidance within the party of ideological discussion was also reported in Włocawek.[112].

Such developments were not new, and the deep-seated ideological crisis was identified as the root cause of the complex of problems that came to envelop Poland. The neglect of the Higher School of Social Sciences attached to the Central Committee was noted in this respect and the failure to draw on its resources to help in the training of apparatus workers, even those directed to work in KW propaganda departments, was deplored.[113] Higher School graduates were explicitly mentioned by the first secretary of Kalisz province – but he sent them to work as secretaries in construction enterprises.[114] The weakness of the ideological aspect of Gierek's rule was therefore not a new factor in the situation, but it became considerably more important with the failure of his economic strategy and the growing sense of impotence within the party. It contributed to the growing sense of alienation from the population felt by the provincial secretaries and the uncertainty they felt as to their role in the late seventies. The disorientation and sense of unreality at provincial level are hinted at in some statements made at the XVI CC Plenum, held towards the end of 1979; KW secretary Szałańska (Nowy Sącz) stated that the pre-Congress provincial committee meetings had been somewhat disturbing: 'the favourable political atmosphere which we observed during the campaign has given rise to a certain anxiety among the *aktiv* as to whether all the problems current in society were really articulated at the meetings'.[115] Reports from another conference suggested, in addition, alienation from the party centre on the part of the provincial committee and frustration at the concealment of information: in Gdańsk one speaker called for an 'honest evaluation of the state of affairs in the country and in the region', complaining that the provincial authorities were able to satisfy such demands only with regard to their own area.[116]

The growing sense of political failure led to criticism and conflict at national level. We have already noted some of the criticism made by KW secretaries at the IX Plenum in October 1977 of continuing centralism and errors in economic policy. Their dissatisfaction with the poor state of food supplies, something that had a direct bearing on the mood of the population, was also strongly expressed.[117] At the same time an appeal from former Politburo and Central Committee members called for a programme of economic and political reforms and directed attention to the 'bureacratic party machine' which 'encourages insincerity, torpor, and causes party organisations to lose their natural initiative'.[118] Disagreements within the central leadership were also reported, and these were associated with the departure of Tadeusz Grabski from the apparatus in 1979 and the removal from the Politburo of Stefan Olszowski the following year.[119] Such disorientation and conflict within the party involved not just the attitudes of party officials but also their political efficacy and the power of the party as an institution. From early 1978, it appears, the party became increasingly reliant on the army and its political apparatus to maintain its position. The provincial party committees came under the partial jurisdiction of regional military commanders and a system of regular military supervision was instituted.[120]

Nevertheless, the VIII PZPR Congress, held in February 1980, was characterised by much of the conventional official party optimism and carried a considerable sense of unreality. While the existence of major problems was not denied and some personnel changes were made, including the removal of the Prime Minister, the tone of Gierek's statement was remarkably positive. 'Party meetings', he claimed in his report on behalf of the Central Committee, 'are to an increasing extent the forum for authentic and honest discussion about all the everyday matters that closely concern party members, the place for critical and self-critical evaluation of attitudes and opinions which lead to the formulation of constructive conclusions and tasks'.[121] The collapse of his regime, however, occurred in a matter of months as a result of the wave of strikes that followed the introduction of higher prices for some meat products on July 1st. One observer argues that the measure was essentially determined by the leadership's sensitivity to the authority crisis and its awareness of the serious condition of the party, 'the growing realization that any further delay in reasserting its authority could only cause further decay'. It was this 'preoccupation with authority-building, combined with a strong overtone of disregard for social protest, that eventually was to undermine the position of the leadership'.[122] So while the depth of the economic crisis was unquestionable, the price rise itself was a relatively minor affair (involving a transfer of 2% of the total amount of meat marketed from ordinary to 'commercial' shops, where prices were higher) and the immediate trigger of the crisis was a political one, directly linked to the leadership's perception of an authority crisis. The wage increases that the authorities were content to grant on a piece-meal basis to end the spate of industrial disruptions that followed the announcement of the price rises in any case soon outweighed any economic impact the rises might have had.

The wave of strikes that broke out in July 1980 caused the longest and most widespread disruption of industrial production that had occurred in the People's Republic.[123] It would appear that the central leadership, aware of the failure of their political tactic from the beginning of July and immobilised by their political impotence, were left with little possibility of making a political response to the workers' growing challenge. No general political position towards it was taken up until well into August when a news briefing was given by Politburo member and CC secretary Jerzy Łukasiewicz. He took care to emphasise the purely economic nature of the strikes and to continue with the claim that the party was in full control of the situation. This was not the view taken by the leadership in communications with its members. A message sent from the CC Secretariat to all members on 19 August indicated rather the 'anti-socialist elements in the strike committees' and the threat posed to the 'foundations of the system of People's Poland'.[124] Central party authorities thus adopted a highly ambiguous attitude towards the strikes which reflected their indecision and inability to bring the situation under control.

As in the case of the disruptions during the winter of 1978–79, material problems and political pressure caused central leadership to emphasise the role of provincial committees and to decentralise its problems. A meeting of the Warsaw committee on 12 August called for firmer party leadership at local level and passed resolutions binding on members within the province. Stanisław Kania, Politburo member and CC secretary responsible for security affairs, visited the Gdańsk committee on 18 August and admitted that 'adventurists' had gained influence with the strikers because of the weakness of the party and its alienation from society. To understand the cause of this, though, reference was made in the first instance to 'inadequacies in the work of the provincial committee and to administrative defects'.[125] The central leadership was clearly still unwilling to accept responsibility for the political situation that had developed.

Kania, moreover, had been appointed to head the party commission set up to deal with the disorders. He was clearly playing the key coordinating role within the leadership at this time and spoke at the IV Plenum of the Central Committee held on 24 August at which four key members of Gierek's leadership team were dropped from the Politburo. At the meeting Kania set the tone for the party's strategy for political recovery and rejected the use of force as a solution – 'only one weapon is important, one force – the force of authority and trust in power-holders, the force of the party's influence on the masses. That is what is decisive and what is most lacking to us today'.[126] It was at this stage that the significance of the party's regaining the strength of confidence was introduced, underpinned by social credibility (*wiary-godność*, the word that was to become a major party slogan throughout the first phase of the post-Gierek period). Clearly, in Kania's view, the party would have to retreat some way in order to make an exit from the impasse in which it now found itself. Before suggesting any such measures he sought to reassure the provincial committees (despite his more critical remarks at the Gdańsk plenum) that they had so far 'passed their exam well'.

Whatever the analysis of the causes of the August crisis, or of ways out of it, it was clear that the focus of political conflict now lay at provincial level. Of the twelve speakers at the Plenum, five were KW first secretaries and the problems experienced in preceding years both with central leadership and with the local population were very much in the forefront of their attention. Władysław Kruk (Lublin, soon to be elected candidate member of the Politburo) referred to the familiar theme of over-centralisation and the extensive development of the bureaucracy under Gierek, while Zasada, first secretary in Poznań since 1971, complained of the absence of 'dialogue' between KW and central party authorities: information communicated on the worsening social mood 'remained without echo or was accepted only unwillingly'. Antoni Połowniak (Elbląg) complained rather that it was dialogue 'with the people that has become more and more difficult', a major complaint being that the authorities simply repeated themselves and would not answer questions concretely or unambiguously.[127]

A major speech was made by Gdańsk secretary Fiszbach, who concluded that 'the content, form and language of our dialogue with society has too often departed from its opinions and sentiments, too often been more a reflection of our desires than a response to the thoughts, needs and problems of working people'. A report was sent on the same day by the Gdańsk KW secretariat to the Central Committee urging communication with the strike committee and stressing the growing problems the provincial committee was encountering in maintaining any relationship with the working class.[128] Considerable importance was therefore attached to the reception of Fiszbach's speech in Gdańsk, not least by the strikers in the shipyards. It was also commended at the Plenum itself by CC member Drozdowicz, Chief Petty Officer in Polish Shipping Line, who stressed that without the efforts of the Gdańsk provincial committee the party would have found itself considerably more isolated from the workers than had already become the case.[129] On the other hand, Fiszbach's speech was received far less warmly by others within the party leadership. At a meeting two days after the Plenum, his view that the crisis had essentially social origins came in for strong criticism and leading party officials were still inclined to identify much of the crisis as an anti-socialist political diversion. The feeling that the party apparatus had been hamstrung by Gierek's centralism received much support, though, and the provincial secretaries continued to argue for a greater measure of autonomy.[130]

While the position of the Gierek leadership had lost its relevance and virtually ceased to exist in political terms, there was clearly no consensus on what should replace it. The CC Ideological Department sent local party organs a directive on 28 August outlining the dangers of accepting any agreement that permitted the establishment of 'free trade unions'. They would perform 'in effect the function of an opposition party' and would introduce a 'destructive element' into the country's political system.[131] At a Politburo meeting on 29 August, Stefan Olszowski, just returned to the party's leadership at the IV Plenum, argued for the use of force in hastening the restoration of party control.[132] At the VI Plenum, which opened on 5 September immediately following Gierek's heart attack, Olszowski again insisted on the need to strike hard against anti-socialistic forces but was forced to affirm general acceptance of the independent workers' movement and follow the strategy laid down by Kania, who was elected PZPR first secretary to replace Gierek.[133] The attempt at a forcible solution, as both Jaruzelski and naval commander Janczyszyn understood, was too dangerous and likely to prove politically fatal for those who adopted it.[134] The alternative, conciliatory solution, argued for successfully by Kania remained very imprecise and was characterised by much uncertainty as to how far the party should go to achieve understanding with the workers and their leadership, now formalised within the rapidly growing organisation of Solidarity.

At the IV Plenum of the Central Committee, Rakowski had drawn attention to the similarity between the 1980 discussion and that which had followed the 1970 events. He had called for an examination of the systemic factors which brought about such ruptures, arguing that the causes could not just be reduced to personal weaknesses. After the signature of the Gdańsk agreement and the fall of Gierek this became a major topic of discussion and it was clear that extensive change would have to take place also within the party if it were to retain any semblance of leadership and if political authority were to be restored within communist Poland. Major points mentioned at an early stage were the election of party authorities 'in such a way that party members could influence their composition in a more realistic manner', and the establishment of an effective division of labour between the party and state apparatuses. This, it was thought, could involve a ban on holding more than one post in the apparatuses of power, greater opportunities in public life for those not in the party, limited tenure in the ocupation of major political offices and apparatus employment only after work in other spheres, a ban on those leaving the party apparatus being guaranteed a more elevated job in other areas.[135] Neither was the desire for less bureaucratic authoritarianism in party life restricted to those with more conciliatory views. The secretary of a miners' cell and member of Wałbrzych KW complained of the party's underestimation of KOR influence and the failure of the KW staff to provide material with which to fight it. He also criticised KW procedures under which anyone intending to make an intervention had to have his speech vetted by a KW instructor or the head of the organisation department.[136]

These and other matters were aired at the lengthy second part of the VI CC Plenum held in early October, the first session having been adjourned after the election of Kania and the admission of two new full Politburo members: Kazimierz Barcikowski, Cracow first secretary, and Andrzej Żabiński, CC secretary since the VIII Congress but previously first secretary of Opole KW. The second part was held on 4–5 October, although proceedings did not end until 6.25 am on 6 October. As may be gauged from the length of the session, the discussion was full and wide-ranging. The debate was varied and often acrimonious, the need to evolve a policy to cope with the worsening economic crisis and unstable political situation vying with the desire to settle accounts with the former leadership and adopt positions for the developing conflict within the leadership. The session hardly provided a forum, then, for a balanced assessment of shortcomings in party organisation and activities, although it did provide the opportunity for extensive discussion and criticism, particularly of the deformations of the recently discredited Gierek regime. Academics were particularly critical of Gierek's dictatorial practices: thus Ney, Rector of the Cracow Mining Academy, traced the problems in internal party relations back to 1973, when discussion at the First Party Conference had been censored. Rechowicz, of the University of Silesia, complained that the pre-1970 style and methods of party work had simply been continued by the new leader, with the possible exception of practices in Gdańsk (although these, he suggested, had also been temporary).

The views of the provincial first secretaries were well aired – twenty-two KW first secretaries either spoke at the session or had their statement entered on the record. Further sensitivity of central party leadership to the position of the KW secretaries was shown by the addition of Kruk, Lublin first secretary, as candidate member of the Politburo (this was balanced by the removal of KW Katowice secretary Grudzień, a close associate of Gierek, his position in Katowice now being taken by Politburo member Żabiński). Established themes of KW criticism were restated and elaborated. The extent to which centralisation was carried under Gierek and the lack of trust shown in the provincial organs was again attacked by Połowniak (Elbląg). Judgments were also passed on the centre's refusal to take account of the growing weight of information about the worsening state of public opinion, and on the growing formalisation of the national leadership's consultations with the provincial committees – which, according to one speaker, became so tenuous that they degenerated to the level of farce.[137]

The weakened position of the provincial committees following the 1975 reform was a persistent theme. Drewniowski (Przemyśl) described the problems of economic backwardness affecting his province which were exacerbated by the organisational reform. He suggested that problems of interference by the party in government activities may well have worsened: the *wojewoda*, state executive who was the first secretary's counterpart in the administrative hierarchy, was relatively powerless and in some ministries the situation was such that branch directors were generally 'not available' to speak to them. Under these conditions 'the only recourse was to telephone calls from the KW first secretary'. Grochmalicki (Wałbrzych) admitted that in past years the 'leadership and control functions of the party were not properly performed', and that attempts to cope with the economic situation had been the major preoccupation. Severe pressure had been imposed on them during the winter some eighteen months previously, when transport and energy supplies had been seriously disrupted, as a result of which the 'provincial committee virtually became an office for the reception and processing of applications from numerous work centres'. The weakening of the provincial secretary and his diminished autonomy were clearly felt by Bolesław Kapitan (Toruń), whose resignation as first secretary was recorded as having been accepted the day after the Plenum ended. He spoke of the climate of rumours and demogogy which had affected the party and its *aktiv*, influencing elections within the party and discrediting its activists at all levels. He resented the tendency of the central leadership to move the blame for the party's crisis of authority on to the provincial committees and suggested that blame should be placed where it belonged – on the shoulders of those who had occupied the leading positions of party and state. He concluded with the plea that the Politburo should 'define its relationship with the KW first secretary, the KW secretariat and the entire executive of the provincial party committee'.[138]

This is presumably what Staniszkis refers to when, discussing the Plenum, she alludes to the 'open rebellion' of the apparatus and its demand for 'structural modernisation'.[139] While Kapitan's demand clearly implied a higher degree of institutionalisation of party activities, more relevant in fact was his objection to the practice of party leaders of devolving problems to the regions and isolating themselves from locally derived political threats. It was by these means that leaders had shielded themselves from the consequences of the weakness of party leadership in Poland and its lack of political authority. By late 1980 it was becoming apparent that such techniques would no longer work, either within the party or within the system as a whole.

Reform and resistance in the party organisation

The process of leadership change at provincial level had begun before the resumption of the VI Plenum in early October. While many KW first secretaries felt they had rather unjustly been landed with the responsibility for the shortcomings of the Gierek era, as their capacity for action and freedom of political manoeuvre had been considerably restricted after 1975, the removal of some was clearly well merited and hardly premature. The first two to go, in September, had been in post throughout the Gierek period and had been responsible for the major centres of Katowice and Poznań. Grudzień (Katowice) had been a Politburo member and close associate of Gierek's and had, moreover, shared the taste of many of Gierek's entourage for expensive country villas. Zasada (Poznań) had also been well entrenched in the local establishment in an area where stories of corruption had been circulating for some time.[140] Many provincial secretaries, it transpired, had not only experienced problems in exercising 'control' over the administration and economic processes but had entered into the laxness and indiscipline that had characterised the late Gierek period and had derived considerable benefit from it. The name of twenty-five first secretaries, just over half, could be found in the material on corruption collected by the Supreme Control Chamber (NIK).[141] This record contributed to the accelerating rate of turnover at provincial level and to the growing frustration of the local population in some areas where established leaders refused to budge.

During October a further ten KW first secretaries resigned or were replaced, and in November another seven. This was about twice the number one would have expected to have been changed in one year under normal conditions. But, not surprisingly, the process of personnel change in the provincial apparatus and the reform of local power structures encountered considerable resistance. Early reports suggested the existence of much ambivalence within the party towards the Gdańsk agreement, resistance to its implementation and continuing hopes that, if measures to put the reform into practice were delayed as much as possible, this threat to conventional party practice might eventually be crushed.[142] The return to the leadership of people like Olszowski, who had favoured alternative ways of dealing with the strikes, clearly gave hope to those who were unhappy with the strategy of the new leadership. The switch in party policy, and the evidence of conflicting orientations within the leadership, gave considerable scope for local variations to the rapidly changing political situation. The formation of the Solidarity organisation in Łódź was obstructed by a virtual 'press blockade' and the attitude of the authorities 'could be best summed up as one of wait and see'.[143] The Gdańsk MKS (regional Solidarity coordinating committee) reported radical differences between centres like Gdańsk and Cracow and others like Krosno province, 'there NSZZ [that is, Solidarity] activists are continually harassed'.[144] Nevertheless, change was occurring at provincial level, although not always in the way one might have expected with the establishment of new reformist party leadership.

Twenty-two first secretaries were replaced between mid-September 1980 and the end of the year, the same number in three and a half months as had been appointed in the five years following the 1975 reforms. Their average age was forty-eight, rather older than those appointed in 1975 or during the 1975–80 period. Amongst the new first secretaries was Stanisław Opałko, a former member of the socialist party (PPS) and manager brought out of retirement to head the Tarnów committee at the age of sixty-nine. His birthdate, 1911, was the earliest of any of the secretaries appointed either in 1975 or subsequently. Throughout the whole 1975–80 period only three appointments (of which this was one) were made over the age of fifty-five and, after Opałko, the next oldest secretary was born in 1921.

A smaller proportion of the other secretaries changed in the immediate post-August months, which suggests that the attention both of central leadership and of the citizenry was focussed primarily on the senior-ranking party officials. Those appointed in late 1980 were also quite young and there was no discernible tendency, as there had been amongst the first secretaries, for the wave of younger appointments in the late Gierek period to be succeeded by a large proportion of older cadres. The proportion of those born before 1934 fell from 33% to 23%, and the number of those born between 1934 and 1938 among the other secretarial appointments rose from 27% in the 1975–80 cohort to 36% in the late 1980 group.

Amongst the first secretaries appointed after the August strikes a dominant part was played by those who had joined the party in the years of late Stalinism (1953–55) and who had been in the party for

Table 3.2 *KW secretaries (1975–80, 1980): date of birth*

| | First secretaries | | | | Other secretaries | | | |
| | 1975–80 | | 1980 | | 1975–80 | | 1980 | |
	N	%	N	%	N	%	M	%
1911–25	2	9	2	9	6	5	–	–
1926–30	4	18	4	18	13	11	3	5
1931–33	7	32	6	28	20	17	10	18
1934–38	4	18	8	36	32	27	20	36
1939–51	5	23	2	9	46	40	23	41
Total	22	100	22	100	117	100	56	100

Table 3.3 *KW secretaries (1975–80, 1980): date of joining party*

| | First secretaries | | | | Other secretaries | | | |
| | 1975–80 | | 1980 | | 1975–80 | | 1980 | |
	N	%	N	%	N	%	N	%
1944–49	3	14	3	14	4	3	1	2
1950–52	6	29	3	14	11	10	6	11
1953–55	3	14	8	36	19	16	7	12
1956–59	2	10	4	18	12	10	7	12
1960–73	7	33	4	18	71	61	35	63
Total	21	100	22	100	117	100	56	100

(Date of joining party of one first secretary in 1975–80 group not clear)

some twenty-five to twenty-eight years at the time of appointment.
Indeed, the history of party membership, an average of twenty-four
years, was longer in this group than in either of the two preceding
groups (each with an average length of membership of twenty-three
years). The other secretaries, being younger, were much less likely to
have joined the party during the Stalinist period in Poland. Only a
quarter had party membership extending back to before 1956. Relatively few, too, had joined in the years immediately following 1956, the

Table 3.4 *KW secretaries (1975–80, 1980): higher education qualifications*

	First secretaries				Other secretaries			
	1975–80		1980		1975–80		1980	
	N	%	N	%	N	%	N	%
Economics	8	35	8	36	42	35	15	26
Industrial	1	4	4	18	12	10	11	19
Agricultural	3	13	2	9	20	16	4	7
History	2		1		7	6	4	7
Education	–		–		6	5	4	7
Law	3		2		2		4	7
Sociology	2		1		5		2	
Language	–		1		4		–	
Arts	2		2		5		2	
Administration	1	48	–	37	9	26	3	
Political science	–		1		3		4	27
Geography	–		–		–		1	
Medicine, social science, philosophy, psychology, journalism, unspecified.	1		–		4		3	
No higher education	–	–	–	–	2	2	–	–
Total	23	100	22	100	121	100	57	100

period of Gomułka's first years of post-Stalin rule characterised by a more reformist spirit. The concentration of party commitment for the secretaries appointed in late 1980 came between 1960 and 1967, the years when 64% of the 1980 secretaries joined the party (56% of those appointed between 1975 and mid-1980 had also joined in this period). Despite their younger age and later date of party membership, then, the other secretaries resembled the first secretaries in showing a rather thin representation of the immediate post-1955 generation of party members.

In terms of the secretaries' educational qualifications (table 3.4) the first secretaries appointed in the immediate post-August months showed a pattern broadly similar to those appointed under Gierek, but with a greater prominence of those with qualifications in industrial and technical subjects. The number of those with degrees in economics and, we presume, often with party-school training was in fact the same, but several more had technical backgrounds. A similar pattern

Table 3.5 *KW secretaries (1975–80, 1980): main non-apparatus experience*

| | First secretaries | | | | Other secretaries | | | |
| | 1975–80 | | 1980 | | 1975–80 | | 1980 | |
	N	%	N	%	N	%	N	%
Industry	2	9	5	23	31	26	12	21
Agriculture	1	5	2	9	19	16	8	14
Government	10	45	8	36	27	23	15	27
Education	2	9	3	14	17	15	11	20
Youth organisations	5	22	4	18	21	18	10	18
Military	–	–	–	–	1	1	–	–
Parapolitical	1	5	–	–	–	–	–	–
No non-apparatus experience	1	5	–	–	1	1	–	–
Total	22	100	22	100	117	100	56	100

could be seen in the appointment of the other secretaries. A high proportion had industrial qualifications, although a smaller proportion had a background in agricultural subjects. Fewer, too, held economics degrees and those with more diverse arts degrees were more strongly represented. The large number of changes in the provincial party leadership between September and December 1980 therefore brought few major alterations in the composition of the KW secretariats.

The career background of the first secretaries appointed in late 1980 showed greater experience in agricultural and industrial production than for secretaries appointed in the late Gierek period (see table 3.5). Nevertheless, the proportion of secretaries with such experience (32%) was still less than had been the case with those appointed in 1975 (36%). Nor was any greater level of production experience apparent amongst the other secretaries. In terms of experience in the party apparatus the secretaries appointed after August had more extensive political training (see table 3.6). Twice the number than in the preceding group had more than twenty years experience of party work, a characteristic we can associate with the higher age of those appointed after the fall of Gierek. But the other secretaries appointed after August also had higher levels of apparatus experience, 26.5% having spent over fifteen years in party work compared with 18% amongst those appointed between 1975 and 1980. These secretaries, on the other hand, were not any older than those appointed earlier. There appears

Table 3.6 *KW secretaries (1975–80, 1980): time from first party appointment*

| | First secretaries | | | | Other secretaries | | | |
| | 1975–80 | | 1980 | | 1975–80 | | 1980 | |
Years	N	%	N	%	N	%	N	%
0–5	3	13	5	23	42	36	15	27
6–10	5	23	3	13	28	24	14	25
11–15	6	27	4	18	26	22	12	21.5
16–20	5	23	4	18	13	11	12	21.5
over 20	3	14	6	28	8	7	3	5
Total	22	100	22	100	117	100	56	100

to have been a consistent attempt to maximise the political experience of secretaries appointed in the wake of the August strikes. Slightly fewer first secretaries, though, had experience in responsible party posts (77% compared with 86%), although the same number of first secretaries in 1980 had previously worked as provincial committee secretaries.

The KW secretarial appointments made after the fall of Gierek and the emergence of Solidarity, then, show some divergence from the patterns that had developed in the 1970s. Fewer first secretaries had been born in 1939 or after, and there were more appointments from the pre-war generation; fewer secretaries had joined the party in the sixties or after; they were more likely to have had qualifications relevant to employment in industry or agriculture and the first secretaries were more than twice as likely to have had production experience. They included twice as many who had been given their first party post more than twenty years previously and fewer first secretaries with party experience of intermediate length. Slightly fewer had not held posts in the party apparatus before (equivalent to 14%). Indeed, three had had no full-time experience in equivalent socio-political organisations at all: one (Opałko) had been brought out of retirement following a career as an industrial manager and two had spent almost all their working lives as Polytechnic academics. But in terms of lengthy party experience and tenure of party membership this group, as we have seen, included some secretaries with highly specialised political backgrounds.

Much of this rather contradictory image was due to the fact that six of the twenty-two first secretaries appointed between September and December 1980 had already served as KW first secretaries earlier in their careers. This was not unprecedented but it was unusual – only three of the preceding sixty first secretaries had served in the same post already, and this was most likely associated with the difficulties involved in establishing the new teritorial units and setting up their party organisations. In short, central party authorities in late 1980 were responding to the threat posed by the rise of Solidarity and the demonstration of party impotence by reappointing those already experienced in leading political positions to the provincial party apparatus. All six reappointments involved people more advanced in their career than was normally the case with those posted to the provincial committees: all came from central ministerial, CC Secretariat or foreign diplomatic posts. As such, they had above-average levels of experience in party work and accounted for four of the six who had received their first party job more than twenty years previously. If the six are excluded, the average length of time from first apparatus appointment for the 1980 group falls to twelve years, lower than the average for the younger group of 1975–80 secretarial appointments. The smaller proportion of those who had not previously held responsible party positions, already evident in table 3.7, would also become more pronounced, falling to 69%. The pattern of appointments in late 1980 therefore showed marked diversity in this respect.

The political implications of this diversity are, of course, another matter. However, it does accord with the response within the party noted by one observer. Thus Misztal identifies both the promotion of moderate and pragmatic officials and a process whereby a 'group of hard-line politicians, long eliminated from the administration, found their way back into executive positions'.[145] It was, indeed, the hard-line orientation that seemed to dominate in the closing months of 1980 and it was often at provincial level that the resistance to Solidarity appeared to be based. Old apparatus habits persisted, despite the soul-baring that had taken place at the VI Plenum. In the new situation the practice of parachuting in a new KW first secretary (that is the imposition of a centrally decided appointment on a local committee) provoked resentment – particularly so in Toruń when this happened one day after the end of the reform-minded VI Plenum.[146] But within the provincial apparatus there were many with severe doubts about the viability of a democratic solution to the crisis in any case.

Some within the provincial committees, it was suggested, did not

Table 3.7 *KW first secretaries (1975–80, 1980): previous apparatus experience*

	1975–80		1980	
	N	%	N	%
Provincial committee secretary	15	68	15	68
First secretary of other party committee	12	55	7	32
Responsible party post, i.e. either provincial committee secretary or other first secretaryship, or both.	19	86	17	77

realise the intensity of public feeling and that, in the absence of any possibility of a rapid improvement in the material solution, people were looking for a 'moral recompense' and concentrated their attention at this level.[147] BBC reporter Kevin Ruane reported views on the resilience of the provincial party apparatus to the forces of change and quoted such statements from one party meeting as 'the middle layer is like a belt of clouds around the earth, preventing the rays of the sun from getting through'.[148] Professor Kołodziejski, state governor of Gdańsk throughout 1980 and 1981 (he was removed from this post in the early stages of the State of War), described the state of mind of established officials at this time in the following way:

> they were not as a whole prepared psychologically or politically for the realisation of the agreement, either centrally or at regional and local level. In this area, the good will of the group constituting the political leadership of state in the precise sense of the term was just not enough. Some of those making up the power apparatus at this time clung to the conviction that they could break this kind of agreement with impunity.[149]

If this is true, as seems to be likely, the conciliatory group around Kania was challenged not only from within the central leadership by those sympathetic to Olszowski's approach but also by the bulk of the national party apparatus. To this extent, Kania's position was even weaker than Ascherson suggests and it is unlikely that he commanded 'the loyalty of much of the provincial apparatus'.[150] At the very least, provincial secretaries cannot have been eager to see the early convocation of an Extraordinary Party Congress, one of the immediate demands of the conciliators and reform-minded party officials, which would put them through a series of party conferences and almost certainly threaten their tenure on the Central Committee.[151]

The programme of reform, acknowledgement of the necessity of which was signalled in the discussion at the VI Plenum, thus met with considerable obstacles both in its formulation and in initial attempts to put it into operation. But it was clearly necessary if the allegiance of party members was to be retained and if there was to be any hope of reestablishing party authority. The case of one working-class member, Albin Terk, gained extensive publicity. He was a long-standing activist whose views had received press coverage at the time of the VIII Congress a few months earlier, but which had changed as a result of the political developments over the summer. They provide an apt illustration of how the experiences of the seventies had failed to sustain party authority and of how the lack of authority had suddenly become critical:

> I have been let down. Many times I have spoken out in defence of what the party was doing, even though I did not fully agree with it. But I believed that behind every decision were reasons which were deeper than my own or those which my friends and neighbours put forward. So I defended the party line. I accepted that as my duty. Now, not for the first time, I have been let down. And, speaking frankly, I no longer have the strength or the conviction.[152]

Terk's words reflect the processes that had led to the crisis of 1980 and identify the sentiments that until the summer of 1980 had imbued the Polish party, never very popular or solidly rooted in Polish society, with a certain measure of political authority.

This situation thus placed a weighty political burden on the provincial committees which they were poorly equipped to deal with and, in many cases, often in any case unwilling to face. That does not mean that some efforts were not made. Measures were taken to raise the status of the provincial party control commissions (WKKP) and boost mechanisms of internal party supervision and control that had encountered such resistance under Gierek. 'The WKKP', wrote on provincial chairman, 'does not ignore any letter and reacts immediately to every one . . . The Lublin WKKP does not even suspend its activity for an hour'.[153] Efforts were made to liven up provincial committee sessions, although these hardly involved dramatic innovations. In Opole, for example, it was decided to start circulating the report of the committee executive before plenary sessions.[154] But the transformation of the status of the provincial committee was in any case no easy matter. Some of the contradictions involved were summed up by Professor Lang, of Łódź University: it is demanded 'from the KW plenum that it plays a more active role in the election of the KW secretary and of the WKKP, that it settles accounts with all, starting from the rank-and-file member and going up to the secretaries – but, at the same time, the current KW plenum is regarded as quite unrepresentative and the WKKP is seen as an offshoot of the party establishment, and therefore quite incapable of performing the tasks demanded of it'.[155] The provincial committee could easily be overwhelmed and disoriented by the new pressures placed on it, even if its staff was sympathetic. One official admitted that communication channels were becoming 'silted up', full of detailed information that the 'leading organ at province level simply should not know'.[156] The hierarchical structure of the party and the political practices this had fostered were not appropriate for the demands of the new situation.

At the same time the traditional status of the party official himself was coming into question. The role of the apparatus and its association with one of the major foundations of the communist party–state, the *nomenklatura* system, had been one of the preoccupations of the Gdańsk strikers and caused enormous complications in the drafting of the agreement, not least because they did not want to be seen as challenging the basis of communist political rule.[157] But by December 1980 doubts about the continuing viability of established career patterns within the apparatus were being expressed even in party organisational publications. Proposals emerged to end the traditional career path of the apparatus worker which was described as 'unhealthy and bad . . . because it had fostered the false belief that real political wisdom is characteristic only of the professional apparatus'.[158] Thus not only were the role and practices of the provincial committee open to question, but also the status and prospects of its associated staff themselves. Neither were such ideas just the property of Solidarity activists and critical social forces – they also appeared to be gaining strength within the party, helped along, no doubt, by the apparatus's unwillingness to go along with the reform strategy articulated by the Kania leadership. The scene was therefore set for the development of further conflict within the party itself, in which the provincial apparatus would play a crucial role.

4   Indecision and *odnowa*: obstacles to reestablishing party authority

The issue of internal party reform

The situation within the party had not moved significantly towards a solution when the VII Plenum of the Central Committee was held early in December 1980, nearly two months after the extensive deliberations that had taken place at the VI Plenum. As some speakers pointed out, Poland was now in its sixth month of crisis and although the leadership had from the outset taken the decision to find a way out of it by *political* means there was as yet no identification of the form this might take. This lack of progress was emphasised at the VII Plenum by, amongst others, the recently appointed KW first secretary in Poznań.[1] Earlier attempts to achieve some internal reform and democratisation within communist parties (for example, Poland in 1956, the late Khrushchev period in the Soviet Union, and Czechoslovakia in the sixties) had shown the process to be an extremely difficult one likely to meet with opposition both internal (largely from the party apparatus) and external (from the more orthodox constituents of the 'socialist commonwealth', particularly the Soviet Union). In the case of the East European countries, the Soviet influence has been an especially strong inhibiting factor, although in Gomułka's Poland the leaders' own inclinations and personality played an important role as well. The Polish experience in 1980 and much of 1981 was unusual however, in that direct Soviet intervention was absent and the internal problems of party reform emerged in their full complexity. They demonstrated the stubborn authoritarianism of a party–state run on the pattern of democratic centralism and the power of the resistance that could be offered by its operational core, the party apparatus, even when (as appeared to be the case with Kania) its leader was by no means ill-disposed towards a policy of reform. By the time of the VII Plenum, after five months of overt crisis, such problems were clearly coming to the surface.

Kania's own speech at the Plenum demonstrated the problems involved in accommodating a reform-oriented policy with the obligatory principles of democratic centralism. He admitted that, while a significant reactivisation had taken place within the party organisation, 'the party as a whole has not found itself'. He identified 'conservative resistance' (by implication, within the party) and confirmed that this should be resolutely overcome. In order to enhance the democratic aspect of party activities he made proposals that would raise the status of the elected party authorities and increase the role of the party membership: when half the members of the appropriate committee agreed, party organs would be permitted to elect their first secretary, executive and secretariat by secret ballot; the professional party apparatus was enjoined 'above all' to be an organiser of the social *aktiv* and executor of tasks set by the party organs. Fractionalism, however, was strongly condemned, as were 'anarchic' attempts to blame the entire leadership and the mass of party activists for the current situation.[2] This, it turned out, caused some consternation in local organisations where the idea of political renewal had already been taken seriously. Measures already taken in Gdańsk to enhance democratic practices and identify the roots of the crisis were now reviewed in the light of this mention of fractionalism.[3] But even Kania's measured attempt to push forward the cause of renewal (*odnowa*) contrasted with the resistance that was latent, though nevertheless widespread and becoming more coordinated, within the party apparatus.

It was particularly strong amongst established party officials in the centre and at regional level. Amongst the KW first secretaries a general distinction in terms of their appraisal of the situation could be made between those with lengthy tenure and those appointed more recently. During the VII Plenum some of the most vehement attacks on Solidarity and its claimed relationship with forces out to undermine party leadership, the strongest doubts concerning party democratisation and the suspicion that it meant harbouring anti-socialist forces, fears of Polish political instability and threats that this might cause 'global' or 'national catastrophe' – such views were more commonly expressed by the secretaries who had been in post for some years and were dismissive of the need for extensive change. They called rather for firmer party leadership and less tolerance of those calling for change in established party practice, for the rejection of attempts by Solidarity to encroach on any sphere of activity where jurisdiction could be claimed by the party. The scope of their tolerance was, therefore, very limited.

Hebda (Zielona Góra, in post since 1972) saw a weakening of the party and a threat to the socialist order posed 'in consequence of the failure of Solidarity to observe the agreements signed at Gdańsk, Szczecin and Jastrzębie', and retreat by the authorities in the face of the movement's demands. Prokopiak (Radom, appointed in 1975) also saw much of the current problem as stemming from Solidarity's illegitimate involvement in political strikes and the influence on the union of 'Kuroń, Modzelewski and others'; as a result of this, 'Instead of the extension of the principles of democracy and social cooperation, participation in strikes is made obligatory, anarchy spreads, there is lack of respect for the law and for the authorities.' Swiderski (Chełm, 1975) declared that it was time to put an end to the mud-slinging against the party and socialism, and for the party – 'out of concern for the nation and our friends' – to adopt 'decisive and offensive political and ideological attitudes in relation to the enemies of our system.' One of the major steps he suggested to stabilise the situation was central to the concerns of those committed to repel such 'anti-socialist forces' – the adoption of the position that 'the party will not resign from its powers over the cadres policy deriving from the practice of *nomenklatura*, which conditions the leading role of the party'. Szablak, a secretary in the Warsaw organisation who had served in the capital's party apparatus without interruption since 1963, called attention to the centrifugal tendencies within the party which meant that party ranks were 'increasingly indoctrinated and infiltrated by centres alien to the party and to socialism'; he was emphatically of the view that Solidarity was headed by people antagonistic to the party and that its ideologists were, as a body, of an 'anti-party orientation'.[4]

Many established provincial secretaries therefore held and expressed views which were in sharp contrast to the commitment to renewal proclaimed by Kania. But Kania's stance, as noted above, showed some ambiguities, too. This was also evident in some of the practical measures he took with respect to local party organisations. Notable here was the case of the Warsaw organisation, which developed a reputation for considerable conservatism and resistance to political renewal in 1981. Kania took a close interest in the leadership of the Warsaw organisation and carefully supervised the succession to Karkoszka, former Politburo member and associate of Gierek who had led the Warsaw organisation since 1976. His priority in this case appeared to be less political renewal than the desire to establish a stable political base in the capital. After November 1980 the first secretary in Warsaw was Stanisław Kociołek, who had initially been its leader in

1964 (at the age of thirty-one) and had joined the Politburo in 1968. In December 1970 he had been sent to coordinate the party's response to the revolt on the northern coast and played a particularly ambiguous role in the massacre of workers outside Gdynia railway station. Kania alluded to this in his speech nominating Kociołek in November 1980 and took pains to stress his virtues as a party activist and his unblemished record as a leading representative of the party. Nevertheless, he returned as a 'leading figure amongst the conservative groups of the apparatus' and, although not a member of the Central Committee, took part from that time in Politburo meetings.[5] It seemed clear that Kania was securing the Warsaw party base with the appointment of an experienced political figure who was unlikely to be carried away by arguments for party democratisation – a safeguard against the situation that developed in 1956, when the Warsaw organisation played an important role in the apparent victory of reformist forces and the transformation of the existing leadership. Kania's initiative, however, left the position of the Warsaw organisation with regard to *odnowa* open to considerable doubt.

Other KW first secretaries expressed more conciliatory views. Nowak (Wałbrzych, appointed in November 1980) affirmed that by its very nature as a working-class movement, Solidarity could not be an anti-socialist force – certain anti-socialist elements had attached themselves to the movement in his province, but they had been expelled. Dąbrowa (Cracow, February 1980) pointed out that renewal had been necessary in the party long before the summer strikes, although the need had been ignored by the leadership, and that resistance to it had still not disappeared – 'there exist within the party people who have still not associated themselves with the process of change in the country and who, in objective terms, are obstructing it'. He argued that the restriction of early elections to the basic party organisations, as had been suggested by the leadership, would mean that the situation would worsen elsewhere and that later elections to the superior organs, including the provincial committees, 'will take place in an atmosphere considerably worse for the leadership as currently constituted than it would be at present'. Kusiak, appointed to the important province of Poznań immediately after the downfall of Gierek (although he had previously been Kalisz first secretary until 1979 – his removal coinciding with Grabski's demotion following criticism of Gierek), also observed that there were 'arising in the party new, negative and disquieting phenomena'. Local party organisations were again becoming active and were gaining a position where they could exercise political leadership, which in the industrial context was generally not questioned by local Solidarity chapters. What was causing disquiet in local party organisations was not Solidarity but the 'overly slow recuperation by the party of its lost position at provincial and especially central levels'.[6] The crucial lack of party authority was also located by a secretary from Płock at levels higher than that of the local party organisation – it was, he said, the Central Committee and the provincial committees that were thought of when members talked of restoring confidence in the leadership.[7]

The conservative stance of many provincial committees thus received extensive substantiation at the VII Plenum, and many recognised the problems this produced for the restoration of some kind of party authority. Doubt may be expressed, though, about the relationship between the opinions expressed by some KW first secretaries and their actions as local leaders. While Kusiak, for example, commented on the weakness of the provincial committees he had held back measures which would have helped to strengthen the committee's position in Poznań: an electoral campaign had begun within local party organisations in early November, but had only progressed against the resistance of the provincial committee.[8] Nevertheless, even amongst those occupying provincial leadership posts for some time, recognition of some positive response to the tide of popular opposition was not lacking. Haładaj (Tarnobrzeg, appointed 1976) thus spoke of the 'unjustified resistance of parts of the party apparatus and its *aktiv* in the face of necessary democratisation and the natural extension of Solidarity influence'.[9]

In this view, the call of the more conservative-minded members of the Central Committee, which included a sizeable number of the longer-serving KW secretaries, for stronger party leadership and greater discipline to be exerted over Solidarity supporters and reformist party members was largely beside the point. So long as the need for a *political* solution to the crisis was agreed upon within the leadership (and this was not publicly disputed for the time being), party authority was simply inadequate to restore the conventional form of political order that was demanded. As many recognised, there was no clear division between Solidarity and the party in the country as a whole (by this stage around a third of party members were also members of the independent trade union). The major political division lay more between the higher levels of the party organisation – the Central Committee, and the provincial committees – and the lower level party organisations and the rank and file. If a political solution was to be found the party leadership had little freedom of manoeuvre unless serious attempts were made to strengthen the national character of the party organisation. It needed to forge vertical links that could help establish the party's authority within the country as a whole. This, in turn, implied the introduction of the kind of intra-party democratisation and restructuring of party activity for which the reformists were clamouring.

Within this conception, the role of the provincial committee, as the 'leading organ' with most specific responsibility for local activity, called for special attention. This fact was not lost on Gdańsk leader Tadeusz Fiszbach. He identified three levels of party activity that would determine its immediate future. One was the occupation of party posts by people who were honest and disinterested; a second was the proper apportionment of blame for past infringements of party morality; third was that the 'provincial committee should recognise as necessary the extension in practice of democratic principles, in addition to amendments to the party statute and additional rules for the regulation of intra-party life'.[10] Thus, there were at least some within the party apparatus, as well as rank-and-file members and other Polish citizens whose lives were inevitably conditioned by the workings of the party–state complex, who were committed to extensive change in the nature of the Polish party, its structure and methods of operation. Even more conservative members of the Central Committee were eager not infrequently to remove dishonest and ineffective members of the apparatus, and to introduce sufficient changes to ensure that the party was not again infiltrated by such people and the party brought into the critical situation in which it now found itself.

Amongst some of the earlier proposals for party change within the context of *odnowa* were those brought forward from earlier periods, when they had not been given any publicity. One had been composed by former party leaders (including a PZPR first secretary, Edward Ochab) and had been sent to Gierek in February 1971. One of its main themes was the need to assert the political primacy of the party's elected organs – the Congress, Central Committee and committees at other levels of the hierarchy – over executive organs such as the Politburo and provincial secretariat. To help achieve this there should be less representation in central and provincial committees of 'party functionaries and high state officials; similarly, Politburo or KW executive members should be treated as others on the full committee and not be regarded as a leading group within it; the electoral principle should be extended to other areas of the party apparatus, for example CC and KW department heads and their deputies'.[11] Similar points were made in 1980 when the causes of the failure of leadership were identified. It had been noted that 70% of the membership of provincial committees was drawn either from the party apparatus or from the state administration: 'Thus the controlled became the controllers.'[12] The nature of the apparatus and the possibility of limiting executive autonomy were, therefore, the topics to which most attention was paid. The development of the group of full-time apparatus workers as a self-sustaining elite answerable only to itself was identified by those committed to *odnowa* as the greatest threat to the healthy development of party life.

A number of suggestions recurred in this area. Firstly, there should be a simple reduction in size, which would be facilitated by discouraging the apparatus from involvement in economic decision-making other than that of a strategic nature.[13] Secondly, there should be a general limitation in the occupation of responsible party posts to two terms of office. Thirdly, following on directly from the above, party office-holding should be rotated on principle and there should be no expectation of repeated election to party posts.[14] Fourthly, those accepted for work in the apparatus should have had occupational experience elsewhere and have proved themselves to be professionally able. As high a minimum as ten years' work prior to apparatus entry was suggested by some. It was felt that the recruitment of those proven in other spheres would make the insistence on the rotation of office-holders less necessary. First secretary Białecki (Olsztyn) made the related suggestion that the 'worker *aktiv* should not only occupy elective party positions in large numbers . . . but should enter full-time, professional party work'. Worker access, he said, had been obstructed by formalised criteria for entry to the apparatus, according to which it was 'easier for those coming directly from the lecture theatre to become a nominal worker activist – and that happens with us – than for an experienced worker who enjoys the authority of his fellow-workers'.[15] A particular focus of attention in this connection were the changes that had taken place within the party apparatus during the Gierek period, aspects of which we have already identified in relation to the provincial secretaries.

One of the most direct diagnoses was that of former first secretary Ochab: 'a considerable majority of the old revolutionary cadre has in recent years been removed from active work, at great cost to the party but with great advantage for revisionists and opportunists'.[16] This process, confirmed by others, was closely associated with Gierek's emphasis on the development of a qualified party cadre and the particular stress laid on the possession of education diplomas. As we have already noted, this emphasis appears to have been interpreted in a narrow way with implications for the activities of the apparatus which were highly dubious. It certainly caused strong resentment within the party. The chairman of the Radom Party Control Commission recounted that 'There exists unconcealed regret and bitterness that . . . people with a long party record and experience but without education were removed. We, the hard core, did not have degrees, we were not in the *nomenklatura*.' The dominance of this newly-constituted 'party intelligentsia' had a serious impact on the party, as it contributed greatly to the opening up of a wide gap between the apparatus and ordinary members. Such a conception of the *nomenklatura* had negative effects in other ways: it narrowed the pool of people available for appointment (in the sense that those not possessing diplomas were excluded) and made its members virtually invulnerable to criticism – even if discredited in one job they would always find another attractive post.[17] This practice, it seemed, had not been touched by the fall of Gierek and still served to protect 'completely compromised people from the former apparatus', as a further memorandum from the 'Experience and the Future' group noted in November 1980.[18] Indeed, it was questioned whether there had been any proper cadres policy at all, in the sense of people's qualifications being fitted to particular tasks. The main problem had been, wrote E. Szeliga, that 'we do not really have anything that would deserve the description of personnel policy, there does not exist any real list of people qualified to occupy posts'.[19] The diploma, plus appropriate connections, was often a sufficient basis for an elite career.

While the criteria for elite entry and service in the apparatus appeared to bear little relation to performance, the benefits derived from the occupation of such positions under Gierek were far greater than had previously been the case. This intensified the resentment felt within the party and in society at large. It was only under Gierek that the Polish apparatus became privileged in quite this way, that its 'employees began to derive real benefit from their position within the power structure'.[20] Indeed, claims M. Hirszowicz, the Polish party officials had had fewer privileges than their counterparts in other East European countries under Gomułka and, prior to 1970, 'the concept of the new class and its economic privileges found less support in Poland than elsewhere'.[21] This changed dramatically during the Gierek decade. Anger at social inequality and undeserved privilege, particularly within the party, was a constant theme and underlay demands from local party organisations, which were also repeatedly expressed at CC meetings, that such injustices should be eliminated and innovations like the 1972 provision for general pensions for members of the elite and their families should be annulled. Miśkiewicz, a local secretary from Szczecin, referred to two hundred individuals within the party who should be divested of such privileges.[22] While, then, the machinery had yet to be put in motion to remove most of these individuals from their positions of power, their motives for resisting change were strengthened by the combination of political and material self-interest. As we have noted, this system involved a sizeable proportion of the provincial party leadership, many of whom were quite young and had little desire to relinquish their recently gained advantages.

Their position was strengthened by the reluctance of the party leadership to introduce further elements of conflict within the party and to risk losing what elements of control they still had. The lessons of 1956 were again relevant here. Stanisław Wroński, editor of the party's theoretical monthly, recalled that there had been 'excessive cadre losses at the intermediate level in 1956' and, while acknowledging that an improper cadres policy had been in operation under Gierek, warned that this time 'we must not permit unfounded, excessive cadre losses in the party at the intermediate level'.[23] He was not specific about 1956 developments, but in connection with the position of the provincial committees the literature refers to their general 'defensiveness, and even demobilisation', to the fact that the growing tide of criticism exposed their leaders to severe scrutiny and that meetings became 'virtual plebiscites' as to whether they were worthy of a vote of confidence.[24] With the rapid growth of Solidarity and the enfeeblement of the party by late 1980 it was not difficult to see why such a situation would not be welcomed again. It is understandable why, even if determined to persist with the policy of political renewal, Kania was wary of confronting the resistance to it developing within the apparatus and the provincial committees. A further 'Experience and the Future' report from this period thus refers to the party's 'fear of new people – the downright instinctive tendency to rely on known people, even though their unsuitability has been proven'.[25] There were deeprooted reasons then why a wholesale reform of the provincial committees and their cadres was not welcome to sizeable numbers within the central leadership. This naturally encouraged existing KW resistance to rank-and-file demands, and those emanating directly from local party organisations, for party democratisation – an understandable enough response to the party leaders' formal espousal of renewal and partnership with Solidarity in meeting its legitimate demands. The issue of internal party reform in Poland in 1981 thus turned out to constitute no less of a political problem than it had on earlier occasions in the European communist states. The long period over which the situation developed, moreover, made it even more complex and gave increasingly clear indications as to the political stance of the party apparatus, within which the provincial secretaries played a major political role.

The party response in the provinces

Despite the ever-rising tide of criticism of official political practice, both past and present, and the continuing discussion of diverse reform proposals, the attitudes of many provincial party leaders showed little change and few showed any inclination to modify established modes of behaviour. At a meeting of the Cracow Party Committee it was noted that 'less informed people' were becoming suspicious that, in view of the protracted nature of internal party investigations and delays in decision-making, attempts were being made to protect discredited people 'especially in the party'. The government, too, was judged to be dilatory in connection with the issue of work-free Saturdays, the major bone of contention between Solidarity and the authorities during January 1981.[26] Growing dissatisfaction led to the occupation of the town hall in Nowy Sącz and the subsequent outbreak of a region-wide strike. This was caused by the slow and very partial accommodation of the Nowy Sącz provincial committee to the demands of political renewal. Conflict concentrated around the exclusion of personnel matters from the agenda of the local reform commission, composed of members of the People's Council with some coopted Solidarity members, and their consideration only by a special group of the KW executive. This was distinguished by the tolerant view it took of such matters as the housing privileges enjoyed by some party activists and members of the administration, and the popular conviction grew that some individuals were being treated with unwarranted leniency.[27] The conservative role of the intermediate party organs was also identified by national Solidarity spokesmen. Gwiazda, national vice-chairman, affirmed that the opportunity to effect change in the socio-economic system did exist, but such chances had existed in the past and 'they were always killed off by the lower and intermediate organs of the power apparatus'. They were able to resist the most enlightened initiatives of the Central Committee.[28]

Critical views of the strength of the conservative forces were not restricted to local party activists and Solidarity spokesmen. Rakowski also called for the authorities to 'respect their partner' (that is, Solidarity), using this as the title of his front-page article, and warned that 'there is a growing anxiety among many people that the whole renewal is being reduced to cosmetic measures'. This he linked with the hardening of sentiments that was evident at the party base, especially in large industrial plants and in the universities.[29] Some differences could be seen in the response of the provincial committees to the activisation of the party base. In the case of Gdańsk, where first secretary Fiszbach had taken pains to stress the importance of the role of the KW in the current situation, the first meeting of a pre-Congress commission took place three days after the last day of the VII Plenum, at which an Extraordinary Party Congress had been called for the end of the first quarter of 1981. The commission consisted of over 250 members and represented local organisations from factories and educational institutions from all over the province. Although it was established in accordance with a resolution passed by the provincial committee, the initiative had been taken by the local organisations. KW employees were described as providing only 'technical assistance', whilst one KW secretary participated in the work of its presidium 'in the role of advisor'.[30] Fiszbach and the Gdańsk KW clearly saw the need to retain links with the grass-roots movement which, if opposed or left to develop completely on its own, was likely to come into conflict with the provincial committee. The emphasis in the attitude of the Gdańsk KW was reflected in the commission's suggestions for the reformulation of the Party Statute, which was to include the statement that 'The leading role [of the PZPR] is based not on power but on its authority. This is the authority of reason and of correct ideas, which is achieved through discussion and rational conviction'.[31]

However, this was not the approach taken by other committees. Six weeks after the first meeting of the pre-Congress commission in Gdańsk a political and theoretical conference was held in Poznań, organised by the University party committee. Although the discussion concerned proposed changes in party structure and involved much criticism of the existing apparatus and its style of work, the KW staff present (who included a secretary and the director of the science department) remained silent.[32] Some of the discussion of the existing apparatus was highly critical in tone – there was talk of 'anti-socialist elements who had ruthlessly dominated the party in recent years' – and a radical reduction in the size of the apparatus was called for.

Other suggestions called for the simplification of the party structure, including the abolition of some KW departments (whose work could be carried out by social commissions) and the elimination of urban district committees to facilitate closer contact of the provincial committee with the party grass roots. The idea that there was an excessive number of party committees had already been aired in the party press and the abolition of the district committees had been mooted in discussion of changes in the party statute.[33] Reform proposals also began to receive more publicity in the party press as the work of the pre-Congress commissions got under way and the question of intra-party reform received more serious consideration as an aspect of forward party planning.

An initial focus of attention was the reformulation of the concept of party leadership, which suggested that a new view of party activity was called for. This was encapsulated in the change in terminology by which leadership was referred to not as *'kierowanie'* (leading/directing) but as *'przewodzenie'* (leading/guiding). This shift had been in train for some years and was reflected in the formulation used in the amended Constitution, introduced in 1976. With the changing political situation of 1980 and 1981, though, this different conception gained new significance and implied, it was stated, 'greater scope for movement from the base upwards, on activity within a social movement'.[34] Closely related to the current criticism of past and present forms of party leadership was the complex of problems surrounding the apparatus, whose most important aspect, according to Erazmus, head of a department in the party Higher School of Social Sciences, was the duplication of party and state activities. This, of course, is a perennial problem frequently noted by both internal and external observers of communist systems, and is one for which a viable solution has yet to be identified. A crucial feature noted by Erazmus was the formulation of a proper cadres policy, both in terms of recruitment and of the transfer of cadres out of party work into other employment.[35]

Further reports amplified the reformist proposals emanating from Poznań and Gdańsk. Attention was directed to the usurpation of the powers of the elected provincial committees by the executive, the secretariat and, ultimately, by their first secretaries, and to the means by which such 'autocratic' tendencies could be countered. These included clearer definition of the competence of the party apparatus and specification of the individual responsibility of its members, supervision of the activities of the apparatus by elected organs, the principle of limitation of the length of time spent working in the apparatus, and the need for apparatus workers to belong to party organisations outside the Central Committee and the provincial committees – which organisations should then conduct a systematic evaluation of the work of the apparatus members.[36] Reports on the work of the Gdańsk pre-Congress commission showed that considerable attention was being paid there also to cadres policy and its application. Particular criticism was made of the *nomenklatura* system of appointment and of the allocation of posts within the party apparatus in general. The account of the Gdańsk recommendations itself was not uncritical, however, and some surprise was expressed at the warning that higher education should not become a fetish in apparatus appointments.[37] This, it should be noted, stood in some contrast to views expressed by Fiszbach (noted above) on the requirements under modern conditions for party cadres to have a background in higher education. The development of a new kind of 'party intelligentsia' under Gierek had turned out to have made an extremely strong negative impression on Polish public opinion.

But while discussion continued throughout the local organisations of the different ways in which renewal within the party could be achieved, and as proposals for reform received greater publicity within the party press, hopes of achieving significant change within the provincial committees went largely unrealised. As it often appeared to be impossible to achieve change through the provincial committees, some local organisations began joining forces in order to press their case independently, bypassing the intransigent provincial organ. Following the example of Solidarity, which had drawn its early strength from the inter-factory committees established during the August strikes, the formation of horizontal links between local party organisations developed (in conflict with the established practices of democratic centralism) as a means of expressing grass-roots opinion and articulating the interests of the party rank and file. As the debate on reform and renewal within the party intensified, the 'horizontal movement' gathered momentum and became a political force in its own right. Its origins were associated with the experiences of Zbigniew Iwanów in Toruń who, having been elected a factory committee secretary in 1980, was expelled by the provincial party control commission (WKKP) for factionalism and public avowal of his Catholic faith. The expulsion was not accepted by the local party organisation and, although the provincial decision was upheld by the central control commission, he continued to play the part of an active member and party official. The major point of this action was, he said, to change 'the Party constitution and the role of the Party in society'.[38]

The secretary of the local university party committee described the advantages of the movement as being to overcome the isolation of small local organisations, which were 'susceptible to manipulation by portions of the professional apparatus' and to 'protect society against threats and the pathological functioning of the party–state apparatus'. Under the excessive influence of the apparatus, 'conservative and even destructive attitudes' were generated within the party.[39] Documents published by the Toruń organisation accused middle-rank officials ('that is, the Central Committee, provincial committees and the departments of the Central Committee') of being a true social force 'which has placed its own interests above those of the party and society as a whole'.[40] It was clearly no accident that the 'horizontal movement' got under way as it became evident that the party apparatus and the provincial committees were not generally interested in reform and that the commitment of the post-August leadership to renewal had produced very limited results. Thus, in the words of the Toruń University committee secretary, there was still 'much ground for mistrust' in February 1981, and it was felt that it was time to 'translate declaration into the language of practice, particularly at the middle level [of the apparatus]'.[41] The movement had originally got under way in Toruń, and soon involved Bydgoszcz and Łódź. By November, Radom, Cracow, Katowice and Poznań were also reported to have generated such movements.[42] By early 1981, then, the continuing resistance of the provincial committees had stimulated the development of an increasingly strong counter-movement.

Resistance to reform: delays over party elections

One of the earliest demands associated with the movement for *odnowa* within the party had been the calling of an Extraordinary Party Congress, as the highest political authority of the organisation, which alone would have the power to decide on and implement the degree of change demanded. Many had hoped, and even expected, that the Congress would be held before the end of 1980. They had, however, underestimated the strength of the resistance to this taking place within the Central Committee (many of whose members were likely to lose their seats) and the party apparatus – even when the top leadership had formally committed itself to the holding of the Extraordinary Congress. This resistance was a major factor in convincing a significant proportion of the rank and file membership of the need for a 'horizontal movement'. One of the immediate objectives of the movement was, in turn, the election of new officials at all levels of the party organisation in order that the demands of the membership should have clearer and more immediate expression. As preparations for the Congress finally got under way, too, further demands for preliminary elections were heard, the Poznań pre-Congress commission, for example, placing particular emphasis on their need at provincial level. As noted above, Kania had proposed in December that elections be held ('with secret ballot') in party organisations where half the members requested them. But even this delayed proposal ran into obstacles as attempts were made to put it into action.

Shortly afterwards, the Central Committee released provisional election regulations based on those drawn up in 1971 and slightly modified in 1975. From the outset it was clear that they did not provide unambiguous guidance. As the introduction to the regulations itself pointed out, 'amongst a large number of the proposals there are many which are mutually contradictory'.[43] Instead of the former directive that the election of secretaries was 'confirmed by the superior party organ', for example, in the new formulation it was stated that the superior organ merely 'confirmed the correctness of the election procedure'. The meaning of this was not particularly clear and, as noted in the introduction, it actually conflicted with the existing Party Statute while implicitly rejecting conventional *nomenklatura* procedures. This form of presentation, with clear indications of the confused arrangements for party elections, did not help the smooth starting up of election procedures. It is difficult to avoid the suspicion that at least some of this confusion was intended. The form in which the regulations were published suggested that, whilst the Central Committee had finally produced the directives in reasonably good faith (although in the awareness that under current conditions they could only be of a provisional nature), the subsequent presentation and promulgation of the regulations served to emphasise their temporary and partially contradictory nature. This reflected the interests of those in the CC Secretariat who were committed to restricting the influence of the grass-roots membership and restraining those pressing for unrestrained party democratisation. In some cases, moreover, the regulations ran directly counter to reform proposals. A longer period of party membership (seven years) was now demanded of potential KW secretaries, with the further requirement that they should have held elective office in party or other social organisations. This conflicted with the currently popular proposal that secretaries should more frequently be drawn from amongst those established in other careers and that appointments should not further the establishment of a caste of political officials. As Toruń secretary Witkowski had written in his article endorsing the validity of the 'horizontal movement' within the party, the 'higher organs have not recognised and do not recognise the general need for such elections'. The regulations as published appeared to reflect this reluctance.

The response of the local party organisations to these proposals was often highly critical. A group of organisations from Poznań queried their legitimacy as party documents, as it was not clear whether they had actually been endorsed by the Central Committee or had simply emanated from one of its departments. Particularly scathing criticism was expressed of the proposal that the local influence could nominate a number of candidates for the executive at a level of 50% of those nominated by the first secretary himself. As existing regulations allowed for nominations at the level of 15%, this was sarcastically described as a '35% increase in democracy for party members'. Surprise was expressed at the total failure to mention two principles generally regarded as fundamental in any conception of renewal as it affected the apparatus – the rotation of officials and the imposition of a ban on the permanent occupation of party posts, and the ending of simultaneous office-holding in the party and the state administration.[44]

The election regulations were only one sign that the central party authorities were not willing to be pushed along by grass-roots forces and were resolutely opposed to certain of their proposals. From their point of view the central Congress Commission was in the safe hands of Olszowski, who was clearly opposed to aspects of *odnowa* within the party that would weaken the power of the central authorities and their major instrument of rule, the apparatus. Some proposals were decisively rejected, as they threatened the party's unity, coherence and discipline and weakened the obligation placed on lower party organs to implement resolutions passed by central authorities. Basic principles of democratic centralism were invoked here: 'democracy without centralism would be of no greater worth than centralism without democracy'.[45] A similar line was taken by a professor from the party's Higher School of Social Sciences who, emphasising that the 'party must always emerge as a unified, coherent force', described as 'primitive and, to say the least, naive certain impressions about direct democracy within the party which are now circulating'.[46] The early weeks of 1981, preceding the VIII Plenum of the Central Committee (which opened on 9 February) thus saw a strengthening of the conservative line amongst the central authorities.

Although, from the point of view of many local party organisations, progress towards renewal was slow and patchy within the party and the conviction that the apparatus was blocking change had not weakened, CC Secretary Barcikowski claimed that improvements in relations with the provincial committees had taken place since December. He reported that KW secretaries were meeting more frequently with the CC Secretariat and that more CC staff were being directed to intensive work in the localities with which they were familiar. The amount of information sent from the centre to the provincial committees had also risen 'many times'.[47] It is likely, then, that what the party leadership regarded as organisational improvement and elements of reform were precisely what local organisations interpreted as a general stiffening of resistance and continuing intransigence at provincial level. This makes it clearer why exceptional figures within the apparatus, like Gdańsk secretary Fiszbach, who had a conception of *odnowa* closer to that of the rank and file, were careful to maintain formal KW control over local initiatives within the party, which thus enabled them to maintain the claim that the principles of democratic centralism were still in operation. The speed with which Fiszbach set up or associated the KW organisation with the Gdańsk pre-Congress Commission is instructive in this respect, as such groups had a close resemblance to local horizontal movements. Indeed, in a memorandum sent out to provincial committees by the CC Organisation Department in November, Gdańsk had been identified (together with Radom, Toruń, Warsaw and Łódź) as one of the centres of the developing horizontal movement.[48]

The Politburo report this time was delivered by Tadeusz Grabski (now a CC secretary) who, like Olszowski, had clashed with Gierek but who was similarly not to be identified as some kind of 'liberal' willing to modify existing conceptions of democratic centralism. The overall tone was markedly more offensive than had been the opening address at the VII Plenum. Mention was made of a 'process of disintegration' occurring within state and society, and the creation of a situation which provided the 'conditions for the activisation of political forces whose policies clashed with those of socialism'.[49] In general, then, he turned attention away from the forces which were continuing to block renewal and condemned those who sought the roots of the crisis in the traditional conception of communist rule and the long-established dominance of the apparatus over the party. It was, he declared, a time of choice when the option of 'socialist democracy' (with the implicit emphasis on the first word) was counterposed to a future of chaos, the dismantling of the power structure and the undermining of the position and role of the PZPR. Grabski was not alone in adopting this approach. Kania's address, which wound up the Plenum, also carried a stronger ideological tone than on the previous occasion. He stated, in phrases with significant historical overtones, that 'Poland has become a weakened link within the socialist community' and warned that 'one weak link weakens the whole', emphasising that 'Counterrevolution will not pass in Poland'. Barcikowski also alluded to Solidarity's 'terrorisation of party members' and warned that this was associated with the 'paralysis of the power apparatus'.[50]

Amongst the provincial first secretaries there were some who alluded to the role of the apparatus in preventing change and prolonging the crisis, although they were less numerous than they had been at the VII Plenum. Thus KW secretary Zawodziński (appointed to Białystok in October 1980, having also served as first secretary in Łomża from 1975 to 1978) spoke of the prevalent feeling that *odnowa* was being obstructed by conservative groups amongst the authorities – 'in the party and the state, economic administration, particularly at the centre' – while Czechowicz, first secretary in Łódź since November 1980, emphasised the continuing need to ensure the responsible behaviour of those occupying positions of responsibility and to develop a system of supervision that 'covers *nomenklatura* cadres at all levels'. He pointed out that cadres were looking for ways of preventing reform rather than ways of seeking to implement it, as they could see no place for themselves in the reformed system. Gajewski, foreman in the Warsaw steel works, made a similar point when he alluded to anti-socialist forces who were obstructing renewal within the party and reported that since November his party organisation had put forward many proposals to higher organs without receiving any answer. This, he said, had contributed to the 'many reservations' and 'strong criticism' concerning personnel within the party and administrative apparatuses.[51]

Of the statements made by provincial secretaries at the Plenum, though, the most forceful was that of Żabiński – and that was emphatically one of defence of the party's position within the power structure. Politburo member and party leader in Katowice, Żabiński had participated in the strike negotiations in Szczecin and had been apparently sincerely sympathetic to the demands of the strikers and their actions in August 1980. By 1981, his views had seemingly undergone a major change which, moreover, was documented in the free trade union press.[52] At the February Plenum his view was that 'The party and the people's authorities can retreat no further'. The key issue was to prevent further demoralisation among the party *aktiv*: 'we realise in the province that we cannot take up the position of a capitulator – we will not by doing so gain the trust of the masses but we will lose the confidence of the *aktiv* . . . we are paying too little attention to strengthening the position of those who are supporting us'. A further element in this necessary reinforcement concerned the approaching Extraordinary Congress. The conditions under which it was likely to be held were, he said, becoming steadily worse and he suggested that the party programme should first be worked out and consolidated, and that only then should the plans for the Congress be finalised.[53] Although Żabiński had said that this proposal was likely to be an unpopular one in general, this was not necessarily true of Central Committee members amongst whom the party apparatus was well represented and many of whom were likely to lose their positions at the coming Congress. Several KW first secretaries thus welcomed his proposal and alluded to the need to reinforce the party in the immediate future in the face of the 'counter-revolutionary elements' now associated with Solidarity. Comments along these lines came from Gawroński (Kalisz), Łabuś (Gorzów) and Solecki (Leszno). Żabiński's declaration provided a rallying point for conservative forces still located in the regional party apparatus and well represented on the Central Committee.

It was at this meeting, too, that Pińkowski was replaced as Premier by General Jaruzelski, the long-standing Minister of Defence. In terms of the prevailing political climate in the Central Committee and the views expressed by many of the provincial first secretaries (who themselves made up nearly 20% of CC membership) the changeover cannot be regarded as particularly surprising. The reference at the Plenum to social disintegration, the weakening of Poland as a link in the socialist commonwealth and the threat of counter-revolution all pointed to the likelihood of efforts to reinforce the coercive capacity of the Polish party–state, while the evident weakness of government leadership and its failure to master current problems also suggested a shift to stronger leadership. The occupation of the key government post by a military figure was nevertheless obviously unusual in the communist political context. The change has been seen as marking a new phase in the political situation and the creation of a new role for the party. Thus, Ascherson described a new separation between party and government, in which 'the Party reserved for itself the unpopular duty of challenging and opposing Solidarity, while the government was seen to pursue its own, more liberal policies'.[54] While Jaruzelski had associated himself and the military with Kania's conciliatory position during the August strikes and had showed no clear signs of deviating from this, it is doubtful that the epithet 'liberal' is here the appropriate one. If by that was meant a lower degree of commitment to the imposition of the Soviet political model in Poland or any weakening of Poland's political and military links with the Soviet Union, such a conception was misleading. Appointed head of the army's Main Political Administration in 1960, Jaruzelski had played a key role throughout the reformation of the Polish armed forces which was designed to prevent the possibility of any recurrence of the Polish army's nationalist posture in 1956. His role as Minister of Defence from 1968 was weighted against political adventurism rather than in favour of anything that could be described as liberalism. In his last statement at a CC Plenum, in October 1980, his tone had been centrist and his main emphasis had been placed on the importance of the Warsaw Pact in underwriting Poland's national existence. At the VII Plenum in December the statement of his colleague General Baryła, vice-minister of defence and head of the army's Main Political Administration, had been relatively hard-line. He had warned that any disturbance of the stability of the socialist state could give rise to the threat of counter-revolution and stressed the role of the army in preventing this. It did not provide evidence of a liberal orientation.

Developments at the VIII Plenum, both with respect to government and the party, thus showed a stronger tendency within the leadership to the maintenance of democratic centralism and disciplined leadership. There were no signs that the pressure for elections throughout the party organisation were to be allowed to get out of hand and, indeed, it appeared that established party authorities and the apparatus were preparing a more aggressive form of defence. The shifting position of the central party authorities gave the provincial committees grounds for hope in maintaining their position, and their attitude to local demands remained, to say the least, a hesitant one. As a secretary in the Poznań Cegielski works put it, when members demand that renewal should occur at province level before the Congress, 'the climate becomes chilly and somewhat misty – it really is still not clear, despite the pressure exerted by many party members, whether elections will take place within the provincial organs or not'.[55]

The costs of centralism

Criticism of the leadership position was not restricted to local party organisations. It was clearly implied in articles by such party intellectuals as Professor Erazmus. In one on the timely subject of party elections, he distinguished between the democratic and centralist currents which had been characteristic of the workers' movement and emphasised that it was the former which had been dominant in the Marxist-Leninist tradition. The dominance of democratic practices was, he argued, associated with the careful development of practices to effect the harmonious transfer of power and ensure that candidates secured the confidence of electors.[56] His explicit linkage of the democratic current with Leninist practice was, of course, a strong argument in its favour, as party pronouncements made constant reference to the need to return to 'Leninist norms'. The precise meaning of the phrase was never made clear, however, and it provided conservative forces with a useful slogan when they wished to link formal approval of *odnowa* with commitment to a more orthodox practice of democratic centralism. Such use of the phrase also came in for criticism. It was pointed out that 'Leninist norms' had never been properly applied in the Polish party and that therefore it was not possible to return to them.[57] Democratic centralism might also, it was pointed out, take different forms according to levels of political development, the composition of the party and characteristics of its membership.[58]

Continuing resistance in defence of the interests and position of the party apparatus prompted more searching analyses and more radical political demands from the pre-Congress commissions and branches of the horizontal movement. The editor of *Polityka* (M. Rakowski) was coopted by Jaruzelski in February to become deputy premier. Meanwhile, his paper called for a renegotiation of the Gdańsk and other agreements to iron out 'ambiguities', although proposals from other quarters appealed for prospective Congress delegates to raise again matters that the strikers and their expert advisers had dropped for fear of appearing excessively provocative.[59] From Poznań came the suggestion that demands for the abolition of the *nomenklatura* system should be examined by the Congress, with the intention that the powers of party organs should be properly codified. Clarification of rights and duties within the party was felt to be called for in the contemporary situation, when there was a noticeable contrast between the positive stance both of the leadership and of the lower organs, and the 'passive attitude of the intermediate organs and the state administration'. The developing political situation was encouraging radicalisation amongst some groups, with calls for the specification of central and regional powers and a greater devolution of political power.

Another response to the problems of securing political change was an increase in the numbers of those leaving the party. The work of

Central and Provincial Party Control Commissions had intensified since the VI Plenum, both because of the party's desire to review and verify its membership and because of the feeling on the part of individuals that complaints submitted by them were more likely to be seriously considered and that justice would be done. Whilst, during the first nine months of 1980 the Opole control commission had received 204 submissions, in the month of October alone it received a further 121.[60] Members of the commissions adopted a more rigorous approach. One commission had previously responded only to written submissions and ignored verbal statements concerning 'some people in executive positions'; it had generally been clear that 'requirements of managerial cadres had until recently been at an inappropriate level'.[61] In the last six months of 1980 over 30,000 had been excluded (*wydaloni*) from the party, a relatively high proportion of those removed from party lists during this period. For the last three months of 1980 a total of 62,000 removals was reported.[62] It would seem that the rate of departure from the party remained at the same level in 1981, as Barcikowski reported to the VIII Plenum (held in early February) that 93,000 had left the party since the end of September, offset by a total of 26,000 who had joined.[63] The growing rate of departure from the party was directly linked with the problems encountered in furthering political renewal. In one factory a large number of resignations from the party was reported from the end of 1980. If things did not improve, according to the committee secretary, the organisation of 1,400 would be reduced to 500 – 'the remedy', he stated, was 'democratic elections'.[64]

Not all those excluded from the party were associated with the former leadership. Shortly after the VIII Plenum, the Central Party Control Commission supported the provincial decision in Toruń to expel Zbigniew Iwanów, the Towimor factory committee secretary who had played an important part in originating the horizontal movement. Not all provincial commissions were as committed to *odnowa* as they might have been: some were unwilling to press charges against their colleagues, while some sanctions applied by provincial commissions were, it appeared, likely to be lifted when errant managers appealed to the central authorities.[65] It was not surprising, either, that the provincial control commissions were sometimes reported to associate themselves with the political tendency of colleagues in the provincial apparatus. The inclination of some WKKP members, particularly it appeared of those with a shorter period of party membership, was to concentrate attention on the defence of party members, 'especially those in the apparatus, from undeserved attack'. They were reported to see themselves as some kind of 'party guard'.[66]

The Bydgoszcz crisis and its outcome

A change in the political climate and a shift in the attitude of the party leadership took place towards the end of March as a result of some dramatic developments in the town of Bydgoszcz. They brought about the most serious confrontation between Solidarity and the forces of the party–state since the August strikes. While the origins of the action remain unclear, it is at least accepted that it was linked with the conflicting orientations we have detected within the central party leadership and with the continuing resistance of major portions of the party apparatus to the pressures for change and renewal. The background to the events lay in an occupation that had been taking place in Bydgoszcz to press for the registration of Rural Solidarity. A long meeting between their representatives and some members of the People's Council was drawing to a close when the room they occupied was suddenly cleared by the police. By the time its occupants reached the street three Solidarity representatives had been severely beaten. Solidarity members throughout the country were infuriated and their leaders were on the verge of declaring a general strike. At the time of the police action several key figures in the party leadership were out of the country, although a deputy premier was present in Bydgoszcz. The apparently planned nature of the intervention and the severity of the beatings gave rise to suspicions that some kind of political provocation was involved.

Official accounts of the incident were briefly descriptive and a formal investigation was set up with the brief of finding out more about its origins. The publicist, J. Urban, ascribed the action to those seeking to transform the economic and political crisis into a 'crisis of Polish statehood', although he was not specific about the identity of such people.[67] Solidarity leaders immediately stated their view that the events represented a provocation by hard-liners of the moderate and apparently reformist Jaruzelski government. A similar opinion was expressed by the influential chairman of the Journalists' Association, Stefan Bratkowski, who pointed the finger at those who were afraid of the party's rank and file. He referred to their desire to avoid the experience of honest elections and to their attempts to delay the convocation of the Extraordinary Congress, taking the position that they were 'the only ones capable of protecting the apparatus from the loss of positions and influence'.[68] Staniszkis also refers to the attempt of the anti-Kania faction to use the frustration of the party apparatus 'as a political lever', while W. Kuczyński also associates the developments with the 'revolt of the intermediate apparatus, horrified by their prospects'.[69] The logic underlying this conception was that Solidarity would take action in response to the Bydgoszcz beatings and that Jaruzelski would be driven to take harsher action to restrict the influence of the union and preserve the communist order in Poland.

Not all took this view. Some ascribed the Bydgoszcz events directly to Jaruzelski and identified March 1981 as the date when he 'probably set the course towards a decisive battle'.[70] Certainly, there were indications of quite extensive preparation for repressive action in March. Reserve militia units (ROMO) had been called up, Solidarity had noted several incidents when military or security agents harassed their members, and announcements of Warsaw Pact manoeuvres were made.[71] Most, however, see Olszowski as having played the leading role in the crisis, with the possible contribution of such party figures as Grabski and Żabiński who had spoken against the conciliatory line promoted by Kania.[72] Particularly tight control was exercised over the mass media at this time – and this fell under the control of Olszowski in his capacity as CC secretary. He is reported to have maintained close telephone contact with the provincial committees during this period and to have attended a meeting of the army's Main Political Administration.[73] The Soviet Press agency TASS released lurid stories of various kinds of counter-revolutionary activities and it was on the express orders of Olszowski that the Polish media were forbidden to carry denials of such allegations.[74] Suspicions that Olszowski and his sympathisers had played a major part in setting up the government–Solidarity confrontation were also supported by the fact that Olszowski and Grabski tendered their resignations at the hastily convened IX Plenum of the Central Committee. The resignations were not accepted however, and it appears that Soviet representatives had exerted considerable pressure to prevent any kind of split within the party leadership.

The political implications of the Bydgoszcz events flowed directly from the long-standing resistance of the party apparatus to political renewal, the problems encountered by the Kania leadership in attempting to solve the conflicts of the post-August period by methods of conciliation rather than confrontation, and the general lack of progress in following any line of policy consistently. The failure of Olszowski to force the party leadership into a position of confrontation opened the way for a greater degree of acceptance of rank-and-file demands and a clearer endorsement of political renewal within the party. This, however, was only decided by what were described as the highly dramatic proceedings of the IX CC Plenum, which opened on 29 March.[75] In addition to the attempted coup from the hard-line position, the leadership was also subject to an unprecedented level of criticism for its failure to maintain intra-party democracy and its obstruction of political renewal. 'Fratricidal conflict' was reported from within the Central Committee and the Plenum was clearly a major turning-point.[76] It was also the period, CC secretary Barcikowski later admitted, when the party came closest to collapsing as an organisation.[77] On this, as on previous occasions, open conflict within the party and public disunity were seen as the most dangerous threat to the survival of the Marxist-Leninist organisation.

Unlike the previous Plenum, then, when the key address made by Grabski lent a harder-line tone to central leadership policy, the IX Plenum was introduced by Barcikowski who dwelt on the achievements and prospects for party reform and adopted a more conciliatory attitude towards the rank-and-file movement. With respect to 'horizontal' developments he affirmed that links between party organisations were positive if they served to enliven the ideological content of party life and developed within the framework established by the Party Statute. He shared with many local organisations the view that 'the crisis has arisen from a definite mistrust on the part of primary organisations and party members of the higher organs and their apparatus', and repeated that the 'main source of the present crisis and of previous crises has been the failure of intra-party democracy'. 'Numerous changes' had already taken place amongst occupants of leading party posts (15% of organisations had conducted elections since the VII Plenum), but he stated that it was still necessary to do everything necessary to 'eliminate the distance and mistrust between the higher organs and their apparatus and (on the other hand) primary organisations and the broad *aktiv*'.[78]

It should be noted again that when mention is made of the alienation of the higher party organs from the party base and of the excessive dominance of the apparatus, it is the provincial organisations of the party that play by far the greatest part in numerical terms. Whilst the political resistance of the party apparatus had been a constant theme in the post-August conflicts, it was the provincial committees that had stood at the centre of these conflicts. If we accept that the total number of those employed in the party apparatus in a political capacity stood at between 11,000 and 12,280 in 1980, only between 560 and 650 were placed in posts of national responsibility, attached to the Central Committee. Of the rest 32%, between 3,270 and 3,710 individuals, were attached to the intermediate organs of the party, at provincial level.[79] Whilst, then, provincial staff made up around a third of the total of apparatus workers, they constituted the overwhelming majority, 85%, of the body of people representing the 'higher authorities', the central and intermediate organs of the party. As Barcikowski admitted at the IX Plenum, their resistance to *odnowa* had not yet been broken. Since the VII Plenum, following which the pre-Congress commissions began meeting and the rank-and-file movement gained momentum, change had been slow and only fifty-two appointments had been reported amongst KW secretaries (including nine first secretaries), representing 18% of the KW secretarial cadre. This was not an insignificant rate of change over four months, but it was little more than the 15% that had occurred over October and November when, it was now clear, *odnowa* had not got under way. All in all, the KW secretarial cadre had remained intact since the VI Plenum in ten of the forty-nine provincial committees: Biała Podlaska, Chełm, Ciechanów, Łomża, Opole, Piotrków Trybunalski, Poznań, Przemyśl, Rzeszów, Sieradz. These were mostly provinces with smaller party organisations and in general may be regarded as being among the more peripheral areas politically, although this was not the case with Poznań. Here the former first secretary, Zasada, had been replaced immediately after the fall of Gierek but no further change in the secretarial cadre had taken place, a fact undoubtedly reflected in the continuing complaints about the negative political attitude of the Poznań party apparatus and the increasingly vociferous criticism from areas like the University.

Thus Barcikowski called for greater activity on the part of apparatus workers. There were still those, he said, who avoided meetings and criticised party authorities and the basic organisations without doing anything to eliminate what they regarded as negative phenomena. The date of the Extraordinary Congress was now fixed for mid-July (Zabiński having been successful in this part of his demand), the election of new party leaders was called for at all levels, the restriction on the number of candidates who could be nominated from the floor was lifted, and the principle of the secret ballot was reaffirmed. Extensive criticism was made of the recent performance of the central authorities and this was not absent from the statements of the KW first secretaries who spoke at the Plenum (a total of five, with a further four entering their statements on the protocol of the meeting). Thus Kruk (Lublin) alluded to the 'wall of mistrust between the apparatus and the party *aktiv* and rank-and-file membership', while Cypryniak (Szczecin) saw the cause of the continuing crisis lying in the failure of the party to regain popular confidence. Dąbrowa (Kraków) went so far as to defend aspects of the horizontal movement and argued that its claim should not be rejected too hastily. The remedy for the current hiatus in intra-party relations was seen to lie in particular with the speeding up of preparations for the Congress (the lack of progress in which came in for wide-spread criticism), the holding of elections throughout the party and continuing cadre change. The demand of the Płock KW for further changes in personnel at central level was also transmitted by a local representative.[80]

The Bydgoszcz crisis had added a further element to the situation in the party and some KW secretaries, particularly Dąbrowa and Bryk (Siedlce), were far from happy with the way the party leadership had handled the affair. A particular target of criticism was the lack of information and presentation of conflicting accounts in the mass media which, complained Dąbrowa, brought official propaganda and news to the 'far borders of implausibility'. Many expressed their awareness of the failure of the party leadership to align itself with the reform movement and restore its authority over the mass of party membership. Rakowski summed up the situation by saying that, in the event of a general strike, the Central Committee and provincial committees would be left to their own devices in their offices.[81] But, of course, KW secretaries were by no means unanimous about the need for further change in the party or about developments in the country as a whole. From the place of origin of the current crisis, Bydgoszcz secretary Henryk Bednarski (ideology specialist and former director of the party school) saw developments reflecting the transition of some elements associated with Solidarity to a 'new level of conflict, to the weakening and destruction of the nation's political structure and statehood'. Luciński (Ciechanów) returned to the old theme of what was seen as the threat to party cadres and spoke of the weakening 'psychological condition of the party apparatus', complaining that cadre changes had been compelled and made necessary 'by the threat of the "strike pistol", in consequence of which we have lost many good cadres'. Not surprisingly, a similar opinion was expressed by Prokopiak, who had resigned from the Radom committee two weeks previously in the face of a threatened strike (although he had gained a vote of confidence from a KW Plenum in January). His complaint was that 'internal party discipline is getting worse . . . Contact between many people in the leadership with party members is becoming increasingly weak'.

Not unrelated to Prokopiak's position was the demand from a Bydgoszcz machinist that 'members who had in the past performed various party functions' should now be removed from the Central Committee, and the statement that it was such 'compromised comrades' who were holding back renewal in the party. Further support for Prokopiak's position, however, came from Olszowski, who denounced the 'campaign waged against party cadres' and establishment stalwart, the writer Jerzy Putrament, who described the apparatus as the backbone of the party. In an instructive comparison with 1956 and its aftermath, he dismissed that threat of the 'so-called conservatives' and directed attention, as had Gomułka in 1957, to the 'more real' problem of revisionism. An indication of the line that conservative thought was taking in the party was also supplied by Ignacy Drabik, a foreman from Kielce. He stressed the errors that had been made in party work and alluded to the 'liquidation of the flower of the party apparatus at *powiat* level' (a major casualty of the 1975 reorganisation). Particular objects of attacks were those in higher education, some of whom were claimed to originate from the 'former gentry, land-owners and factory-owners'. A menacing tone was introduced by the suggestion that the role of Zionism in the successive crises of People's Poland be examined.[82] The voice of party reaction was therefore by no means absent from the Plenum.

Neither were concerns about military security absent. General Baryła called for a radical attack on fractionalism and reported the highly critical views of military cadres on outbreaks of social disorder and breaches of legality. They were, he said, always ready to defend socialism as well as the independence of Poland.[83] Thus, while the protracted resistance of the apparatus and the failure of what appeared to be the Bydgoszcz provocation finally spurred the leadership to adopt a less ambiguous position, it was not at all clear that the position of the reformers had been really strengthened. The incorporation in the CC resolution of attacks on enemies of socialism and 'various right-wing forces' who were exerting influence on Solidarity, in combination with reaffirmation of the principles of democratic centralism and condemnation of *ideological pluralism*, provided the conservatives with extensive ammunition. Certainly, the reformers were by no means content with the outcome of the Plenum and they suspected that the 'resolution represented a turning away from the discussed reforms and a retreat from the Gdańsk agreement'.[84] The ambiguities and conflicts within the party were far from being resolved.

Developments at the party base

These continuing ambiguities in central policy, despite the more sympathetic view taken of local party democracy and the setback suffered by the conservative initiative in Bydgoszcz, were reflected in the diversity of the situation at local level. As had been the case in the past, a leading role was taken by the Gdańsk organisation. Apart from the qualities of the provincial leaders there and the policy they had chosen to follow, the professional experiences of the provincial staff were also felt to play a part in this. Local apparatus workers were described as being untypical by virtue of their youth and professional experience – they did not feel bound, therefore, to defend their apparatus position as a source of income and material security. Provincial secretaries had made it clear that they did not regard election to pre-Congress conferences as votes of confidence and were not fighting to retain their seats on committees (by April one of the eight KW secretaries had already failed to secure election to the district conference).[85] However, Gdańsk was recognised to be well ahead in its political developments and there were fears among local activists that the party organisation might become isolated because of this. Efforts were made to extend horizontal links outside the province, and Łabęcki, party secretary in the Lenin shipyard, reported that secretarial contacts were maintained with representatives from Poznań, Legnica and elsewhere.[86] Horizontal developments in Gdańsk, however, were different from those in nearby Toruń in the absence of antagonism between local organisations and the provincial apparatus, and in the avoidance of anti-apparatus sentiment as the main driving force behind local links.

Conditions elsewhere were less favourable for the development of local democracy in the party organisation. Professor Dobieszewski, who had previously written in support of the orthodox conception of democratic centralism, now grudgingly accepted the horizontal movement 'as a social fact', ascribing its development to 'reaction against the intellectual incapacity and local lack of political initiative on the part of the vertical structures'.[87] Clearly, this did not suggest the welcome acceptance of horizontal developments as a positive phenomenon. Such reluctance was also evident on the part of many local officials.

Party staff in Katowice were reported to be uncooperative in their dealings with pre-Congress commissions and discussed the political issues involved in terms no more sophisticated than those of a 'political primer'.[88] Criticism continued of restrictions on news and the circulation of information, publication often depending on the disposition of local forces. Attempts to organise elections to the workers' self-government in the Tychy motor plant (Katowice province) met with the KW response that party members there were acting 'in an insubordinate manner' and local workers were clearly not impressed by the progress made towards local party democracy.[89] Some party punishment was dealt out to the Tychy town committee secretary. It was, however, regarded as insufficient and in the autumn he was expelled from the party.[90]

The Warsaw organisation also continued to act as a bastion of provincial resistance. It had been singled out by Bratkowski as a hard-line centre in his Open Letter condemning the Bydgoszcz provocation, while the head of the organisation department (Bolesław Porowski) was later identified as a major source of resistance to all democratising forces and to the apparatus criticism that had been expressed at the February KW Plenum.[91] Porowski mounted a spirited defence of his position, but other criticism of political practice within the Warsaw organisation was not lacking and hopes in Warsaw were pinned to the further development of the horizontal movement.[92] But it is doubtful whether these hopes were ever fulfilled to any great extent on a general basis. The barriers to horizontal organisation remained strong and the party grass roots had no tradition of independent association; passivity and inactivity were wide-spread at the party base: people 'are afraid to stick their neck out. They wait for orders from above'.[93] In places like Toruń and Gdańsk different kinds of horizontal movement developed under very different circumstances. One developed with considerable success in Poznań. Elsewhere, like Łódź, developments did not get very far and the party apparatus remained in control.[94] Nevertheless, the horizontal movement gained some representation in eighteen provinces and a national meeting of members took place in Toruń on 15 April.[95] Under the more acceptable title of the Pre-Congress Forum for Party Understanding it even received some official PZPR patronage and was attended by Łukasiewicz, deputy director of the CC Organisation Department, and Najdowski, Toruń KW first secretary.

The impact of the horizontal movement at the party base and its overall political effect on the party organisation remained quite limited. A contributory factor here was the sharply expressed Soviet criticism of developments within the PZPR. After the IX Plenum the first charge of revisionism to be directed at the PZPR came from a fraternal party, that of Czechoslovakia. Shortly after that, the first direct criticism of the Polish party appeared in the Soviet press. As it was directed at the rather improbable target of the Warsaw party organisation, this was probably a sign of displeasure with the party leadership as a whole.[96] The Toruń conference prompted a visit from Suslov, the long-standing ideology expert and guardian of Marxist-Leninist orthodoxy. Further Soviet expressions of displeasure at Polish party revisionism followed soon afterwards. Similar to the way in which it provoked sharper criticism from the Soviet Union, the growing salience of activities within the horizontal movement and increased central tolerance of grass-roots democracy at the party base did nothing to diminish apparatus resistance to such aspects of *odnowa* within the PZPR. In many ways, the threatened activisation of the party membership and the rise of anti-apparatus sentiments were considerably more worrying to established officials than was the registration of Solidarity or even its development along more explicitly political lines. From the point of the party apparatus, the August strikes and their political consequences represented a weakening of its position but 'in general it did not constitute a direct threat to it, if only because union activists had no intention of becoming party secretaries'.[97] This was not the case with the movement for change within the party. Even if they did not intend to become party officials themselves, those active in the movement were decided on limiting the powers and tenure of existing incumbents of party posts. The fear and dislike felt by most of the apparatus to this gave them further incentive to restrict the development of the horizontal movement, and it seemed that in many areas they were quite successful in this.

A further factor weakening the influence of the horizontal movement as a separate current, distinct from official party activities, was the growing tolerance of the movement expressed by the party authorities. This was particularly notable at the X Plenum of the Central Committee, which met on 29 April, two weeks after the conference of representatives of the horizonal movement. If, stated Łabęcki, the 'Central Committee is capable of foresight, of what it might gain and what it might lose, then it should immediately take the decision to accept such gatherings as part of its own activity'. Central authorities had already taken several significant steps in this direction and, at the X Plenum, the deputy director of the CC Organisation Department spelt out the conditions that had brought the movement into existence:

the suspicion of the rank and file that no renewal was really taking place in the party, doubts concerning the position of the central and provincial authorities, the desire to accelerate preparations for the Extraordinary Congress. In view of the self-criticism made by the leadership over preceding weeks and months the implication was that many aspects of the horizontal movement were legitimate while others were due to errors made by the party authorities. This point was underlined by Gdula, recently elected first secretary of Bielsko, which earlier in the year had been the site of serious conflict and had seen a general strike directed against the existing political leadership. Since then, said Gdula, the reformed KW secretariat had succeeded in defusing social conflict and, by maintaining close contact with local party organisations, had forestalled the formation of local links without KW participation, 'which we would have regarded as showing a lack of confidence in our effectiveness'.[98] A similarly active stance on the part of the provincial committee in Bydgoszcz, it appears, also forestalled the development of the horizontal movement there. According to KW secretary Bednarski, its activity 'practically ended in June 1981' and was largely absorbed in the activity of the pre-Congress conferences.[99] In some ways, then, the success of the horizontal movement in promoting its arguments and publicising its case concerning the harmful political effects of apparatus conservatism led to its eclipse as a separate tendency and its decline from April 1981.[100]

5 Renewal and party authority: the Extraordinary Congress and its consequences

The position of the party apparatus

In addition to pursuing the stronger commitment to renewal articulated at the IX CC Plenum and reflecting the semi-formal acceptance of the horizontal movement by the leadership (and its consequent neutralisation as an autonomous political force), the X Plenum looked ahead to further change by finally determining the dates of the Extraordinary Congress and discussing the programme guidelines set out for it. By this stage, too, the election process was well under way within the local party organisations and was shortly to begin at province level. Already at the Plenum some disquiet was expressed at the early results. The small number of workers elected to the provincial conferences was commented on by Kania, and KW first secretary Zawodziński deplored the fact that workers made up only 12% of the total of those so far elected in Białystok. Some saw this as the result of the continuing crisis of confidence in the party and doubts concerning the effectiveness of activity within the party, attendance at party meetings now being at a level of 30% to 40% in many areas. Łabęcki, a leading activist from Gdańsk, ascribed their reluctance to lack of confidence in the prospects for renewal within the party and unwillingness to risk distancing themselves from their workmates.[1] Local party organisations, on the other hand, were far less troubled than central party authorities by the limited number of workers elected and did not share the assumption that higher worker representation was in some way a guarantee of party democracy. They seemed more inclined to the view expressed after the Plenum by P. Moszyński that 'even if the authorities were made up 100% of workers there would still remain the fundamental problem of the capacity of the party masses to control the activities of the authorities'.[2]

Others linked the election of workers with general problems surrounding the low level of party authority and the position of the apparatus. Ciupa, first KW secretary in Konin, saw the problems involved in attracting workers to stand for election as symptomatic of a weakness that was likely to become more pronounced in the future: 'I fear that in coming years many difficulties will emerge in the selection of comrades for work in the apparatus of our party.' A major cause of this was the current position of the apparatus which, 'to put it delicately, has for many months been totally criticised for everything'. He found the Congress programme guidelines weak in this respect as they were not sufficient to tackle the issues involved. The guidelines did, indeed, have relatively little to say about this important and controversial topic. The party apparatus, they said, 'should assist in the implementation of [party] resolutions. Work in the Party apparatus should be based on temporary leave granted to people who have worked at least five years in their respective institutions. The Party apparatus should consist of a considerably larger number of blue-collar workers'.[3] That was about it. It seemed clear that the leadership was not eager for this topic to receive particular emphasis at this stage.

Neither were the views of the more conservative forces absent from the stage. Siwak, the persistent voice of hard-line populism, thought the elections in most local party organisations were being conducted 'under the aegis of those who are out to dismember the party in a premeditated manner. We are being lost by those who have demanded so much.' In general, the election regulations and the party programme proposals (its main formal business on this occasion) met with approval, although there was no lack of disagreement here either. The new election regulations, amended after the IX Plenum, proposed the ending of the practice whereby members of higher party organs had to be invited to participate in the activity of the presidium of the conference or meeting, and had the right to sit on the newly elected party committee. Invitations to participate in this way were now a matter for the meeting or conference to decide. Similarly, provincial conferences were left to decide how many KW secretaries they wished to elect and the decision was taken out of the hands of the CC Secretariat.[4] This clearly weakened central control over provincial and local 'elections' and, if rigorously applied, would spell the end of conventional *nomenklatura* practices. It also meant the removal of the career security that the professional party worker had enjoyed once he had joined the caste of officials. Party elections could henceforth be conducted, at least in theory, without the participation of any higher party official. Further demands were expressed at the X Plenum that candidates for party office should not be introduced from outside those formally identified as participant in the election meeting and that candidacy should be limited to those elected to the meeting or conference from local party organisations.

This, of course, was intended further to limit central control over elected posts and to maximise local influence over party appointments. It was indignantly challenged by one central official – 'Does this mean that the Central Committee should only represent the party and not have the right to direct its activities?' – and was interpreted as an attempt to undermine the ideological and organisational unity of the party. Jaruzelski was also emphatic on this point: 'we must protect all those occupying positions of popular authority who are working honestly and effectively. The apparatus should be improved but it is not permissible to wreck it'.[5] Demands for changes within the Central Committee itself were rejected, as a new Committee would be elected at the Congress, now only ten weeks hence. Four members were, however, expelled for past misdemeanours (two former KW first secretaries among them) and a commission set up under Tadeusz Grabski to evaluate the activity of CC members as members of the political leadership. Four members of the existing top leadership were dropped, three of whom who had been appointed candidate members of the Politburo and/or members of the Secretariat already at the VIII Congress. They were replaced by two worker members of the Central Committee and two KW first secretaries, both of whom had an un-broken record of service in the party or state administration extending back nearly twenty years each.

The extent of change at local levels was considerable, but not necess-arily as dramatic as some speakers at the Plenum suggested. In Lublin province 75% of the executive in primary and shop-floor organisations was changed, many of the incomers being appointed for the first time. But amongst the first secretaries elected at the sixty-six primary organ-isation conferences held in Poznań, only ten came from outside the party apparatus. In Kraków, of the forty-three first secretaries elected in local organisations, only fifteen had not held that office before. Overall, around 50% of the first secretaries of primary organisations were changed during the election campaign and 38% of those in committees of the 'first level' (ie at factory, town or commune level), the level of change settling in fact at a lower level than finally emerged in elections to the provincial committee secretariats.[6] This still reflected a striking rate of change and a far greater involvement of the party rank and file in the election of officials than was normally the case. The possibilities of affecting the outcome of elections were eagerly seized and there were constant rejections of the practice of higher party organs 'bringing secretaries in their briefcases': that is, descending on local organisations to supervise the installation of centrally-determined candidates.[7]

The determination of officials to defend their position was, however, far from broken and, as the X Plenum had shown, there were serious misgivings within the leadership as to the eventual implications of the grass-roots movement and the threat it might pose to the position of an apparatus capable of operating within any normal conception of democratic centralism. The atmosphere was hardly one to encourage incumbent officials to participate in the ongoing process of change and the fate of former party leaders served as a warning to them. One case that gained some publicity was that of Jerzy Zasada, formerly Poznań KW first secretary and ex-Central Committee member, who was unable to find work as a qualified driver and had no alternative but to draw his pension.[8] The article in which this information appeared, entitled 'What is to be done with the apparatus?' understandably evoked considerable comment. It was argued that the apparatus had become a general scapegoat 'on whom everything could be blamed and at whom anything could be thrown', and it was pointed out, as we have noted above in connection with KW secretarial appointments, that over recent years the apparatus had become younger and better educated, frequently with political experience gained in the youth organisation. Their insight, however, had made the signs of impending crisis that more obvious to them and that was why, it was claimed, so few attempts had been made to explain the situation to the public and why meetings with the population had been avoided.[9]

This particular combination of apparatus sensitivity and fatalism was not particularly convincing as a defence of the recent record of party officials, and justifications of the permanent staff of the communist establishment carrying any popular conviction were notably lacking at this juncture. Nevertheless, despite the acceptance by the leadership of election procedures that allowed for far more local autonomy within the party than had ever been the case before, it remained committed to defending major features of the position of the apparatus as expressed within the conventional practice of democratic centralism. At issue here were the continuity of party leadership, the consequent necessity of central leaders to be able at least to stand for re-election to the Party Congress, and the maintenance of some basic conditions for the centralised direction of the party organisation. These conditions even a relatively reformist party leadership could hardly let slip and it could not afford, therefore, to ignore the protests and concern expressed by conservative forces whose priority was the defence of the party establishment and the traditional dominance of the apparatus. The leadership thus showed considerable ambivalence towards the question of reform as it concerned the party apparatus, and in practice tended to preserve the conventional position of the apparatus, if not that of all its individual members, wherever possible.

The provincial party conferences

The series of electoral conferences at province level began on 30 May and started off with those in Szczecin, Olsztyn and Włocławek. They were to evaluate both past performance of the party organisation and the prospects outlined in the Congress guidelines, and to elect delegates to the Congress and new provincial authorities. While there had been extensive activity at local level with elections throughout the country, turnover in the provincial secretariats in the first months of 1981 had been quite restricted, certainly compared with the twenty changes in first secretary and the fifty-one other secretarial changes recorded in the last three months of 1980. So far in 1981 only seven KW first secretaries had been changed (three of them to lose their position during the June elections conducted with the newly elected conference delegates), with a further nineteen other secretaries being changed during the first four months of the year. Although it is not possible to know precisely how each of these changes took place, it is clear that by May the manner in which secretarial changes were made had altered drastically, with the practice of nomination from the floor and secret election becoming established. The 'parachuting' of experienced officials into provincial trouble-spots, still prevalent in late 1980, was clearly no longer the general practice and local control over the election was becoming stronger. When the KW Secretariat was reconstituted following the strike in Bielsko-Biała in February the emergence of the new first secretary had been a surprise even to himself. Andrzej Gdula, former agriculture secretary, had stood, he said, largely as a 'procedural alternative candidate' and had not expected to win the election.[10]

When the round of conferences began, the disagreements that had already emerged over the election procedure, and which reflected the differing political views of the appropriate role of the apparatus, were not slow to make themselves apparent. In Szczecin, where leading Politburo member and Kania ally Barcikowski was proposed as a delegate to the Congress, a well-publicised conflict erupted over whether his candidacy should be permitted, as he had not been elected a delegate to the provincial conference. As local Solidarity figures had made their views on the matter known, the objections to his candidacy were seen by party stalwarts as a provocative challenge and a threat both to the continuity of party rule (this becoming the standard chorus with which further challenges were countered) and to the viability of party leadership. As *Polityka* put it, any such rejection of experienced candidates would 'close the path to further political work on the part of both the good and the bad, to all who had not retained their political virginity and were not starting their career from zero'.[11] From this point of view, Barcikowski was a positive example in that he had a good reputation among party reformers – having successfully negotiated the August agreement in Szczecin in the company of Żabiński and maintained, unlike Żabiński, a relatively clear commitment to renewal through the following nine months. There was, indeed, some evidence that his candidacy was put forward at an early stage with the encouragement of party hard-liners in the expectation that it would provoke conflict within the Szczecin organisation and hold back Barcikowski's chances of election.[12]

The situation was finally resolved in his favour when, with due regard to the recently established protocol, Barcikowski was first elected to the list of candidates for election to the Congress and then elected as a delegate. A rough ride was also given, despite the protests of the recently elected KW first secretary, to the report of the outgoing provincial committee. It was criticised for its generality, sense of superiority and lack of information on members of the now discredited provincial leadership. It was claimed that more of them deserved to have their reputation examined and that this included some who had occupied leading posts.[13] At the same time, practically all the candidates from the horizontal movement failed to gain election as delegates to the Congress, for example, not one of the six candidates from Szczecin Politechnic succeeding.[14] A further object of criticism was the practice established under Gierek of forming direct links between the Central Committee and its apparatus and the larger industrial plants (which also had the right to elect delegates directly to the Congress). This was thought to give preferential treatment to workers in the large plants and was resented as a breach of party democracy. The conference therefore prevented those plants which had already elected delegates directly from electing any further representatives.

This development threw more light on the low level of worker representation in the provincial conferences, as the preference shown during the Gierek period for the recruitment of workers to the party now seemed to have provoked general sentiments of resentment against the favouring of any particular social group. Workers, it appeared, were now not willing to stand for election both because they felt unqualified for responsible positions and because they felt misused and manipulated by the party leadership over recent years.[15] Considerably more value was attached to the importance of democratic procedures rather than to the more dubious advantages of numerical representation. Interestingly enough, this insistence on democratic procedures was often seen as obsessive and excessive by writers in the party press, and its origins were clearly not understood. An exception to this, however, was Gutkowski's report on the Szczecin conference in which he made clear his conviction that the delegates' punctiliousness showed a concern for real rather than formal democracy.[16]

Another of the early provincial conferences was held in Olsztyn, where the official report was rather less sympathetic. Under the heading 'A new "infantile disorder"?' the reporter complained that 'procedural matters dragged out endlessly' and that delegates showed an 'obsessive mistrust', although he acknowledged that these features were perhaps natural consequences of the slow process of renewal.[17] Olsztyn bore out well Grażyna Pomian's observation that the party election conferences became transformed into 'people's tribunals'.[18] Olsztyn's had been one of the nine provincial party leaderships investigated by the Central Party Control Commission, whose enquiry had by May led to the removal of fifteen individuals from their official post.[19] The character of the former leadership may be gauged from the fact that the first meeting of the provincial committee which gathered to evaluate the situation following the August strikes was not called until October. After considerable unrest the first secretary was finally removed in January on the basis of clear evidence of illegality and abuse of office.

The report of the outgoing first secretary (who had only in post since January) was attacked for its lack of self-criticism and 'downright alarmist representation of the threat facing the country'.[20] Conflicts within the provincial party organisation remained acute and it was clear that the party *aktiv* had not yet evolved a 'unified ideological and political platform'. Another report gave more concrete indications of the views of the former leadership that had elicited local criticism. When, for example, Kania had laid a wreath at the foot of the monument erected to the memory of the Gdańsk workers massacred in 1970 one member of the provincial committee had called for the destruction of the monument and the erection of one in honour of those members of the militia and the security forces who had been killed. Unlike in Szczecin, the Olsztyn party organisation firmly rejected the proposal of the outgoing committee that six members of the central party authorities should be proposed to the conference for election as delegates to the Congress. If this were permitted, it was pointed out with a certain measure of irony, the chances of local representatives, 'particularly workers and farmers', to gain election would be correspondingly limited.[21]

But neither did the Olsztyn conference represent a victory for the horizontal movement, or the Association for Party Action as it was known locally. Only a few of its representatives had been elected to the conference, fewer than the forty-three members of the party apparatus who were amongst the 348 delegates. No-one from the horizontal movement was elected to the new provincial committee and only one person from Olsztyn itself (the first secretary) entered into it. Thus a 'new alliance' was defined in these terms: 'the apparatus with a base of small rural centres and small work plants'.[22] Similar outcomes were noted elsewhere, for example in Radom.[23] As had been the case in Szczecin, the new KW first secretary in Olsztyn had previously been a member of the KW secretariat, and the choice of the provincial conference electorate in this way favoured the continuity asked for by the party leadership. Part of this continuity could be explained by the continuing strength of the local apparatus, which was often able to secure the election of its preferred candidates. The lack of success of the horizontal movement, though, was also associated with tendencies amongst the party membership which counted against the election of well-known politicians. This sentiment cut two ways. It acted, firstly, to express a strong feeling against all those who had been associated with the old regime; party activists who had previously held office at even local and shop-floor level were in 'the great majority simply mown down'.[24] Particular problems were experienced in some cases by party officials – town and province officials were defeated at an early stage in Cracow just because they were members of the apparatus.[25]

But, ironically, this tendency also appeared to count against candidates who represented the horizontal movement. It was suggested, indeed, that people were beginning to suspect that the movement itself was threatening to become an alternative establishment.[26] The publicity that some figures from the movement had received appeared to act against them and made them a 'natural target for "deletion" from ballot sheets'.[27] The new voting procedure itself, which invited electors to cross off the names of candidates additional to those required to fill the number of seats available, probably encouraged this tendency.[28] The reputation of the horizontal movement was not helped by the behaviour at the town conference of Toruń by Iwanów, the ebullient plant committee secretary who had been expelled from the party, and who now resigned his mandate to the provincial conference. His self-presentation and certain statements ('I have never been a communist. My ideas are closer to those of the social democrats') had provided useful ammunition for those eager to condemn the whole movement. The indictment received full coverage in the party press.[29] Others active in the Toruń movement, like Witkowski, though, resolutely defended their position against charges of factionalism.[30] The underlying principle of the horizontal movement, that of a loyal opposition which continued to accept the patterns of party behaviour suggested by 'democratic centralism', also proved to be a considerable obstacle in conflicts with less scrupulous members of the party establishment. Several causes contributed, then, to the political eclipse of the horizontal movement.

Developments at Włocławek followed the general pattern. The new first secretary, 32-year-old K. Łuczak, was a previous member of the apparatus – not at provincial level but the secretary of a local organisation. Here, too, the elections did not go in favour of the central organisation – of the 105 members of the new provincial committee only sixteen came from the town party organisations, although it provided a third of the province's party membership.[31] This pattern of representation, though, did not prevail in subsequent elections and eight members of the new KW executive came from the town organisation, seventeen of the new first secretary's eighteen recommendations for the executive being accepted by the conference. The four new KW secretaries were all from outside the provincial apparatus (although three had been first secretaries of local organisations). The other KW provincial conference that was held before the XI CC Plenum (which opened on 9 June) was that in Gdańsk. Sixteen members of the party apparatus and twenty-five from the government and economic administration were elected to the new KW committee, which totalled 121. The relatively low level of worker participation was also a feature of the Gdańsk results – amongst the forty-seven delegates elected to the Congress there were only six workers, although thirty-seven were elected to the new provincial committee. Workers had made up 23% of

the 415 members of the conference itself. The low proportion of workers was held in the party press to be responsible for the shortcomings
of the conference, which was said to be preoccupied with criticism and
the apportionment of blame for past errors.[32] This was judged by the
party commentator to express an excessively negative attitude in view
of the current political situation.

An attempt to pre-empt the Congress: the Moscow letter

The pre-Congress elections, controversial as they were in
Poland, were a source of further displeasure in the Soviet Union.
Towards the end of May, it appears, Soviet tolerance of Polish developments finally evaporated.[33] The outcome of the local party conferences clearly played the major part in bringing this displeasure to the
surface with the final implementation of procedures by which key
members of the party establishment were threatened with removal.
The apparatus, though, as Sanford has pointed out, was the 'only
guarantor of Communist rule' and the activities that were taking place
throughout the party organisation in preparation for the Congress
were in this sense threatening vital Soviet interests.[34] The result was
the widely publicised 'Moscow letter', dated 5 June and referring
specifically to the results of elections in the local organisations and the
composition of the delegations to the Congress selected at them. Soviet
dissatisfaction was directed towards 'interference' within the ranks of
the party, 'enemy attacks' on its cadres, opportunists elected to the
local conferences and the Congress, and the removal of numerous
activists with 'unblemished reputations'. The 'so-called movement of
"horizontal structures"' was roundly condemned as a tool for the
destruction of the party.[35]

Although, as noted above, the political consequences of the horizontal movement should not be exaggerated in terms of its impact on the
outcome of the local conferences, it remained influential in some
regions. Towards the end of June it played an important part in the
Poznań conference, where 25% of the delegates were Solidarity
members.[36] Despite strong pressure from Grabski and his erstwhile
rival Kania, the party leader, the conference refused to elect as delegates to the conference two strongly favoured candidates, CC Department Head Tokarski and leading party intellectual Professor J. Wiatr.[37]
On the new 121-member-strong provincial committee sat only two
people who had formed part of the outgoing leadership. The atmosphere therefore remained extremely uncertain for the party establish-

ment and guaranteed considerable support for the Moscow letter from many members of the continuing Central Committee, which was rapidly convened to receive the letter and assembled on 9 June. As the focus of political change was now firmly on the provincial conferences and the nature of the political upheaval was now becoming clear, it was not surprising that the views of past and present KW first secretaries were very much to the fore.

Of the first six speakers at the XI Plenum four were or had been KW secretaries and were clearly not sympathetic to the direction the changes had taken. Najdowski (Toruń), the first speaker in the discussion, set the tone by challenging the basis of Kania's whole policy which had remained committed to finding a *political* solution to the crisis. It was time, he proposed, to change the formula: instead of seeking to overcome the 'crisis independently and by peaceful means', the emphasis should now be placed on 'overcoming the crisis independently' *tout court*. This was a call for a turn away from the commitment to a 'political' solution and for the contemplation of coercive means of solving the crisis. Łabuś (Gorzów Wielkopolski) suggested that the rot had set in when the leadership had failed to act on the line laid down at the VIII Plenum in February, when Kania and Barcikowski had moved to adopt a harder-line position and the definition of the 'counter-revolutionary threat' posed by Solidarity had been clearly expressed. Głowacki (removed from Słupsk KW in November) traced the 'degradation' of the party further back to the V Plenum in August 1980. This also implied that the leadership should have rejected agreement with the strikers at Gdańsk or Szczecin and brought the disruption to an end by further persuasion or, more likely, by force. He also called for the annulment of the election of Congress delegates by 'invalid means', the strict observance of the Party Statute and the election regulations, and the guarantee of the party leadership's 'passive right' of election to the Congress on the basis of the functions they performed within the central party organs.

Prokopiak (now removed from the leadership of the Radom committee) asked whether *odnowa* had to mean that power was steadily given away by the party at all levels and compared its position to that of the 'British queen, who has the title but not the power to do much'. Żabiński, one of the two KW first secretaries in the Politburo, spoke of the mass of apparatus workers who had done nothing to deserve the campaign that was now being waged against them.[38] The Moscow letter had clearly given further strength to the conservative forces on the Central Committee and to the threatened provincial secretaries, many of whom now faced removal from the leading party body as well as from their local post. Some managed to overcome the new election regulations. Although the outgoing first secretary from Słupsk, Alfred Wałek, had not secured election to the provincial conference from the town meeting (and did not, therefore, have the right to stand for further election) he managed to persuade the conference to allow his candidature and he was subsequently re-elected first secretary.[39] Disregard for the formal election regulations, then, was not the prerogative of the reform forces within the party.

By no means all the views expressed at the Plenum were unfavourable to the outcome of the elections. KW first secretary Opałko (Tarnów) thought that 'The newly elected party authorities are composed in the great majority of good party members, while the newly elected secretaries at all levels provide a guarantee of solid party work'. Jadwiga Nowakowska, a factory worker from Łódź, confirmed that some 70% of the party authorities were now composed of new people, but they generally had a 'good political preparation', particularly in terms of experience gained in the youth movement. Some felt that the renewal of the party authorities should be carried forward as fast as possible and that the Central Committee should not escape the process. For steel worker Kazimerz Jarząbek the priority was to remove, 'possibly even at today's plenum', from the Central Committee those members who had already lost their party offices, 'particularly the KW first secretaries'. Barcikowski, clearly unshaken by the rigours of the Szczecin election, also had some harsh words for the hard core of the provincial apparatus: 'I listen with sadness and shame when KW secretaries speaking at the Central Committee complain to the Politburo that the primary party organisations in the provincial organisations they lead are falsely electing delegates, diverging from the principles of the statute and neglecting party regulations'. Responding directly to Żabiński he asked who, if even Politburo members were unable to control the party organisation in their area, should feel responsible for ensuring correct party practice in their area: 'Perhaps we should put it all down to Kania?'[40]

The party leader himself did not express strong criticism of developments in the local organisations. While condemning 'electoral demagogy' and the tendency to eliminate experienced activists and apparatus workers, his overall evaluation of the elections and their outcome was a positive one: 'Taking into account the fact that we are applying the principles of such freely conducted elections for the first time, we may conclude that the results are not bad.' The difficulties experienced by some members of the leadership in gaining election as delegates to the Congress and the refusal to allow the candidacy of those who had already served two terms in party office were, however, condemned as endangering the continuity of party leadership.[41] This relatively favourable view of developments within the party organisation exposed him to virulent criticism from the strong forces of conservatism within the Central Committee, whose views were amplified by the criticism expressed from the Soviet authorities. This gave Grabski the opportunity to launch the most direct attack on Kania and his leadership to date, although Kania was again able to resist the threat to his position by avoiding the call for a vote of confidence.

Nevertheless, with views expressed like those of present or past KW secretaries such as Najdowski and Głowacki, the XI Plenum saw the most direct expression of the conflicts and disagreements that had persisted within the post-Gierek leadership of the party. Some attacks, like that of Głowacki with his condemnation of the whole leadership line since the V Plenum, were clearly the desperate expression of defeated politicians who were soon to lose all contact with the apparatus of power. Others, like that of Najdowski with his implicit call for the use of force to restore central control within the party and over political life in general, had more direct relevance in terms of party policy and the range of choices open to the leadership. Both, however, were a direct response to the dispute over the role of the party apparatus and the exposed position contemporary party officials found themselves in with the spread of political conflict and contested elections within the local organisations. The 'Moscow letter' was clearly bound up with this political threat, although views on its precise role, on the intentions behind it, and on its effects do differ. The fact that it reflected strong Soviet displeasure with developments in the PZPR and that it was associated with a failed attempt to challenge Kania's position would seem to suggest that it represented an unsuccessful attempt to exert pressure on the Polish leadership.[42] The fact that it resulted in the apparent strengthening of Kania's position has given rise to the belief that the letter may even have been solicited by Kania himself with that particular intention.[43]

Other views of the circumstances surrounding the June letter and its consequences during the XI Plenum, however, suggest a more balanced evaluation of Kania's position. Moreton, for example, points to the fact that Kania was actually unable to command a majority in the Central Committee at this point but survived because of general fears of a split within the party that would have endangered the position of all, while MacDonald maintains that the effect of the letter was to 'drive the party's reform movement into wholesale retreat' by marginalising all groups not closely associated with the position taken by Kania personally.[44] Holzer also finds it difficult to believe that the Soviet authorities were so unable to affect the course of events in the Polish party and that their influence was so roundly rejected. On the contrary, he detects a strengthening of conservative tendencies (if not of the personal position of Żabiński and Grabski) at this time and a resumption of the 'party offensive'.[45] Another indication of some shift in the approach of the central leadership at this stage was deputy premier Rakowski's speech at the municipal party conference on 6 June – immediately after the receipt of the Moscow letter but before the proceedings of the XI Plenum. It was seen, as Rakowski continued to point out four years later, as the 'first visible sign of the government's turn towards offensive action' and took the form, as Andrews describes, of a 'scathing attack on Solidarity' following a period 'marked by an absence of strikes and by continuing Government–Solidarity negotiations on diverse subjects'.[46] Other sources support Holzer's proposal that, while the Moscow letter can be seen to have failed in that it inspired an unsuccessful coup against Kania's leadership, the clear statement of the real threat of Soviet intervention had a crucial impact on the approach taken by the top Polish leaders.[47]

While the XI Plenum may well have marked a victory by the Kania leadership over the die-hard conservatives in the Central Committee, who had in any case often lost their position in the party by this stage and thus passed on to the political sidelines, it is therefore unlikely that the Moscow letter was as counterproductive as many observers have suggested. It was notable that at the XI Plenum, as on earlier occasions, military representatives reiterated the availability of the armed forces to act to support the Polish socialist state and indicated that the army was in a state of readiness far superior to that of the party in so far as the defence of socialism was concerned. At the same time the support of the military remained committed to the joint Kania–Jaruzelski leadership. It was significant in this respect that it was Rakowski who spelt out the military solution hinted at by Najdowski but who also reaffirmed that he was 'still a supporter of political solutions', while Vice-Minister of Defence (and head of the Main Political Administration) Baryła took pains to point out the stabilising role played by Rakowski as reflected in his recent statement at the Bydgoszcz conference.[48] Such a clear convergence of views and endorsement of the line pursued by the leadership suggests that the centrist strategy evolved by Kania was not so distasteful to the Kremlin as a brief reading of the Moscow letter might indicate, while its role in exerting a less direct influence on the leadership should also not be ignored. Whatever its effect, though, it was clearly too late to restrain the sweeping changes that were under way within the local organisations, which had now reached the stage of bringing about large-scale changes within the leadership of the provincial committees.

The new generation of provincial party secretaries

The turnover of KW secretaries during this period certainly represented the most sweeping changes that had yet taken place in the party authorities. Of the forty-nine first secretaries, twenty-five were replaced from the last days of May to the end of June. All were new to the post, although in Szczecin Miśkiewicz acquired it slightly earlier than the rest following the entry of Cypryniak to the CC Secretariat (Miśkiewicz was elected on 12 May and confirmed in post on 30 May). Turnover amongst the other members of the provincial secretariat also assumed considerable proportions. Excluding the first secretaries, there were around 194 KW secretaries during this period. Fifty-one changes had taken place between October and December in the wake of the 1980 summer strikes but then, as was the case with the first secretaries, the rate of change slackened and only an additional twenty-two were changed in 1981 up to the end of May. At the provincial conferences, however, extensive changes took place and as many as ninety-one new secretaries were elected in June.

Indeed, a high rate of change at the conferences was unavoidable as a result of the outcome of the elections held at lower levels of the party organisation. Extensive change was inevitable as almost 50% of the provincial leading party cadres (secretaries and control commission chairmen) were not elected to the provincial conferences. While only 24% of KW first secretaries failed to get elected to the conferences the rate was far higher in other cases: 54% of economic secretaries, 55% of organisational secretaries, 61% of propaganda secretaries.[49] In the course of the conferences a further half of the leading cadres present failed to gain re-election, finally leaving amongst the leadership 73 of the 292 leading cadres who had been in post at the beginning of May. While twenty-four first secretaries were returned to their post, the totals for other secretaries were far lower: eleven (of the original forty-nine) organisational and propaganda secretaries, nine economic secretaries and eight agricultural secretaries. The conferences thus saw

Table 5.1 *KW secretaries (1980, 1981): date of birth*

| | First secretaries | | | | Other secretaries | | | |
| | 1980 | | 1981 | | 1980 | | 1981 | |
	N	%	N	%	N	%	N	%
1911–33	12	55	4	16	13	23	16	18
1934–38	8	36	9	36	20	36	18	20
1939–41	1		6	24	12	21	15	16
1942–45	1	9	4	16	9	16	23	25
1946–59	–	–	2	8	2	4	19	21
Total	22	100	25	100	56	100	91	100

Table 5.2 *KW secretaries (1980, 1981): date of joining party*

| | First secretaries | | | | Other secretaries | | | |
| | 1980 | | 1981 | | 1980 | | 1981 | |
	N	%	N	%	N	%	N	%
1944–55	14	64	3	12	14	25	16	18
1956–59	4	18	4	16	7	12	8	9
1960–63	2	9	11	44	18	32	17	18
1964–67	2	9	4	16	12	22	25	27
1968–70	–	–	3	12	3	5	9	10
1971–76	–	–	–	–	2	4	16	18
Total	22	100	25	100	56	100	91	100

very extensive change within the leadership of the provincial party committees.

The average age of the first secretaries elected in May–June 1981 was forty-three, rather younger than that of the other cohorts on appointment (discussed in chapters 2 and 3). The great majority, 76%, were born during the years of the world war and those immediately preceding it, and were between the ages of thirty-six and forty-seven at the time of appointment. Only 16% were born before 1934 and could have had anything more than a child's experience of the war, a marked difference from the preceding cohorts studied, in each of which well over half had been born before 1934 and on whom the war could have had a clear intellectual and political (as distinct from emotional) impact. In a country like Poland, where geo-politics and *Realpolitik* have been constant themes, and 'idealism' and 'realism' have been seen as major alternating poles of action, such a generational transition may well have considerable political relevance.

In comparison with the first secretaries elected in May and June 1981, the other KW secretaries were generally younger (46% born after 1941 compared with 24% of first secretaries), although there were also slightly more older party workers (18% having been born before 1934). Comparison with the secretaries appointed only a few months earlier, the September-December 1980 cohort, indicates that those elected in June 1981 were considerably younger than them as well (62% having been born after 1938 in contrast to 41% in the preceding group). The changes made in the KW secretariat as a result of the pre-Congress elections thus bear out Kania's comments made at the XI CC Plenum on the rejuvenation of the party authorities.

In terms of political generations, table 5.2 indicates the small number of first secretaries elected in 1981 who joined the party during the Stalinist period. The pattern of recruitment to the party shows a sharp reversal from that of the first secretaries appointed in 1980: 88% had joined the party in 1956 or later, a contrast with earlier appointments when the highest proportion of those joining after 1955 had been 43%, during the late Gierek period. The largest number had joined between 1960 and 1963, before Gomułka's regime had settled into its final period of dictatorial stagnation. The first secretaries elected in May and June 1981, then, appeared to reflect the advent of a new generation at this level of the apparatus in two ways: firstly, of those who had reached adolescence and maturity in the post-war years and, secondly, of those who had joined the party after the period of Stalinist rule in Poland. Their characteristic experiences were probably not greatly different from those of the Solidarity leaders and militants: they 'belonged mostly to a generation that matured in the 1970s . . . [which] inherited political expectations expressed during the October 1956 uprising and the March 1968 students' revolt, as well as the wave of strikes and protests in 1970 and 1976'.[50] According to one analysis there were two distinct groups among the Solidarity leaders in terms of age and political experience. Around a third of the union's leaders were aged between 35 and 44 in 1981, also the largest age group of the

Table 5.3 *KW secretaries (1980, 1981): higher education qualifications*

| | First secretaries | | | | Other secretaries | | | |
| | 1980 | | 1981 | | 1980 | | 1981 | |
	N	%	N	%	N	%	N	%
Economics	8	36	3	12	15	26	14	15
Industrial	4	18	6	24	11	19	13	14
Agricultural	2	9	8	32	4	7	19	20
History	1		1		4	7	7	8
Education	–		2		4	7	9	10
Law	2		1		4	7	2	
Sociology	1		–		2		2	
Language	1		–		–		2	
Arts	2		1	28	2		–	
Administration	–	37	–		3		3	21
Political science	1		1		4	27	7	
Military	–		1		–		2	
Medicine/psychology	–		–		1		2	
Philosophy, journalism, geography	–		–		3		–	
No higher education	–	–	1	4	–	–	11	12
Total	22	100	25	100	57	100	93	100

provincial first secretaries elected in May and June 1981. Unlike their more numerous younger colleagues, the older Solidarity leaders had participated extensively in official political activities. Their 'political socialization . . . occurred before the government-controlled quasi-participatory organizations managed to discredit themselves in the eyes of the rank-and-file participants' and, suggests Pakulski, their work with Solidarity could be interpreted as a 'continuation of their previous ("official") political involvement'.[51] Such similarities in background and approach increased the likelihood of the new first secretaries being inclined to develop stronger links with the Solidarity organisation and increase sympathy for its objectives.

The greater youth of the other new provincial secretaries was also reflected in their party experiences. In contrast to the first secretaries a majority, 55%, had joined the party during the second half of Gomułka's period of rule and the first part of the Gierek regime (1964–76). They included considerably more recent recruits to the party than had

Table 5.4 *KW secretaries (1980, 1981): main non-apparatus experience*

| | First secretaries | | | | Other secretaries | | | |
| | 1980 | | 1981 | | 1980 | | 1981 | |
	N	%	N	%	N	%	N	%
Industry	5	23	8	32	12	21	25	27
Agriculture	2	9	7	28	8	14	16	18
Government	8	36	3	12	15	27	9	10
Education	3	14	3	12	11	20	23	25
Youth organisations	4	18	2	8	10	18	11	12
Military	–	–	1	4	–	–	2	
Parapolitical	–	–	1	4	–	–	2	8
Health	–	–	–	–	–	–	2	
Library service	–	–	–	–	–	–	1	
Total	22	100	25	100	56	100	91	100

been the case just a few months previously, when the new KW secretaries appointed in the autumn of 1980 included only 9% who had joined the party after 1967.

The first secretaries elected in 1981 were more likely to have educational qualifications than the preceding cohort in industrial (technical and scientific) subjects and, particularly, in agriculture and forestry. The number of those with the more general 'economic' qualifications showed a marked decline, probably indicating a lower proportion of those trained through party channels (table 5.3). The greater production experience of the new first secretaries in industrial activity and (again) particularly agriculture is also apparent (table 5.4). Considerably fewer came from employment in the government and state structure. Unlike the other secretaries appointed in the late seventies, those elected in June 1981 had fewer educational qualifications relevant to industrial and agricultural production than the first secretaries, and also less direct production experience in those areas. Quite a few of the other secretaries, eleven in all, had not acquired any higher education qualifications at all, a marked change from the trend in KW secretariat appointments under Gierek although not one that was surprising in view of the bitter criticism that had been expressed of the 'party intelligentsia'. As was the case with the first secretaries, more of the KW other secretaries than the 1980 cohort had production experience

Table 5.5 *KW secretaries (1980, 1981): time from first party appointment*

| | First secretaries | | | | Other secretaries | | | |
| | 1980 | | 1981 | | 1980 | | 1981 | |
Years	N	%	N	%	N	%	N	%
0	4	18	4	16	10	18	27	30
Up to 5	1	4	5	20	5	9	26	28
6–10	3	14	7	28	14	25	22	24
11–15	4	18	6	24	12	21.5	6	7
16–20	4	18	1	4	12	21.5	6	7
over 20	6	28	2	8	3	5	4	4
Total	22	100	25	100	56	100	91	100

in industry and agriculture and fewer came from a background in local
government and the state administration. Experience in education and
the youth movement was also very common. Unlike the appointments
made in late 1980, those elected to the KW secretariat in June 1981 were
more likely to have followed agricultural than industrial courses of
study, a tendency reflected in the higher proportion of those following
agricultural careers. This was clearly a function of the tendency evident
at the party conferences to vote down candidates from the main political and industrial centres and to favour those from the smaller towns
and rural areas.

The first secretaries elected at the party conferences in 1981 had
considerably less experience in the party organisation than those appointed during earlier periods. Fewer than 36% had held jobs in the
party apparatus when Gomułka ruled and four had no previous
experience at all, a further three having taken up party work only in
1980. Two came directly from work in industry and forestry. Only two
had experience of party work which extended as far back as the fifties.
Table 5.6 shows that this less extensive apparatus experience was
associated, not surprisingly, with limited service in responsible party
positions (secretarial appointment at province level or first secretary of
a local party organisation). Those elected in 1981, though, were more
likely to have headed local organisations than the preceding cohort. It
was at province level that their lack of experience was most marked, an
observation that lends further support to the view that it was at

Table 5.6 *KW first secretaries (1980, 1981): previous apparatus experience*

	1980		1981	
	N	%	N	%
Provincial committee secretary	15	68	10	40
First secretary of other party committee	7	32	12	48
Either provincial committee secretaryship or other first secretaryship, or both	17	77	16	64

province level that the decline in party authority had become most evident, with correspondingly fewer provincial secretaries succeeding in the elections for the new first secretaries. The outcome of this process of renewal within the provincial secretariats was even more striking in the case of the other KW secretaries. 30% of those elected at the 1981 provincial conferences had never worked in the apparatus before, an unprecedented figure for a post that lay within the *nomenklatura* of the CC Secretariat.

Even amongst the KW secretaries elected from those who had worked in the apparatus before, a relatively small minority had a lengthy record of apparatus employment, with no more than 18% having received their first party job more than ten years earlier. The background of the secretaries elected in June 1981 contrasted particularly strongly with that of the KW secretaries appointed in late 1980, who had a longer party record (in terms of time elapsed since commencement of work in the apparatus) than those selected to serve as KW secretaries during the latter half of the Gierek period. Although, as we have noted, the first secretaries elected in May and June had considerably less apparatus experience than preceding cohorts, they were far more experienced than the other KW secretaries elected at this time. Indeed, it appears that Kania's calls for continuity in party leadership were not disregarded. Delegates to the provincial conferences were relatively cautious in their choice of first secretaries and were often disposed to re-elect experienced officials (provided that they had not been discredited by their past behaviour and had not aligned themselves with the conservative resistance to local party democracy), although their career backgrounds were clearly not identical to those of their predecessors. On the other hand, in their choice of other members of the KW secretariat they were more inclined to opt for those with fewer apparatus connections and in favour of those with more direct experience in production and closer acquaintance with Poland's current social problems. The growing proportion of those from educational occupations, a traditional source of social activists and 'concerned' members of the public, is instructive in this respect, as is the appearance of some secretaries with experience of the medical service.

At the end of the pre-Congress election round, only six KW first secretaries remained in post who had been there at the fall of Gierek ten months earlier. This was, obviously, a far higher rate of turnover than would have been expected under normal conditions and with the operation of the processes of cadre replacement associated with the conventional practice of democratic centralism. One informed view was that the normal rate of turnover at this level would be 18% per annum, equivalent to the replacement of nine provincial first secretaries each year.[52] In the ten months which followed the fall of Gierek, though, forty-three first secretaries had been replaced, and this left only three KW secretaries who had been in post at the time of the VIII Congress, which had taken place less than a year and a half earlier. This clearly deepened concern within the party about its effectiveness as a political organisation and its institutional coherence.[53] Later accounts indicated how long it in fact took to develop effective working teams within the provincial leadership. Even under the exceptionally favourable conditions for change in Poland after the fall of Gierek it reportedly took Bednarski, the new first secretary appointed to the Bydgoszcz provincial committee in October 1980, some eight months to assemble a new leadership team.[54]

While, too, there obviously were extensive changes at provincial level during this period their impact should not be exaggerated. At the XII CC Plenum, Barcikowski acknowledged the significance of the changes that had occurred, but also pointed out that they did not go beyond those which had taken place in 1956–57.[55] Somewhat surprisingly, Malcher claims that as a result of conflict within the army between the military leadership and the political administration turnover of leading cadres in the military party committees was even higher, and he notes that 'similar elections in the civilian party did not produce such drastic changes of directing personnel'.[56] This is an unexpected observation in view of the fact that the military presence was clearly an element of growing political importance in the party leadership following the appointment of Jaruzelski as Premier, while military pronouncements at successive CC plenary sessions had stressed readiness to act to preserve socialist orthodoxy. At any event the growing political role of the army which acted to support the party centre was also evident, while the slightly greater prominence of the military in the new provincial leadership (table 5.4) in fact suggested a stabilising influence rather than the converse.

The survival of only six first secretaries from the Gierek period and of only three from the time of the VIII Congress does show, nevertheless, personnel change of massive proportions within the provincial leadership. In fact, these figures slightly (but only slightly) mask some elements of continuity within the KW leadership, as some first secretaries appointed in late 1980 had previously held the same position in other provinces. Żabiński (Katowice) and Zawodziński (Białystok) had first been appointed KW first secretary in 1973 and 1972 respectively, while Kociołek (Warsaw) had initially been appointed first secretary in Warsaw in 1964 (before spending three years in Gdańsk from 1967 to 1970). Two KW first secretaries had remained in the same position since the reorganisation of the party structure in 1975. One was Fiszbach (Gdańsk), who had become a deputy member of the Politburo and gained some prominence both as a leading proponent of party reform and for his able (though ultimately unsuccessful) leadership in Gdańsk prior to 1980. The other was Zdisław Luciński (Ciechanów), who was considerably less prominent as a member of the party leadership. He had, for example, not spoken at a single CC Plenum in 1981, although at the IX Plenum (held during the Bydgoszcz crisis) he had recorded a statement to be entered on the CC protocol. The views he expressed were quite different from those of Fiszbach and his sentiments clearly in line with those of the apparatus conservatives. He thus complained that 'leading cadres at all levels who are defending the party's line in a principled manner are subject to continual attack' and held that the cadre changes that had taken place so far had been 'essentially compelled' and had occurred under the threat of the 'strike pistol'.[57] Despite the wide-ranging changes that had taken place amongst the provincial secretaries, then, the staying power of some of their more conservative representatives should not be underestimated.

Nevertheless, there can be no doubt that the elections conducted during the 1981 party conferences, starting at the party base and continuing through to the provincial meetings, brought about enormous changes amongst the occupants of the leading party positions. In the country as a whole, 13% of KW secretaries were new to the party apparatus, a percentage similar to that in a number of local party

organisations (in Poznań province, for example, 15% of local secretaries came from outside the apparatus). The elections affected
directly only a relatively small part of the apparatus, though, as the
majority of party workers were appointed and not subject to election.
Obviously the newly elected leaders would have an impact on the
organisation, but the extent of this was difficult to gauge. Some indication of the extent of change within the apparatus as a whole over
this period was given by the deputy director of the CC Organisation
Department. Writing in the early stages of the martial law period he
stated that some 4,400 members had left the apparatus since the fall of
Gierek.[58] This meant an annual rate of departure of 3,106 employees
per year, slightly over a quarter of the party staff. While, of course, we
do not know how this turnover was distributed, in view of the slow
pace of political renewal in late 1980 it may be concluded that a large
part of the changes took place in association with the preparations for
the Congress and were thus linked with the turnover of elected party
leaders.

The Extraordinary Congress and the reformation of the party authorities

The other main task of the provincial conferences was the
election of delegates to the IX (Extraordinary) Party Congress, due to
open a fortnight after the provincial meetings ended. It became clear at
an early stage that the composition of the Congress delegates would
reflect the balance that had emerged in the provincial conferences,
decisively favouring the representation of smaller towns and rural
party organisations to the detriment of the larger provincial centres
(conventionally favoured in party representation).[59] While fewer
workers and members of the central 'party, political and ideological
aktiv' were elected, the representation of middle management, local
government personnel and the secretaries of factory party committees
was increased. This form of representation appeared to be in accordance with the wishes of the party rank and file. In view of the increased
number of newly elected KW secretaries with employment history in
education and health, it was significant that the number of Congress
delegates with these backgrounds also rose markedly. The proportion
of delegates from the party apparatus at the level of province, town
and commune in fact also increased, including some former apparatus
members who had just failed to secure re-election at the recently ended
provincial conferences. A total of 20% of the delegates were full-time

party workers.[60] Whilst the composition of the Extraordinary Congress was therefore an unusual one, it by no means implied a marginalisation of the party apparatus, but rather a shift in the way it was represented which counted against its central cadres.

When the Congress opened on 14 July 1981 its proceedings reflected the recent establishment of democratic practices in the party and the strong attachment of Congress delegates to them. Elections were contested and held by secret ballot in the more important cases and, as had been the case at the provincial conferences, were the source of some major political clashes. Kania's plea for the CC first secretary to be elected at the outset of the Congress, for example, was rejected by delegates who insisted that the new Central Committee be elected first. A major theme of the Congress was party democracy and the clear determination of leadership and delegates to reappraise the role and operation of the party apparatus and to lay down agreed principles for its future development. Kania alluded in his introductory address to the 'clear principle' that the party apparatus 'must perform a service role with regard to the party organs'. In the programme affirmed at the close of the Congress it was clearly stated that it was necessary to implement 'new principles of apparatus activity and the selection of cadres, to put into practice its subordinate role in relation to party organs and primary organisations, to eliminate practices whereby it replaces elected organs and supplants the state apparatus'. Following discussion within the specialist groups into which the Congress delegates were split these principles were built into the new Party Statute. This document confirmed the requirement for democratic elections in the party, limitation of the period of tenure for party officials, and restrictions on multiple office-holding in party, state and social organisations – particularly those located on the same plane of activity. Kania, though, took care to reaffirm the importance and continuity of democratic centralism and stressed that it was an excess of bureaucratism that had proved to be the undoing of the party rather than centralism. In this way he countered the demands made by the more radical 'horizontal' voices and proponents of the anti-apparatus movement.[61]

The new, and enlarged (to 200 full and 70 deputy members) Central Committee voted in by the Congress, however, was influenced in its composition precisely by sentiments of anti-centralism rather than by anti-apparatus feeling. The degree of renewal within the Committee, with only eighteen members of the former Committee voted on to the new body, certainly gave scope for considerable change. Only one category of members of the old Committee were successful in retaining their position – 80% of the generals and admirals continued their membership of the central party body.[62] The most notable change was the ending of the traditional dominance of central party and state authorities and of provincial party leaders. Only eight KW first secretaries were elected to the new Committee, while the outgoing Committee, although smaller, had contained twenty-five KW secretaries as voting members. The shock of this change was so sharp that Kania felt constrained virtually to apologise for it in his closing address, stressing that 'it was not an expression of a personal judgment on these comrades'.[63] A further ten first secretaries were elected deputy members. Of the eight full members four were newly installed in the provincial post, having been elected at the pre-Congress conferences, and none had been in post prior to October 1980. This outcome clearly did not reflect a neglect of provincial interests, as care had been taken to secure representation of all forty-nine provinces (bar one, which only had a deputy member).[64] It appeared to stem from the feeling that the provincial party leadership (in effect, its secretariat) should no longer have a monopoly on the representation of local interests, a task it had so obviously failed to perform in the late seventies.

In some contrast to this result four KW first secretaries (from Łódź, Tarnów, Wrocław and Olsztyn) were elected to the Politburo, succeeding the former provincial representatives (Żabiński and Fiszbach), neither of whom succeeded in election even to the Central Committee. As Żabiński had placed himself firmly on the side of the party conservatives and experienced considerable difficulty in securing election to the Congress as a delegate, this was perhaps not surprising. The absence of Fiszbach from the Committee was more notable and reflected the feelings, prevalent among party activists, against well-known public figures (of whatever tendency) and against representatives of any of the more clearly defined political wings of the party. An exception to this generalisation appears to have been the acceptance by the Congress of Kania's plea for the preservation of continuity within the party leadership, which facilitated the election of Jaruzelski, Barcikowski, Olszowski and Kania himself to the Politburo. The relative success of KW first secretaries in elections both to the provincial conferences and to the new KW secretariats may also be attributed to the acceptance of his request.

The rejection of Fiszbach's candidature showed the rigorous way in which party members intended to apply the agreed principle of the rotation of cadres, accepting the need for continuity only in the case of those who could be construed as absolutely essential politically. At the same time it reflected a definite fundamentalist strain within the party reform movement. The reception of the news about the new party leadership was received with some satisfaction in Gdańsk province, the absence of Fiszbach from it being seen as a good thing 'for at last he will have time to occupy himself with the Gdańsk organisation. After all, before he was practically always in either the Central Committee or the *Sejm* [parliament]'.[65] The feelings against members of the central and provincial leaderships that were expressed in the Central Committee and Politburo elections, though, did not extend to other categories of local official who were less prominent. The representation of the first secretaries of factory party committees on the Central Committee was considerably increased, as it had been amongst delegates to the Congress themselves. The persistent pressure for democratic elections throughout the party, which had finally been accepted as necessary by Kania and which had indeed been used by him to restrain such opponents as Olszowski and Grabski, thus culminated in a freely elected Congress and Central Committee which, in accordance with demands long expressed within the party, was notably free of the numerical dominance of the representatives of the central party–state complex and its key organs.

A major question now was whether the Central Committee, in its role as the supreme organ of the party between Congresses, would be able to decide policy and have it implemented both through the central party apparatus and through its local and provincial branches. The question of the status of the Central Committee in relation to the major organs of government and state was also an open one. One consequence identified as following directly from the non-election of many of Kania's opponents to the Central Committee was the shift of 'factional games' to provincial or district level and a series of local conflicts provoked to embarrass the central leadership. Examples of such diversions were the confusion over the issue of food coupons in Katowice and Łódź.[66] Further problems arose from the fact that central supervision over the provincial apparatus and control over local appointments were in the hands of the harder-line conservatives within the central party leadership.[67] All this pointed to problems arising from the reduced links that now existed between the Central Committee and the provincial apparatus. From the provincial point of view the changes also promised a different political role. Following the exacerbation of Poland's economic crisis and the attenuation of the provincial committee's traditional economic role with the party's formal withdrawal from direct economic administration, the reduction of the provincial committee's role on the horizontal plane was now followed by the paring down of its vertical links with the central party organ and the slimming down of its role in this respect.

The reconstitution of the Central Committee, the enforced political retirement of many prominent party officials and the firm commitment to a service role for party workers seemed to indicate a significant diminution of the political role of the apparatus and a defeat for the aspirations expressed by some of its representatives. One view of the immediate post-Congress period was that the 'inner core of the communist establishment must have been close to despair . . . they had lost the certainty that the Party machine could respond coherently to any plan of action'.[68] But others took a very different view. Bielasiak observed that the Congress's 'relatively open process masked the reassertion of the political apparatus', while Mason claimed that the new, socially representative (but also politically inexperienced) party leadership was 'incapable of restraining the Party's bureaucratic apparatus, which had remained largely unchanged through 1981'.[69] While the latter statement was something of an exaggeration in general terms, it was probably not far off the mark so far as the central party apparatus was concerned. Moreover, the apparatus had now become freed of its major opponent. The reconstituted party leadership had more solid political credentials than its predecessor and internal party critics stood on much shakier ground. Most important, 'without a congress to prepare for, rank-and-file groups had no institutional means in the party to contribute to policy'.[70] The democratically conducted Congress had, it appeared, left the party apparatus as a body relatively unscathed.

Its effect in terms of party structure was to differentiate between at least two main forces within the national organisation, one 'composed of workers, peasants and the biggest operators of the Central Committee and the other the enormous central and local apparatus, in whose eyes the current Central Committee [was] something artificial, alien and antagonistic'.[71] The apparatus was not slow in taking steps to tame the anomalous creature the Extraordinary Congress had produced. At its first plenary session following the Congress new regulations were introduced whereby it was agreed that invitations to the CC sessions should be sent also to the Chairman of the Council of State (who had previously been a member of the Politburo), directors of CC departments, the head of the army's Main Political Administration (which had the status of a CC department), all KW first secretaries, editors of the leading party publications, and 'party activists occupying leading positions in social organisations'.[72] Clearly, the isolation of the Committee from the major party structures was not intended to last long and the enlarged deliberative body (the additional participants added up to a hundred individuals) came more to resemble its predecessors.[73] At the same time, thirteen permanent commissions were set up to involve CC members and the coopted officials in ongoing policy studies. Each commission was to elect a presidium and be provided with a secretary from CC staff. In this way CC members were further integrated with the staff and activities of the CC Secretariat.

Not only, then, did the apparatus emerge relatively strong from the party renewal process, but it also moved quickly to exercise this strength over the new central party body. Thus, wrote one observer, the '"worker-peasant-military" Central Committee came under the strict control of the apparatchiks'.[74] Within the Committee itself the leadership also adopted a more offensive stance. With the elections over and extensive turnover in occupants of leading party posts, it no longer had to fear charges of conservatism or of resistance to renewal if it exerted firmer control over local party activities. Barcikowski was therefore quick to condemn the continued existence after the Congress of 'various kinds of "forum" on one hand and "structures" on the other', as their persistence threatened the party with fractionalism. There was also an ominous reference to instances, 'by no means rare', of people who remained in the party and 'not only failed to participate in the implementation of party policy but conducted activity that was openly antagonistic to it'. This attitude was accompanied by the expression of greater criticism against Solidarity and its 'aggressive centres', while the Central Committee was invited to repeat an earlier condemnation of party members who took part in political strikes.[75] Having consolidated its position, at least in formal terms, through holding party-wide elections and the Extraordinary Congress, the leadership clearly saw itself as being in a stronger position to counter the political challenge of Solidarity and to influence the political climate as the union prepared for its National Congress which was to open on 5 September.

Party renewal and political authority

In many ways the results of renewal within Polish political life and its impact in terms of the democratisation of the party were highly ambiguous. Democratisation had, finally, been carried through within the PZPR to culminate in an unprecedented party gathering, a truly Extraordinary Congress. No sooner had it been brought into being, though, than the dramatically reconstituted Central Committee appeared to discover that the conditions for its effective operation were not present and that other forces within the central party organisation had a determinant influence on its mode of functioning. The top leadership, moreover, and the handful of experienced politicians in the Politburo now felt freer to adopt a more aggressive party policy and to abandon former ambiguities in their treatment of the horizontal movement and the more outspoken proponents of the radical conception of party democratisation. The outcome of the democratisation movement within the party and the circumstances of the Extraordinary Congress had little positive effect on the level of party authority and did not bring about any improvement. Indeed, the protracted conflicts within the party, the delays in organising party-wide elections and the reluctance of the leadership to summon the Congress had exacerbated the weakness of party authority and suggested the growing political irrelevance of the party in the face of Poland's multi-faceted crisis. By the second half of 1981 the problem was not so much that the party had been unsuccessful in restoring or establishing its political authority, but more that increasing numbers of people did not see the party as a valid basis for the exercise of political authority. A major public opinion survey found 53% of respondents in favour of a system without the leading role of the party, with 60% in favour of limiting the role of the party. Even amongst party members 46% were in favour of such a limitation.[76]

The twelve months that followed the August strikes certainly saw no resolution of the authority crisis that conflict indicated. What was perhaps most noteworthy about the attitude of major portions of the party establishment during this period, though, was that they seemed largely unconcerned about the party's authority deficit and set their face against the conciliatory approach adopted by the Kania leadership, clearly underwritten by the military authorities. While on the face of it this might have appeared politically suicidal, it was decidedly less so when account is taken of the political and military dominance of the Soviet Union within the region and the fate of earlier attempts at political reform within communist systems. The attitude was taken by many within the party–state bureaucracy and probably the majority within the higher ranks of the party apparatus, the bulk of which would be composed of staff attached to the provincial committees but which would exclude officials situated in the local organisations, where they might be expected to be more exposed to the sentiments and views of the working class and rank-and-file members.

The leadership of the provincial committees, the elected authorities (KW secretaries), also showed considerable variation in their attitudes during this period. As the crisis deepened the longer established provincial leaders showed growing signs of anxiety and dissatisfaction with the conciliatory stance of the Kania leadership, however qualified and tentative it seemed to those anticipating a brisker pace of renewal. Such anxieties intensified as it became clear that an Extraordinary Congress could not be avoided and that the political forces growing within the party would not be containable within the conventional practices of democratic centralism and its tightly organised elections. At times, such as that of the VIII Plenum in February 1981, it seemed that their desire to restrain the party democratisation movement was having some success, but their failure to block the process of change the following month with the challenge to Kania's leadership in the wake of the Bydgoszcz crisis in fact opened the way to more extensive renewal within the party. The more recently installed KW first secretaries, on the other hand, appeared to be more convinced of the need for reform within the party organisation and showed greater sympathy for the forces contained within the Solidarity movement. The intermediate character of the provincial party organ, drawing support from its links both with the party centre and the provincial membership and seeking to establish its authority on the basis of this dual relationship, was thus reflected in the divergent positions taken up by its leaders as the crisis continued.

The biographical characteristics of the provincial secretaries installed in 1981, many of whom gained their position under conditions of relatively free political competition, suggest a closer relationship with the provincial membership than with the party centre (or, at least, the full-time CC staff) and the possibility of their establishing political authority within the province and its party organisation by building on this local base. But the position of the provincial secretary was also crucially dependent on his status as a member of the national party organisation and his position with respect to the national power centre. The composition of the new Central Committee, though, left the provincial secretaries as a body with only limited access to the party's central decision-making body and the prospects for the functioning of the reconstituted party organisation remained very much open. The central party apparatus had taken steps soon after the Congress to reestablish its conventional links with and forms of influence over the

Central Committee. Its relations with the new secretaries and largely reconstituted provincial secretariats had to be faced next, and any chances the party had of reestablishing its authority on a national basis would be strongly influenced by the form the new relationship between the party centre and province would take.

Institutional reform and political conflict

Questions of organisational change and institutional reform were priority items on the agenda of the new provincial secretaries, their attention naturally being concentrated on arrangements at province level. Previous discussion had identified the key problems – the solutions, however, were not easily identified. A KW secretary in Koszalin pointed to the role of the provincial committee branch departments as an aspect that had come in for much criticism, particularly for duplicating the work of other institutions and administrative departments and supplanting their function. The answer, admitted secretary Chmielewski, was not easy to find and KW departments had not yet found the means of formulating and implementing strategies of economic development. One improvement would be to stop tolerating incompetence amongst those in economic management and he was clear that the party should not divest itself of its 'right of recommendation' for such appointments.[77] This had a direct relation with the work of the provincial party control commissions which was also coming under scrutiny. As the new WKKP chairman in Katowice indicated, they had come in for particular criticism at the pre-Congress conferences for not bringing members of the former leadership properly to account. Their actions had been interpreted as being those of an 'executive organ' of the KW Secretariat, a view that had been given some basis by the reinstatement of members who had received party punishments before August 1980.[78]

Appointment procedures were also highlighted in a closely argued article in the party's theoretical monthly. Much of the blame for the parlous state of the party itself was placed by J. Doliński on *nomenklatura* conventions, whereby 'an official became a leader not due to any virtues of intellect or character but thanks to the function he performed, while he performed this function not through any prior personal authority or by democratic choice but from recommendation'. Several negative consequences followed from this, the most obvious being the dominance of administrators over activists in party organs and the overlapping of the hierarchies of the party and the state administration.[79] Measures to reduce the administrative character of the provincial committee apparatus were taken in Płock. The KW branch departments there were scrapped and five 'lines of action' were established, which covered organisational, socio-occupational, propaganda and information affairs and local activities. Apart from the first secretary only two other KW secretaries had been elected to take charge of these areas and, as a result of this and other forms of staff reduction, provincial staff were reduced from sixty-three to fifty, thus releasing personnel for work in local organisations. A second major initiative was the abolition of the KW secretariat, 'which had often usurped the competence of the KW executive', and the elimination of the chancellery of the secretariat as a separate organisational unit, which had similarly tended to usurp responsibility for the work of the branch department and had even 'operated in some ways over their heads'.[80]

Such discussions and activity clearly indicated that the question of party renewal, now less prominent on the agenda of the Central Committee, was still an important issue at province level and its continuation regarded as a major determinant of both the party's authority and public views of the party's claim to exercise overall leadership within Polish society. KW first secretary Skrzypczak, elected in Poznań where the horizontal movement and Solidarity supporters did manage to secure a major victory at their provincial conference, later indicated the extent of the difficulties this involved. The major element in them was, as ever, the position and treatment of the party apparatus within the province. Around half of those employed in the provincial committee itself were changed, and particular attention was paid to the previous occupants of the secretarial positions. Most of them had skeletons in their cupboards and Skrzypczak hoped to sack them directly. The Central Committee did not want to allow this, though, and encouraged him to find ways of transferring them to work outside the party organisation. No easy task, as he noted, at a time when Solidarity controlled cadres appointments. At the same time, in addition to the hundred provincial committee employees, he was expected to take responsibility for the fate of the hundred or so local secretaries who had been displaced in the recent elections. This itself was, in his words, 'a hellish problem'. Apart from anything else, it was a major financial drain and he made it clear that he would not pay their salaries later than the end of 1981.

In the end, alternative employment was found for many of them and, amongst a total party staff in the province of five hundred, only thirty received outright dismissal notices. This whole process provided a major item of business throughout 1981 and involved him in negotiation and conflicts with the central organisation. Despite an apparently satisfactory solution, the affair in fact dragged on and it was one of the factors that provoked his removal in 1982 (the account from which this information is drawn derived from an interview conducted before his departure for Nigeria as a trade representative). He did not, he recognised, realise the degree of resistance put up by the party 'reaction' and the danger it represented. Those not capable of the level of activity shown by Skrzypczak and the Poznań organisation met other political fates. According to the account of M. Jagiełło, reformist deputy director of the CC Culture Department from late 1980 to the announcement of the State of War, the provincial party establishment in most cases was quick to exert control over the newly elected KW secretaries and the 'democratically elected provincial committees hardened their attitudes as each day passed'. Developments in the newly elected Central Committee followed the same process and a 'colourless Central Committee fell into the hands of the central apparatus – and later those of the provincial apparatus'.

As it had been for some months, then, discussion and disagreement over the role of the apparatus and measures necessary to achieve the appropriate changes in its mode of operation was at the centre of the concern about renewal. As Kolankiewicz pointed out, the bureaucratic establishment of the party-state was far from shaken by the Congress and events surrounding it, as the 'democratic elections and statutory changes in the party are little more than the first steps in rolling back the power of this "bureaucracy"'.[81] The level of change in the elective posts was one thing, but the response of the appointed staff to the new political expectations was another. The question that arose was 'how comrades working for years in the party apparatus and with their own habits will fit in with the new, more difficult conditions . . . whether they are willing and able to accommodate themselves to new demands and will be sufficiently open to the necessary changes in party structure?' The writer's response was, 'I admit, I am far from optimistic.'[82]

This view was not an isolated one. One article contained a bald statement of three 'theses' about the character of the apparatus: that it does not like real change, that it does not take kindly to theorists and theorising, that it objects to criticism and the diversity of opinions. The persistent hope of the apparatus following the August developments had been, it was claimed, to return to the state of affairs that had pertained under Gierek and it continued to regard its long-established patterns of behaviour as essential principles of action and the only conceivable form of operating.[83] Even those within the apparatus who reacted strongly against these theses were willing to admit shortcomings that had developed within the activities of the apparatus over past years. Clearly condemned was the practice of people passing straight from educational institutions to work in the youth movement and then to the party apparatus, with no alternative occupational experience. It was also argued that only those with higher education should gain employment in the apparatus.[84]

But in several ways the changes within the party that occurred as a result of the provincial conferences and the Congress enhanced the role of the apparatus. It had, indeed, been recognised at the conferences that in a situation where large numbers of provincial secretaries and even whole secretariats had been changed it would be only the KW department heads, their deputies and instructors who would have the experience of organising political work in local areas, factories and communes. Moreover, not all the secretarial positions had been filled at the conferences and, while such vacancies existed, KW departments were working without the leadership of elected representatives of the provincial committee (whether recent or more established) and were thus operating as autonomous segments of the apparatus. It was not made clear how many KW secretariat posts remained unfilled, although it had been stated that only forty-three members of the pre-Congress KW cadre (excluding first secretaries) had secured re-election, leaving around 151 posts to be filled.[85] Published biographies confirmed the election of only ninety-one secretaries in June, with a further twenty-five and ten elected in July and August/September respectively. This meant that by the end of September there might still have been as many as twenty-five secretarial posts unfilled – although this did not necessarily have to be the case as provincial committees now had the right to determine themselves the number of secretaries appropriate for the particular province. As we have seen, some committees, like that in Płock, had opted for a different organisation of the provincial cadre and deliberately not filled 'vacant' posts.

The climate of public opinion with regard to employees in the party apparatus also played a part in this. Those who had left apparatus work during 1981 found no sympathy for their plight and were described as encountering extensive, and by no means deserved, public disapproval. Never, including the situation following the events of 1956 and 1957, had such people been 'in such a difficult position as they are now'.[86] This was understandably associated with difficulties experienced in recruiting new staff to work in the apparatus – and in securing the agreement of people to stand for elected positions. The position of first secretary of at least one factory committee was still unfilled for lack of those willing to stand for election. The older party activists who refused to go along with the practices that developed under Gierek were still not eager to occupy leading positions, and available candidates were reported to be mostly those who were young and inexperienced or older fanatics who were content to go along with whichever orthodoxy prevailed.[87] In neither case did this promise close control or consistent reform of the apparatus.

The Congress, therefore, had not resolved the issues that had arisen around the apparatus, and to this extent had not succeeded in appearing as the watershed of party renewal that the wide-spread changes in the composition of the committees and the procedures used to conduct the elections might have suggested and as the leadership was eager to claim. This, indeed, was the basis of the reserved attitude taken by the rank and file towards the Congress and its outcome. The Congress and the new Central Committee were accepted as positive developments, but they were seen as representing only the beginnings of a solution to the persistent problems that had surrounded party rule in Poland. Workers in the Wrocław Pafawag factory were described as receiving the outcome of the recent Congress with mixed feelings and taking a wait-and-see attitude, some threatening to resign if things did not improve.[88] Party members, in common with most of the rest of Polish citizens, were not overly impressed with the results of political renewal, while they were definitely frustrated with the growing material hardship of everyday life. The central leadership, on the other hand, with the elections and the Congress now over, were more inclined to reduce the emphasis on renewal and to build up what could be conceived as a more normal state of party unity to face the continuing political challenge of Solidarity and the exigencies of the worsening economic situation.

Indeed, the adoption by the party leadership of a more combative attitude was partly justified by reference to the increasingly 'aggressive' and 'anti-socialist' opinions and actions emerging from Solidarity circles. Certainly, the public mood in the immediate post-Congress period was more bitter and frustrated with the growing problems experienced in getting supplies of food, which were not helped by cases of evident maladministration and what seemed on occasion to be acts of deliberate provocation by the authorities. Such feelings naturally fed through to the Solidarity leadership and played a part in the debates and disagreements that developed within it. The more interesting question is whether the party leadership or elements within it played some part in making sure that Solidarity criticism of the authorities and aggression towards them did not die down. The behaviour of the central leadership during this period leads observers like Ash and Holzer to conclude that in all likelihood the breakdown in relations with Solidarity in early August 'was premeditated' and that the intensification of conflict 'does not seem to be accidental'.[89] Clear evidence of the authorities' misrepresentation of Solidarity's part in the disagreement is also available, and censorship agencies during this period banned publication of material on the Orwellian grounds that it was 'abstractly objectivist' – that is, true but inconvenient.[90]

Neither were the Soviet leaders likely to have been passive observers of this situation. They were surely pleased to see Olszowski continue his work in the Politburo and would not have been dissatisfied with the treatment Solidarity received in the mass media during August. Soviet naval manoeuvres began off Gdańsk the day before the Solidarity Congress began and the friction between Solidarity and the Polish party leadership was, concluded Ruane, 'very definitely in the interests of the Soviet Union'.[91] Thus it would be a mistake to accept that the tougher stance of the party leadership was simply a response to the adventurism of Solidarity forces or the 'failure' of the Extraordinary Congress, in the sense that it did not swing public opinion round to its side or provide a new basis for agreement with Solidarity. The general commitment of the leadership to renewal, particularly on the part of the Kania-dominated centre, had helped it succeed in what must have been its prime objective – staying afloat on the swelling movement of democratisation within the party and organising the survival of a leadership team with recognisable features of 'continuity' through the sequence of dangerous uncontrolled elections.

Kania had certainly been committed to a 'political' (that is non-coercive) solution to the conflicts of the post-August situation, but he was also a full-blown democratic centralist and had been the archetypal Central Committee senior official since the 1960s. Therefore, while his commitment to renewal and the more definite pro-reform stance taken from the IX Plenum should not be seen as pure political window-dressing, it was surely not to be expected that this hitherto conventional member of the higher apparatus would turn into the Zbigniew Iwanów of the Politburo. The demands of the situation had probably taken him further in the direction of party democratisation than he would originally have wished, but there had never been any indication that the leadership during the period of the greatest dominance of this political tendency immediately before the Congress had contemplated any revision of the principle of democratic centralism. Sanford is probably correct, therefore, in concluding that Kania's great achievement had been 'to out-manoeuvre the genuine reformist elements within the PZPR who were willing to make the post-1980 system work'.[92] While the party reformers had from the outset been the group most eager for an Extraordinary Party Congress to be held it was in fact the prospect of its meeting that provided them with their greatest source of strength rather than the fact of the Congress actually being held. It was similarly its opposition to the established party leadership and its apparatus that sustained the horizontal movement; once it came under central patronage and gained a semi-official status its momentum was halted. Equally, while Kania had steered the party through the Congress and achieved some success in assuring a measure of leadership continuity, the democratic tide left him in something of a political backwater and it was logical that after it his role was a diminished one. He did not, for example, deliver either of the major Politburo reports at the II and III plenary sessions of the Central Committee as he had at the X and XI meetings immediately before the Congress. But his lower profile was not a consequence of the 'failure' of the Congress or of a personal lack of success so much as a reflection of the fact that the party now found itself in a different political position.

It was, nevertheless, by no means clear in which direction the party, as a body, should or could develop from the position it now occupied. The response of the CC apparatus was, clearly, to restore its position with the party's central decision-making body along former lines. That, however, was the response of one of the party's constituent groups and it was not one that could be shared by the party as a whole. One view was simply that it lacked the will or ability to develop a clear view of what to do at this stage and, in consequence, 'the Party once again lost initiative'.[93] Yet it seemed to be very much on the initiative of the central leadership that relations with Solidarity were sabotaged in early August and that attempts to take the heat out of the situation were rejected. The changes in party outlook at the tenor of its relations with different political actors were, of course, by no means wholly determined by internal factors. Soviet displeasure at Polish developments and impatience at the inability or unwillingness of the leadership to restore what the Kremlin would view as a 'normal' situation had been demonstrated on numerous occasions, most notably in the

June letter which had been followed by a direct challenge to Kania's position in the Central Committee. Kania and Jaruzelski conferred with Brezhnev during mid-August in the Crimea, a normal practice for East European party leaders though not for their prime ministers. Jaruzelski's presence, it has been suggested, was an important sign of Soviet doubts as to the capacity of the party to retain control over the situation.[94] While further Soviet economic aid was promised, its provision was linked with demands that the Polish leadership establish firmer political control. In retrospect it seems highly likely that the meeting marked, if not a definite decision to apply a military solution to the crisis, at least its promotion to the status of the most viable remedy.

The Soviet response to the first round of the Solidarity Congress (which included reference to the possibility of setting up free trade unions throughout Eastern Europe and in the 'nations of the Soviet Union') was also fierce, prompting Soviet ambassador Aristov to deliver a strong note to Kania and Jaruzelski concerning unacceptable anti-socialist and anti-Soviet developments. It asked why 'no decisive steps' had been taken by the official authorities to stamp out such activities and noted that the instigators of 'anti-Soviet provocations' had not in one single instance met with a sharp response from the authorities or been punished.[95] It was probably a measure of the importance of the note, and of the consequent Declaration released by the Polish Politburo, that the issue of the party journal in which both documents were published appeared a week ahead of schedule. The position of Kania and Jaruzelski, which had hardly been a comfortable one at the outset, was now a particularly difficult one. The idea of further alliance with the grass-roots party radicals had now lost its political point – having held free elections throughout the party organisation it was now no longer possible to plead the necessity of going along any further with this current. It was difficult, then, to find political arguments, as there had been in June, to muster against Soviet complaints. Kania's own position was, as we have noted, now somewhat marginal within the Polish leadership. The centrist policy he had become identified with, reflected in his statement at the III CC Plenum in early September that 'Our declaration for understanding is an offer of alliance with all those who are not against socialism', also contrasted strongly with the more aggressive attitudes expressed by the party leadership following the Extraordinary Congress.[96]

Such an arrangement of forces served to strengthen Polish sensitivity to the Soviet charges and, in conjunction with the deepening conflicts in Polish political life, to encourage the Soviet leadership to increase their pressure. A further factor strengthening the Soviet position was the material support they were providing for the Polish economy. As economic decline continued and consumer shortages worsened the leadership had little chance of gaining any popularity or even establishing its credibility as a political force – and without Soviet assistance the position would have been much worse. This fact was emphasised by Kania at the III Plenum, when he announced that the Soviet Union was rescheduling debts of over one and a half thousand million dollars until the mid-eighties and was supplying consumer goods Poland did not have the resources to buy elsewhere.[97]

These circumstances made Kania's personal position increasingly problematic. At the IV CC Plenum, which opened on 16 October, he condemned party members who had 'lost their party identity' as simultaneously members of Solidarity, a phenomenon he described as 'highly worrying', but nevertheless refused to place all responsibility for the lack of confidence which 'paralyses the party from within' on the 'anti-socialist elements' lurking within and behind Solidarity or on the failure of the party leadership to deal with them more severely. Certainly, Solidarity was developing a political role, a tendency which had in no way been diminished by the tenor of its recent First Congress, but Kania accurately appraised the differentiated character of the union, which was described at this time as hesitating 'between a desire for negotiation, which was constantly disappointed, and the response of revolt and the temptation to break off all relations, which were particularly strong at local level'.[98] Kania was also aware of weaknesses in the party's approach to this matter (not just in its implementation of agreed policy) and in its view of *odnowa*. He seemed to think that the party control commissions were still dragging their feet and their operation should be more effective in promoting the renewal of the party, although he did warn against 'hastiness'. He made it clear that he had no desire to see the party purged in such a way that there would be a need in a subsequent period, as there had been 'in previous decades' (and would be again only a few months later under the radically different political conditions of the State of War) to rehabilitate unjustly expelled members. He condemned attacks on deserving party activists, but followed this by reminding the Committee that the party, 'its organs and local organisations have the obligation to control and check people appointed to responsible positions, demanding of them that they carry out their duties honestly'. It was relevant that the word used for 'check' (*rozliczenie*) could also be translated as 'bringing to account', the watchword for those demanding a more thorough purge of corrupt and discredited politicians who still remained in the party.

He took care, though, to distance himself from some of the more radical demands of the party reformers and stressed, as he had at the III Plenum, that the party could never abandon its 'cadres policy', which he presumably meant to include its *nomenklaturist* control over appointments. The resolution produced by the Plenum carried a considerably stronger tone. It noted that the 'general activity of the mass of the membership which accompanied the preparation and proceedings of the IX Extraordinary Congress of the PZPR has not been properly put to use' and was attributed directly to the 'violent attacks' launched against the party by the opponents of socialism. The 'causes of our lack of success', it was claimed, 'are also to be found in ineffective action and the irresolute implementation of the decisions taken by party and state authorities'.[99] The party leadership was clearly increasingly worried by the ineffectiveness of its action and its failure to reassert control over the development of the political situation in Poland. Hopes of greater unity and the objective of concerted action expressed at the Congress and proclaimed with some apparent confidence immediately afterwards were so far largely unrealised. At the same time, the adoption of a more offensive attitude towards Solidarity suggested the development of a political situation marked by the greater likelihood of relations of competition and political conflict occurring. In the light of continuing, and intensifying, party weakness this was a dangerous prospect indeed for the PZPR leadership. Yet in some ways this threat was very much of its own making. The inability of the party to increase its popularity and regain some authority (and even to keep its members) was very much bound up with the feeling that there was little commitment amongst much of the leadership to pursue the policy of renewal. There were clear signs that this was occurring within the provincial committees – but they were now far less well represented in the Central Committee and it was unlikely that their relations with the central apparatus at this stage were particularly close or effective, at least so far as the KW elected leadership was concerned. The relegation of party reform to a lower level of priority was therefore closely linked with the greater emphasis placed on political competition and conflict.

6   The advance of the military

Crisis within the party leadership

The opening of the IV Plenum of the Central Committee on 16 October 1981, at which General Jaruzelski was to assume leadership of the party, took place four days after the annual Day of the Polish Army. Army Day was marked in the party press by an article from the pen of General Honkisz, deputy head of the army's Main Political Administration and, since the IX Extraordinary Congress, a member of the Presidium of the Central Auditing Commission of the party. In the light of the weakening of the party's position and of the critical exchanges that were to take place at the IV Plenum his comments on the political atmosphere within the army were particularly interesting. The party, he wrote, had always been the ideological and political leader of the armed forces, and the effectiveness of political work within the army was currently being demonstrated by the fact that the military was playing an 'unquestioned role' as a stabilising factor in Poland's political predicament. In this, of course, he was not thinking of party leadership simply as an external influence on the army – particularly as General Jaruzelski was one of the longest-standing members of the Politburo and had played a prominent political role since the beginning of 1981. The healthy ideological views prevalent in the army were due 'in large measure' less to external party guidance than to the services of 'party members in uniform', that is the party organs and their apparatus within the army (of which, of course, Honkisz as deputy head of the political administration was a prominent representative).

The party organs of the military had been strengthened as a result of the proper conduct of *odnowa*, during which the party organisation had been refreshed by the election of 'many new people from outside the professional political apparatus'. If, though, as claimed, renewal had been responsible for an even higher rate of turnover than in the civilian party it had clearly not been associated with the same level of organisational disruption. The correct political stance of the army was attributed to the fact that 'there had been no interruption in the party life of the military', a clear reference to the internal divisions within the PZPR and its leadership and to the conflicts that had arisen over such developments as the horizontal movement. All in all, Honkisz implied, not only was the army in good political shape but, due to the effectiveness of internal party work, it was in a better position to exercise party leadership and stabilise Poland's political life than the PZPR itself.[1] Having emphasised these points, his article ended with the portentous statement that the 'Day of the Polish Army has not only symbolic significance'.

This confident assertion had considerable relevance to the situation within the party, in which there were wide-spread feelings about the ineffectiveness of its actions and fears of the total meaninglessness of its 'leading role'. In the context of the disquiet expressed at the IV Plenum about the paralysis of the party organisation, Honkisz's views received considerable support. The address made by Olszowski on the problems of ideological activity followed closely the phraseology and approach taken by Honkisz, expressing approval of the stabilising role of the army and its high level of ideological fitness, reflected in its continuing educational activity. 'We should', stated Olszowski, 'make active use of these military experiences'. Borowski, an electrician from Konin, pointedly reminded Honkisz's superior, Jaruzelski, that in his ministerial role he was responsible for the defence of the nation, and thus of the party and of socialism as well. Towards the end of the second day's discussion Bańko, a machinist from Katowice, claimed that the institution of a 'state of war' was the surest way to prevent bloodshed in Poland and proposed that power should be handed over to the army for the period of a year.[2] Together with some more conciliatory statements at the previous Plenum, Kania's concluding address had contained a surprising reference to a 'state of emergency' (*stan wyjątkowy*) and the emphatic confirmation that 'in the defence of socialism the authorities will use any means that are necessary'.[3] Such views were far more prominent at the following CC gathering.

The proposal of these and analagous solutions to the problems surrounding the erosion of party authority reflected a hard-line response to a situation in which party decisions and actions did not evoke public support. Other members of the Central Committee, however, were more concerned with the reasons for this lack of support and analysis of the causes of the lack of leadership credibility. They continued, in particular, to focus attention on the objectives of the apparatus and its role within the party, both of which were perceived to have negative consequences for the political position of the party and its leading organs in Polish society. The strongest spokesmen for this view were the worker members of the Committee and secretaries of factory party committees. Thus, local committee secretary Kucharski spoke of people's suspicions of a fifth column 'composed of people who should long ago have been placed outside the party', who were providing those who had been ousted with a comfortable retirement and protecting them from criminal proceedings. Others, also from industrial locations, spoke aggressively of the apparatus 'at all levels which provides a comfortable retreat for compromised activists', of 'conservative forces which cannot be moved by any action whatever', of the 'increasingly open and unconditional mobilisation and offensive of the reactionary forces in the party, which describe themselves as "the only true communists"', and of the 'growing lack of confidence in the newly elected authorities, overgrown by an elderly apparatus now swollen by undeserving comrades who had to leave their posts as a result of the electoral campaign'.

The overwhelming impression given by those who spoke in this vein was of an apparatus dedicated primarily to its own protection, fending off criticism from below and relatively undisturbed by the elected party organ to which it was formally subject. Such an apparatus was an ineffective instrument for the implementation of CC decisions and gave the impression of little coordination of any sort within the party organisation. The problem facing the Central Committee, said Edward Banicki, a locksmith from Leszno, lay not in the passing of political resolutions but in inducing 'the central party *aktiv*, members of the Politburo, the whole party apparatus – particularly at the centre – to adopt a united line of action in those matters which concern us. Can we say at the present time that such an interpretation and such a line has been adopted by the central apparatus, or by the majority of the apparatus at the intermediate level? Personally, I feel that this has not been done, and it represents a great danger to the party'.[4] The apparent inactivity and continuing powerlessness of the party was therefore associated in this view with the resistance entrenched within the apparatus to the policy of political renewal and to the pursuit of any policies which did not accord with its own immediate interests.

In conjunction with the problems experienced within the Central Committee of achieving unanimity and hammering out a coherent political approach this left the Politburo itself with little capacity for effective national action. As Kucharski pointed out at the beginning of the plenary session, one of the fundamental criticisms currently made of the party was that the Politburo was isolated and, despite all the declarations made at the Congress and the resolutions passed there, acting without consultation with local organisations. As local cells were, after democratic elections and the assertion of democratic forces in the organisation, expecting to play some part in the determination of its line of action this meant that the decisions of the leadership were 'in reality not capable of implementation'. Further, the Central Committee itself was not finding it easy to establish its own identity or define an appropriate mode of operation. As we have already noted, steps were taken soon after the Congress to compensate for the 'amateur' nature of the new Committee by extending its membership and including key figures from the apparatus, in conjunction with the establishment of a series of commissions that would involve members in regular contact with staff of the CC Secretariat.

Many members were not happy with the implications of these measures for the status of the Central Committee, and discussion at the IV Plenum reflected grievances about the way the Committee was being managed and apparently reconstituted, in breach of the spirit if not the letter of party democracy. The first issue that arose concerned the participation of non-CC members in the commissions set up soon after the Congress. The composition of the Resolution Commission for the IV Plenum which had been proposed by the Secretariat (and which included nine non-CC members) was rejected and it was decided in future to form CC commissions only from members of the Committee. This also reversed the earlier decision that all KW first secretaries should participate in the work of the permanent commissions. The question of the relationship between the Committee and the Politburo was further raised by Marian Orzechowski (University of Wrocław) who suggested that the Politburo, in publishing a political declaration in response to the criticism of the Soviet ambassador the previous month, had usurped the function of the Committee and further exceeded its powers in preparing for the recent parliamentary debate on self-management without consulting the Central Committee.

Politburo member Łabęcki, formerly party secretary in the Gdańsk shipyard, turned the question back on those present and argued that the initiative and 'strength of will' had to come from the Committee itself. The very structure of the meeting, though, and the way it was organised made this far from easy. Arendt, party secretary in a Toruń factory and activist in the horizontal movement, indicated this when he argued for the necessity of providing information on who the CC 'guests' were and why they had been invited, for different seating arrangements to make it clear who the CC voting members were, for earlier circulation of Plenum materials and for some systematisation of the order in which members were permitted to speak.[5] Openness and clarity about CC proceedings had not been helped, as one local secretary pointed out, by the suspension of the convention that had been established before the Congress of publishing a stenographic account of CC plenary proceedings in standard issues of the party's monthly journal. The practice was, in fact, resumed for the IV Plenum. Such demands gave an indication of the problems faced by the 'amateur' Central Committee in exercising its formal powers and controlling the resources that remained at the disposal of the CC Secretariat.

While the interest of central party staff in the work of the Central Committee and its outcome seemed to be a particularly close one, inappropriately so in the eyes of some of its members, the opposite appeared to be the case with most local organisations. Indeed, the ambiguous relationship that existed between the central secretariat and the Committee made relations between the centre and organisations at local level more problematic. Telex messages and directives were being received in local organisations from the office of heads of CC departments who had yet to be confirmed in their post by the Committee itself. Neither were the new provincial committees receiving the central assistance they had expected. Kałkus, from the Cegielski works in Poznań, complained that the new provincial committee received no support or backup in its work from the central apparatus.

Poznań, now led by Skrzypczak, had been the site of the greatest success of the horizontal movement in terms of the outcome of party elections. Practically the whole of the provincial committee had been replaced, and all the KW secretaries and department heads were new, as were most of the district first secretaries. Obviously, as Kałkus pointed out, the new Central Committee had a major call on the services of the central apparatus, but it did not meet every day – and neither, he noted, had any great change taken place in the central apparatus which might have affected its capacity to provide assistance elsewhere. It may well have been possible to maintain organisational links between the centre and province which bypassed the provincial committees and even, in cases like Poznań where extensive change had occurred and the influence of the horizontal movement had been significant, the apparatus itself. Such a possibility had been hinted at in June at the XI Plenum in a cryptic exchange between Barcikowski and Kusiak, the incumbent KW first secretary who would have been well aware of the imminent end of his tenure as provincial leader. This hinted at the existence of some plan of action involving the Poznań committee but which excluded party centrists like Barcikowski who went along with the reform movement.[6]

Kusiak's successor Edward Skrzypczak, who had previously been party secretary in the Cegielski works, felt that at the time of the IV Plenum not only was his organisation not receiving appropriate support from the central authorities but that its position was effectively being undermined. Following his removal in 1982 he wrote that 'During the months preceding the declaration of martial law the control of regional party bodies over the local security structure had diminished, as apparently the security forces were given instructions directly by the central authorities'. After Skrzypczak's removal and following his promotion to the Politburo, Kałkus distanced himself from his former colleague, stating that 'comrade Skrzypczak had authority and inspired confidence' but that he also had 'an impulsive character and was too aggressive for many people'.[7] The feeling of isolation from the central authorities at least was also present in other provincial organisations, and calls were heard for greater participation by members of the Central Committee in the work of local committees.[8]

In view of the determined efforts made to restore the position of the provincial secretaries on the Central Committee these complaints are particularly interesting, as they suggest that the central apparatus was less interested in integrating the party nationally as a political force than in incorporating local party leaders to sustain the traditional centralism of the party structure and to perpetuate its leading role according to the orthodox conception. The net result of these different trends was declining activity on the part of local organisations and growing passivity amongst rank-and-file party members. Thus, reported Ciechan from Toruń, many organisations had failed to hold a single meeting since the IX Congress and, said Kaźmierkiewicz from Płock, the local party organs had virtually passed out of existence – with some ten or twenty percent of members now attending meetings and 'they, including the secretaries, already prepared to hand in their resignation'. This state of affairs, commented provincial secretary Fiszbach, was not surprising when members' opinions and sentiments were not properly reflected in resolutions passed by the leadership:

one 'cannot defend decisions which do not convince him'. If, Fiszbach concluded, the link between central authorities and the party base was again becoming weak, 'this was not the fault of the base'.[9]

But there were marked differences at the Plenum in how the responsibility for this state of affairs was to be apportioned. Many members were critical of the way the party organisation was currently run and, sometimes more by implication than outright statement, held the apparatus to be largely responsible. Others, as we noted above, directed their fire at anti-socialist forces and the behaviour of Solidarity leaders, and often expressed their dissatisfaction with the way the party leaders were dealing (or failing to deal) with the perceived political threat. The statements of eight KW first secretaries appear on the Plenum record and, apart from the notable exception of Tadeusz Fiszbach, fears about the deteriorating economic and political situation and dissatisfaction with the performance of the leadership (for whatever reason) led them to pronounce in favour of a more clear-cut and, often, hard-line strategy being adopted. Kociołek (Warsaw) and Dąbrowski (Zielona Góra) both called for the suspension of the right to strike, Czech (Przemyśl) attacked the resolution currently on the table and declared himself in favour of such decisions as would 'mobilise the party and state authorities to a real political offensive', Mróz (Opole) directed attention to the 'strength of our ideology' and emphasised the necessity for all in Poland to realise that 'our country, for good or evil, is tied to the Soviet Union'.[10]

From the disturbing situation of 1981 some harked back to the more reassuring vision of the early period of Gierek's rule, before the reform of the party apparatus in 1975. A farmer-member of the Central Committee dated the origins of the crisis to that year and referred positively to the pre-reform structure. Unlike present times, in the early 1970s there had been 'a strong authority in the countryside and everything worked organisationally, unlike the present situation'. The question of reversing the 1975 reform had been raised during the pre-Congress election campaign, although Politburo members at that time had expressed different views on the advisability of this.[11] It was also suggested that some such administrative change had to occur before any serious economic reform could be considered.[12] Associated with this view of the pre-1975 structure was the desire to strengthen the local party *aktiv*, the implication being that a *powiat*-based *aktiv* would facilitate the mobilisation of former activists and apparatus members whose services had been dispensed with since 1975. Kania himself appeared to favour this view and stated that the Politburo was considering the establishment of 'regional associations of party action', which would be particularly concerned with assisting the party's organisational work.

The notion of a broad offensive in party activities was also associated with proposals for a review of party members. This was put forward initially by Kania, who suggested an exchange of party cards in the process of which only those who wanted to be active and 'fight for the party's ideals' would retain their membership. 'We do not have to be a three-million strong party', he stated, and 'we are not one now in real terms'. While receiving the support of some hard-liners like Siwak and Bednarski (Bydgoszcz KW first secretary), many other speakers felt the suggestion was irrelevant and likely to be counter-productive, particularly representatives of industrial and local organisations. Marian Arendt pertinently asked who would verify whom and according to what criteria, and warned of tendencies to developing a 'cadre party, which would have to exercise power without social support'. This he linked with the views of the hard-liners who sought immediate social confrontation, taking as a pretext for this the aggressive wing of Solidarity. This criticism reflected the awareness that the harder line adopted by the party leadership since the Congress was not restricted in its programme to sharper conflict with Solidarity – it also involved clearer lines of division within the party.

There were clearly conflicting approaches and diagnoses of the major political problems within the Central Committee, but such disagreements were not absent from the Politburo either. This is evident just from the record of the IV Plenum exchanges, and the extent of the differences between Politburo members clearly took some members of the Central Committee by surprise and was a source of shock for others. The most serious attacks were made on the reformists, including those elected to the leadership at the recent Congress, and on the whole the progress of developments strengthened the line favoured by the anti-reform forces. Thus the weekly *Rzeczywistość*, established by Olszowski and associated with the hard-liners, published a suggestion that Politburo member and CC secretary Kubiak (Kraków University Professor) was a CIA agent, an allegation condemned by *Polityka* in strong terms but one for which the weekly's editor received only a 'warning conversation' from the Central Control Commission of the party.[13] The affair was further raised by Arendt at the VI Plenum when he queried the attitude taken by the CKKP, which he regarded as particularly dubious in the case of a journal established originally on the basis of a recommendation from the CC Secretariat. On this occasion Siwak attempted to disguise the issue by accusing Arendt's Toruń colleague, Ciechan, of further sowing division in the party leadership by publicising an innocent mistake of Siwak's at a local meeting.[14]

Apparent infringements of discipline on the other side met with more serious sanctions. Stefan Bratkowski, chairman of the Journalists' Association who had spoken out strongly against the political influence of the apparatus since the time of the Bydgoszcz crisis in March and persistently condemned the hard-liners' manipulation of the mass media, was expelled from the party altogether. It was hardly coincidental that this occurred two days before he was to lead the delegation to an international conference in Moscow, a visit the party leadership was particularly eager to prevent. This was far from being seen as a manifestation just of Warsaw politics, and the Gdańsk shipyard party committee (where Politburo member Łabęcki had been secretary) registered a protest at the expulsion.[15] Conflict, then, was rife throughout the party but was particularly evident at the level of the top leadership and was seen by many as a prime cause of the leaders' inability to take control of developments, associated with the feelings of paralysis and ineffectiveness that were pervading the party.

It was in this context that dissatisfaction came to be focussed on Kania's leadership capacity and at this juncture he tendered his resignation. He had fully recognised the problems within the party that undermined its action: 'Lack of confidence . . . is paralysing the party from within. We must break our way out of this position . . . No-one can have faith in a party that will not believe in itself'.[16] Judgments on the mechanism of the leadership change are varied, though. One view was that the change was caused as much by medical factors as by politics, as 'Kania himself . . . became ill and torpid, sinking into depression'.[17] Certainly a marked change in leadership attitudes appeared to take place towards the end of September and a change was clearly anticipated by some, probably in favour of Olszowski.[18] A major factor in this, as we have noted, was Kania's weakened political position following the Congress and the growing weight of Soviet pressure. An important part was most likely played in this by growing doubts about Kania's personal leadership capacity from June onwards and Moscow's support only of Jaruzelski within the Polish duumvirate. Ploss concludes that the Soviet leaders 'expected Jaruzelski or Olszowski to impeach Kania at the Polish Central Committee meeting', and it is broadly accepted that 'Soviet pressure was a major factor in the October decision to replace Kania'.[19] Polish–French journalist K. S. Karol suggests that the Kremlin leaders were specifically displeased with Kania's refusal to go along with their policy of waging a war of nerves, designed to bring the country to the verge of civil war.[20]

The question of Kania's role in these arrangements and the possibility of his agreement to stand down remains very much open. One source claims that the vote of confidence, and particularly its timing, was just a mistake and that Kania had misjudged the extent of the criticism that surfaced during the early part of the Plenum.[21] This explanation, although claimed to be derived from internal information, is hardly convincing. At all events, Kania's resignation was accepted, although not by an overwhelming majority (by 104 votes to 79). Far more decisive was the vote in favour of Jaruzelski taking on the party leadership (180 to 4 against). Yet the circumstances surrounding the choice of Jaruzelski were by no means clear, either. Nor was it immediately evident how the change in leadership would serve to eliminate the numerous problems arising within the party structure. Fiszbach, present at the Plenum only as a coopted KW secretary, observed that some seemed to think that the 'premier-general' simply had to give the order and 'everything would be arranged', but he foresaw a less optimistic situation – one in which the commander might be left with an order that could not be carried out.[22] Indeed, while the general carried full defence as well as prime ministerial responsibility and thus had full control over Poland's military and security forces, he had also allied himself with Kania's commitment to a political solution to Polish conflicts and the refusal to apply coercive measures to them. It is very likely that, even if this was not the intention of Jaruzelski himself, many of those who voted for the leadership change did so in the expectation that the existing policy commitment would be shown to have failed: 'According to their calculations, when General Jaruzelski calculates that the policy of dialogue will not succeed, he will set to and implement his real programme . . . and the time of the state of emergency will at last be proclaimed.'[23]

The extent to which these expectations were shared by Moscow is not fully clear. One view was that the Soviets 'do not appear to have dictated his choice. Rather, his election was primarily influenced by domestic conditions in Poland at the time . . .' Further, it was suggested that from the Soviet point of view Jaruzelski was a 'less than fully trustworthy comrade'.[24] On the other hand, Soviet doubts should certainly not be exaggerated and their desire for firmer communist party leadership control, if necessary using methods so far eschewed by the Polish ruling group, was well established. So far as Soviet doubts did exist, it is likely that they had arisen following some of Jaruzelski's more unconventional measures: for example, his decision to retain the Defence Ministry when appointed Premier in February and his refusal to back up Gierek in August 1980 when the latter still enjoyed the confidence of Moscow.[25] Neither of those decisions, however, should have raised doubts concerning his fundamental loyalty to Moscow or his commitment to the leading role of the party exercised through orthodox channels of democratic centralism.

Moreover, by October 1981 the situation in Poland had developed to the stage where the Soviet leadership must have been desperate for any change that promised to strengthen the possibility of firm communist control being restored. Even if Jaruzelski might not have identified himself with all the anti-Solidarity views of his hard-line colleagues, he was nevertheless the representative and commander of the portion of the communist establishment in Poland in which the Soviet authorities appeared to have the greatest degree of trust. It was, for example, the army party daily, *Zołnierz Wolności*, that provided them with the appropriate Polish material when they wished to affirm that 'Poland has been, is and will remain a firm link in the socialist community', and it was party members in the armed forces who were often singled out as stressing 'the need to strengthen state power and resolutely end attempts to undermine the basis of the socialist system'.[26] The change in party leadership was also presented by the Central Committee as one likely to reassure the Soviet allies. As Barcikowski stated before Jaruzelski's election, he was known 'both by our friends and in the world as a whole, which will undoubtedly help him to perform his incredibly responsible and difficult functions'.[27] This view was presumably shared by the great majority of CC members as they cast their vote for Jaruzelski, the election itself being overseen by the Scrutiny Commission whose chair was in the safe hands of General Księżarczyk.

On election as party leader Jaruzelski reaffirmed his commitment to Kania's line and overall political conception while introducing certain differences of emphasis. He stated his intention to steer 'the same *general* course' (emphasis added) and also said that 'we have always avoided confrontation and today also we do not seek it. But one thing is sure – that the possibilities of retreat are exhausted'. The statements of those most closely associated professionally with Jaruzelski suggest which concerns were uppermost. General Honkisz thus singled out for criticism the 'statements of "Solidarity" pseudo-specialists on defence', especially those who criticised the Warsaw Pact and suggested that reductions of military expenditure would ease the path of economic reform. General Siwicki, Chief of the General Staff and Vice-Minister of Defence (who would be brought into the Politburo within two weeks), noted how the 'bad faith of the opponent' had been underestimated and how it was 'proceeding with premeditation to destroy the material substance of the state'. General Kiszczak, Minister of Internal Affairs (brought into the Politburo in early 1982), emphasised the outcome of the Solidarity Congress, which had been marked by the promulgation of the 'doctrine of a political party aiming at the destruction of the structures of the socialist state and the gradual assumption of power'. Jaruzelski's promotion also prepared the way into the Politburo, then, for a number of military colleagues markedly antagonistic towards Solidarity. A further step towards militarisation was indicated at the IV Plenum when the heads of the CC departments were presented for ratification and General T. Dziekan was announced as the new head of the Cadres Department.

Taking all these factors into account, then, it is clear that Jaruzelski's occupation of the top party position meant rather more than just the continuation of Kania's general course. The authority crisis of the party had persisted so long and the Congress had proved to be so unproductive in political terms that the conservative forces within the apparatus appeared to have lost virtually all patience with Kania's centrist policy of conciliation. Many of them, indeed, had little sympathy for Kania's policy from the beginning and had done their best to undermine it. By the time of the IV Plenum, though, they were vociferous in their opposition and there were many demands for the leadership to take a more aggressive approach. Of the provincial secretaries who made their views known most appeared to share this attitude. In the Central Committee local and provincial interests were, of course, less represented now by the provincial party staff and more by local secretaries and other activists. They, too, often called for more offensive action. Those who attributed the weakness of the party to the inadequacy of inner-party democracy, however, were also critical both of the leadership and of much of the apparatus.

Kania's centrist position thus found itself without any significant base at the Plenum and the lines of division emerged more clearly than they had in the past. As part of the process of sharpening the identity of the party in relation to other political forces and preparing to tighten up on party discipline, eleven members of the Central Committee, including Politburo member Zofia Grzyb, who were also members of Solidarity were persuaded to leave the independent trade union. Such changes in themselves clearly did little to tackle the problems that had been aired at the Plenum and were the preparation for more decisive action. What precisely this would involve was left unclear, for while many calls for a hard-line approach had been made, Jaruzelski and other members of the party–state leadership also prepared for further negotiation with a view to arriving at some political agreement. In this situation of considerable uncertainty it was announced at the V Plenum, held only two weeks later to resolve organisational matters arising from the previous CC Plenum, that the cumulation of powers in the hands of Jaruzelski would continue as a result of the existing situation 'in which further diverse complications may await us in the coming weeks or months'.[28]

The eclipse of the party

An atmosphere of looming confrontation, in which the decisive exercise of state and military power could be presented as a necessary evil to the broad mass of the Polish public, was certainly becoming evident in the mass media. An article in *Polityka* which appeared in November examined the historical development and nature of the Polish military and suggested that it might have a special role to play in furthering the cause of *odnowa*. It dismissed the views of 'our new right', 'who identify socialism with their own group interests and count on the army to defend them, not in confrontation with "Solidarity" radicals – but with society as a whole'. This was a clear condemnation of those like Olszowski who had more than once tried to harness the force of apparatus resistance and reaction. The ambiguity attached to Jaruzelski's cumulation of party–state posts meant that the political situation could easily develop in very different directions. Thus, military intervention could also play a temporary role in acting as an 'umbrella' to forestall the outbreak of a civil war that would serve the interests of representatives of the 'old régime'.[29]

Such arguments, of which this was but one example, were clearly double-edged. They established some degree of military intervention as a necessary and even desirable development, but also served to distinguish this course from that of the party conservatives who had been urging a hard-line approach and the adoption of 'extra-political' means of solving the crisis since before the Congress. This approach, of course, fitted well with the personal leadership of General Jaruzelski who had been an apparent supporter and close collaborator of the centrist Kania, but whose appointment in Kania's stead opened up the possibility of using firmer methods to achieve moderate ends. In fact, both methods were employed concurrently. On the one hand, negotiations with the main forces of Polish society, including Solidarity and the Church, were undertaken and the possibility of establishing some kind of front of national unity was explored. On the other, the military muscle was flexed by sending operational groups initially into the countryside, to verify the work of the administration and expedite the solution of local problems. The latter move was reported to have caused the 'first confrontations between the armed forces and the lower level apparatchiki resentful of such a major interference', although it was admitted that a 'direct clash was not discernible'.[30] Whatever the validity of this assertion the response of some members of the population was more forthright: 'It's really the first step towards introducing a state of emergency', one farmer and representative of Solidarity was reported to have said. The new leader's approach had other, more general effects. After Jaruzelski had been party leader for one month, it was noted that 'Jaruzelski's style is edging the party itself off the stage. He rules as soldier–Prime Minister rather than party leader'.[31]

There were also growing feelings that the party was 'edging itself off the stage' by virtue of its falling numbers and increasing resignations. Thus, in the autumn of 1981 Touraine and his colleague wrote that 'hundreds of thousands of members left the party', which thereby lost 'a large part of its industrial base'. This was a great exaggeration, though one which some in influential party positions were not unwilling to encourage. Even the experienced analysts of Radio Free Europe appear to have overstated party losses by more than 50%.[32] Part of the problem lay in the sometimes confused categories of party expulsions, resignations and simple removal from membership lists which have not always been clearly distinguished. Details of developments in these areas until the end of September were, however, presented in the party press and, while the overall reduction in membership levels was less dramatic than some have suggested, significant changes in the relationship between the different kinds of departure from party ranks did take place.[33]

The changes in the level of party membership and the total number of resignations, expulsions and removals from party lists (for reasons of passivity, non-payment of dues, 'growing away from the party', etc.) over the fifteen months from the end of June 1980 are reproduced in table 6.1 from the party source cited. Obviously the number of resignations, expulsions and removals (610,000) was greater than the decline in party membership (375,000) – but the difference is not accounted for by the relatively small number of candidates accepted (29,000) over this period.[34] It is possible that the expulsions/removals and resignations categories overlap in some way – but again it is not clear how. There is no way the groups can be combined to iron out the

Table 6.1 *Reductions in PZPR membership (mid-1980 to end of 1981) (in thousands)*

	Expulsions and removals from list	Resignations	Fall in membership	Total members
end June 1980				3,150
end December 1980	74	70	58	3,092
end June 1981	260	137	223	2,869
end September 1981	47	22	94	2,775
end December 1981				2,691
Total	381	229	375	

discrepancies (such apparently erroneous addition was the cause of the misleading conclusion of Weydenthal *et al.*), so the precise meaning of the totals provided cannot be fully defined. There are, nevertheless, some significant conclusions to be drawn from these statistics which reflect on the situation in late 1981.

Firstly, while there had been a steady decline in the total number of party members since mid-1980 and the onset of the strikes over July and August, the peak period of decline had fallen in the first half of 1981 and the rate of decline after the middle of 1981 (and after, in effect, the Extraordinary Congress) slowed down during the next two quarters. Indeed, prior to the declaration of the State of War in December it appears that the rate of decline in party numbers had come to a virtual halt by the end of November, for a total party membership of 2.77 million was announced for the beginning of December.[35] Singled out for comment in the party press, however, was not the absolute decline in party numbers but the fact that a large part in it had been played by resignations rather than by the different forms of discipline exercised by the party authorities. Thus the level of resignations was 'hitherto unknown on this scale' and, most significantly, the majority of these, 71%, were working-class members. Even the rate of resignation was in decline after the middle of 1981, though, and it might have appeared that the Congress had indeed had a beneficial effect on the level of membership. It was also confirmed by a Lódź KW secretary that fewer had been leaving the party since Jaruzelski took over the leadership.[36]

A third factor, however, did indicate a worsening of the situation in the autumn of 1981. In the fifteen months after mid-1980, 29,000 new candidates were accepted by the party, but 25,000 of these had joined before the end of 1980. Clearly, very few were attracted to the party during 1981, and for the third quarter the number of acceptances was even lower than during the first half of the year and as few as 546 individuals presented themselves as candidates. While, then, the overall decline in party numbers was by no means as dramatic in late 1981 as some have suggested, particular tendencies within the party membership did reach critical proportions at this time. The position was particularly bleak in connection with the working class, where the decline in the party's fortunes threatened to wipe out its industrial base completely in certain areas. In one portion of a transport plant in Świdnik, for example, party membership during the year preceding the declaration of the State of War fell from seventy to just three.[37]

But numerical indications cannot convey the full nature of the problem. A key factor in the authority crisis was the 'decomposition of the party', which meant that the party secretary was unable to exert his former authority in the factories and that the party's overall capacity to govern the country had become enfeebled. A major survey conducted by the Academy of Sciences' Institute of Philosophy and Sociology suggested that only 24% of members supported the existence of political arrangements in which the PZPR played a leading role, while 53% would support a situation in which they did not (23% were undecided or had views which did not fit the available categories).[38] Solidarity polls added further details, not all of which fitted together into a coherent picture. In Wrocław, 90% were reported to be in favour of eliminating the leading role of the party from the Constitution but 82% declared their confidence in Jaruzelski and his government. In the Warsaw region, though, only 21% stated confidence in the government and 65% thought that public confidence in it was declining. Jaruzelski, however, was viewed more positively and 41% of Solidarity members thought his accession to the party leadership had eased tensions in the country.[39]

Such results unequivocally demonstrated the weakness of party authority and, more ambiguously, the growing disfavour into which the government was also falling. Both, of course, were now headed by Jaruzelski – yet his personal standing still seemed to be high. But the 'firm measures' whose prospect had been brought closer by his assumption of the party leadership were supported by only a small minority. Amongst the measures that were to be enforced under the State of War, the use of the militia and police forces against street demonstrations were supported by 13%, the banning of public protests and demonstrations by 15% and the use of the army to break strikes by 7%. Such support was concentrated amongst the remaining members of the old, pre-Solidarity branch unions, predominantly those who were also PZPR members and who occupied some managerial position. It was this group, according to one description, who constituted the 'core of the establishment', those 'who are the object of attack by all groups'.[40] Certainly, despite the personal popularity of Jaruzelski, there was little support among Solidarity members (currently numbering some 9.5 million) for the policies the party leadership was now floating. In the Warsaw region only 14% thought that the union should submit to the ban on strikes the party was attempting to get passed by the *Sejm*.[41]

There were few signs, then, that the firmer government and leadership associated with Jaruzelski was commanding much public support or that the decline in the party's authority had been halted, although the actual drop in party numbers was by no means as pronounced as some observers have claimed. Indeed, it is by no means unlikely that the harder-line faction within the leadership was exaggerating the numerical collapse of the party in order to persuade the remaining centrists of the need to act while the party still had some viable kind of social base. Another important factor was the growing crisis fatigue of Polish society, the increasing reluctance of Solidarity members to take part in yet more strike action and the uncertainties among its leaders as to what they could conceivably do to improve the lot of their members amidst the worsening economic and political crisis. It is, of course, not beyond the bounds of possibility that some within the leadership had been dragging their heels over agreements with the different parties involved and delaying the introduction of remedial measures with precisely the intention of producing such an outcome. While there were many signs of the growing weakness of the party, then, it should also be noted that the political basis of the Solidarity movement was also in some ways becoming less secure. This had happened less because of any political actions taken by the authorities than because of the effects of continuing economic and social crisis by means of which Solidarity had been denied a great capital asset, 'the capital of hope, which society had placed in it'.[42]

Some Solidarity activists, also, were only too eager to suggest that the party should play a drastically reduced role and to demonstrate that its eclipse was indeed imminent. A further phase in this development was reached in late November, when the Solidarity organisation at the Ponar-Żywiec plant in Bielsko-Biała proposed a referendum on the removal of the party organisation from the plant, including leaving its current headquarters, conducting political work outside of factory hours, doing without financial support from the enterprise, and divorcing 'party leadership' from the conduct of plant affairs. The signal for this action, it was later admitted in the party press, was the party leadership's recent demand that party members should sever their links with Solidarity, which resulted in local Solidarity's requirement that their members should leave the party.[43] The referendum on the withdrawal of the party was held on 23 November. Of the 1,421 plant employees, 1,119 took part, and of these 970 supported the Solidarity proposal. The party organisation, which comprised 350 members (or rather fewer on some accounts), had called for a boycott of the referendum but some clearly took part in the vote.[44] This measure had a considerable impact both on the party leadership and on local Solidarity organisations; by the end of the month demands for such removal of party organisations had been made in twenty-one provinces, nearly half the Polish regions.[45]

The VI Plenum of the Central Committee opened on November 27, shortly after these developments. Although it was intended to be devoted to economic affairs and the issue of reform, it was Solidarity's challenge to the party and the state of the organisation that dominated the discussion and, in the words of one reporter, transformed the Plenum 'into a platform for the mobilisation of forces which were now understood to be not only of a political nature . . . the voice of the "moderates" during the VI Plenum was swamped by war-like shouts and calls for action'.[46] The views of the reformers and horizontalists (now represented largely by Arendt and Ciechan, the secretaries of Toruń factory committees) were not absent, but their statements were restricted (at least in the published text) to criticism of economic reform plans and to exchanges with the hard-liners Olszowski and Siwak. Olszowski attempted to defend the role of *Rzeczywistość* in attacking Kubiak, while Siwak provided some camouflage by making similar criticisms of Zbigniew Ciechan. At all events, the overall political strategy of the party leadership received little discussion at the Plenum, and attention was focussed on the growing challenge of Solidarity and the direct attack being mounted on the party by 'counter-revolutionary forces'.

The prime issue here, of course, was Solidarity criticism of the position of the party committees in the factories – organisations which were, according to CC Secretary Mokrzyszak, 'the foundation of our party, the source of its strength and leading role. This is therefore an attack on the Leninist foundation of the party structure'. But the problem did not lie solely or even primarily in such attacks, but rather in the fact that the foundation was crumbling of its own accord and that the 'source of party strength' was running alarmingly dry. Indeed, he himself deplored the fact that local party organisations and even their leaders were less capable of undertaking active work. The primary significance of conflicts and divergences within the party was emphasised in the first issue of the party journal under the State of War: 'it was not extremists from "Solidarity" but "our" theoreticians . . . who formulated proposals and the requirement of removing the party from the work-place', whilst party groups too often agreed with the programme of the 'anti-socialist opposition'.[47] The growing weakness of the party organisation at local level was highlighted by other speakers and, faced with a further demand from Solidarity for a referendum organised by the organ of self-government on the continuing presence of the party and related organisations in a Katowice plant, a local representative was adamant that 'We shall certainly lose the referendum . . . we must come out directly with a resolution that we do not allow this and indicate what we shall do, because otherwise we shall not have anyone to defend or anything to defend them with.'[48]

There were several calls for emergency measures to be taken (including one for a personal dictatorship to be exercised by General Jaruzelski) and clear warnings from Barcikowski and Jaruzelski that special arrangements would be made in the event of a 'national understanding' not being reached. The Plenum resolution called for application of all resources 'at the disposition of state and party' for use against those organising and inspiring actions designed 'to remove the party from socialist work places'. It also directed the PZPR parliamentary group to act to introduce a draft decree on the undertaking of exceptional measures to ensure the defence of citizen and state (although the party group had of late been encountering difficulties in implementing their plans within the increasingly independent *Sejm*).[49] On 2 December a notable pointer to future action was the use of ZOMO (*Zmotoryzowane Odwody Milicji Obywatelskiej*: Motorised Units of Civil Militia), the riot police set up after 1970, to break the students' occupation of the Warsaw Fire Officers' Academy. On 3 December recordings were made of Solidarity leaders in Radom apparently announcing the inevitability of confrontation with the party–state, and perhaps advocating the use of force in any such encounter. These received wide publicity to strengthen the leadership's claim that Solidarity was indeed in the hands of counter-revolutionary forces out to subvert party leadership and dismantle the socialist state.

Under these conditions, in the early hours of Sunday, 13 December, Jaruzelski announced the establishment of a Military Council of National Salvation which would rule Poland for an unspecified period under the conditions of a State of War. This, it was claimed, was 'not a substitute for the constitutional government. Its only task is to protect legal order in the country, to guarantee restoration of order and discipline'.[50] On this basis thousands of people were rapidly interned (particularly Solidarity leaders and activists), a strict curfew introduced, the freedom to travel suspended, and a stop put to virtually all means of communication. While the Polish Constitution did not provide for a state of emergency or 'martial law', it did embrace the State of War resorted to in this case which, therefore, lay within the bounds of constitutionality. Its legal basis was somewhat shaky, as its introduction should have passed through the *Sejm*, which had been sitting in the immediately preceding period, and Jaruzelski acted before convoking the Council of State, which otherwise had the authority to suspend the normal rights. In general terms, though, Jaruzelski followed the correct procedures with a military thoroughness that contrasted with the political arbitrariness of the leadership over the preceding weeks and months.[51]

In more practical terms, it seems most likely that the *coup* was prompted by the desire to regain firmer control of the situation before the dissolution of the party had progressed to the extent where there would be no national organisation to speak of and, therefore, no local network to protect from further challenge from Solidarity and no basis for rebuilding a more orthodox party–state structure. The early days of the State of War, though, were characterised by a range of wild assertions about Solidarity intentions: that capitalism would be restored and Poland withdraw from the Warsaw Pact, that the old estate-owners would return and that the future would be impoverished and fascisised (all this in one of the few remaining media outlets, the party–military organ *Żołnierz Wolności*). Yet the assertions were not accompanied by evidence for the claim that Solidarity had any offensive intentions towards state power at all.[52] Similarly, in the Soviet-produced explanation of *Who Pushed Poland to the Brink*, an analagous justification for the *coup*, the only section in the documentary Appendix in which there is no photographic evidence is that referring to the conspiratorial intentions of Solidarity and their intended use of violence.[53]

Immediately following the declaration of the State of War, 'military commissar-plenipotentiaries' took overall control of the state administration, with the suspension of the right to strike key enterprises were militarised, while social life was virtually immobilised. Careful attention was paid to the control of strategic groups and to those holding key institutional posts. Of the 5,000 or so who were interned immediately, most were Solidarity leaders and political figures defined as those who had posed the 'counter-revolutionary threat' to the survival of the socialist state, although a token group of leaders from the discredited Gierek administration were also taken into custody. Some plant directors were replaced (in Gdańsk, Warsaw and Łódź) on 14 December for failing to carry out their duties and two days later a larger group was sacked for not implementing the military rule directives. Four provincial governors (the state equivalent of the KW first secretary) were replaced from the outset by military personnel. A summary of these developments was published in the first issue of *Polityka* to be published during the State of War, on 20 February.[54] The former head of the Polish 'red berets' was posted to Gdańsk as military commissar.[55] For some time there was barely a mention of the party and the Politburo was not reported to have met before 23 December.

At provincial level the main initial moves were made in January. Żabiński and Fiszbach resigned their first secretaryships in Katowice and Gdańsk, and twelve other KW secretaries were replaced during January, among them four in Katowice (which had been the location of the major resistance of the State of War), two in Gdańsk, and one each in six other provinces. The new appointments did not have the strong party background that characterised many secretaries, and the military connection was apparent. Of the new secretaries in Katowice, one had served in the army since 1954 and had held until recently the post of deputy head of political affairs at the provincial military HQ. Two others had no previous party apparatus experience, one coming directly from the University of Silesia (an arts Ph.D), the other from work in the mining industry. Of those appointed in Gdańsk, one had also served in the army since 1961 (coming directly from the post of deputy commander of political affairs within the Coastal Defence), the other transferring from the directorship of an industrial construction association (having worked in the party apparatus before 1975). The appointments made during the early period of the State of War also tended to have less marked local commitments.[56]

In various ways, then, the institution of the State of War furthered the eclipse of the party that had become evident during the autumn of 1981. The military had gained greater prominence within the Politburo, with the promotion of Jaruzelski to first secretary and the inclusion of other generals in the ruling party body, and moved into some strategic positions in the provincial party apparatus. Relatively little was heard of the party for some time and the bypassing of the party gave developments the clearer appearance of a military *coup d'état*.[57] Despite its underpinning by the military forces the leading role of the party had been seriously compromised and the lack of party authority fully demonstrated. The *coup*, as Michnik pointed out, had substituted 'the argument of force for the force of argument' and confirmed the absence of any kind of party authority normally claimed in the European communist party–states (Michnik's comment was a pertinent, though probably unintended, reversal of Jaruzelski's statement to the VIII Congress that the socialist states 'do not play the role of a supplicant, nor do they use the argument of force; they use the force of argument').[58]

A very different interpretation was placed on these developments by party representatives and, particularly, by leading military figures. According to a military academic appraisal the entry of the military occurred 'exclusively with the intention of facilitating the state's exercise of its constitutional duties without any interruption . . . the army did not act under the specific conditions of the State of War as an independent political force directed against the state, but as the armed branch of the party and the state'.[59] In the same way as the overlapping structure and composition of party and state bodies in communist countries has helped sustain party authority by associating the 'leading force' with an operating state system, so the association of the party leadership and, increasingly, its national apparatus with the armed forces has supported the idea of its privileged relation with military power. In view of the organisation of the armed forces within the East European systems, though, the Polish military was also an established political force in its own right by virtue of its Main Political Administration which served both to exercise political supervision over the armed forces and to express military interests within the leading organs of the party. As we have noted, these views were consistently expressed at the successive plenary meetings of the Central Committee held during and after the August strikes. They had regularly reflected condemnation of all anti-socialist forces (conceived, it seems, rather broadly) and punctilious concern for security interests. They had also shown consistent suspicion of both conciliatory moves towards Solidarity and tolerance of unorthodox activities within the party, placing them close to the attitudes associated with the conservatives and hard-liners of the party establishment.

Thus, it is certainly misleading to conceive of the military and its Main Political Administration as a force opposed to or even distinct from the party as a whole. Soviet evidence also suggests that there is no reason to assume the existence of any significant conflict or competition between the MPA, or military party apparatus, and the military commanders, the professional soldiers.[60] A more appropriate view is that 'the military elite participates . . . not as the party per se, but as part of the party, the party-in-uniform'. If anything, this statement and the view taken of Polish politics, that 'the role of the armed forces became pivotal, beginning with Jaruzelski's promotion to party leadership', underestimates the role of the army. Its 'pivotal' role can be traced back further than that, certainly to the vote of confidence won by Kania in June, when the official account took care to point out that 'members of the central party organs in soldiers' uniforms expressed in a decisive way their full confidence in and recognition of Stanisław Kania and Wojciech Jaruzelski'.[61]

Thus there is little cause to think of the army acting against the party. The course of events in Poland suggested that 'the political function of the military would not be opposed to that of the Party; in fact they were what was left of the party'.[62] Spielman's contrastive judgment on Jaruzelski, that 'far from a typical communist, he is much more a typical general', avoids the main point.[63] Yet, the greater political salience of military figures and the declaration of the State of War clearly did have political implications for the institutional character of the party and the prospects for it regaining authority. While the military and MPA are in part fully integrated with the party they also have their own identity, both organisationally and politically. Simes has suggested that the Soviet military elite is increasingly 'becoming a separate group in Soviet society' and that, while it is clearly subject to the overall authority of the Politburo, it is more than just a branch of the apparatus and 'does not take guidance from the Central Committee Secretariat'.[64] The Polish MPA, as we noted above, had its own political viewpoint throughout the crisis and did not appear to diverge from the attitudes expressed by its Soviet equivalent, which has been noted for its suspicion of détente and has been described as 'one of the centres of neo-Stalinist sentiment'.[65] It was not surprising, then, that the State of War brought sharp changes in the nature of party life.

The party reaction

Within the party as a whole normal procedures were suspended on the basis of the transmission of a central Instruction on 'Party Leadership Under Conditions Arising From the Threat To State Security', which gave exceptional powers to the executive organs. An early act was the dissolution by the Toruń KW executive of the whole party committee of the University, which had played a leading part in the development of the horizontal movement. The specific charges made of the committee throw an interesting light on the precise features of the horizontal movement which worried so many within the party leadership. It had adopted a 'capitulationist line' towards anti-socialist forces, neglected inner-party work and failed to adapt to the new requirements made by the militarised system. In particular it was criticised for having paid too much attention to 'national, provincial and urban' activities and failed to carry out obligations within its own sphere of competence, notably in taking charge of the student movement, failing to perform its 'proper role' during student strikes and not exercising its 'prerogative of influence' over cadre appointments within the University.[66] The leadership of the party committee *within its designated area* was therefore strongly emphasised as was the control over appointments.

The need to restore party control over cadres was also reflected in the fact that the first CC commission which was reported to have met (in the middle of February) was that concerned with internal party affairs, its major conclusion being that a new cadres policy based on different principles should be worked out and applied. The weakening of the conception of party leadership was a major theme at this stage and it was associated with the speedy reversal of some of the leadership changes made during the pre-Congress electoral campaign, which were described as occurring under 'unnatural conditions' as a result of which there had been elected to leading positions people 'under the influence of Solidarity extremism, susceptible to opportunism'. Measures to rectify these errors were soon taken and in the first month or so of military rule, 349 secretaries were removed from district or town committees and 307 from plant committees, while 2,091 first secretaries of primary party organisations were changed. A further 1,800 members of diverse party committees were also changed. The rectification of recent party errors was thus swiftly carried out after the *coup*.[67]

Particularly strict discipline was applied by the secretariat of the Katowice provincial committee, itself having been extensively changed. On 24 December the party organisation of the Katowice steel works (Huta Katowice), which in the seventies had been the largest in the country, was dissolved and carefully reconstituted. In this process it was downgraded from a *Komitet Fabryczny* (Plant Committee) to a *Komitet Zakładowy* (Factory Committee), which had the effect of placing it under the direct control of the local town committee. In the first months of 1982 around a quarter of its members left the party, most of these being expelled or removed by the leadership from party lists, and formal party approval was withdrawn from many *nomenklatura* appointees. In January the Soviet consul general had visited Katowice and conferred with the first secretary. It appeared that the Soviet diplomatic corps had played 'an active watchdog or even participatory role in the reshaping and reinvigorating of the PZPR'.[68] In Gdańsk four members of the KW executive were removed, seventeen from the provincial committee and eighty members of the first level organisations, while eighty-one secretaries of primary organisations and over two-thirds of the apparatus were changed. The party organisation in the Lenin shipyard was losing members during the first half of 1982 at a rate more than half as high again as it had suffered during the eleven months following the 1980 strikes.[69] One of the leading military figures appointed to the KW secretariat was particularly critical of the persistent influence of the horizontal movement in the province, which continued well after the Congress and had a significant effect on the work of the provincial committee. The roots of such 'deviations' clearly went deep into the party organisation and Auditing Committee Presidium member Stępień, from Gdynia, spoke in February of a deep and continuing division within local party ranks.[70]

The situation was a similar one in other provinces, particularly those with large concentrations of workers. The dissolution of the party organisation in the large Elwro factory in Wrocław was also undertaken by the KW in the early days of military rule, and six teams of the provincial control commission were sent to work in the plant. Party membership in the plant, whose employees numbered some 6,000, had fallen from over 1,000 in 1980 to around 450 by the time of the December *coup*, and then to under 300 as a result of the verification.[71] It has also been claimed that a significant number of military officers, as many as 20%, were also expelled from the party, largely because renewal had brought into the military party committees those who were more inclined to restrict the politicisation of the army and had shown resistance to preparations for the State of War.[72]

The 'verification' of party members proposed by Kania at the IV CC Plenum, which at the time had attracted considerable criticism, was therefore swiftly carried out in early 1982. Party membership fell to 2.597 million in mid-February 1982, which meant a rate of decline under the State of War more than twice as rapid as had been seen in the second half of 1981.[73] As well as being responsible for an intensified rate of decline, the verification had another special characteristic. Instead of the large number of resignations, which had previously been a cause of concern to party commentators, the bulk of the decline occurred as a result of 'a planned cleansing of the ranks'. In consequence of this nearly 12,000 members were expelled and a further 85,000 removed from party lists in 'a little over two months'. By the end of February the level of party membership had declined by 129,000 since the declaration of the State of War. The new leadership under Jaruzelski had applied the kind of party discipline called for by hard-liners like Siwak and representatives of party orthodoxy such as Bednarski. The review of staffing and appointment procedures was the first step in what was described as the return to the 'normal functioning' of the party. While this involved a rejection of the 'traditional, formal and bureaucratic approach to *nomenklatura*' it did mean that central control over appointments to party posts was to be fully restored and that the aberration of the unfettered pre-Congress elections was not to be repeated.[74]

After the resolute measures which followed the introduction of the State of War the members of the Central Committee, which finally met on 24 February, showed marked divergences of opinion on the developments now taking place in the party and the direction that future political developments should take. The Plenum itself met some two and a half months into military rule and had been awaited, as several speakers emphasised, with considerable impatience by the party rank and file. The delay, it was suggested, had been caused by major differences within the party leadership which were also reflected in the general nature of the decisions with which it concluded.[75] The move taken by Jaruzelski in declaring the State of War, resolutely acting against the 'counter-revolutionary threat' and thus removing the threat of civil war and a 'national tragedy' were, naturally enough, unanimously welcomed. But the precise significance of these developments for the party and the prospects they presented it with were the basis for the expression of differing views amongst those present at the VII Plenum (it was, too, the last one at which the diverse views expressed received broad coverage – after this the full proceedings of plenary discussions were no longer published in the standard party journal).

One source of disagreement was the nature and conduct of the verification of party membership outlined above. Koziołek, a pensioner from Bielsko-Biała, called for the purge of all who had stood on the sidelines or had been in opposition to the party in its moment of crisis, and suggested that mere expulsion from the party was not enough for those who had brought the country to the edge of disaster. Others, including the miner Skwara – expelled from Solidarity following his attacks on the union at the IV Plenum, demanded a similar verification of the Central Committee and the application within it of a military rigour. Three members of the Committee were indeed 're-called' from it (including the horizontal movement activist from Toruń, Marian Arendt) on the basis of a proposal put forward by CC secretary Barcikowski. But others, such as KW first secretary Wojtal, questioned the ideological basis of the verification, and criticised its reduction to the simple expulsion of members of the now suspended union.[76] The issue remained a controversial one and another provincial first secretary, Zawodziński (Białystok), later stated that 'personally I am against the word and whole idea of verification'.[77] The official view, however, enunciated at the end of the year by CC secretary Mokrzyszczak, was that the decline in party membership at this stage had occurred as a result of normal internal discipline procedures and that no 'verification' had taken place, thus leaving open the possibility of a more rigorous purge of party ranks if advisable.[78]

A second area of disagreement concerned the nature of the 'reinvigoration' of local party organs that many CC members noted and welcomed. Several reports stated that a relatively large number of primary organisations had held two or three meetings under the State of War, which was taken as an encouraging sign. The party *aktiv* had, said Witosławski (employed in a Piła porcelain factory), undergone a 'spontaneous enlargement' with the announcement of military rule as specially convened executive groups conducted interviews with members and expelled as a priority those who had been Solidarity activists. As such developments might suggest, the State of War had been received (in the words of school teacher Zdzisława Gębska) 'especially positively' by party members of long standing and they had been quick to take up active work, including the formation of 'groups of self-defence'. All this sounded suspiciously as though the new political conditions were merely providing the pretext for the return to active party work of those excluded from activity or restrained from traditional practices by the former pro-reform stance of the party leadership. A secretary of the Warsaw University party organisation who was interned for his unacceptable political activities noted how, on the second day of the State of War, a visit to provincial party headquarters showed that 'all those sectarian party functionaries who had long ago been democratically voted out of office were now back'. KW first secretary Kruk also expressed his view at the VII Plenum that, party unity having been previously threatened by the 'non-statutory structures of the younger generation' (a reference to the horizontal movement), it was now being threatened by analagous groupings amongst the older generation.[79]

Others also warned of attempts to return to the discredited practices of the Gierek period, of those 'who would like to regain the positions they had occupied before, to restore their power and former influence'. Łabęcki regarded as particularly dangerous to the party those who claimed to be 'true communists' but who in fact simply wanted a return to the pre-August situation. For some, said a foreman from Kraków, military rule had been celebrated as a victory and others began to 'conduct affairs as they had in the good old days of the 1970s'. He quoted in his support a well-known article by Colonel Kwiatkowski which had appeared in *Żołnierz Wolności*, the daily organ of the military authorities, and stated that 'there are still reasons to accuse the cadres of the party apparatus of acting in the old, inadequate ways'. In the guise of defending the party from external threats, it was stated, there should be no pretext for the 'defence of compromised administrators, of party and state pseudo-activists', an approach that had cost the party dear in the past and would again prove extremely harmful.[80] It seems evident that the positive view of party developments taken by some members of the committee was very much a reflection of the satisfaction of some groups at the crushing of the reform movement and the relaxing of the pressures previously exerted on the conservative forces. As the director of a CC department at this time later admitted, the VII Plenum was followed by a period when a decidedly rose-tinted view of developments was accepted within the party.[81]

The resurgence of conservative forces and the adherence to the line pursued by the harder-line faction within the party leadership provokes a number of questions about the political significance of the State of War, the intentions held by the joint party–state leadership dominated by Jaruzelski in introducing it, and the nature of the commitments and the pressures that had influenced developments within Polish political life and brought about its formulation. As suggested earlier, there is every reason to suppose that Jaruzelski shared Kania's desire for a political solution to the crisis, was willing to develop a conciliatory relation with Solidarity as a mass worker-based movement and to countenance the extension of democracy with the party. On the other hand, he was clearly not willing to tolerate any abandonment of the principles of democratic centralism, the political challenge of Solidarity to the leading role of the party or the continuing collapse of the economic and political structure. Both the political status of the regime and the military position of Poland within the alliance, moreover, would be more secure if the 'apolitical' role of the armed forces were preserved and the influence of the military was exercised behind the scenes rather than having to act in such a way that it could be interpreted as having usurped the position of the civilian party leadership. In itself the declaration of the State of War did not contradict these commitments or signify some *coup* against the party, although it clearly reflected the recognition of some degree of failure of the approach adopted by Kania and of the weakened position of the party leader after the IX Congress.

The situation was complicated, however, by the fact that a harder-line response to Solidarity and to the forces weakening central party leadership had long been argued for by such critics of Kania as Olszowski and Grabski. This had initially been reflected in the unwillingness to sign an agreement with the strikers at Gdańsk and elsewhere, in the support for the resistance offered by the apparatus both to Solidarity and to grass-roots pressure for renewal within the party, and in the lack of enthusiasm shown for the proposal of the Extraordinary Congress. It is highly likely that the Bydgoszcz crisis was engineered by these forces to provoke a confrontation between Solidarity and the party leadership and to discredit, if not eliminate, the Kania line. Having failed in this, criticism of the Kania approach continued during the preparations for the Congress and was further strengthened at the time of the Soviet letter in June, when a further direct attack on his leadership was mounted and calls for a forcible solution to the Solidarity problem were made. When Kania's resignation was achieved the implications for his critics, of which (as noted above) they were well aware, were somewhat ambiguous. The election of a party leader in uniform indicated the possibility of stronger party action and less tolerance of political indiscipline, but Jaruzelski had been closely identified with the now discredited approach taken by Kania.

Immediately after the declaration of the State of War, stories circulated that the act was not so much an attack on Solidarity as an attempt to 'forestall plans by the party's orthodox wing to take over power', or to forestall a 'confrontation' prepared by the party apparatus whose target was not only Solidarity but also the 'Jaruzelski group'.[82] Jaruzelski himself apparently persuaded the Church and Archbishop Glemp that his action had prevented a *coup* planned by 'Olszowski and a group of hard-liners, who had direct support from Moscow'.[83] While any such hard-line *coup* could well have provoked fiercer confrontations with the Polish public and Solidarity forces, and imposed sharper discipline within the party, the State of War introduced by Jaruzelski itself produced the conditions for quite a rigorous verification of the membership and facilitated the return to action of a sizeable number of 'experienced activists'. If there was a hard-line *coup* planned for December 1981, it is tempting to conclude that much of it was implemented by the Jaruzelski leadership and that talk of an alternative, anti-Jaruzelski action was designed to provide an alibi for those whose sympathies it wished not to alienate. It is quite possible, however, as Staniszkis suggests, that there were originally two scenarios in existence, one intended by Jaruzelski to develop a 'new control structure at the expense of the party', the other prepared by the 'ideologically oriented section of the party apparatus', which were in the event combined, possibly under Soviet influence.[84] Combination of the plans at a late stage may help to explain the sharp divergences evident at the VII Plenum.

Far less credible is the claim that the State of War was a 'catastrophe for the Polish party apparatus' and that Jaruzelski 'undertook a massive purge of apparatchik ranks' – if by that was meant the apparatus forces associated with the hard-line conspiracy. Although little evidence has been provided for such assertions they have been repeated by some observers. But such interpretations of the effect of the military *coup* have been based on misunderstandings of Jaruzelski's comments at the VII Plenum on staff changes in the party apparatus since 1980, some observers assuming that they referred to the few weeks of military rule.[85] Equally unlikely is the claim that the 'political army' (that is, its political administration) had undertaken a process of political infiltration that would by the mid-1980s have placed it in a position where it would 'have taken the place of the Communist Party and ruled Poland'. This scenario, it is asserted, was interrupted by the emergence of Solidarity and replaced by a military intervention that took place earlier than planned.[86] There is no real evidence to suggest that either the army or its political wing had ever contemplated any large-scale move against the party and its apparatus as a whole and it is by no means clear that the two forces could be differentiated sufficiently for that to happen.

The precise relationship between the military, particularly the Main Political Administration, and the party apparatus as a whole, and the way in which this relationship changed over time, must therefore remain something of a mystery. It is probably significant that Michnik was content to pose the question rather than provide the answer in this area: 'it is interesting to speculate whether Jaruzelski . . . has also destroyed the power of the party apparatus. Until now, the party apparatus ruled while the military functioned as its armed tool. Now, the military apparatus is at the helm while the party is a mere front'.[87]

Nevertheless, in view of the political prominence of Jaruzelski and other military figures, and of Jaruzelski's association with the reformist party centre in conjunction with other military pronouncements of a harder-line character, there must surely have been some tension both between the military and the civilian party and also within the army's political administration (as there had been within the central party establishment). In view of the advanced state of disintegration within the party–state leadership in the seventies and conflicts reported between the CC Secretariat and the General Staff over the nature of party control, it is likely that the army did retain considerable autonomy, although its voice could hardly be decisive.[88]

The political importance of the army in 1980 and 1981 had already given it an important position within central party organs. After the IX Congress it had nine members and seven deputies on the Central Committee, six members on the party Auditing Commission and sixteen on the Control Commission, the latter giving the military a particularly high representation (18% of the Commission) on a party organ that had special significance during the State of War and the exercise of extended disciplinary powers over the party membership.[89] The military occupied, then, important positions in leading party organs but were hardly able to dominate them by their level of representation. Military leaders were well placed to influence and act in consort with the party apparatus, but hardly to replace it or usurp all of its functions. Staniszkis states, indeed, that Jaruzelski had claimed in December that the apparatus was 'the only group where he could find support', although the level of cooperation rapidly declined, as the apparatus 'especially on the provincial level, felt that its interests were in jeopardy'. Both forces, it seemed, embarked on the State of War as a defensive operation, the 'last chance of preserving a relatively integrated apparatus of rule'.[90]

A major part of any argument against either military or party apparatus embarking on a course of action that would involve dominating the other or seriously undermining its role was the importance of both to the Soviet Union and the perception that both constituted priority Soviet interests. The significance of the military and its political apparatus to the Soviet Union is perhaps evident, but the importance of the party and its apparatus operating according to orthodox principles of democratic centralism is no less crucial: 'In dealing with Eastern Europe, the Soviet First Secretary has found that control over the policies and personnel of the fraternal parties is precisely what control over policies and personnel is in Soviet politics: the means and ends of all his endeavours'.[91] Control over policy and personnel could effectively be reduced to the intimate relationship with central party leadership, its apparatus and national staff that has persisted in Eastern Europe. The Soviet leadership thus understandably expressed disquiet from an early period not only about the political threat of an independent trade union, the diverse military and strategic implications, but also about the weakness of party leadership and the inadequacy of central party control.

Assessment of Soviet responses and intentions throughout the Solidarity period must also play a part in an evaluation of the State of War, as these are likely to have had a strong influence on both the hard-line orthodox and the military groups. Both had particularly close Soviet links and must have had a very good idea of their ally's intentions. The State of War was, moreover, declared with the specific objective of averting a 'national catastrophe' and the threat of direct Soviet intervention was certainly claimed to be a real one in late 1981. But while Soviet interest in Polish developments was a close and urgent one throughout the period, and had clearly given rise to growing disquiet as 1981 progressed, the precise nature and timing of decisive Soviet influences remain uncertain. Some observers were of the opinion that a Soviet invasion was imminent in December 1980, based on United States information that plans for such an intervention had already been completed and leaks from Polish CC members that the Soviets had been 'within hours of an order' for invasion.[92] Most, though, on the basis of more thoroughgoing analysis are sceptical of this claim and conclude, for example, that the threat of Soviet military intervention was 'never particularly credible' or that Soviet leaders simply showed 'an inability to take a decisive step'.[93]

While the possibility of invasion was obviously on the agenda and was probably favoured by some groups, it is more likely that the majority opinion had decided against such an option and chosen instead something like a 'great campaign of psychological pressure on Polish society as a whole' and a 'long-term strategy of indirect interventionism'.[94] The dangers of a Soviet military intervention were obviously great, given the size and location of Poland within the constellation of East European forces and national Polish attitudes towards their Eastern neighbour. The Soviet military was also embroiled in the Afghanistan conflict and was unlikely to risk a further confrontation, while the political leadership was still trying to preserve the remaining elements of detente and did not wish further to upset its international relations.[95] Nevertheless, there were clearly some who favoured a more direct early solution to the Polish problem and their inclinations were by no means politically insignificant, particularly in view of the coalitional nature of the Brezhnev leadership and the weakening of the leader's grip over the ruling group towards the end of a lengthy period of dominance.[96] According to one account, the Soviet military's preference for a solution by force of arms was the inspiration for Jaruzelski's eventual *coup*. Conflict within the Soviet leadership certainly seemed to be important in deliberations over the appropriateness of a military solution. Nor is it beyond the bounds of possibility that the disposition of forces within the United States administration favoured the exaggeration of the likelihood of Soviet invasion. The role of a Polish National Security Advisor, Z. Brzezinski, in the final weeks of the Carter administration could also have been crucial.[97]

Whatever the doubts over the preparedness of the Soviet leadership to settle the Polish problem by military force, there can be little uncertainty that they were impatient to see the restoration of communist order and that some contingency plan had to be made to secure strategic and military interests in the event of a general strike and the paralysis of communications with the German Democratic Republic – events threatened by developments in Poland in November 1980. Some analysts assert more definitely that the Polish military takeover was arranged in December 1980 following a decision not to go ahead with a Soviet invasion.[98] More likely, however, was the acceptance of the military option as one alternative and final Polish solution if developments got totally out of hand and Soviet pressure became irresistible. In late 1980, though, Kania was still developing his tactics of effecting some measure of compromise with Solidarity, while not actually conceding too much, and bowing to demands for an Extraordinary Party Congress, but not pressing too hard with arrangements to make sure that it actually took place. The diverse forces involved in these conflicting claims gave him some room for manoeuvre and the military outcome might well have seemed distant at the outset.

Nevertheless, it seems clear that some military plans were laid at this time. Immediately after the VII Plenum (1–2 December 1980) an unusual official reference was made to the national 'Military Council'.[99] More elaborate plans followed, and it was clear from the eventual internment process that lists had been drawn up in the spring of 1981. Military preparations were raised to a further level in April with the establishment of an independent Soviet command structure within Poland that would release domestic forces for internal activities, while unusually detailed vetting procedures of the Polish military were undertaken by the Soviet command in June and July.[100] It seems most likely, though, that a more definite decision for military rule was taken in the summer or early autumn. The relevant joint operational council is reported to have been established in late August or early September.[101] A sequence of developments in Soviet propaganda behaviour also suggested that decisive moves were being taken from early September to resolve the crisis, and these 'became clear-cut after Jaruzelski's advent to the key Party job in Warsaw'.[102]

While contingency plans involving some form of military rule had probably been drawn up to meet the possibility of national emergency in late 1980, then, it seems most likely that what was virtually a final decision on the use of the military to resolve the continuing conflicts was taken in August 1981. Kania's tactical freedom to play off the various political forces was greatly reduced after the Congress and both Soviet and domestic hard-line pressures were stepped up at this time. Following the conclusion of significant agreements with Solidarity further discussions were, as we have suggested, sabotaged by state representatives in early August and a policy of party offensiveness and continuing tension pursued. But this emphasis was also abandoned in the following month, with a surprising degree of agreement being reached on self-management and ideas of coalition rule being floated. As Ascherson had noted towards the end of September, 'Something has happened in the party leadership.'[103] This was the near-final decision on military intervention and the extended militarisation of the party leadership. The final attempts at 'national agreement' made in November cannot have been undertaken with much chance of success nor, on the part of much of the party–state leadership, can it have been hoped that there would be any major compromise.

The subsequent revelations of Colonel Kukliński shed further light on this and tend to bear out the sequence of developments outlined above. Preliminary preparations to introduce some form of State of War were, in fact, according to Kukliński, begun in August 1980 before the signing of the Gdańsk agreement. The plan developed further, though, as Soviet dissatisfaction and pressure increased in November of that year. Soviet plans to reconstitute the Polish leadership took shape and preparations to secure this by military intervention in early December were well advanced. Not surprisingly, the discovery of this had a traumatic effect on the Polish leadership and on General Jaruzelski in particular. It led them to intensify preparations for an internal military solution and it was only with the promise of this, timetabled for the spring of 1981, that Soviet invasion plans were shelved. As the time approached though, states Kukliński, the Polish government did not judge that the right conditions for a military solution had developed – although in the second half of March, in Bydgoszcz, some hard-liners seemed to think that the original plan should be followed. As the Polish leadership chose a line of relative conciliation and compromise with Solidarity the Soviets proceeded in early April to raise their level of military preparedness in Poland and to upgrade their forces and equipment. This background military presence remained a major factor throughout the subsequent political developments.

Thus, Jaruzelski and Kania were both committed at an early stage to a military solution but were horrified at the prospect of introducing it prematurely in the face of a massive and united domestic opposition. Kania's distaste for this 'solution' was, writes Kukliński, maintained and even hardened throughout 1981. Jaruzelski, though, became less resistant to its introduction and was more persuaded of the necessity for its introduction by mid-June (the time of the 'Moscow letter'). His views increasingly diverged from those of Kania and the contrast became critical, writes Kukliński, in early September. Kania's continuing opposition to the imminent introduction of a State of War put an end to his career as party leader and his replacement by Jaruzelski merely confirmed this in October. By November, then, the decision to apply military methods was 'virtually irrevocable'.

General Kiszczak was, perhaps, not essentially wrong when he asserted that 'The preparation of plans is not contradictory with the truth that the decision to introduce the State of War was taken at the last moment', but the 'final decision' claimed to fall at the end of November must have been one of a series that brought the military solution into ever greater prominence.[104] Jaruzelski's claim to be following Kania's original policy of conciliation in the autumn of 1981 cannot therefore be seen as an accurate reflection of the tenor of his leadership and the ruling group as a whole had moved significantly in the direction of the policy long argued for by the hard-liners and supported by the higher levels of the apparatus. Nor can the State of War be interpreted as an attempt briefly to suspend 'extremist activity' in order to permit any further development of political renewal as conceived by the party centre before the Congress. The State of War reflected the aspirations and activities of the forces of reaction in the party and represented the application of decisive measures against the process and political threat that had got underway in the summer of

1980. It was also, by this stage, very much a move for self-preservation, as any form of crisis-resolution undertaken independently by the Soviet Union would surely have resulted in the political demise of much of the party centre, as well as its revisionist wing and the Solidarity movement.[105]

The provincial view of the State of War

Apart from disagreements over the verification of the party membership and the effect of the State of War on inner-party life, exchanges at the VII Plenum also exposed differences between provincial secretaries in terms of their appraisal of its implications for the role of party. One view, put by first secretary Wojtal (Krosno), was that 'The State of War does not place any restriction on party activities and has been very helpful for us in working out many problems. It has facilitated the settlement of many internal affairs'. The party, in fact, could operate 'normally' as if the State of War did not exist (and as if, presumably, there had been no Solidarity and the 1980 strikes had not happened). This view was shared by General Łukasik, deputy chief of political affairs in the air force, and later in the year to be appointed KW first secretary himself, who similarly disagreed with views that the State of War 'encumbers the operation of the party, restricts its role and jurisdiction'. He again used the description of the militarised regime as providing an 'umbrella' for the party, 'protecting it to some extent from the odium for taking some necessary, though unpopular decisions'.

The view of first secretary Zenon Czech (Przemyśl) was rather different. His prime concern was with the public presentation of the role of the party and this, he felt, was detrimental to party interests because party action was portrayed by some writers ('not excluding those in party publications') as only an 'auxiliary force, alongside a state administration which was actually ruling'. The motives for not publicising the role of the party during the early military period were, he felt, understandable to party members but this was not the case with other views that had appeared, some suggesting that military rule reflected the political collapse of the party and that the army had emerged as some kind of 'third force'. Czech stated that the military could not simply be presented as some kind of non-party force in Poland as 'The army is not just the military branch but in its whole ideological identity constitutes a section of the party'. The notion of the party as an auxiliary force, moreover, was not simply antithetical to the principles of socialism but also threatened the 'generally expressed [acknowledgement] of the needed democratisation of social life'.

A related point was made with considerably more emphasis in *Polityka* which argued that the Politburo's *Instrukcja* meant a 'significant restriction of inner-party democracy' and warned that 'it is easy to become accustomed to extraordinary powers'.[106] It was suggested that the restrictions were not intended to remain in force throughout the whole State of War period but only during the 'first weeks (months ?) of party work under the new conditions' (uncertainty in the original). Reference was made, however, to a speech by Barcikowski delivered to CC workers in which it was indicated that they were essentially unrestricted in their scope, which was left to the decision of the party's executive organ (in fact, the *Instrukcja* remained in force throughout the period of the State of War and was not withdrawn until August 1983). The writer (an academic from Poznań University) drew further attention to the danger of perpetuating the alienation of the Polish people from the authorities and the need to develop the party as a force of integration.

This, indeed, was a point emphasised by many of the KW first secretaries who spoke at the VII Plenum. While many of the worker-activists, from amongst whom were found most of the speakers at the meeting, endorsed the party purge and were eager for the leadership to pursue the hard line it now seemed to be espousing, the KW secretaries displayed more awareness of the politically exposed position of the party and the dangers of the minority position it was placing itself in. The party, stated Brożek (Nowy Sącz), was only surviving 'from meeting to meeting' and the life of the organisation in a broader sense was far more problematic, while Kamiński (Zamość) noted that the 'rejuvenation within the party ranks' (much applauded by some activists) had a very closed character and did not feed into any dialogue with the rest of society. Kruk (Lublin) also wondered how far any rejuvenation was just the 'effect of the work of the organisational *aktiv*' and emphasised that the basis of future party activity had to be the aspiration towards social acceptance.[107] For the provincial secretaries, then, it was not so much the lack of party authority and the unpromising nature of the State of War in this respect that was worrying, as the disregard of the problem itself by many on the Central Committee and their willingness to rely on the power of the military and security forces to ease the way for the party. This, however, could never help the restoration of the leading role of the party and merely ignored the continuing authority crisis.

Kruk was one of the most experienced provincial secretaries, having been in post since 1977 and, following the departure of Fiszbach, being one of the two longest-serving KW first secretaries. This kind of plain speaking was significant and reflected an awareness on the part of the more seasoned members of the Central Committee of the obstacles facing the party in restoring its position. As General Milczarek had emphasised, the party suffered its greatest losses where Solidarity had been strongest, in production plants and amongst the working class, and this imposed particular difficulties on the party in the reassertion of its identity. This fact was not glossed over either by the vice-director of the CC Organisation Department, who placed particular emphasis on the 'deep disorientation' of workers in the larger industrial plants. The number of strikes following the declaration of the State of War was estimated at some 200 and resistance was officially admitted to have been encountered in eight provinces. Where such developments had happened they had been joined by party members, 'including members of the party executive', and in some cases 'their organisers had even been the secretaries of the party'.[108]

As the experienced members of the party staff were well aware, the situation in which the party had been placed was a grim one and it is significant that at the VII Plenum their attention was caught by the prime need of the party to gain public acceptance and to establish itself as a viable political force in the eyes of Polish society. It provided a clear parallel to the theme of 'credibility' (*wiarygodność*) that had run through the 1980 VI Plenum – although for obvious reasons the analogy was not drawn in February 1982. Developments since September and October 1980 had certainly not contributed to the restoration of party authority but had left it further weakened in terms both of membership numbers and of political effectiveness. The disappointing outcome of the policy of renewal in the party and of the Congress, closely linked with the resistance of much of the party establishment and the resistance of the apparatus, placed the party in some ways in a worse position than it had been in 1980 when much of the responsibility for the failure could be laid at the door of the former leadership. The hard-line activists could to some extent close their eyes to this problem, but this could hardly be the case for provincial secretaries who were supposed to assume general political responsibility within the locality and to exercise an overall leading role.

KW secretary Basiak (Tarnobrzeg) directed attention to the 'wall of indifference' that stood between the party and the industrial workforce and the importance of winning over the 'non-party *aktiv*, which enjoyed a high level authority'. In this, he said, it was essential for the party to press for the implementation of reform although in this area, he plainly admitted, it had a distinctly poor record: 'From the very beginning, burdened with the habits of old ways of thinking and acting, we have concentrated our whole intellectual effort on finding ways to dismantle reform'. Dąbrowski (Zielona Góra) stressed the importance of concrete party activity and the presentation of a coherent plan of action rather than reference to vague plans concerned with 'rebuilding public confidence in the party' which, he said, was in itself more likely to engender mistrust. Specific positive suggestions, however, were not made at the Plenum.

The provincial committees were, in contrast, given specific directives of a negative character and the resolution of the Plenum allotted a particular role to the committees in bringing to a halt 'all movements, structures, forms and seminars of a non-statutory character'. They were, therefore, enjoined to continue with the process of increasing central control and purging the party of all undesirable members. A decision related to the organisational interests of the provincial committee was the endorsement of the development of the 'regional centres of party work' (ROPP: *Rejonowe Ośrodki Pracy Partyjnej*) proposed by Kania at the IV Plenum. Favourable comments about their work were made at the VII Plenum and the growth of their activities appears to have coincided with the early State of War period. In Rzeszów province seven such centres had been set up in the second half of December drawing on the 'large group of experienced social and political activists who had been with the former *powiat* committees', that is, the old district committees which had disappeared in the 1975 administrative reform. It was precisely this group of former party workers ('whose activeness had declined for various reasons – often because no tasks had been suggested to them') that was targeted for the ROPP in order not to poach staff from other local committees.[109]

The establishment of the regional party centres at this time seemed to indicate that under the protection of the military not only were some endeavouring to return to the conditions of party work that had pertained prior to August 1980 but that there were also tendencies to return to the situation that had existed before the administrative and party reform of 1975. CC member Mikulski, himself an individual farmer, complained that since the reform party organisations in the countryside had been deprived of effective supervision.[110] Certainly, Jaruzelski had little specific to say at the Plenum about the intended direction of future developments. Not surprisingly, the horizontal structures were unreservedly condemned as 'they would have led sooner or later to the liquidation of the party' and the threat of civil war strongly emphasised, both factors underwriting the perceived need for party centralisation and the leadership's determination to strengthen its control. Yet there was no disavowal of the former political line: 'There is not and cannot be any turn away from the policy of reform, which is an integral part of the programme of socialist renewal.' Neither were there any negative comments made on inner-party democratisation – he identified no specific faults in the pre-Congress election campaign, which was strongly criticised by others. Other statements made by Jaruzelski were notably vague, though. Charges that socialism was not susceptible to reform were dismissed and socialism was described as 'reformable in the best sense of the word' (although what this meant was not made clear), the need for democratic centralism was summed up in the imprecise phrase 'as much democracy as centralism', and the need for 'a new style' of party work was noted.[111] It was evident that a militarised form of rule had been introduced without any clear conception of how the party was to develop under the new conditions.

The reassertion of central control

The process by which the central authorities enhanced their control over the party organisation met with a number of obstacles. One important one was the view held by key party organs on how discipline should be exercised within the party under the State of War. The IV Plenum of the Central Party Control Commission met on 4 March and commented on the problems in this area, one of which concerned the improper attitude taken by provincial control commissions at the start of the State of War. Most of them had been preoccupied with the investigation of party members suspected of abuse of office and had neglected political and ideological problems, although 'as is known, the ideological and organisational state of the party was highly worrying at the time'.[112] Before redirecting the activities of the provincial control commissions, the central party control organ often had to effect changes in the composition of the provincial body. In the case of the Wrocław commission this meant the expulsion of 14 of its 43 members, 7 of whom had been in the commission's presidium. The vetting of provincial authorities also extended to the verification of KW members, of whom many in Gdańsk for example were loath to sever their links with Solidarity.[113] Following the extensive changes that had been made in the composition of the party organs prior to the Congress the reassertion of central control under the State of War involved changes in the nature of the provincial authorities as well.

In the process of restoring party unity within this conception the main target was the 'opportunist-revisionist tendency which has always constituted and may still constitute the main threat to the real consolidation of the party'. The most fearsome manifestation of this was the horizontal structures which by the summer of 1982 had been expunged from the party. Nevertheless, there were still 'tendencies to anarchistic behaviour in inner-party life' associated with particular ways of interpreting the principles embodied in the Party Statute. The consolidation of party unity, even under the conditions of the State of War and the exercise of special executive powers, thus seemed to be less than fully secure. An article gave full details of the development of the horizontal movement in Toruń (where the Consultative-Coordinating Commission of Party Organisations had been officially wound up after the VII Plenum) and stressed its fractional character. It admitted, though, that traces of the movement still remained and created problems for the recovery of party identity. Some key questions remained unanswered: 'Why could the opportunist current take the initiative in many party centres so effectively, why did it not meet with more decisive resistance?'[114]

Problems involving the local party organs which impeded the imposition of party discipline were not restricted to the provincial committees and provincial control commissions. Local party revision commissions, concerned more with the effective operation of the party as an organisation rather than with its political side, were composed of activists elected in 1981 who required considerable preparation and training before they were thought capable of executing their duties. In the middle of 1982 many of the local commissions were still 'little active or operated only in a narrow range'. The provincial auditing commissions were judged to be in a better state, although the formal requirement of the WKR (*Wojewódzka Komisja Rewizyjna*: Provincial Auditing Commission) chairman's participation in KW executive meetings was not always met. Party organs were sometimes unwilling to submit to WKR scrutiny, while apparatus workers often showed an 'improper attitude' to commissions' tasks and competence. The power apparatus still included 'certain groups with an interest in weakening social control over their activities, of avoiding this control, of placing themselves above work people'.[115] The State of War and the militarisation of party leadership did not seem to have helped the solution of this perennial problem of inner-party discipline, which had been a critical point of weakness under Gierek and to which the horizontal movement and freer elections within the party seemed to offer an alternative solution. Now, however, they were clearly off the agenda.

In a situation where the purification of party ranks was a major priority and much concern was shown over the recent attractiveness of 'opportunism and revisionism', it was not surprising that matters of ideology received new emphasis. The draft of an ideological programme ('What we are fighting for, where we are aiming') was presented to the VII Plenum and provided a focus for discussion throughout the party in the following period. In April the first All-Poland Ideology and Theory Party Conference was held in Warsaw. As part of this effort renewed interest was paid to the youth organisations, the younger generation having been particularly susceptible to the political views current in Solidarity and having made up a large proportion of those who had recently left the party. The IX Plenum of the Central Committee, held in July, was also devoted to youth affairs. Underestimation of the role of ideology was seen by some as a major failing of the Gierek approach which had been responsible for the incapacity of the party to act as a mobilising force when faced with the political challenge of Solidarity.

The ideological emphasis, however, was associated particularly with the approach of the orthodox party faction and hard-liners rather than the centre with which Jaruzelski had identified himself. It was espoused by those who wished to see a more extensive party purge and were happy to see the formation of a more limited but ideologically purer party organisation. It arose, therefore, from a limited part of the leadership and did not gain the more general sponsorship within it that might have been anticipated. Many were suspicious both of the implications of the ideological emphasis and of those who promoted it. It was not, for example, seen as any kind of solution to the authority deficit suffered by the party – the recent experience of the party had shown that 'its social authority depends less on the ideas it promulgates than on the degree to which they are realised'.[116] The renewed emphasis on ideology therefore appeared to have little direct relevance to the building of party authority and to the practical problems facing the organisation, as many activists were aware. The loss by the party of its ideological identity was not really reversed during this period and 'the long process of de-ideologization of the PZPR was completed under martial law'.[117]

The main line of development within the party structure that facilitated the enhancement of central party control concerned the ROPP,
the regional centres of party work. As noted earlier, the *aktiv* drawn on
by the ROPP was predominantly that discarded or ignored following
the 1975 reform and, in view of the acute shortage of party lecturers
that developed after August 1980, the function of *lektor* was more and
more performed by 'activists from the former *powiat*, whose value had
not always been perceived or recognised in the past, and who after the
elimination of the *powiat* were sometimes just expelled or forgotten'.
Work-ties formed within the *powiat* had, it appeared, not necessarily
disappeared with its abolition and the 'links had survived, the ROPP
now having sanctioned them in some way'.[118] The operation of the
ROPP, then, not only compensated for more recent shortcomings but
also filled a 'natural gap' in the party organisation between provincial
centre and local organisation that had persisted since 1975. Graver
problems had emerged more recently, though, including the 'low level
of leadership effectiveness of party organisations', the 'inadequate use
of the instruments of the cadres policy', and 'inappropriate response to
the infringement of ideological/moral principles and norms'. In Skierniewice, it appears, this involved considerable reorganisation of the
party in the countryside: 213 small organisations were amalgamated or
dissolved and 186 placed under constant surveillance 'as proper independent operation could not be assured' – the great majority of these
involving rural organisations.[119]

In some cases measures had been taken to make good these defects
at an early stage, and a KW post in Kielce was earmarked for the
coordination of party work on a regional basis as early as September
1981. According to the official account, the ROPP were established by a
CC Secretariat decision in December, but it is clear that steps to reas-
semble the former *powiat* workers had been taken soon after the Congress and that the project was under way before December 1981. It was
decided, for one thing, that cadre issues were a category that could be
resolved more easily within the ROPP framework as 'there began again
to emerge the view that elective posts did not necessarily have to be
filled by local people'. The regional centres, in short, facilitated the
resurrection of the practice of 'parachuting' officials into local organisations.[120] The ROPP fitted easily into the conventional system of staff
appointments and party records showed that they had strong links
with the pre-reform party structure. Thus, during the next two years or
so, four people were appointed KW secretaries who had been ROPP
secretaries in 1982. In three cases they had directed a ROPP based on a

powiat in which they had formerly worked as secretary. In two cases they had left the apparatus after the 1975 reform for training at the party's Higher School of Social Sciences.

While this line of activity helped the party 'to move on to the offensive' it did not happen without some degree of friction. Criticism was heard from the Szczecin provincial committee that the establishment of the ROPP showed a return to the old *powiat* structure, an allegation denied by a former *powiat* worker. The incumbent party secretaries, though, were by no means all enthusiastic about the innovation. It left the role of the commune secretary and his capacity for independent decision-making considerably open to question and there were complaints of the '"administration" of party organs by comrades from the region'.[121] Accounts which contained nothing but praise for the new structure also took care to note its consultative character and to dissociate its activity from the new executive powers endowed by the Politburo's *Instrukcja* of December 1981. The new ROPP directors, wrote one observer, were 'not so much "super-secretaries" as older and more experienced comrades who could prompt and even advise some people'. They had a tendency to 'approach matters in too much detail', informed another report which stressed that the ROPP director should not 'take over the statutory duties of the local party organ'.[122]

From the point of view of the peasants, it seemed that 'under martial law the old system came back into normal operation'.[123] The early experiences of the regional centres gave further evidence of the problems facing the Jaruzelski leadership in its commitment to the principles of party action elaborated at the IX Congress while also dedicated to halting the organisational dissolution of the party. By destroying the horizontal movement and purging or neutralising the forces most committed to party reform there remained little to counteract the tendencies which sought to preserve the conventional dominance of the apparatus and to restore its personnel to their former position in the party organisation. In the terminology of a slogan current at the time, the old was coming back.

7   Political normalisation and party authority

Military rule and party leadership

Jaruzelski's *coup* had not been mounted against the PZPR leadership or against the party as an institution; it had more the nature of an internal rearrangement of party–state forces and an upgrading of the role of the 'party in uniform', led by the army's Main Political Administration. Nevertheless, it did direct attention to the party's association with institutions concerned with the concentration and mobilisation of the power resources of the Polish state and it de-emphasised the role of the party as an institution of political authority and an agency of political and ideological leadership in orthodox Marxist-Leninist terms. The *coup* represented a departure from the normal procedures of party–state rule in so far as it meant a qualification of the party's claim to exercise general leadership on the basis of a dominant political authority. As communist rule departed from its association with party authority some of the major party organs found themselves bypassed and their leaders downgraded in political importance. Provincial first secretaries had shown themselves to be divided at the VII Plenum in their views of these developments; there could be little doubt, though, that the militarisation of party rule affected their political standing and gave rise to some significant tensions and political conflicts.

Observers differ in their views of the significance and permanence of the changing political position of the provincial party leadership. In keeping with his hypothesis concerning the well-elaborated plan for the militarisation of the Polish political system, Malcher does not minimise the political role of the army and notes reports that 'confirm that the WKOs [*Wojewódzkie Komitety Obrony* – Provincial Defence Committees, the provincial equivalents and subordinate agencies of the supreme military body, the Committee for National Defence, KOK] are concerned with all aspects of life in a region in the same way as did the Regional Party Committee in the days when the party was still fulfilling its leading role'.[1] They were headed by the provincial governor (*wojewoda*) and composed of 'deputy Governors, provincial PZPR First Secretaries, the provincial MO [police] commander and the chief of the military provincial staff'. Sanford also reports an informal Polish government briefing which stated that some 18,000 officers and NCOs had taken over decision-making functions from 'discredited party *apparatchiks*'.[2] This statement is hardly credible in view of the fact that the entire party apparatus did not officially reach this total, but is perhaps more reasonable if it was really staff in government and state institutions who were referred to. Some noted the 'major consequences' of the formal elimination of the overall political responsibility of the provincial first secretary, particularly in relation to his control over *nomenklatura* appointments.[3]

Others have maintained that the State of War 'did not remove power from the three major components of the "inner party": the party apparatus, police and security officers, and the economic administrators'. Rather, it erected for them a 'protective screen' and did not produce any fundamental redistribution of power within the 'inner party', although it clearly brought about some change in the relations between them.[4] According to some views the party retained considerable autonomy and resisted initiatives of what was described as the 'military junta'. Certain social commissions, originally established in work-places as 'a "purely technical" apparatus of the economic administration' were taken over by local party organs and used by them as a means of self-rehabilitation. There were also examples of 'three-cornered battles' between the military commissar, the executive of the local party organisation and the district party apparatus.[5] A further report of the 'Experience and the Future' group (*Doświadczenie i Przyszłość*) concluded that 'one thing is certain – that as a result of the State of War the position of the cadres of the power apparatus, both of the military and party, has been strengthened and reinforced'. Because of the greater freedom of action now available to the party apparatus it appeared to be securing the removal against the policy of the central authorities of good experts from the administration whom it did not regard as ideologically desirable.[6]

The fate of party personnel themselves has also been subject to conflicting interpretations. One claim was that 'by June 1982 no less than 5,000 out of the PZPR's 11,000 full-time political party workers had been replaced', a figure that in fact approximates with the turnover that had occurred in the apparatus since the fall of Gierek. The head of the CC Cadres Department actually announced at the end of 1982 that so far 750 had been removed from the apparatus during the period of military rule, most of these having entered party service under the special conditions of the post-August 1980 interlude.[7] In terms of established party workers, then, the 'military threat' may well have been very limited indeed. General Łukasik, who replaced Skrzypczak as KW first secretary in Poznań in May 1982, claimed that his appointment was in fact the only one made in the KW apparatus under the Politburo *Instrukcja*.[8]

But even if the power of the provincial committees and the party apparatus was not fundamentally changed or undermined by the State of War, this does not mean that the role of the provincial secretary was not diminished and qualified by the new mode of rule. The erection of a 'protective screen' for the central agencies of communist rule was accompanied, Morawski suggests, by a redefinition of relations between them. Economic administrators and the state apparatus were, for a number of reasons, far less vulnerable to the interference of the party staff. In terms of individuals it was the influence of the party secretary that was most dramatically reduced, particularly at province and commune levels. The formal party monopoly was suspended and relations were equalised between the representatives of the major power structures – local governor, police chief, military commissar, party first secretary. The situation was complicated, however, by the fact that the pattern of relationships was not identical in all provinces and that any one of those figures (or none of them) might dominate in a given province, according to local conditions and the individuals involved.[9] Such indeterminacy and local variation contributed to the broadness of the range of views expressed on the position of provincial secretaries during this period.

Some provincial secretaries expressed their doubts about the militarisation of communist rule at the VII Plenum, while Białystok secretary Zawodziński admitted that the events of 13 December had been a 'certain defeat for the party' and that some 'felt themselves pushed aside after the taking of power, in a manner of speaking, by the military'. In the first weeks there had been, he stated, some 'sharp discussions and differences of opinion', although a 'common language' with the commissars had been quickly found. Relations had been less than smooth in some areas where 'there had been attempts to restrict the role of the committees'.[10] In contrast to some of the expectations expressed in late 1981 (and noted above in chapter 6) which had foreseen the resort to some kind of exceptional or military regime, the political role of the military was not restricted to a short, one- or two-month period. Over three months after the announcement of the State of War, in late March, a further set of military operational groups was set to work to check agricultural preparations for the spring, while detailed military checks on the system of administration in individual provinces continued. The precise reason for this was by no means apparent to all party workers. 'Why', asked one commentator, 'must the army do what the party and its members should and are obliged to undertake; why does not the party inspire such activities?' It was difficult to understand, he went on, why local party organisations numbering several hundred members could not muster thirty or forty individuals, possibly involving some members of the KW problem commissions, to carry out such checks.[11]

The same writer provided part of the answer to this question himself some three months later, when he reported on the rechecking of the Piła province administration by the military authorities. The results of the first investigation had been received passively by the Provincial Office and 'its conclusions and recommendations treated offhand-edly'. In consequence of the second check the military governor, his deputy and numerous directors and other employees were dismissed. Such investigation involved, of course, the operation of the state administration and not of the party. But the supervision of the admin-istration was a prime responsibility of the provincial party committee which military rule had not removed from it. It was not realistic to claim that the party was able to resume its leading role in this respect.[12] Toruń province was also subjected to a second check. As the results of the first appeared to have been ignored or had not been acted on properly, the governor and his deputy were also fired there.[13] By the autumn six provinces had been checked by the Armed Forces In-spectorate, one consequence being that five people were expelled from the party and twenty received some form of party punishment.[14]

It was, apparently, Jaruzelski himself who introduced the concept of the reinspection and stressed that an inspection was completed only when the conclusions of the initial inspection had been acted on and its recommendations implemented.[15] In contrast to the party, it could be claimed that the military 'turned out to be an efficient administrator' and were successful in keeping the bureaucrats on their toes.[16] On the other hand, the fact that stern measures had to be taken after the recheck in Piła and Toruń suggested to others that the military representatives had themselves 'rapidly succumbed to the influences of corrupt local coteries'.[17] Despite its modified role under the State of

War, the party was by no means unaffected by the exposure of these shortcomings. Apart from the application of various forms of party punishment, the recheck of Toruń province was also followed by the resignation of KW first secretary Heza. Much of the blame, it appears, could have been attached to the Provincial People's Council and ascribed to the inactivity of its chairman (this was certainly the opinion of the party journalist who reported on the case).[18] But the acceptance by the KW first secretary of the responsibility for the state of affairs in the province was no act of cavalier self-sacrifice and reflected the continuing failure of the party to resume its leading role.

In formal terms, the KW first secretary still held overall responsibility for what happened in the province, while something over half the employees in the Toruń province office (*Urząd Wojewódzki*, the government body responsible for local administration) were party members (as many as 230 of the 426 employees). Moreover the 'leading and directing role of the party released it from the obligation to undergo that form of administrative control' and the State of War clearly did not imply lowering of the expectations held of leading party personnel or of major party organs. As the chairman of the Central Auditing Commission (*Centralna Komisja Rewizyjna*) stated soon after these developments, the effectiveness of party checking and its ability to carry through decisions 'has not been and is still not one of our stronger suits'.[19] Under the conditions of the State of War it was clearly the military rulers who were carrying the major responsibility for the workings of government and the state administration. The party's role was now a more specialised one and it was concentrating on the enhancement of ideological and organisational unity within its own structures, leading to a reduction both of its interest in and its capacity to influence other political and administrative institutions.

The continuing weakness of the party and its ineffectiveness as an agency of political rule was only one aspect of the uncertainty surrounding the issue of how far the militarisation of the Polish political system had penetrated and of how long military rule might be expected to last. Disagreements persisted about the nature of the approach that should be taken by the authorities as a whole towards Polish society, and there appeared to be little resolution during 1982 of the ambiguities in Jaruzelski's position that were apparent at the beginning of the year. Under the restrictive conditions imposed by the State of War, moreover, there was little opportunity for the public airing of the different views. One means that was available, however, was the examination and description of relevant historical experiences and the passing of historical judgments on situations that were not so distant from the contemporary Polish situation. A leading example of such parallels was the post-1956 development of Hungary. Numerous articles on its economic policies appeared, and some also paid attention to the political aspects of the comparison.

One article, in particular, stressed Kadar's refusal to take the apparently easier way out of the crisis by relying exclusively on 'administrative methods' of maintaining power, and the importance of his 'open', centrist political approach which prepared the way for subsequent economic reform. A major point repeatedly enunciated, with obvious import for the Polish situation, was the Hungarians' determination to fight a *'simultaneous* effective battle on two fronts: against revisionism and dogmatism' and the determination not to treat 'dogmatism as something less harmful than revisionism or a less threatening disease'.[20] These statements, with their obvious allusion both to the ideological orthodoxy that was being imposed under military rule and to the position taken by Gomułka in 1957, were a reflection of the continuing conflicts within the central political leadership and a clear criticism of the leadership's current line.

Another indication of the dilemma facing the Polish leaders was the reference to Kadar's view in 1957 that local party organisations were concentrating so much attention on 'the elimination of alien elements from the factories that they were not capable of devoting sufficient attention to political work amongst the masses'. The major slogan associated with the Hungarian approach was, of course, the statement that 'he who is not against us is with us'. Without direct rebuttal this view received a major qualification in June 1982 by the deputy head of the army's Main Political Administration, who concluded an article with the statement that '"he who is not against us may be with us". That is our historical opportunity and our necessity.'[21] There was clearly no inclination from this quarter towards excessive tolerance of unorthodox political forces. It was clear that under the cover of historical analysis the existence of major differences in political orientation were being marked out and the conditions of future party leadership defined.

The references to Hungary were relevant not only because of the parallel with the post-1956 developments but also because, in 1982, Hungary was able to present an example of a relatively successfully reformed communist economy, in marked distinction to the progressive deterioration of Polish economic conditions. Although a reform programme had been slowly worked out in 1981, conditions under the State of War were not propitious for its implementation. Blazyca concluded that, in fact, 'throughout 1982, the economic reform barely functioned', while Ryszard Bryk, the Vice-Minister of Mines who had previously served as a KW first secretary between 1976 and 1981, suggested that economic performance might in fact have been better if no attempts at reform had been made at all.[22]

Political developments had affected the possibility of reform in several ways. Not surprisingly, the opportunities for extending workers' self-government under military rule were severely restricted. In a highly critical survey of the situation published in June 1982, one contributor suggested that, whatever the policy adopted at the centre, any moves towards self-government were countered by the practice of the administration and by local political forces. Included in this was the practice of local party organisations who interpreted the need to recover their political position as meaning that they should 'rule by strong-arm methods in all matters'.[23] Many good managers had been sacked or demoted as a result of political conflicts in such places as Warsaw and Gdańsk through the imposition of the State of War.[24] Managers were replaced on more than one occasion in some plants and the process of administration was clearly weakened for much of 1982.[25] Others directed attention to the attitudes of central authorities, whose position was clearly strengthened by the conditions prevailing in 1982, and were not always cooperative when plans for self-government were actually agreed within the plant and with the participation of the local party organisation. The position of the branch ministries, indeed, was thought to have undergone further strengthening from the mid-point of 1982.[26] As the year wore on, the reformist credentials of the military regime grew increasingly difficult to sustain and more doubts were expressed about its capacity to retain its autonomy from conflicting tendencies within the party and its apparatus. It is possible, wrote one commentator in November, that the 'post-December system and those operating within it may be gradually pushed towards "harder", more conservative positions, distancing themselves from reformist projects'.[27]

References to the experience of other communist countries were also brought into the debate over this issue to highlight positions it was otherwise difficult to develop under current Polish conditions. An article on party–military relations in China was clearly relevant here, its major point being that the lengthy involvement of the military in political rule that had begun with the Cultural Revolution was proving very difficult to undo and that the political role played by the army had given rise to significant ideological differences between the military and the party authorities – an important point of divergence having been the army's resistance to economic modernisation.[28] This view has also received some substantiation in Western sources which have identified a group of critics centred on the Chinese army's General Political Department who attacked the abandonment of orthodox ideological values and the new emphasis on materialism that was associated with the modernisation programme.[29] Foreign parallels thus suggested a military association with ideological conservatism rather than reform tendencies within the party and, moreover, a reluctance to restore the more conventional leading role of the party in situations perceived as politically uncertain.

Resistance appeared to be mounting to the indefinite extension of military rule in Poland, and even gained some expression within the public arena. But others were determined that there should be no premature military withdrawal. One indication of this was the leaked views of Colonel Wiślicki, military commissar of radio and television networks. He stated in March that 'The State of War in Poland will last until the Party is reborn, and I'm not thinking here about the Party's bureaucracy for that will be reborn quickly – I'm thinking here about [the] rank and file in big enterprises.'[30] More official views from within the military leadership also confirmed that the rebirth of the party would be a lengthy process, one that was 'complicated and diverse, both as to its social content and the rate of change in the different fields of party activity'. This view was not restricted to military representatives and could also be heard from party leaders, including those in the provinces. KW secretary Krenz (Koszalin) thus affirmed that, while the State of War had put a halt to the growing tide of anarchy which had severely weakened the party, 'it would be an error to assume that the opponents are defeated', and pointed to the continuing need to verify the work of party groups, 'many of whom lead only a formal existence'.[31]

The political stability that was created by military rule was therefore a precarious one. There was clearly some conflict involved in the relations between the party and the military, even if, as argued earlier, the party–army complex within the communist political system may most constructively be seen as a 'dual-role élite'. To judge from some of the statements reported above, there would appear to have been at least a certain tension between the views of General Jaruzelski, who seemed to have some genuine – if highly qualified – commitment to economic reform and political centrism, and the harder-line views of those like Colonel Wiślicki, who were more decisively committed to the imposition of unchallenged central control and for whom the undoubted priority was the eradication of all political opposition. Similar conflicts, of course, were clearly evident within the party itself. Thus, while the military solution had preserved the political system and defended parts of its apparatus from further democratisation and social criticism, the stability it achieved was a temporary one that appeared to promise little for a more viable consolidation of the system which would involve the restoration of party leadership and the assertion of party authority over Polish society.

It was not surprising, in view of the military threat to their formal political position combined with their political openness to local pressures, that a number of provincial party leaders voiced their awareness of the tentative nature of the military stabilisation and the dangers of shelving the reform proposals. Thus, the protests emanating from provincial party leaders at the slow progress made towards reform in 1982 were by no means identical with the more radical reformist currents of the previous year but were a more sober response to the absence of party authority and the problems of maintaining the semblance of party rule under current conditions. Nevertheless, even this muted criticism seems to have been sufficient cause for the central authorities to step up the rate of turnover of provincial first secretaries. The leading provincial reformer, Tadeusz Fiszbach, had been removed from Gdańsk at the commencement of the State of War. Both Kruk (Lublin) and Kamiński (Zamość), who had expressed reservations about the implications of military rule at the VII Plenum, had been removed from the provincial leadership by the end of the year. Skrzypczak, the horizontalists' candidate in Poznań, lost his position in May, while in Kraków, Krystyn Dąbrowa, one of the last major reformist figures, resigned in October.

Of the eleven KW first secretaries who left their posts in the year following 13 December 1981, seven were clearly of a reformist bent and had either publicly expressed some doubts about current policy or else carried party responsibility for areas which had seen major local resistance to the central party and military powers. A further two had been elected during the democratically organised party conferences of June 1981 (Jasiński in Legnica, Kropnicki in Chełm), as had Skrzypczak and Kamiński. Gawroński (Kalisz) reportedly resigned for family reasons, while Kociołek lost his post in Warsaw as a result of conflicts in the central leadership. From the point of view of many provincial leaders, a year of military rule thorughout 1982 brought little improvement. In December the Wałbrzych committee produced a gloomy assessment of the progress made towards workers' self-government in the province – only 53 out of the 323 plants and factories in the province had taken any action in this respect.[32] Some KW secretaries protested that it was not from their committees or from the provincial governors that the measures taken to block reform initiatives were emanating. Wrocław secretary Mazur re-emphasised that the continuing poor political atmosphere in the factories made the possibility of any viable self-government a very distant one under military rule.[33]

The experience of military rule, in fact, placed the KW secretaries in a situation not unlike that they had occupied after 1975, when central decision-makers had faced provincial secretaries with equally intractable demands for the 'enhancement' of party authority but had chosen to extend the powers of parallel state institutions. It was significant that one of the main developments in party organisation at this level in 1982 was the establishment of the regional centres of party work (ROPP) – which resembled nothing so much as an attempt to restore the structure and conditions of work abolished by the 1975 territorial reform.

Sources of party weakness

While it was possible to draw certain parallels between military rule in 1982 and the inter-war dictatorship of Marshal Piłsudski (the *Sanacja* regime), links that some in Jaruzelski's entourage were by no means unwilling to encourage, there were signs that the modern military regime was far from providing a *sanacja*, a 'purification' or 'healing' of the political system, that its instigators had claimed it would. Public opinion did not swing round to the regime or to the party, and attitudes changed little for much of 1982. 'The divisions and conflicts from the end of 1981 remained frozen', and the 'democratically-inclined majority' remained separate from the minority who had supported the authoritarian remedy.[34] Amongst public opinion surveys carried out in 1982, the greatest concentration of uniform opinions was found in answers to the question of whether the party had been compromised in the eyes of society by its actions at the beginning of the year. At least nine out of ten in most groups by education level thought that the party had been thus compromised. The proportion was slightly lower among union members, but it did not fall below 85% in any of the groups.[35] Combined with the purge of the party and the verification of its membership, this lack of support contributed to the decline in PZPR membership.

While there is no doubt about the downward drift of the membership total, there is some uncertainty about the actual state of affairs at the end of 1982.[36] Sanford suggests that they were 'intentionally kept murky by the authorities' and that, in any case, internal returns were unreliable during this period.[37] It is likely that the last statement is the more relevant to this confusion. One of the later figures provided for the end of 1982 was from Cypryniak, head of the CC Organisational Department, which was reproduced in subsequent statistical annuals. This was presumably as accurate as any other and it indicated that the membership total at the end of 1982 was 2.327 million.[38] This represented a slightly higher rate of membership decline than in the second half of 1981, but not so high as between January and June 1981. In September 1982, CC secretary Barcikowski noted that the sharp drop in membership numbers that had been evident earlier in the year had then been halted and that the departure of some 20,000 members each month was 'approaching the norm'. What was different about the current situation (as, indeed, had been true for most of 1981) was the continuing lack of party popularity and its failure to attract new members.[39]

The lack of interest in party membership was most evident among industrial workers. KW first secretary Brożek (Nowy Sącz) stressed the need for change in a situation in which, while the party 'represented' the working class, the 'external expression of this representation' was barely discernible.[40] The membership situation was illustrated by the state of the party in the Lenin shipyard in Gdańsk, where a party membership of 3,300 before August 1980 had officially fallen by some 36% – although more realistically (removing pensioners and the retired from the total) it had declined by as much as 55%. So long as 'honest, realistically minded workers and former members of Solidarity cannot be brought over to the side of the party', wrote one party commentator, 'we shall not make any further progress'.[41] Party materials from Gdańsk showed a declining rate of attendance at party meetings, while with the threat of further strike action the shipyard was again militarised in December 1982.[42]

Nor were the central party organs satisfied that the party members who remained were of adequate quality. The Central Party Control Commission (CKKP) identified the weakening of party ranks as a 'consequence of ideological ferment' and noted the continuing threat presented by 'opportunist, reformist orientations' amongst party members.[43] Indeed, some observers thought that the number of expulsions from the party was small in comparison with other political crises, a sign of the political weakness of the party in 1982.[44] Soviet spokesmen seemed to agree with this analysis and by the late summer there were signs that 'the purge was not proceeding fast enough or thoroughly enough for Moscow's liking'.[45]

The party organisation itself was identified as a second source of weakness. Much of the criticism was directed at the provincial committees and concerned their failure to stimulate local party organisations and direct their work under the difficult conditions imposed by military rule. A joint Central Party Commission and military check undertaken in Olsztyn province uncovered 'poor organisation of party work with inadequate supervision activities'. A fundamental problem was its failure to develop a 'conception of collaboration with local party organisations', a defect that also appeared in KW relations with the ROPP, who often failed to implement party resolutions and KW recommendations.[46] The weakness of party organisation in the Lenin shipyard was also linked with the 'rather ineffective assistance provided by the KW', propaganda activities being particularly poorly conducted and described as the 'Achilles heel' of current party work.[47] Provincial control commissions (WKKPs) were criticised by the central commission for making insufficient use of the results of the military operational groups, and they were called upon to check 'at least twice a year' the attitudes of party members who were responsible for implementing the recommendations of the control organs.[48] Military rule had reduced some of the pressures on provincial organisations and protected the position of the apparatus, which was beginning 'once more to give up the good work habits about which there had been so much discussion at the IX Congress of the party'.[49]

A third aspect of party weakness was the continuing conflict within its higher echelons and the criticism of its leadership by such prominent political figures as Kociołek. He lost his provincial post and was removed as Warsaw Committee first secretary in June having, according to Adam Michnik, attacked the leadership for ignoring economic cooperation with the Soviet Union. Appropriately enough, he was dispatched to Moscow as Poland's ambassador there.[50] In July, Olszowski left his job as CC secretary and moved to head the Ministry of Foreign Affairs. A further departure was that of Tadeusz Grabski, former CC secretary and Politburo member, who failed to gain election to the IX Congress and was sent to Berlin to take up a post in foreign trade. Before leaving he wrote a 'letter of farewell' to his local party organisation, which was also circulated to members of the Central Committee before the October 1982 Plenum. It was highly critical of recent developments in the party and blamed the leadership for not using martial law to defeat the 'forces of counter-revolution', allowing the party to sink 'into a deep coma' and suffer 'progressive atrophy', and implementing a 'programme of self-liquidation of the party'. According to Sanford, this criticism expressed the sentiments of 'discontented sections of the party apparatus'.[51]

Grabski's views and action were, not surprisingly, roundly condemned by CC secretary Barcikowski – not least for providing a basis for popular belief that there was a power sturggle within the party. Further discussion of Grabski's views appeared in the party journal under the title 'One Just Man in Sodom?', and particular mention was made of Grabski's call for a 'revolutionary purge' of the organisation and his apparent desire for a 'small, cadre party'.[52] The letter was not an isolated incident and he also took part in a press conference organised by the hard-line weekly, *Rzeczywistość*, concerned to promote the 'elimination of right-wing tendencies within the Polish left'. Fractionalist tendencies were clearly persisting under military rule, despite the condemnation of diverse 'structures' and 'forums' made immediately after the IX Congress and repeated on subsequent occasions (the resolution of the VII Plenum in February 1982 had also rejected all such signs of party fragmentation as impermissible and contrary to the party statute). Conflict was not absent from some of these groups themselves: relations within the leadership of the Grunwald 'Patriotic Association' developed to the extent that an extensive law suit was launched by one member.[53]

The only member of the Politburo to leave during 1982, though, was Jan Łabęcki, first secretary of the Gdańsk shipyard party organisation, who had formed part of the reformist wing of the leadership. He resigned and returned to the shipyard as a simple worker in order, he later said, 'to break down the barriers of suspicion'.[54] Despite the distancing of some of the hard-liners from central party positions, then, it is not possible to agree with Taras that the 'strategy of clipping wings did not succeed in eliminating reformist as well as dogmatist forces'.[55] In view of the protection given to the apparatus by the military rulers and their success in routing local party reform forces, it must be concluded that the dogmatic forces were the more successful in surviving the rigours of the State of War. This, however, represented a holding operation rather than a process of reconstructing the party and restoring in some way its authority. 'The process of rebuilding a vital communist party', wrote one informed observer, 'had made little progress in the first eleven months of martial law and was likely to require several years before the task was really accomplished.'[56]

Problems of party organisation

The State of War was 'suspended' on 31 December 1982 and was fully revoked in July 1983. Obviously this did not signal a return to the *status quo ante*. Legislative changes and constitutional measures had been introduced to strengthen the powers available to the civil leadership and to enable it to retain control of the political situation short of the resort to military force. Military figures remained in key positions throughout the system, with two acting as KW first secretary and as many as ten placed amongst the forty-nine provincial governors.[57] Important central posts were still occupied by the military – including, of course, that of party first secretary. Stronger parallels with the 1981 situation existed, though, in terms of the continuing weakness of the party and the problems it faced in attempting to establish any new form of political authority. Rather than any increase in party strength it was the growing problems experienced by the opposition, notably underground Solidarity, in organising demonstrations and otherwise bringing political pressure to bear on the authorities that made the suspension of the State of War possible. Particularly notable here was the poor response to the call for a day of protest on 10 November 1982. The party itself remained weak, with steadily falling numbers and (perhaps more important) no clear idea of how it was to re-emerge as a 'leading force' with a new role that was not merely a resumption of that which it had signally failed to perform on several occasions in the recent past.

Soon after the suspension of the State of War, in January 1983, provincial party conferences were held throughout the country and provided some guide to the state of the party after a year of military rule. The picture officially presented was a patchy, though not a wholly disheartening one. Provincial first secretary Zenon Czech (Przemyśl) later described the conferences as a watershed in the rejuvenation of party life.[58] Nevertheless, the reports from them also carried some more negative comments. A decline in party discipline was noted in Bydgoszcz, warnings that the party 'should not identify itself with the administration' were issued in Gorzów Wielkopolski, while it was noted in Lomża that the 'reason for the weakening of party work is the departure of some of the experienced activists, the lack of skill of many new party workers and a decline of party commitment on the part of state and economic administration cadres'.[59] A 'lack of political skill' was also identified in Poznań, as well as an inability to make use of the statutory rights 'so energetically pursued two years ago'.[60] As Jaruzelski stated at the Katowice conference, 'there is still a lot to be done in our ranks. We need to devote a lot of effort to grubbing out and overcoming everything that prevents our getting through to the masses and gaining their complete confidence', while in Warsaw he made the common statement that a number of organisations 'do not show a sufficient degree of activeness'.[61]

Barcikowski pointed to the different social situation in which a weak party found itself: 'We must put our own ranks in order and at the same time occupy the social vacuum that has developed with the dissolution of Solidarity . . . The exceptional situation of the party today consists in the fact that there are no intermediate links between it and allied parties on one side, and society on the other; meanwhile, the social sphere cannot tolerate a vacuum'.[62] In describing the problematic position of the party in terms of the broad gulf between state and civil society in Poland Barcikowski recognised the extent of the task that faced the leadership in achieving political 'normalisation' and the restoration of some credible version of party rule. The emergence of Solidarity had been followed by the germination and flowering of a range of autonomous social organisations and activities in the face of which party authority and its claim to exercise a leading role in society rapidly evaporated. Party–state power, we have suggested, was less damaged by this process, but was able to reassert itself only by bringing the military authorities into greater prominence and tacitly acquiescing in the collapse of party authority. If 'normalisation' meant the reimposition of basic features of the Soviet system and the restoration of some form of party monopoly, the withdrawal of military representatives from key posts in the party and state structures (a process by no means completed by the revocation of the State of War) meant that the party had to acquire new sources of authority if it was to resume more of a leading role.

In this situation the views of the KW first secretaries gained more publicity. Their views on the provincial and local party organisations reflected, naturally enough, the difficulties outlined above; they also showed considerable divergence in what they regarded as the best way to tackle these problems and in the conceptions they had of the appropriate path of development for the PZPR. In this they echoed the conflicts apparent at the higher levels of the party. The major worry of

Miśkiewicz, first secretary in Szczecin since May 1981, was the mood of the working class: 'there exists a climate of mistrust which surrounds the party on all sides. The workers have no faith in words. It is facts which build confidence.'[63] From other industrial centres both Brigadier-General Łukasik (in Poznań from May 1982) and Stanisław Bejger (Gdańsk from January 1982) also pointed to weaknesses in local party organisations and continuing unevenness in their level of activity.[64] In terms of the response of the KW staff to this difficult situation, it is interesting that both Łukasik and Mróz (Opole first secretary from June 1981) admitted that apparatus staff showed some reluctance to enter into direct contact with (in the case of Poznań) workers and (in Opole) peasants.[65] The isolation of the party and the extent of the tasks facing it were clearly presenting the provincial authorities with some difficult choices.

It was also clear, though, that the first secretaries' responses to the situation differed considerably. Skrzydło, Kruk's successor in Lublin, seemed to be particularly aware of the 'conservative tendencies' that were gaining strength in the party and of the likelihood that a 'return to the old administrative methods of realising the leading role of the party would again lead us into the wasteland of political error and increase the mistrust of the party'.[66] Manifestations of arrogance and pomposity were similarly denounced by Mróz. Opałko (Tarnów first secretary from October 1980) traced the roots of successive crises to the deficiencies of the party educational system. Party members and society as a whole, he thought, were 'still incorrectly prepared for understanding the socialist idea and bringing it to life'.[67] A more general survey of KW first secretaries' attitudes, however, uncovered some degree of suspicion about the effectiveness of 'ideological formulae and dogma', and a feeling that the political hopes attached to the new formulation of the party programme were rather excessive.[68] Miśkiewicz also emphasised that 'the attitude of workers was most mistrustful and antipathetic to decisions and activities of a political character'. It appeared that many did not feel that the authority of the party might be restored by placing greater emphasis on ideology.

A few other KW first secretaries did argue for a stricter ideological line and suggested solutions which did not appear to place greatest priority on counteracting the isolation of the party. Bejger (Gdańsk), for example, called for greater inner-party discipline and more respect for the principle of democratic centralism. Wałek (Płock first secretary from October 1980) endorsed a line of development that carried even less promise of reconciliation with the workers and argued that 'in such a revolutionary period as that in which our party finds itself, there is a temporary necessity for a cadre party which would be able . . . to lead the country out of the crisis'.[69] The phraseology and sentiments contained in Wałek's statement were reminiscent of the views expressed in Grabski's letter and it was clear that the fractional conflict that persisted within the leadership had not left untouched the leading cadres at provincial level.

Both positions, of course, were responses to the continuing weakness of the party and to the problems it was faced with in gaining the capacity to exert some 'leading role' as the military partially withdrew from advance political posts. The problems involved considerably more than just a lack of social support – of central importance was its institutional weakness associated with the persistent authority deficit from which the party had suffered. This raised factors other than the failure to gain popularity among the working class and the public at large, and crucially affected its relations with other agencies of political rule and administration, concerning particularly the party's lack of organisational coherence and its autonomy as an institution. As on previous occasions, one of the main ways this was expressed was in the party's problems in exerting its functions of checking and verification ('control'). The failure of elected party authorities to exercise supervision internally and thus to ensure that their decisions were implemented by subordinates within the organisation, and also to carry out checks on the institutions of the state and economic administration, was clearly an important factor in the difficulties faced by the leadership in rebuilding the party and asserting its authority.

Concern over this problem had already, as we have noted, been aired during the State of War. With its official suspension and the retreat of the military from the political foreground, the party's lack of capacity in this area again became more obvious and was a source of more public worry. Why, it was asked following the control of a tenth province (Słupsk) by the armed forces inspectorate in late November 1982, had the party again proved itself incapable of conducting some kind of effective check here, thus forestalling yet another highly negative conclusion from the military inspectorate? (Nine of the ten checks had uncovered serious deficiencies in the administration.) Grzelak had first raised the question in May 1982 but now, with the passage of time and the suspension of military rule, it clearly required an answer more urgently.[70] It soon became evident that the issue was a complex one and that several factors were involved.

One of these factors was the committee work-load of the KW secretaries. According to the head of an Elbląg committee department, the secretaries 'had never before . . . taken part in so many meetings', with the result that there was just 'not enough time for the verification of the execution of plenum decisions'.[71] Another was the composition of the WKKP which, since the IX Congress election campaign, had been staffed by non-professional activists. Previously their makeup had been different; in Warsaw, for example, there had been four full-time deputy chairmen in addition to the WKKP chairman. WKKP checks could demand considerable resources in terms of time and, on occasion, specialist knowledge of particular environments which could produce, as the committee's vice-chairman admitted, a 'basic problem'.[72] The general approach of the WKKP was not without fault, either, as the CKKP had pointed out at the VII Plenum, and some provincial commissions were still 'so concerned with bringing individuals to account that they failed to evaluate ideological attitudes'. They were also prone to apply unnecessarily severe punishments and to 'exceed their authority in withdrawing *nomenklatura* recommendations'.[73]

A related problem which was by no means a new one, was the 'resistance of party organs and the apparatus' to verification and the tendency of apparatus workers illegitimately to represent the organs, which was 'contrary to the service role of the apparatus defined by the IX Congress', and to adopt arrogant attitudes towards the new activities of the party revision commissions. A strong attack was made by Professor Kozakiewicz on 'sections of the central, province and commune power apparatus who understand normalisation as the recreation of the socially compromised system of government from the "good old days" before August 1980, which had been unmasked as ineffective and harmful for the development of socialism in Poland'.[74] Evaluating the significance and consequences of the IX Congress, however, Rakowski was at pains to emphasise the 'enormous cadre changes' that had taken place in the party since 1981 and to deny 'schematic' views of the apparatus worker as an archetypal conservative and 'anonymous party official'.[75] Many changes had, of course, taken place, although our analysis had suggested that their impact was rather smaller than some have claimed. It was also clear that the persistence of old habits could not be denied.

It is interesting in this respect that it was the element of the pre-1975 party structure reintroduced in 1981–82, the ROPP, that came in for particular criticism. Thus the Central Auditing Commission (CKR) had a 'series of reservations about the lack of effectiveness of the political and coordination activities undertaken by the ROPP and improper relations between ROPP and party organs'. At the local conferences they were criticised for supplanting rather than helping primary party organisations and local organs, and one call was made for their dissolution as they were seen as an 'attempt to rebuild a party administration'.[76] Such criticism was, of course, premised on a conception of the party as a social movement as well as, or rather than, an administrative organisation. But, certainly in terms of the state administration, there was an increasingly strong current of opinion in favour of a return to something like the pre-1975 territorial structure, with calls for the return of the *powiat* and some positive comments on the 1981–82 ROPP innovation. A similar reorganisation, it was noted, had also occurred in the police forces.[77] The nature of the state administration, its growing strength relative to the party under the conditions of the State of War, and its current tendencies of development all tended to militate against the less administrative conception of the party promulgated at the IX Congress. The relative weakness of the party also encouraged its workers to revert to the established mode of operation, especially as it had few reserves of social authority on which to draw. The party was therefore subject to conflicting pressures which were reflected in the conflicts that persisted within the party and its central leadership, involving also the provincial secretaries.

Conflicting views of party development

Following the Grabski incident, party disunity was condemned and fractionalism once more proscribed by the Politburo in December 1982. The importance of this declaration was underlined soon afterwards at the VII Plenum of the Central Commission for Party Control (CKKP), and it was made clear that disciplinary proceedings would be taken in the case of further infringements. Barcikowski branded such signs of inner-party struggle as 'politically criminal' in the light of the current political situation.[78] But despite the leadership changes that had been made in 1982, the signs of dissension within the PZPR and, indeed, echoes of Poland-related conflicts within the Soviet bloc as a whole did not disappear. Mention was made from within official circles of the 'government's political adversaries, present within the party itself'. Mink, indeed, has suggested that openness about such conflict has been a distinctive mark of Jaruzelski's mode of normalisation. In the spring of 1983 the Soviet press published a hard-line article that had previously appeared in *Nowe Drogi*, combining this with attacks on *Polityka* and the person of Rakowski. Noting the *Kommunist* reprint of Kraszewski's article, though, *Polityka* condemned the Western media for stirring up trouble.[79]

In view of the developments outlined above, official denials of continuing inner-party conflict are difficult to believe, as is the allegation of *Polityka* that it was the Western media who were the ones busy painting a picture of 'hard-liners and reformists' at loggerheads within the party. Some uncertainty over the Central Committee policy-making agenda also appeared to be present and, despite earlier publicity, the XII Plenum of the Central Committee was not devoted to ideological matters, these being postponed until the next meeting. It was also necessary at the May Plenum for both Jaruzelski and CC secretary Czyrek to condemn yet again all manifestations of fractionalism and demagogy. Underlying conditions here were not just the clash of forces predominantly within the Polish party but also influences from elsewhere in the Soviet bloc. One factor in this was the apparent reluctance of the Kremlin to tolerate the continuation of a militarised form of rule. On several occasions, according to Rupnik, Moscow 'expressed its concern about some implications of the Jaruzelski approach: the stress on military authority and efficiency overshadowing that of the party; reverting to a nationalist discourse and away from a Marxist-Leninist one; seeking a compromise with the Church . . . instead of "rooting out" the heresy'.[80] In more practical terms it was not difficult to imagine the Soviet military leadership 'vigorously objecting to the persistent use of the Polish military technocratic elite as public administrators' because of the effect on the military preparedness of Warsaw Pact forces. Rice's analysis also suggests the likelihood of basic political objections to the virtual identification of the party and military elites in Poland, as she saw such links having formed in Czechoslavakia in the 1960s 'at the expense of Soviet power and influence'.[81] The Soviet Union was likely to be reluctant to permit such developments to happen again.

It was not unlikely that continuing hard-line forces within the PZPR were deriving some encouragement and sustenance from Soviet politicians. But arguments that these uncertainties and continuing conflicts were a grave embarrassment and represented a series of defeats for Jaruzelski, leading to him losing face with Moscow, were probably exaggerated. He was, after all, awarded the Order of Lenin in July 1983 on his sixtieth birthday. But the postponement of ideological matters for Central Committee deliberation until October was rather more than an affair of political confusion or stalemate or, as Taras suggests, just a reflection of Jaruzelski's desire to 'avoid making ideological decisions'. Those eager to bang the ideological drum were precisely those who also favoured a more selective party which maintained its distance from the mass of the workers – that is, the hard-liners who did not fight shy of disrupting the surface unity of the party. By delaying the ideological Plenum Jaruzelski was in fact helping to consolidate his position and promote what seemed to be the majority view in the party. On the other hand, towards the end of 1983 Staniszkis detected a 'visible return to ideology amongst the leadership' and a growth in attacks on the Jaruzelski leadership for its non-ideological style of operation.[82]

It should not be assumed, however, that all Soviet pressure was exerted in favour of the hard-liners and their higher-profile ideological offensive and against the line pursued by the Jaruzelski leadership. There were differences within the Soviet theoretical establishment over the origins and nature of the Polish crisis, and there were those who agreed with the conclusions of the PZPR 1981 Congress about 'the "structural causes" of the crisis', endorsing its strictures against the deficient developments of intra-party democracy, the prevalence of bureaucratic centralism throughout the party–state system and the lack of institutional controls on the party leadership. The changes in leadership after the death of Brezhnev also brought shifts in emphasis within Soviet policy, with Andropov (in power during 1983) stressing the need to revitalise production processes in contrast to the greater emphasis placed by Chernenko on intensifying ideological work.[83] In early 1983, then, there was clearly an easing of the restrictions not just on ideological debate itself but also on discussion of the centrality of ideological matters to the process of political recovery and the restoration of party leadership, most likely in anticipation of the lifting of the State of War in July 1983. A more empirical approach to party affairs was generally suggested.

One analysis contrasted the tendency to erect ideological stereotypes which, in fact, often degenerated to forms of self-advertisement (an obvious reference to Grabski was here included) with more 'realistic' ways of giving expression to anxieties about the current state of the party – ways which might help identify practical steps that could be taken to improve the condition of the party. Current problems were not attributed primarily to the weakness of ideological discipline. In this view, the complexities of the current situation flowed from the 1981 renewal process and the consequences of the pre-Congress election campaign, the latter regarded as having had an overwhelmingly positive effect. But, in the nature of things, some of those ejected as a result of this process had been treated unjustly and with excessive haste – although most of the injustices had since been rectified. Current problems, then, derived from the situation that had developed immediately prior to the suspension of the State of War, when those restored to their position had shown signs of relapsing into bureaucratic habits and arrogant attitudes. This was permitted, it was implied, by the weakening of democratic processes and the interruption of political renewal. In working out current problems the writer warned against restoring order in the party by tolerating the continuing dominance of the apparatus and the erosion of democracy, or by waving the banner of democratic centralism – as there had hardly been a period when its principles had been satisfactorily applied.[84]

Another writer warned against the belief that full ideological unity could really be achieved in a given political situation. This idea was dismissed as illusory, as such unity could only be achieved by a sect 'in which religious fanaticism was raised to a virtue and was capable of embracing all members of a collectivity without exception'. This, it was noted, could hardly be the case with the PZPR. Involved in the problems surrounding the party membership were not just the declining levels of membership but also its changing age-structure. The PZPR had lost many of its younger members between August 1980 and mid-1983, although its leadership at all levels had undergone considerable rejuvenation. This also was the basis for some inner-party conflict. By the end of 1982, only 11% of party members were under thirty, while in 1978 they had made up 24% of party members and in 1970 and 1960 had provided over a quarter of its membership. The proportion of working-class members had also fallen. In 1978 they had provided 46% of the party's membership. In the second half of 1983, however, it was announced that the proportion of working-class members had fallen below 40%, whilst workers made up 43.2% of the nation's work-force. Others, on the basis of more confidential information, claimed that once pensioners were discounted the true proportion of workers in the party was as low as 14% and that overall party membership had already fallen below two million.[85]

By this stage official returns showed that 9% of the adult population was in the party, lower than other countries in Eastern Europe where membership ranged from 10% in Hungary to 17% in the German Democratic Republic. In many workplaces and areas of society, then, the party retained only a minimal political influence. Many of those who had resigned or been expelled were, according to one contribution to the party journal, among the more 'active' members who were 'motivated by the interests of society, inclined to collective action, [and who] had enjoyed authority in their environment. At the same time, there had remained in the party many who were passive and of uncertain quality.' This was indeed a different view from that put officially in the months that followed the announcement of the State of War. As the party continued to show few signs of political recovery it was clearly felt by many that a more realistic view of its problems was required and that steps had to be taken that could provide the basis for a more effective political development. The same writers noted the continuing political impotence of the party and the fact that it had stabilised its position only by reverting to its former state. Contradictions in its role were identified (that in some ways it acted as an extension of the state apparatus while in others it claimed to emerge as a representative of society, as a social pressure group against 'the authorities'). Within the party, pressures were clearly growing for a more coherent path of development to be marked out.[86]

There could be little doubt that this would have to involve some conception of a more autonomous role for local party organisations. In one view, the continuing weakness of many organisations threatened to create a party 'inspired' only from above, suggesting a degree of centralisation that could well turn into bureaucratisation. This could involve attempts to block economic reform in order that local party organs might retain what influence they had over the work-force. It also meant the continuing dominance of the executive organs of the party and the political apparatus as, in common with some of the other views expressed over recent months, there followed the observation that the 'party has not freed itself of opportunists and those less active'. It was, indeed, noted that 'there may now be communists outside the party as a result of their own errors and those of others'. This meant that some had been wrongly excluded from the party and that their return might therefore 'be an important turning-point in rebuilding the link with the working class and the authority of the party'. Not surprisingly, this conception of who was a proper communist did not pass without challenge, and it was questioned whether the authority of the party would really be strengthened by admitting those inclined to oppose the regime. Others also expressed doubts on this matter, but accepted the starting points about the weakness of local party organs, existing tendencies towards centralism and the return of former administrative methods, and the need to consider the readmission to the party of at least those workers who enjoyed full authority in their work-place.[87]

Pursuing the issues identified in these exchanges, material emanating from investigations conducted by the Central Auditing Commission indeed confirmed that 'revitalisation' was occurring (in the words of the title of the report on its activities) 'with minuses'. The weaknesses in the work of the local organisation were confirmed, as was their tendency to evaluate the performance of members employed, particularly in management, 'according to the old methods'. It also clearly emerged that some activists were eager to return to the former practices according to which the party could intervene directly 'in all decisions of the administrative management'. The analyses current in 1983, then, had a number of points in common, notably in terms of their emphasis on the doubtful quality of the party rank and file (particularly of its working-class members) on the return to administrative methods within the party, and on the growing dominance of the apparatus. Jaruzelski's statements at the XII CC Plenum in May also reflected this perception. We do not expect people, he said, 'to rush to join the party': they must feel 'that they need the party . . . each time a good cause is defeated that is a defeat for the party'. He appeared, therefore, to identify himself with the realistic view of the party's problems and its possibilities for development, and to maintain his distance from those who sought a solution in the intensification of ideological demands and the pursuit of stricter orthodoxy.[88]

Military review of the party apparatus

As attention turned back again to the condition of the party and its capacity to exercise political leadership, the issue of the party apparatus, its political outlook and the discipline it was subject to, also returned as a topic requiring major scrutiny. Military figures retained their responsibility for party cadres within the CC apparatus and Jaruzelski was clearly determined to retain some freedom of action with regard to the party apparatus despite the lifting of the State of War. Specialists who had left economic posts to join the apparatus were found not to have 'sufficient political experience' and there were complaints that they had brought 'administrative and economic methods of work' with them to the apparatus. In practice this might mean that they failed to respond to the inadequacies of party organisations when these fell outside their area of special expertise. However, reports from some provincial committees suggested that by 1983 the tendency to staff the apparatus with those experienced in party work was again gaining strength.[89]

The old problems of arbitrary apparatus action and the inadequacy of the discipline exerted over apparatus staff had by no means disappeared, it seemed. Instead of propagating and explaining the policies and views of the party leadership, some CC and KW *lektors* insisted on presenting their 'own, different and contradictory position'. This sounded like behaviour which, if practised by party reformers or horizontalists, would have been condemned as fractionalist and suggested that either discipline within the apparatus was very lax indeed or party staff were active participants in the party conflict and in-fighting discussed above. Manifestations of 'ignorance and arrogance' on the part of administrators and officials in general were coming increasingly to the attention of the party authorities, and they were reported to have made specific warnings about the dangers of bureaucratism within party life to activists consulted in meetings called prior to the XII Plenum in May.[90] Comments on bureaucratic arrogance and the conduct of party activity 'from behind the office desk' were also made at the XIII Plenum in October 1983.

The position and operation of the apparatus had also been the object of close scrutiny by the military leadership. As well as concentrating on matters of ideology, the XIII Plenum also passed a resolution on cadres policy based on the proposals of General Dziekan, head of the CC cadres department. He recalled the distortions that had developed in this area during the seventies and noted the lack of control over cadres that had resulted from the departure from Leninist principles. He proposed, therefore, the establishment of a systematic method for carrying out party assessments. He wrote later about the changes envisaged and pointed out that, following the 1975 reform of the administration, the number of 'leadership' posts requiring the agreement of party organs – that is, those posts within the *nomenklatura* of the party leadership – had risen from some 10–14% of the total to 16%. (As leadership posts, in the most general sense, were reckoned to number a million this suggested that some 160,000 were on the party's *nomenklatura*.) The total had since declined, and it was Dziekan's recommendation that the process of reduction should continue. It was clear, however, that he was faced with some resistance in this area and it was here that the interests of the military and the party apparatus appeared to be most divergent.

Signs of tension and awareness of the potential for conflict can be detected in the precise wording of Dziekan's statements on this issue: 'Fully sharing the arguments of members of the Central Committee which advise caution in this area and progressing with all due care, it will nevertheless be possible to reduce the number of posts requiring party consultation and acceptance, both at central level and in all the provinces.'[91] He was clearly aware of some opposition to the proposed reduction of the party *nomenklatura* and the resulting reduction in the power of party officials. Dziekan also identified a further task in this area and directed attention to the need for the long-term definition and development of cadre reserves (a process which he was able only to launch, as he succumbed to a heart attack less than twelve months later). There was at present, he noted, no clearly defined pool of cadre reserves, and 'we are at the beginning of their systematic development'. The upgrading of cadre skills and the improvement of management and leadership operations – in the economic administration as well as in the party – was regarded as a matter of considerable urgency and was seen to be closely linked with the poor economic results that had been achieved since the inception of the State of War. Indeed, it was reported of the XIV CC Plenum, held in November 1983 to consider the economic situation, that 'for a long time . . . there has not been such sharp criticism of the economic administration, including the government itself. Neither did the criticism avoid the person of the First Secretary.' The issues surrounding the identification and deployment of specialised personnel, the influence of party officials over these processes and the prospects of social and economic recovery were, therefore, complex and interrelated and entered into the dominant conflicts within the party–military elite.

The party apparatus itself was not passive in the face of these developments. Measures had been taken within the apparatus to defend the position and privileges of its members. Apart from the informal developments noted above, an official union was established by party workers which by the end of 1983 had enrolled over 20,000 members, including retired employees, and embracing 90% of those eligible to join.[92] According to its chairman, one of the major objectives of the union was to improve the public's knowledge about the apparatus, to enhance its popular image and counter 'demagogic attacks' on the organisation. It was intended to further the 'integration of the apparatus' within the party as a whole and, most interestingly, appeared also to include most of those occupying 'elected positions' – although some of them preferred to affiliate to unions based on the section of the work force who constituted the electorate for such officials. The sentiments that underlay this move received some support from other quarters. Despite the enormous changes that had taken place within the apparatus, complained one writer, its workers 'had met with little understanding or recognition, not to speak of civility' over the past two or three years, and it was now time to evaluate their position more objectively.

An important background condition to these developments was the introduction at the IX Congress of the principle whereby 'elected' party officials (the inverted commas appeared also in Kołodziejczyk's article), that is, the secretaries of the party organs and committees, were to be limited to no more than two terms in office. In fact, the restrictions were not quite so rigorous as this suggests, as the Party Statute adopted in 1981 did allow for party conferences 'in specially justified cases' to allow candidates to stand for a third term, which would extend their period of tenure to seven-and-a-half years. This, it was claimed, blocked the career path and 'natural progression' of appointed instructors and department heads up the party hierarchy. After the IX Congress, it was claimed, the PZPR was 'probably the only party' which closed the path of advancement of appointed officials to 'elected' posts, unless the party workers were also elected members of the appropriate committee, which was an extremely unlikely occurrence. This view effectively challenged two of the major principles of the former democratisation movement – the restriction of the apparatus to a strictly service role, its members clearly subject to the elected party authorities, and the rotation of elected party officials, which prevented individuals developing an unlimited claim on party office.[93]

The inheritance from 1980–81 was also, it was claimed, having a direct effect on the staffing of the apparatus. Opałko, the veteran KW first secretary in Tarnów, spoke of the dangers of 'negative selection' (that is, having to select from the small number who did not refuse party work) and of the need to persuade and cajole potential applicants. Similar problems were reported by the Opole first secretary, Eugeniusz Mróz, who stated that 40 of the province's 310 party posts remained unfilled. Financial insecurity played a part in this, as did the better career opportunities for trained teachers with the introduction of a new career contract (those with teacher training having made up a significant proportion of party staff in that province).[94] In the eyes of some, the problematic position of the apparatus was directly attributable to the expansion of the political role of the military, which had 'blocked its paths of traditional career advance'. Elements of conflict between the military and the party establishment concerned not so much differences in political orientation as divergent views on how the apparatus should be staffed.[95] By no means all party staff condemned the new arrangements and some provincial first secretaries, for example, J. Brożek in Nowy Sącz, endorsed the two-term limitation.

Other official views showed a critical awareness of the 'many weaknesses in the functioning of the party apparatus' and stressed that 'its function and role must always be one of service'. This attitude was linked with a strong emphasis on the importance of party unity – the implication being that any rethinking of the role of the apparatus would mean a qualification or rejection of the decisions made by the IX Congress, which continued to represent the fragile base on which the party established itself as a unified institution.[96]

Consolidation of the party organisation: the provincial leadership

The resumption of the discussion about the role of the apparatus and the more vociferous defence of party staff, particularly in relation to the restricted career prospects offered under present arrangements, was hardly fortuitous. It gained momentum in the period preceding the XIII Plenum (the postponed ideological meeting) when a new round of electoral conference was due to get under way within the party organisation. Preparations for the conferences were announced at the Plenum by CC secretary Mokrzyszczak, who emphasised the implications of the elections for the quality of the party leadership throughout the country and called for the election of committees composed of those who were 'principled, ideologically committed and experienced in the organisation of party work', of members who had 'authority within their environment amongst both party members and non-members'. The provincial conferences were due to be held in December 1983 and January 1984.

The hope was expressed at an early stage that the proportion of workers elected to the party organs should at least reflect the proportion of workers amongst party members and the working-class character of the party (itself somewhat limited at the present time). So far, it was noted in the PZPR journal, 'there are more verbal appeals and assurances about the role of the working class than attempts to secure the election of real workers to the leading groups of the party organisation'.[97] H. Bednarski, KW first secretary in Bydgoszcz prior to his appointment as CC secretary in November 1983, also stressed the importance of maintaining the working-class character of the party – although, as befitted the former director of the party school in Bydgoszcz, he was also eager to emphasise the demand in the apparatus for those with academic qualifications. While, he admitted, there had been a time in the party 'when we did not like people with academic titles', such views now seemed to be on the decline. In view of the continuing problems experienced by the party in mustering working-class support, or even interest in party activities, such hopes showed considerable optimism. As Jaruzelski admitted at the Lublin provincial conference, 'before the campaign began a host of doubts was expressed whether the party could stand such a difficult test, whether we would be up to it'. He concluded, however, that 'these anxieties proved to be groundless'.[98]

In the earlier elections at least, though, there was a decided preponderance of delegates from the intelligentsia (or white-collar workers) – making up as much as 65% of conference delegates in contrast to only 15% of workers. If this balance of class composition emerged in the party organs elected by the conferences it was suggested that 'the question of the class character of the leadership of the workers' party would not be one that was out of place'. In the event, workers made up 27% of the new provincial committees elected at this time. Turnover within the provincial committees was extensive at 66%, a higher level than in the party organs at other levels. The level of working-class participation in the new committees could, in fact, be seen as some achievement, as it had formed only 19.9% of the outgoing committees. Working-class participation at other levels was somewhat higher, although it could hardly be regarded as satisfactory as it fell significantly short of reflecting the dominantly working-class environment in which the party committees were elected. Thus, even in the plant committees (KF), workers made up only 41% of the membership and in the executives elected by the primary party organisations only 36%.[99]

In the great majority of cases the provincial committees were elected after the election of the first secretaries – forty-six conferences chose first the KW leader (by secret ballot) and then elected the KW. In only two cases was the first secretary chosen by the newly elected provincial committee.[100] The number of first secretaries elected for the first time in December 1983 and January 1984 was in fact quite low and only seven changes were made in all, bringing the number of KW first secretaries changed since December 1981 to a total of nineteen. Four of the seven changes, moreover, did not occur as a result of the conference election but in consequence of the promotion of the incumbent first secretary, in two cases (Bednarski in Bydgoszcz and Porębski in Wrocław) to the post of CC secretary and in the case of Messner (Katowice) to that of vice-chairman of the Council of Ministers. Of the remaining four who did not get re-elected two, at least, were clearly due for a change. Luciński (Ciechanów), a stalwart conservative, had been in post since the administrative reform of 1975 and had for some time been the sole survivor of that generation. Wałek, in Płock from October 1980, had also held posts in the party apparatus and the youth movement since the forties and had only managed to hang on to his provincial position in 1981 by the use of orthodox means (see chapter 5). Change in the KW first secretarial cadre at the end of 1983 was therefore relatively limited.

The average age of those appointed KW first secretary during the State of War and the following period was forty-nine, considerably higher than those elected in 1981. The age distribution was also quite different, with nearly half (48%) of those appointed after December 1981 having been born no later than 1930. Only 10% had been born in 1939 or after, while nearly half the secretaries newly elected in 1981 (48%) had been born during this period. The radically different political conditions introduced under the State of War had brought to the fore an older political generation to replace those elected in 1981. Nevertheless, amongst those appointed under the conditions of military rule only one, Marian Woźniak in Warsaw, had served earlier as KW first secretary – and then only for a few weeks in mid-1981, before he was elected CC secretary after the IX Congress. Associated with these changes, party membership among the 1981–84 first secretarial appointments often dated back to the Stalinist period (1948–55). During this period, 47% had joined the party, in contrast with only 12% of those elected in 1981. Far fewer, accordingly, had joined during the Gomułka period. Moreover, the recent appointments had been party members for a longer time (twenty-five years on average) on appointment than had been their predecessors in 1981 (twenty years on average).

Also in keeping with the longer period of party membership, the first secretaries appointed after December 1981 were less likely to have educational qualifications with direct industrial or agricultural relevance and showed a return to the situation more characteristic of the pre-1981 secretaries, with a larger number of party officials qualified in 'economics' being appointed. As suggested in chapter 3, this most likely indicates a greater number of secretaries with qualifications gained in party institutions. Yet the post-December first secretaries were, in fact, more likely to have had career experience in industry than the 1981 cohort, although markedly fewer had worked in agriculture (reflecting a return to procedures of central control in contrast to the strong influence exercised at the 1981 provincial electoral conferences by those representing rural party organisations). The first secretaries appointed in 1981–84 also showed a return to the tendency to recruit from those with backgrounds in government and the state administration. In several ways, then, changes made in the provincial leadership after the introduction of the State of War suggested a return to the pattern of appointment characteristic of the pre-1981 period, a reversion that might be expected of a 'normalisation' period.

In some respects, though, the KW secretary appointments made after December 1981 showed considerable diversity. Whilst a large number of KW appointments were relatively new to party work, others had political experience which stretched back a long time. Whilst the 1981 party elections had seen a considerable infusion of new blood into the apparatus, those who became first secretaries after December 1981 were often even less experienced in party work; 47% had less than six years' experience of work in the party apparatus, while only 36% or just over a third had such limited experience amongst those elected in 1981. On the other hand, over a quarter of the post-December appointments had received their first party job over twenty years previously – a level of seniority found among only the 1980 appointees and those appointed even further back at the time of the 1975 reform. Relatively few (16%) lay in the middle range of party apparatus service, from eleven to twenty years.

This suggests that the difficult political situation had been responsible for the mobilisation of those with unusual career backgrounds into the provincial leadership – those with little or no experience in the party apparatus, for example, or those whose extensive party service might have already taken them out of the apparatus or to a level above that of the provincial party apparatus. Slightly more of the post-December group than the 1981 cohort had had either KW or other first secretarial experience, although there were still more (26%, compared with 20%) without any apparatus experience whatsoever. In this sense the post-December group of new KW first secretaries shared more similarities with the 1981 first secretaries than with those appointed before the emergence of Solidarity. Amongst those who had become KW first secretary during the State of War or after and who had no previous apparatus experience, two (Messner and Skrzydło) were academics, one (Janicki) was an industrial manager, one (Zieliński) came from the state administration and one more (Łukasik) had had over thirty years' experience in the air force.

Amongst the forty-nine KW first secretaries as a whole, the nineteen post-December appointments had caused certain changes. By early 1984, 27% of all provincial first secretaries were over fifty years of age compared with 12% in 1981. The proportion of those with career experience in industry had continued to rise, and the number of those with experience in government departments and the state administration had also risen again. Still more (31% compared with 25%) had little apparatus experience, having received their first party post less than six years earlier. By early 1984, however, the provincial leadership cadre contained some apparatus stalwarts who had received their first party posting over thirty years previously, a record possessed by no first secretary in 1981. Yet the number of KW secretaries with no previous apparatus experience before appointment had risen from six in 1981 to eleven in 1984. Similarly, the pattern of apparatus experience showed no sign of returning to the pre-1980 pattern and the proportion of first secretaries with previous KW secretarial or other responsible secretarial experience continued to decline.[101]

While the turnover amongst the first secretaries was quite limited in December 1983 and January 1984 as a result of the changes made at the provincial conferences, renewal was more extensive in other parts of the leading provincial cadre. This could be clearly linked with the radically different conditions pertaining within the party organisation, the emphasis placed on party discipline and the stricter demands made of members. A key role in this process was played by the provincial control commissions, and roughly a third (sixteen) of their chairmen were changed over the two-month period. The level of turnover among KW secretaries in general (that is, secretaries other than the provincial party leader himself) also ran at a higher level. Indeed, the rate of change amongst KW secretaries in general had been higher throughout 1982 and 1983 than for first secretaries. Sixty-eight changes had taken place in those two years amongst the secretarial cadre, while as a result of the provincial electoral conferences a further fifty-one changes were made in January and February 1984. This made 119 changes since the beginning of 1982, well over half the general secretarial cadre and a level of turnover considerably higher than the nineteen new first secretaries (39%) appointed since December 1981.

Of the changes made at the provincial conferences the functions of most of the secretaries concerned, forty-six, are known. The highest rate of renewal was found amongst the ideology secretaries (twenty), while in addition ten organisation secretaries, nine economic, four agricultural and three science secretaries were changed. The large number of ideology and organisation secretaries changed surely reflected the emphasis recently placed on party discipline and ideological orthodoxy, and the importance of ideological matters in the context of the developing conflicts within the party. As with the provincial first secretaries, the other secretaries were rather older than those elected in 1981, 40% having been born before 1939 (38% of the secretaries elected in 1981 had been born before 1939). Only 17% had been born after 1945 compared with 21% of those elected in 1981. Fewer of those appointed under military rule, only 9%, had joined the party after 1970 (18% in the previous cohort). Throughout the provincial secretariat, then, there appeared to be a general tendency after December 1981 to appoint more seasoned political workers and to eject some of the more recent party recruits.

The educational qualifications of the secretaries appointed after 1981 showed little difference from those of their predecessors. Rather more had degrees of a scientific or technical character, and fewer had qualifications in agriculture or lacked any kind of higher certificate. These tendencies were reflected in the career experience of the recently appointed secretaries, many of whom had worked in the industrial, trade or transport sectors. The number of those with experience in the fields of government and education remained constant, but was lower than had been the case between 1975 and 1980. The proportion of those joining after work in the youth organisations also continued to decline. As with the first secretaries, then, there appeared to be an attempt to appoint more experienced political workers who had spent some time in industrial work. The post-December recruits, not surprisingly in view of the prevailing political climate, also included more people with military and security experience, and also a larger number from the 'parapolitical' sector (journalists, editors, cultural workers).

The impact of military-led normalisation, however, can be detected more clearly in the backgrounds of those appointed to the KW secretariat during this period, notably in the reduction of the proportion of those appointed with little or only very recent experience in the party apparatus. Of the KW secretaries elected in 1981, 58% had held no previous party office or had received their first appointment less than six years earlier. The proportion of such newcomers dropped to 41% amongst those appointed after December 1981. This stood in marked contrast to trends within the group of KW first secretaries and suggests that, while the military-led leadership had introduced personnel from outside the established apparatus cadre into the leading provincial position, it had continued to rely on more experienced party personnel for the second-rank positions. It should also be noted that amongst the newcomers to the provincial secretariat were five people transferred from military and security units who were hardly likely to be lacking experience in the kind of political activities characteristic of the State of War and the subsequent months.

Amongst those appointed after December, 32% of KW secretaries had been first appointed to the apparatus more than ten years earlier, compared with 18% amongst those elected in 1981. This did not reflect the level of apparatus experience characteristic of pre-1981 appointments, which had stood at 40% or above, but it clearly represented a return to the mobilisation of the more experienced party worker and the reinforcement of the provincial committees with trusted cadres. To this extent, despite the relatively small increase in the proportion of workers elected to the provincial committees (which was, nevertheless, an improvement on the 1981 results), the outcome of the provincial conferences must have been the source of considerable satisfaction in the party leadership. At the XV Plenum of the Central Committee which opened on 18 February 1984, then, Jaruzelski was able to speak of the continuous and systematic consolidation of party ranks, although this was qualified by recognition of the 'long and difficult road which lies ahead of us'.

Major aspects of these difficulties were the extensive passivity in local organisations and 'flagrant discrepancies' between party organs at different levels of the organisation and in different provinces. A very qualified form of optimism was also evident in the short, published reports on each provincial conference. One substantive criticism that often appeared (for example, in those from Jelenia Góra and Łódź) concerned the resistance to economic reform that persisted and the obstacles the party encountered in demonstrating its leadership within the economic sphere. There were also frequent references to difficult relations with the working class and the problem of engaging the sympathies of young people. A characteristic statement appeared in the report from Rzeszów, where the need was identified for a party programme 'which would be accepted not just by the membership and party organs, but which would also receive the approval and support of society': only then would the party gain 'full authority and a leading role in society'.[102]

This was a theme that was expressed with increasing clarity in the coming months. Under military leadership the party organisation had been disciplined, purged and brought under tighter central control. Its position with regard to society at large had not been improved, though, nor had its role within the political system and in relation to the other institutions of communist rule been enhanced. Arguments for a more flexible conception of the party's role had been aired in the run-up to the provincial conferences and some ways in which the party might reestablish itself as a social and political force with some measure of public support had been identified. In October an article had been published which referred to the changes taking place in the party whose essence lay 'in deepening the comprehension of the party's leading role – above all – as a form of social service'. This referred in particular to the letters of appeal received by the Katowice party organisation's daily paper, which were now said to be being given special attention by the provincial committee and which were regarded as a useful method of gauging the public mood. It was, nevertheless, hardly a new focus of interest in the party (even if it had not been at the forefront of the attention of the party authorities in recent years) and had been the subject of some discussion in its relation to debates over party authority in the late seventies (see chapter 3).[103] Nevertheless, in the search to find some basis of popular support and to restore party authority, it represented a conception of the party's leading role that was of a considerably less 'vanguard' character than had been articulated over the preceding two years – if, indeed, the notion of party activity as a form of social service could be described as forming part of a leading role at all.

Provincial first secretaries, such as Ratajczak (Gorzów Wielkopolski) and Woźniak (Warsaw), did not hesitate to emphasise the need for a party programme that would be accepted by society as a whole, the latter stating that party resolutions and activity should always be linked with 'the state of consciousness of the whole society' and that 'socialism cannot be built without the participation of non-party people'.[104] Even CC secretary Barcikowski, in a relatively sanguine interview, conceded that the problem of 'building a national understanding' was proving to be more difficult than had been thought at the time of the IX Congress.[105] Having concentrated first on reshaping and reasserting control over the party organisation, the party leadership now turned its attention more towards the continuing weakness with respect to the mass of Polish society and the problems it faced in gaining authority as a political force. The leadership's reassertion of control within the party organisation was only the first stage of political normalisation – and even that involved the advance of the military authorities to a position of unusual political prominence. Further development of the normalisation process meant both the development of the party as a political force capable of a greater degree of independence from the military and the establishment of relations with the mass of the Polish population which would permit the establishment of a more conventional pattern of party rule involving at least the capacity to exert a minimal form of political authority by the civilian leadership.

8 The Polish road to political stability: ruling without authority

Sounding out the grass roots: the National Conference of Congress delegates

The leadership's attempt to establish a new relationship with the rank and file and the working class, and thus explore the possibility of restoring its authority by seeking some pragmatic bases of social support, was made public at the Party Conference held in March 1984. This was convened following a decision taken at the IX (Extraordinary) Congress of 1981 that delegates should retain their mandate and meet at a National Conference, roughly half way between that and the next formal Congress. The formal rights of the Conference delegates, deriving from party elections held nearly three years earlier, were not fully clear, although it was obvious that the delegates retained considerable 'moral prestige' (drawn to no little extent from the conditions under which they were elected in 1981) and that the Conference would be a political event of some importance. Pre-Conference statements made by some of the delegates echoed recent concerns of the party leadership, arising for example from the problems involved in controlling bureaucracy and improving cadre policy (where a bold approach was called for by one member of the Gdańsk provincial committee and complaints were heard of the failure to respect decisions of party organs).[1] The limited progress made in the direction of economic reform was noted, as was the party's inability to safeguard living standards, which were felt to be closely linked with the degree of confidence in the party felt by the working class. Anxieties about the state of inner-party democracy amongst the Conference delegates were also evident. One noted that, while their status after the Extraordinary Congress had been somewhat ill-defined, no attempt had been made by the top leadership to make use of their services. Party discipline, said another (from Gdańsk), had been excessive and criticism had been too easily condemned as opposition. In an evident reference to the recent provincial conferences, another noted that there had often been only one candidate ('not only in local committees') in the election of first secretaries. Uncontested elections at the recent provincial conferences had been, it was claimed, very much the dominant form, as there had been two candidates in only four provinces and more than this in only one.[2]

The membership composition of the original Congress was not greatly changed. Of the 1,962 elected in 1981, 16 had died by the time of the Conference, 19 had been subject to some form of party discipline and were disqualified, while 48 were no longer members. As only 1,835 mandates were deemed to be valid by the time the Conference opened on 16 March, this suggested that a further 44 mandates had been withdrawn between that date and CC secretary Mokrzyszczak's statement on the subject on 27 February. At the Conference, Jaruzelski reiterated his realistic view of the possibilities of party leadership and stated that 'it is not sufficient to decree the leading role of the party', admitting that while 'socialism cannot be built without a Marxist-Leninist party, it is not communists who can build it by themselves'. He spoke again of the weakness and passivity of some party organisations and noted that a survey of the views of Conference delegates had shown that more than a third thought that the resolutions of the IX Congress had not been fully implemented. On the other hand, he was more sanguine about the condition of the party apparatus and announced that around 60% of its staff had been employed in it no longer than five years and that, for the first time, a 'cadre review' had taken place in the apparatus.[3]

A major feature of the Conference was that it provided an unusual forum for the expression of rank-and-file opinion and criticism of the state of the party. Some members felt that the authorities were again tending to present a simplified picture of reality and that activists were become increasingly smug; criticisms were made of recent organisational innovations (the ROPP were clearly in mind here) which were 'confusing and ineffective' and served to swell the ranks of the administration and feed bureaucratic pomposity; the apparatus was condemned for its weak commitment to renewal and the Central Committee itself criticised for its readiness to coopt new members; the dominance of management in industrial party organisations was identified as having consequences for inner-party democracy which meant that worker criticism was suppressed, a point which echoed the earlier remarks of the delegates about the way in which criticism was viewed within the party. In their rejection of the way in which the regional party centres (ROPP) had developed since 1981, some suggested that they should just be disbanded or absorbed by the organisation surrounding the provincial committees. In the party press, however, generally positive appraisals of the role and activities of the ROPP continued to be published.[4]

The critical orientation towards the current approach of the party authorities and their direction of the party organisation was continued in views expressed of the recent provincial conferences and the conditions under which the provincial committees operated. A worker from the 'Ursus' factory complained about the stage-managed character of the Warsaw conference and another, also (perhaps significantly) from Warsaw, charged that the results of the conference had been arranged before it opened. From another province, one KW member complained of the inability of the party organ to exert any influence over the apparatus, about whose service role 'we no longer hear anything'. The recent election of the KW first secretary and its political implications were singled out for criticism, and the procedures employed were said to have conflicted with the requirements laid down in the Party Statute (which demanded that there should be more candidates than there were posts). Not only was one single candidate put forward – the 'outgoing' first secretary who was nominated for re-election on the recommendation of the Politburo – but attempts to nominate a second candidate were rejected as infringements of democratic centralism.[5] Such procedures were apparently very much the norm under current conditions and their application at the provincial conferences directed attention to the general question of internal party procedures following the lifting of the State of War.

The critical views expressed were of particular importance not just because of the recent date of the elections or the fact that they were the first to take place since the State of War, but also because it was the task of the Conference assigned by the IX Congress to review the existing, provisional election regulations and to adopt a set of permanent procedures. The arrangements which came in for criticism at the Conference, however, actually represented infringements of the Party Statute which had already been accepted by the IX Congress and there was no formal necessity to amend the electoral regulations to guard against such behaviour – although there were clearly expectations on the part of some delegates that this should be the case and it could obviously have been done to clarify the matter. But the delegates' criticism did not seem to have any effect on the course of the Conference proceedings and the issue did not progress any further, although it obviously made nonsense of the principle of secret ballotting so strongly emphasised in 1981.

The recommendation of the CC Commission was that the provisional rules had stood the test of time and that they could be accepted with minor amendments, one of which was that the number of candidates for committee membership should exceed the number of electoral vacancies by at least 15%. That suggestion was not accepted by the Conference, either. A further feature of the regulations finally agreed was definition of the number of secretaries appropriate to each of the forty-nine provincial committees, which was to vary according to the level of party membership in the province. On the basis of the level of party membership reported at the end of December 1983 this provided for a total of 294 secretaries at provincial committee level. This represented a considerable rise on the 255 (with the possible addition of a further two or so) who had been elected as a result of the December 1983/January 1984 procedures.[6] It was, further, a higher total than the 243 secretaries in post prior to the 1981 elections when, of course, the PZPR had a far higher membership total. This appeared to promise the further expansion of the apparatus at province level and gave at least some credence to fears of a bureaucratic resurgence.

A further basis for criticism expressed by the delegates concerned the processes of checking and supervision of party activities (*kontrola*). The extent of recent changes amongst chairmen of the two provincial control agencies, the auditing commission (WKR) and the party control commission (WKKP), had been quite considerable: twenty-one and eighteen respectively. The basis of this extensive turnover was somewhat uncertain, as the degree to which the work of the commissions and their chairmen had been assessed and evaluated was said to have been far from satisfactory. We have also noted (chapter 7) that the number of changes made at this level of the party hierarchy should be placed in the context of the reassertion of central control pursued under military rule. At the Conference several negative comments were made on the politically motivated character of WKKP decisions and the inability of the commissions to control the executive apparatus and exercise their supervisory influence.[7] Some weeks earlier the Central Auditing Commission (CKR) had also complained about the problems encountered in attempting to establish principles according to which the control agencies could work with party organs. At the Conference the CKR chairman, K. Morawski, elaborated his concern at greater length. A further problem, he said, was that 'in some provinces the party leadership itself showed only a "formal interest" in the revision commissions's and betrayed this in its methods of preparing and selecting candidates to serve with the control agencies. There was, in short, considerable resistance to intra-party control and resentment of such activity.[8]

The situation reflected in the Conference proceedings tended, therefore, to confirm the assertion of central control and the qualification of inner-party democracy that had been introduced under the State of War. Opinions expressed at the Conference suggested a widening gap between current practice and the principles elaborated at the IX Congress, and the consolidation of this disparity into a relatively conventional form of central party rule which gave the apparatus considerable protection and security. In recognition of this process, a number of clearly expressed condemnations of bureaucratic centralism appeared in the party press. 'The process by which the party executive frees itself from the control of party members', warned L. Grzybowski, 'has been the main way in which the principles of democratic centralism have been infringed'; while democratic centralism had on occasion been weakened by anarchist tendencies and fractionalism, the more common and thus dangerous deviation had been in the other direction, 'that is, excessive centralism'. The influence of inner-party conflict on the development of authoritarianism was identified. Discussing styles of party activity, M. Szyszko noted that the authoritarian – as distinct from the democratic – style was generally characteristic of conflict situations and 'conditions of fractional struggle' and was actually preferred by 'sectarian currents and groups'. The relation of this observation to the re-emergence of inner-party conflict in late 1982 and 1983 hardly needed to be emphasised. A further indication of this line of thinking was given by K. Mżyk in his book-length study of democratic centralism, in which he approvingly quoted Tito's gloss on the operationalisation of the concept – the maximum of democracy in policy formulation and unshakeable unity in its implementation.[9] The Conference certainly gave some possibility of sounding out rank-and-file opinions and consulting with those who had played a more important role in 1981, but its proceedings offered little opportunity for broader forms of democratic participation or of influence over policy making.

The search for working-class support

In line with these concerns increasing attention was paid by the leadership to the lack of popular support for the party and policies and to its pronounced isolation from the working class. For two years an official lack of concern had been evident towards the falling levels of party membership and a commitment to quality rather than quantity had been enunciated, but now the tone changed quite sharply. Underlying this change were reports like that from Poznań, where it was noted that party membership in the Cegielski works had fallen from a high of 3,930 in June 1980 to 2,132 in 1984, whilst the proportion of workers amongst them had dropped from 77% to 56%. The number of working-class members had therefore fallen from over 3,000 to 1,190. In this situation, the 'numerical development of the party organisation had stopped being a question one could shamefacedly keep quiet about' and, it was stated, attention now had to be paid to the quantitative development of the party. In late 1984, workers made up only 38.8% of the party membership, well below the place they occupied in the work force as a whole, which stood at over 43%.[10]

Even amongst the workers who were currently becoming party members results were least impressive in the large industrial plants and those most likely to join were to be found amongst those occupying managerial positions.[11] The need for a 'strong immediate link between the party and its parent class' could no longer be ignored, argued another article – it was 'the key to everything: lasting normalisation, the quality and pace of the processes involved in the difficult task of overcoming economic collapse [and] renewal'. Quite simply, 'in order to gain mastery of the situation it is necessary to have the majority of the workers behind us'.[12] Thus, for the XVI Plenum of the Central Committee, held in June 1984, a major departure was envisaged – it was held outside the capital in the Grand Theatre of Łódź and was attended by eight hundred workers from all over the country, both party members and those who were not. In his address to them, CC secretary Porębski emphasised the desire to 'increase the importance of open party meetings', which were a 'very important way of acquainting non party-members with the life of the party'. The implication seemed to be that if the workers were not eager to come towards the party, then the party was willing, if not to embrace the workers of its own accord, at least to open its doors wide to them.

It should be noted, of course, that admitting workers to open party meetings was not the same as giving them rights within the party organisation – what seemed to be at issue was rather an attempt to create some kind of auxiliary rank and file, a development that was not so contradictory to the much-discussed development of the PZPR as a cadre party as might have first appeared. The emphasis within the party leadership was now firmly placed on the virtues of consultation and the establishment of a rapport with the working population as a means of establishing a minimum level of party authority, but there were few signs of the party establishment opening itself to broader participation in terms of decision-making and effective control over executive agencies. The discussion at this unusualy large meeting was, in fact, quite anodyne and tended to be dominated by references to detailed problems of production and accounts of the participants' work situation. Some criticism was made, though, of the extent of the workers' isolation from the party and the newly established official trade unions. In one speech this isolation was attributed at least in part to 'errors committed by the authorities' with the accusation that the party was 'losing the characteristics of a workers' party'.

CC secretary Porębski was careful, however, not to remain uncritical of aspects of working-class development: some sections had fallen prey to the 'influence of demagogy and anarcho-syndicalism' (the latter being the current way in which Solidarity was defined). Parts of the work force were also criticised for their improper work habits and the fact that they had adopted incorrect social attitudes.[13] Nevertheless, the enlarged Plenum showed a considerably more conciliatory attitude being taken by the leadership to the work force and less demanding expectations in terms of ideological conformity. According to one account, party recruitment policy in 1984 was marked by the striking 'lack in any sense of an appeal to ideology'. The extent to which this was due to Polish decision alone, and even against Soviet preference, is the subject of some uncertainty. One account suggests that, accompanying Chernenko's weakening medical and political health, the 'Warsaw Pact countries all showed unprecedented independence'.[14] Others conclude that Soviet influence remained relatively strong, particularly through the links maintained by the KGB and its head, General Chebrikov. This was seen as part of a package of support for the Polish regime following the lifting of the State of War, under which increased economic aid was accompanied by higher levels of political and security 'assistance', which also served to enhance the position of the more pro-Soviet faction within the leadership. Not all agreed that ideology remained as much in the background as others suggested, and some saw the ideological effort becoming intensified after Andropov's death in February 1984.[15] There is evidence to suggest, then, that the more conciliatory attitude adopted towards the workers was part of a stabilisation policy which was agreed not just at the domestic level. Indeed, it is not unlikely that the major part of the resistance offered to Jaruzelski's softer, consultative approach had domestic roots.[16]

The new approach taken towards the working class, though, was not restricted to open meetings and less didactic forms of communication. The effectiveness of party work and the reality of party leadership remained highly questionable, and conceptions of a more active role for workers within the party came increasingly to be associated with the development of a new worker–peasant inspectorate, which would both strengthen party links with the working class and improve the effectiveness of party activities as a whole. Two major weaknesses in party work, therefore, would be tackled at the same time and the programme carried hopes both of gaining greater popular support and publicising the effectiveness of party leadership in a concerted attempt to rebuild party authority. Accompanying this strategy was the objective of making workers again the dominant social group in more than one sense in socio-occupational and geographical environments where workers constituted the majority of the population.[17] The task would obviously not be an easy one. Weaknesses apparent in the party organisation for some time had not been overcome. Behind the protestations that local organisations were more interested in the quality than the number of party members, claimed KW first secretary Łukasik, was a prevalent political passivity and unwillingness to engage with the work force as a whole; the workers themselves showed little desire for participation and most of them, stated the first secretary of a large Lublin plant, 'have a bad opinion of us and see hardly any improvement, any change for the better'.[18]

A series of factory meetings arranged with workers after the XVI Plenum echoed the criticisms that had emerged at that gathering (exasperation with low living standards, bitterness at social inequality, suspicion and dislike of intellectuals, resentment at the private sector – the last two often identified as 'anti-socialist forces') and also uncovered a pronounced lack of enthusiasm for the establishment of yet another control agency. The committees of 'social control' instituted in the late seventies were still remembered as a specious publicity gimmick and the status of further amateur enterprises was much doubted, particularly in its likely influence over the economic administration.[19] These views were lent some support by details of existing control procedures and the maze of control networks; even before the end of 1984 one plant had been checked forty-seven times and, during one period, three different agencies were investigating the same area of activity. Of those questioned in a recent survey, moreover, 62% regarded the existing system of control as already effective.[20]

'Workers' control' and political authority

The proposed new 'worker–peasant inspectorate', however, received enthusiastic publicity from the authorities and was presented as a suitably Leninist solution (with copious references to the original *Rabkrin*) to the problems associated with Poland's ineffective administration and diminished party authority. It was both an 'important aspect of the dictatorship of the proletariat' and seen as representing a 'watershed in the activity of the entire system of social control'. While the CC Secretariat had taken the decision to launch the inspectorate in August 1984, following the XVI Plenum, its roots were traced back to the XIII Plenum, at which major problems of ideology had been aired, and as far back as the pre-Congress discussions of 1981, which had seen many proposals 'for the strengthening of workers' and peasants' rights'.[21] The activities of the inspectorate were also to facilitate the 'direct participation' of the working class in political life.

Initial deliberations, however, did not result in a clear plan for the implementation of the proposals, and consultations did not produce 'unambiguous answers as to the form and location of the inspectorate' in the political system. Variants proposed included an agency based primarily on People's Councils, another based on the Supreme Control Chamber (*Najwyższa Izba Kontroli*), and one more combining elements from different structures.[22] Concern was expressed that the inspectorate should have real rather than formal powers and that it should not be closely associated with existing bureaucratic structures. Thus, arguments that it should be based on the People's Council structure alluded to its constitutional basis as the primary organ of popular representation in a given locality.[23] In the event the inspectorate was placed under the jurisdiction of the Supreme Control Chamber – but also under the 'political and ideological leadership' of the PZPR, whilst it was simultaneously directed to act in close cooperation with the People's Councils. This result seemed to imply close linkages with the existing party–state complex and placed some question marks over its own powers.

Some early experiences also gave rise to public doubts about the usefulness of the inspectorate. What, for example, was to happen after the check? The important thing, concluded one report, was to ensure that the particular check or control was the last one – that is, to ensure that it was successful. 'Up to now this has not been the case.' In general, though, the experimental application of the scheme was deemed successful and the programme was intended to be fully operational by the end of 1985. As it developed it became clear that, whatever the legal basis that had been established, the inspectorate would be under the 'political patronage and leadership' of the party and that direction would be exercised by the legal commissions of the party at CC and provincial committee level.[24] On a national scale, nearly 18,000 inspectorate 'controllers' were chosen, 62% of whom were PZPR members and 70% of whom were recommended directly by the primary party organisations. Local lists of controllers were presented by the executives of the provincial committees and confirmed by the Provincial People's Council. Their training was provided by the Supreme Control Chamber, while 'it was expected' that support for their activities would be provided by the party control and revision commissions. Later reports confirmed the close relationship between the workers' inspectorate and the party control organs.[25]

As the workers and peasants' inspectorate became fully operational, then, it appeared to fit closely into the framework of existing control agencies which, of course, were themselves associated with the range of established political and administrative institutions. It may well have been the case that this form of incorporation tended to nullify its capacity for supervision and effective checking on the operation of the relevant organisations, a danger which had been clearly underwritten by past experience and which had not been ignored at the time of the project's proposal. Certainly, following the full implementation of the programme by the end of 1985, considerably less attention was paid to the inspectorate in the press and fewer ambitious hopes were expressed of its likely impact. Towards the end of 1986 the endorsement of the inspectorate's activities was rather muted, the results of its introduction being described as merely 'confirming the correctness of the party leadership's decision' in putting it into practice. Problems in parallel institutions had not diminished following the lifting of the State of War, and the effectiveness of checking and verifying the operations of the established institutions and bureaucracies was, as in the past, not facilitated by popular apathy and the limitations placed on democratic participation. Public dissatisfaction with the shortcomings of party control procedures was again on the rise, with the CKKP chairman complaining of the failure of local commissions to take action against misdemeanours and the CKR chairman continuing to attack the resistance of local organs and their staff to investigation and the evaluation of their performance.[26]

The limited success of the inspectorate, therefore, was due at least partly to the factors that minimised the influence of other control agencies. It is likely that the effectiveness of the inspectorate also suffered from its close association with the provincial committee and its apparatus. The role of its first secretary, the position of the committee and its capacity to perform a leading role in the locality had all been circumscribed, as noted above, by the diminished status of the party, the continuing influence of the military and limitations imposed by the stringent socio-economic situation. A particular problem seemed to be the bureaucratisation of KW departments and the excessive routinisation of their work – to the extent that there was sometimes little inter-department coordination and little overall leadership from the provincial apparatus. There were complaints of inadequate supervision of primary organisations from the province and the limitation of contacts to routine administrative consultation with local secretaries. As a result, the CC Secretariat issued new directives in early 1985 with the aim of integrating KW activities and improving party leadership within the province.[27]

Some of the disappointment expressed concerning the performance of the workers and peasants' inspectorate was traced to its planned general role, not dissimilar to that of KW organs, and to over-ambitious requirements of being in the position of having to check and verify virtually anything in the locality. These excessive demands, in one view, led directly to the bureaucratisation of the activities of the inspectorate and the well-known dangers of the 'domination of the permanent apparatus of controllers' over social activists. In view of the close supervision exercised by the provincial committee, such bureaucratisation within the inspectorate necessarily meant a close association with the KW apparatus and the effects of its weakened political position. Provincial conditions and the relative position of the KW secretariat seemed to vary over the country, but there were general factors that had led to its lower political status and diminished influence (chapter 7). Low levels of party membership, passivity among the members and organisational weakness, reduced powers over the *nomenklatura* and staff appointments all had influenced the position of the provincial committee, under normal conditions the effective power-holder within local society and the prime agency of the central authorities below national level.[28]

The provincial committee was no longer the centre of the sub-national political network. Bejger, Gdańsk first secretary, was thus able to make the unusual admission that 'at province level, we do not have any controversial problems'. Conflicts arose more at enterprise level, involving relations between the plant committee, director and workers' council – involving also perhaps the trade union. They represented, according to one description, a 'horizontal movement' of local power-holders, being likely to involve, say, the secretary of the local party committee, the provincial governor, or the director of the construction plant. Notable here was the absence of the provincial first secretary. According to Staniszkis, this re-alignment of forces had not only a practical impact in terms of local power relations but it also contributed in more general terms to the fading of the general notion of party leadership throughout the political system; no longer was it thought necessary to turn in all matters to the party committee and consult with 'the secretary'.[29] Underground Solidarity publications also alluded in stark terms to the attenuation of the role of the provincial committees which, it was claimed, suffered more than the central leadership from the decline in party authority 'because they are nearer to "the people". In provincial committees . . . nothing is decided, no-one ever goes there, telephone calls are an even greater rarity.'[30] While according with certain trends we have noted this is, of course, a more dramatic picture of the marginalisation of the provincial committee than we have so far suggested and a very different one from that presented in the party press.

Indeed, official accounts at this time were claiming that provincial committees were increasingly becoming the target of appeals from the local population and the focus of their attention in attempts to secure social justice and practical improvements in their living conditions. As had been the case in the 1970s, emphasis was increasingly laid on the role of the provincial committee as the recipient of citizens' letters and popular complaints as a means of establishing and consolidating links with the population at large (chapter 3). A resolution affirming the importance of such contacts had been passed at the IX Plenum in 1982, but it received stronger emphasis in 1985 as greater priority was ascribed to strengthening the party's social base and making good the decline in its membership. As had been the case some years previously, the number of letters and complaints received by provincial committees was seen not so much as a sign of persisting social and economic difficulties as a mark of the 'growing confidence of society in the party'.[31] Such forms of political communication have been recognised as playing a significant role in political processes within other communist systems, but accounts like White's do not mention as part of that role the expression of confidence in the party authorities. That emphasis appears to be specific to the Polish party and its alienation from national society, which thus brings its leadership to seek various forms of social reassurance not required by organisations like the CPSU.[32]

Much play, therefore, was made of the extent of communication between population and party organs, and its increase over successive years. In 1982, for example, party organs received letters and appeals from 412,044 people, and in 1985, from 423,122. This was indeed an increase, although not one that could be described as very striking. In view of the evident unpopularity of the party in 1982 under the State of War, the slightly higher number of letters and appeals received in 1985 was not an impressive testimony to its enhanced or restored authority. Indeed, there were some signs that the population had been in some places less inclined to turn to provincial committees for assistance. In 1984, the complaints department in Tarnów KW received 15% fewer communications than during the preceding year; a similar decline was noted in Skierniewice – although it was matched by an increase in the number sent to primary organisations.[33] Even if such communications are to be realistically viewed as indices of the population's confidence in the party and thus of the party's political authority, recent signs did not point to any significant upturn in the party's fortunes. What was more significant was that in 1984 and 1985 the party leadership laid emphasis on new, locally-led 'control' procedures and on the provincial committees' capacity to deal with citizen demands and consumer complaints as a means of placing party authority on a firmer footing – as it had some years previously in the late seventies. Again, provincial committees were placed in a contradictory position, encouraged to develop more locally-oriented, conciliatory lines of policy while political power remained resolutely centralised and the national leadership showed little inclination or capacity to alter policy in ways that would provide more lasting grounds for popular satisfaction and thus establish party authority. In both cases party leadership at the provincial level was severely circumscribed and surpassed by the powers devolved to equivalent levels of institutions more firmly located within the state structure. To the extent that levels of party authority were effectively determined by the actions and status of the provincial committees, the outlook for the party's national position in the mid-eighties was somewhat less positive than it had been ten years earlier, although aspects of its political strategy were strikingly similar.

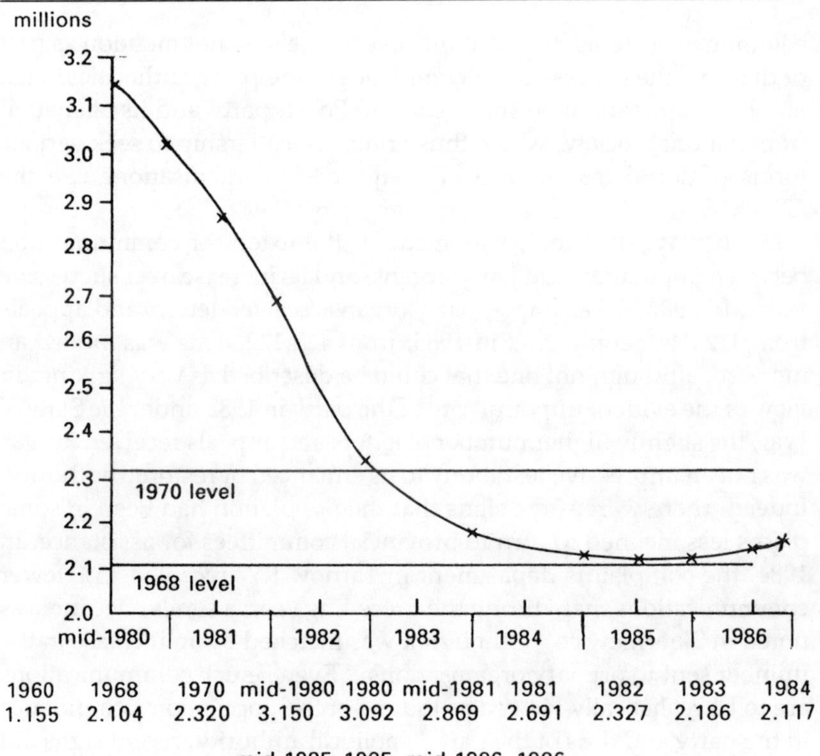

1960	1968	1970	mid-1980	1980	mid-1981	1981	1982	1983	1984
1.155	2.104	2.320	3.150	3.092	2.869	2.691	2.327	2.186	2.117

mid-1985	1985	mid-1986	1986
2.112	2.115	2.126	2.129

Figure 8.1 Party membership, 1960–86
(In millions, end of year totals unless otherwise stated)

The state of the party

The problems experienced by the party in gaining social confidence and rebuilding authority on that basis were illustrated by a number of opinion polls. In response to a question asking which institution served society well and was most congruent with its interests, only 16.6% mentioned the party. More mentioned the Church, the *Sejm*, the army and the government. Below the party itself came only the recently formed official trade unions, security forces, auxiliary political parties and PRON, the recently established 'national rebirth' movement. The following year, 1986, saw some apparent improvement with 'around a fifth' of respondents stating that they had a high level of confidence in the party's Central Commitee (other party organs were not mentioned).[34] But general interest in party matters remained at a fairly low level. Despite all the publicity during the preparations for the X PZPR Congress in 1986, only 44% claimed to be informed about the contents of the outline PZPR Programme, while 10% stated that they had read or looked through it. Dissatisfaction with key personnel was also widespread, and in fact became more acute as attention passed to the higher organs of power at province and national level.[35] KW first secretaries in particular appeared to be the object of public dislike, and a number of them received the lowest vote in their constituencies during the autumn 1985 elections.[36]

While action taken during the State of War and in subsequent years had restored discipline within the party organisation and strengthened central control over the party hierarchy, the nature and effectiveness of party work in the social context left much to be desired. Membership continued to decline through 1984 and the first half of 1985, and the work of local organisations often had little impact on their surroundings. The party, announced CC secretary Porębski to the XX Plenum (June 1985), had 'made considerable progress in rebuilding its internal links and its operational mechanism'. But primary organisations generally were not active enough and there was frequently a lack of discipline in party work which kept them on the margins of social life, this being particularly the case with party cells in the large industrial enterprises. Membership continued to decline and now stood at 2.112 million. The Politburo expressed the view that it was both 'possible and indispensible' that there should be a 'full and consistent stabilisation of the development of our ranks' in the run-up to the X Congress, which was due to be held in a year's time.

By the end of the year, some success in this strategy was reported. October was the third month in a row that membership totals had shown a rise, while 1985 was the first year since 1980 that significant numbers of new members had been accepted in the party. The net rise in itself was not large at 1,000 (64,000 having joined the party and 63,000 having been removed from party lists), but 1985 was the first year since 1979 that the party had ended a year with more members than it had registered six months earlier (see Figure 8.1).[37] The decline in membership was halted, in fact, just around the time of the XX Plenum, as the second half of the year showed an overall rise in the total of party members. The increase continued in 1986, although at a gradual rate, and on the eve of the X Congress at the end of May 1986, membership reached 2.126 million. This was a far cry from the rate of increase in earlier times (106,000 joined the party in the first six months of 1980 – just before the outbreak of the summer strikes) but it did represent a reversal of the downward trend in party membership that had persisted since that time.[38] Significantly, though, no end-of-year totals for 1986 were published in the early weeks of 1987 and the recovery of the party as an institution was a precarious process.

Membership totals were, of course, affected not only by the number of those applying to join the party but also by resignations and expulsions. The number of those joining the party over recent years had, until 1985, been outweighed by the number who had resigned, been expelled or just removed from party lists for passivity or indifference. In fact, after 1982 the fall in party numbers was due rather to the latter factors: resignations and removals from party lists rather than expulsion for serious political infringements of party discipline. Overall, some 40,000 were expelled (*wydaloni*) between the IX Congress and the end of March 1986, most expulsions occurring towards the end of 1981 and during the State of War. In 1983 1,128 were expelled for 'infringements of an ethical nature' and in 1984 a further 1,761. In 1985, a total of 651 people were expelled from the party.[39] Slightly more than half of the expulsions in the recent period (53%) concerned party members performing managerial functions in the economy and administration, to whom increasingly strict criteria were applied in terms of performance as party members. Provincial control commissions were said to be taking a decisive stand on such matters and occupying themselves increasingly with 'control' activities involving checking and verification.[40] Clearly, though, internal party control procedures had become more concerned with the impact of party members' behaviour and the quality of their performance rather than in maintaining party discipline merely by expelling undesirable elements. Moreover, in view of the clear decision to stop the decline in party numbers it obviously made sense to monitor and improve the performance of party members rather than to expel those whose behaviour was less than satisfactory.

The attempt to improve the party's standing in Polish society was also accompanied by calls for more democratic practices and reexamination of the continuing ambiguities in party organisation and the implementation of its principles. An early, and major, contribution to this debate was made by E. Erazmus in an article on the 'ambiguity of the party apparatus'. Avoiding a simple condemnation of the apparatus as the identifiable source of current political problems he nevertheless condemned recurring deviations like the elimination of the distinction 'in terms of decision-making' between the elected and executive bodies within the party. Pertinent contemporary reflections were clearly intended in references to the 1920s, when the extended role of the apparatus was attributed to anarcho-syndicalist tendencies within the working class and views were prevalent that those 'who led the party in the militarisation period . . . cannot and will not be able to promote democratism and should therefore go'. Reference was also made to features noted above concerning the provincial committees and the ease with which centralising tendencies fitted with the KW departmental structure.

Criticism of centralism in connection with the provincial apparatus and implications of excessive bureaucratisation were associated with the continuing attention paid to the status of the regional party centres (ROPP). By 1985 they appeared to be firmly established as 'local departments of the provincial committees', which continued to raise 'misunderstandings' and resentment on the part of a number of local secretaries.[41] It was maintained that at least some of the functions originally performed by the ROPP (formally called into being, it should be remembered, by a CC Secretariat decision of December 1981 and the principles of their operation outlined by the VII Plenum of February 1982) had now lost their relevance and that, the cadre disruption of 1981 now having been countered by the reassertion of normal procedures, the status of the ROPP in the local political system could now be redefined. Others were more forthright in their view and criticised the persistence of the ROPP as non-statutory bodies, exercising unwarranted powers as purely executive organs.[42]

There were clearly a number of issues relating to theory and practice in the party organisation that required clarification – and several deeprooted contradictions inherent in current party work that stemmed from the leadership's claimed allegiance to the reformist principles laid down at the IX Congress and from the insistence on centralism and discipline that abruptly re-emerged with the commencement of the State of War. The persistence of such contradictions raised numerous questions about the reality of democratic practice in party work and contributed to popular mistrust of its organisation and officials. Resolution of such doubts was felt by many to be a necessary condition if the party was to establish its authority and regain an effective leading role. Hopes were attached in this respect to the forcoming X Congress of the PZPR, due to be held in the summer of 1986. A 'business-like discussion' was called for, which would permit a 'solid reckoning' and identification of the causes of specific party failures and reasons for departures from principles laid down at the previous Congress. Behind contemporary democratic rhetoric lay, claimed one critic, 'tendencies to autocracy and bureaucratism, formalism and deceit'.

Justification for these views was sought, as it had been on numerous past occasions, in uncorrupted Leninism, and two specific deviations from Leninism were identified in the Polish situation – the usurping of government functions by the party apparatus and elective bodies by the party executive, and the burdening of the party *aktiv* with bureaucratic tasks and other non-priority duties.[43]

Pressures for such changes were, of course, not restricted in these matters to Polish society and the changes launched by Gorbachev in the Soviet Union gave Polish reformers considerable help and lent them a useful appearance of orthodoxy. His initiative had been welcomed at the XX CC Plenum in June 1985 by Jaruzelski, who noted his encouragement of open, specific criticism both of the administration and of individual members of party organs at different levels. Such measures he described as 'inspiring, innovatory solutions' to the political problems shared by the socialist countries. Another enthusiastically endorsed Gorbachev's thesis that the socialist countries face the 'supreme necessity of implementing essential reforms and changes', and emphasised the need for the party to develop indirect means of performing its 'guiding and leading role'.[44] Such sentiments found support at province level and Mieczysław Czerniawski, appointed first KW secretary in Łomża in January 1986, also criticised habits of unthinking compliance with centrally transmitted directives within the party and the erroneous confusion of this with political leadership; it was necessary, he said, to distinguish between organisational discipline and sheer grotesqueness. The pervasive culture of bureaucratic obedience was singled out by others as a prime cause of the demotivation prevalent in society and amongst young people in particular.[45]

Early indications of how party affairs would be handled during the Congress year, however, did not augur well for the airing of major political differences and for hopes of their resolution. At the XXIII CC Plenum, held in December 1985, it was already announced by the Politburo that the party meetings held in preparation for the coming Congress would not elect new committees and their local leadership as had been the case in 1981. Instead, the elections would be held after the Congress, from September to December. Clearly this was proposed in order to prevent any recurrence of the conflict and uncertainty that had preceded the Extraordinary Congress five years earlier. But it also raised serious doubts about the intentions of the leadership with respect to the discussion of contentious issues and the seriousness with which they intended to pursue the principles established by the IX Congress. This concerned in particular the role of the party apparatus and the steps taken in 1981 to ensure that party officials did not stay in their jobs for unlimited periods of time and develop unwarranted rights of office. By the time of the announcement at the XXIII Plenum, twenty-seven of the forty-nine provincial first secretaries had been changed since the IX Congress. As the party rules adopted then stipulated that party secretaries should, in principle, stand down after five years this meant that twenty-two first secretaries were due to be changed in the run-up to the Congress.[46]

This early decision about the ordering of party business in 1986 meant that any doubts or conflicts concerning the leadership's adherence to the principles of the IX Congress and its treatment of the still contentious issues surrounding the status of the apparatus would be kept away from the coming Congress. It would be correspondingly easier to arrange it as a political set-piece and use it more as a public relations exercise than a forum for the airing of real differences and a means for advancing towards a resolution of the contradictions still implicit in the party's position and the approach of its leadership. This ambivalence was also present in the views of some of the KW first secretaries. Secretary Czechowicz, himself in post from November 1980, well before the IX Congress, affirmed that the party would stick to the principles laid down then, but also claimed that the party needed a 'certain stabilisation of cadres' and stated that he would recommend some flexibility in the application of the rotation principle. At that time the general limitation of five years in post for party secretaries represented two terms of office. In the event, the X Congress reaffirmed its commitment to the two-term general limitation – but unified the terms of office throughout the party organisation to five years, thereby actually departing from principles laid down at the IX Congress and easing the restrictions there placed on officials' careers in particular offices.[47] Arrangements concerning the X Congress, then, did little to provide the conditions for more open debate; nor did they support the procedural decisions taken in 1981 to limit the tendencies of party secretaries and the apparatus in general to develop as a self-serving caste. In neither of these ways did the leadership choose to use the X Congress as an occasion to reinforce the democratic aspects of the party organisation and to enhance the party's authority by establishing a firmer basis of popular participation and support.

The decisive role of cadres

None of the strategies recently mooted had done much to improve the position of the party in Polish society. The more conciliatory approach adopted towards the working class had contributed to halting the decline in party numbers but had done little to extend general support for the leadership or to establish party authority. Despite a range of institutional innovations there was no real change in the location and exercise of power and little genuine extension of democratic participation. Neither did the economy show many signs of recovery and there was little hope for the growth of support for the party on the basis of its performance in this field. In seeking to consolidate its position and enhance its political and managerial effectiveness the leadership again began paying closer attention to groups over whom it had more direct control and who were, at the same time, the instruments for the realisation of its policy. Issues of cadre policy therefore came into positions of greater prominence.

Cadre policy had, in one sense, been at the forefront of the attention of the military leadership at an early stage, but this had concerned primarily the strengthening of political discipline and the reimposition of central control both in the party and in parts of the state structure. It had also entered into the intensification of checking and verification procedures (*kontrola*) and the emphasis on various kinds of inspection activities. The Central Committee's attention had been turned to cadre issues at the XIII Plenum in October 1983 where General Dziekan, head of the CC Cadres Department, had set out guidelines for the development of cadres policy, including the formation of a cadre reserve (chapter 7). A year later, at the XVII Plenum, the commitment of the Central Committee to the development of the policy was reaffirmed as an 'indispensible element of the party's leadership function within the state'. Following Dziekan's death, his successor as head of the Cadres Department, General Honkisz, reported on developments in the two years following the XIII Plenum. A cadre review in 1985 had included over one million individuals and a second check on full-time party cadres had been carried out. Progress was reported also on the creation of a cadre reserve.[48]

The new emphasis was clearly understood to have fundamental political implications and to go considerably beyond issues of technical proficiency. It was the case, for example, that the 'credibility of the party is often determined by its cadre policy', while the majority of the party's defeats, in one view, were the result of 'an inappropriate choice of people for leadership positions'. This opinion was also held by KW first secretary Mróz, who added that, unless it exerted an influence on cadre decisions, the party would be unable to perform its leading role. In his province, Opole, 19% of the overall 'leading cadre' were changed in the period 1984–86.[49] In the current situation in which the party apparatus found itself cadres issues had particular importance. We discussed in some detail in chapter 2 the connection between the changing composition of the KW secretariats, cadres characteristics and the nature of party work under Gierek. We later noted the changes in the nature of the secretariats and the role of party organs under the radically different political conditions of the accelerating renewal movement (1981) and the State of War (1982–83). The importance of these connections was confirmed by current discussions within the party. The sheer pace of change had lent increasing importance to party cadres policy. Most changes had taken place at province level and below, and here turnover in the early eighties was described as having reached the level of 80%. A consequence of this had been, and still was, the 'laborious task' of rebuilding the party apparatus.

Military experience was clearly intended to exert a major influence over the replacement and development of civilian cadres. The attention paid to this in the party under Jaruzelski's leadership and the retention of the leadership of the CC Cadres Department by the military was enough to demonstrate this. Malcher has suggested that the large number of political officers produced by army training establishments, considerably in excess of the army's own needs, has had a close connection with the military interest in civilian cadres policy and the renewal of leading staff throughout the party–state complex. Other sources, though, suggest that the military interest has lain rather in cadre mechanisms and the processes of staff training and placement. The Polish military, claimed one Ministry of Defence representative, had worked out original solutions to the problems arising in these areas by the early seventies, while developments in civilian sectors showed that alternatives to the processes prevailing there might well be usefully applied. Long-term planning, training and verification were essential to the military staff programme and, while this point was not singled out for emphasis, the planned nature of staff development and the 'psychological security' this offered the military officers would seem to stand in some conflict with the principle of elective leadership which still prevailed in the party apparatus.[50]

This was only one of a number of difficult questions that arose in the consideration of cadre policy. The desirability of developing reliable mechanisms for training, appointing and replacing key personnel was evident. It touched on many of the key issues rooted in the structure and operation of the communist party–state, though, and raised topics that had been the source of controversy and conflict in the past. It was regarded as crucial, in one view, to distinguish between a cadres policy and the principle of the *nomenklatura* cadre, the latter referring not to the process of identifying and allocating those with particular talents but rather to the political guarantee of society's general trajectory from capitalism to socialism. The two were clearly linked, as the question of the occupation of leading positions was obviously intimately related with the holding and exercise of political power. Thus, according to Erazmus, it was important that the choice of those selected for leading positions should be made not by the executive apparatus of the party but by its elected organs. The problems posed by the apparatus in this connection were, as was well known, complex and persistent ones. The development of an appropriate cadres policy in relation to the apparatus itself involved equally serious difficulties. As the same writer pointed out, these were by no means solved by internal reorganisation or changing certain numbers of the incumbents of party apparatus positions.[51]

The depth of these problems was confirmed by subsequent comments on the implementation of the cadres policy. The judgment of one party official from a factory organisation on the recently conducted cadres review was a negative one, largely because the criteria applied were excessively 'general and laconic'. The difficulties encountered in applying the policy at local level were considerable – partly because official moves had also been made to enhance elements of local self-government and the cooperative principle in enterprise management. This reduced the potential influence of the party in some production environments. Party influence over cadre affairs could also be limited by the features of enterprise self-management that accompanied the attempts to press forward with various aspects of economic reform. Examples were given of stalemate situations that developed following conflict between the different actors involved. In such a situation, described the secretary of one industrial party organisation, 'the party, of course, loses out'. In that case, he explained, they managed to secure the removal of that director from his post, because 'it was a struggle over who had authority'. The situation was clearly complicated by the leadership's diverse attempts to introduce elements of reform and greater participation in different sectors of the local economy, some of which could easily come into conflict.[52]

Cadres change was also taking place in the party apparatus. Writing in mid-1984 Nowak, first secretary of the Wałbrzych provincial organisation, stated that around half of the party's full-time workers had been replaced in the past five years, and that over the past year their number had fallen from 244 to 235. In view of the level of change in the apparatus during 1981 and 1982 this rate of turnover seemed rather modest and, indeed, it was reported a year later that in the country as a whole nearly two-thirds of party workers had been employed by the PZPR for five years or less.[53] This broadly fitted in with the previously noted report of an 80% turnover in the early eighties affecting staff at provincial level and lower. In apparatus appointments considerable emphasis was paid to educational qualification and training; 80% of party political workers were reported by General Honkisz to have higher education and increasing attention was again paid to party training, a doubling of graduates from party schools foreseen for the year 1995.

As might be expected from the adoption of such a time scale, stabilisation of apparatus development and the regularisation of cadres renewal was regarded by the General as being of prime importance. Increasing numbers of apparatus workers were being employed following service in elective posts within the party organisation, apparently a post-renewal reversal of the previous tendency for experienced party workers to rise and occupy formally elective offices. More were also coming in to work in the apparatus from the state administration. In general, it appeared, the tendency to compartmentalise careers was again on the decrease. People were less likely to be restricted in their employment to the three main career structures: the political, managerial and administrative. This was explicitly noted in the Bydgoszcz apparatus, where people were now less likely to spend their entire career in the party organisation, moving from one apparatus post to another. Turnover here appeared to be taking place at a relatively high level, 120 staff (out of a total of 370 in the province) having been recalled from apparatus posts in a recent two-year period.[54]

It was not clear, however, that the attention paid to party cadres and the development of a more integrated personnel policy had achieved much of an effect in terms of party work. One provincial first secretary complained that the cadres still had not mastered the means of exerting political influence within their environment and tended to restrict their party activities to office work and contacts within party headquarters and local offices. General Baryła, CC secretary newly elected to the Politburo at the X Congress in 1986, noted the continuing marginalisation of many party organisations as a political force and their restriction to a peripheral involvement in matters of major importance. They were still, in many cases, only able to assemble a slender social *aktiv*.[55] The 'strengthening' of the party, said another CC secretary, Henryk Bednarski, was still a highly relative process and far from an even one. Party organisations continued to restrict their activities too often to matters of internal party importance only.[56]

Accompanying the shift to a greater emphasis on cadres policy and the need for a coherent long-term plan in this area was a reappraisal of the role of ideology and a growing awareness of the party's weakness in this area. The adoption of a more conciliatory approach towards the working class and the general population in 1984 had been accompanied by the decision not to place undue stress on matters of ideological principle. Neither of these features were particularly successful in helping the party to mobilise support or lay a new basis for its authority. In keeping with the greater stress on leadership and planned development that the discussion of cadres policy reflected, then, the poor dividends paid by the more pragmatic approach prompted reconsideration of theoretical matters and ideological offensiveness. Discussions on the party's long-term programme included many comments to the effect that it should be of an essentially practical nature, that doctrinal concerns relating to Poland's position with regard to 'developed socialism' were hardly the most pressing issue, or that it would not suffice just to carry on pushing the 'old ideological wagon'. But also recognised to be of considerable importance in this discussion were the changes and developments in the Soviet Union. No longer, noted the deputy editor of *Nowe Drogi*, would it be possible to attribute Poland's problems in pursuing coherent reform policies to the conservatism of the Soviet Union.[57]

Despite Gorbachev's evident concern for practical matters of economic recovery and commitment to efficiency in terms of administration and political management, he has by no means denied the importance or continuing relevance of matters of ideological principle. Concrete issues of economic stagnation and political corruption have clearly received the greatest publicity, but they have also been accompanied by extensive references to Leninist principles and thus firmly located also in an ideological context. He has been reported to be particularly concerned about the extensive role of the Catholic Church in Poland, while the pressures for normalisation in Poland inevitably mean that issues of ideology cannot permanently be laid to one side.[58] A number of commentaries began drawing attention to the continuing ideological inadequacies reflected in party life. A general lack of ideological knowledge was detected amongst party members and complaints were still heard, towards the end of 1985, about echoes of both the revisionist and 'sectarian-dogmatic' views condemned at the VII Plenum in February 1982.[59] Fears were expressed of a decline into 'ideological turmoil' and condemnation of contemporary conceptions of the party's leading role, particularly as it was expressed in the context of current discussions of 'alliance methods' of exercising power.[60] Meetings held prior to the X Congress in the spring of 1986 also gave rise to general expressions of the need for 'greater ideological offensiveness and more effective propaganda activities' as part of the programme of party work.[61] From the point of view of both cadres development and ideological activity, then, stronger party leadership was called for.

Leadership change under democratic centralism

The X Congress of the PZPR was held in the summer of 1986, almost exactly five years after the IX (Extraordinary) Congress which had taken place in the midst of political renewal and the turbulence surrounding the Solidarity movement. In its timing, as in the tight control surrounding both the preparations made for it and its actual proceedings, it was an 'ordinary' party event as much as its predecessor had been extraordinary. It had virtually none of the political conflict and uncertainty that had characterised the IX Congress and was strictly managed by the party leadership. To the extent that it represented an internal party event controlled by the leadership it had little to offer or even interest the mass of the population. As we have already noted in this chapter, only 10% of the public had acquainted themselves with the pre-Congress materials. The Congress had little to contribute, therefore, to the strengthening of the position of the party or to the processes through which the leadership hoped to reestablish its authority. Measures had been taken at an early stage to remove potential sources of conflict and disruption – like the decision made to hold elections for provincial secretaries at a later date. At the Congress the decision was taken to 'unify' party election regulations by proclaiming a general five-year term of office in elected party posts while reconfirming the decision taken at the IX Congress that two terms in office should be the normal maximum for elected party officials. This side-stepped the problem of what should be done about the large number of party officials who were due for replacement by mid-1986, among them twenty-two of the forty-nine provincial first secretaries. This meant that an open clash with the principles laid down at the Extraordinary Congress was avoided – but the consequence of extending the 'normal' period of office for provincial secretaries from five to

Table 8.1 *KW first secretaries (1975–80, 1981, 1983–86): date of birth*

	1975–80		1981		1983–86	
	N	%	N	%	N	%
1911–30	6	27	1	4	5	16
1931–33	7	32	3	12	1	3
1934–38	4	18	9	36	11	38
1939–41	5	23	6	24	3	10
1942–45	–	–	4	16	6	20
1946–59	–	–	2	8	4	13
Total	22	100	25	100	30	100

Table 8.2 *KW first secretaries (1975–80, 1981, 1983–86): date of joining party*

	1975–80		1981		1983–86	
	N	%	N	%	N	%
1944–49	3	14	–	–	1	5
1950–52	6	29	1	4	3	15
1953–55	3	14	2	8	2	10
1956–59	2	10	4	16	–	–
1960–63	6	29	11	44	7	35
1964–70	1	4	7	28	7	35
Total	21	100	25	100	20	100

Sources: Życie Partii did not publish biographies of new KW secretaries for much of 1985 and 1986. In the case of most first secretaries it has been possible to collect most of the relevant details. Information on the other new secretaries has not been available and they are not discussed in this section.

ten years was clearly in breach of the intentions that lay behind the 1981 decision. To this extent the X Congress helped to 'normalise' the position of the provincial secretaries by reducing the pressures on them to leave office or to face special procedures for re-election after a relatively short period of time. A further element of normalisation was their increased representation on the new Central Committee, twenty-

Table 8.3 *KW first secretaries (1975–80, 1981, 1983–86): higher education qualifications*

	1975–80		1981		1983–86	
	N	%	N	%	N	%
Economics	8	35	3	12	7	32
Industry	1	4	6	24	3	14
Agriculture	3	13	8	32	3	14
History	2	9	1	4	2	9
Sociology	2	9	–	–	2	9
Political science	–	–	1	4	2	9
Other	7	30	5	20	2	9
No higher education	–	–	1	4	1	4
Total	23	100	25	100	22	100

seven of them gaining representation on this occasion in contrast to the eighteen elected in 1981.

Further change in the provincial committees was postponed until the local conferences met, the process beginning in the early autumn. Official satisfaction was expressed with the composition of the new provincial committees, almost exactly half of which (49.8%) were made up of workers and peasants, slightly more than their level of membership in the party as a whole. This was also larger than the part workers and peasants had played in the committees whose life had just ended. As many as 77% of the new provincial control commissions' members, and 64% of the committee members, were elected for the first time. According to CC secretary General Baryła, this showed that 'the party was achieving the desired rotation of cadres'. In the light of the changes just made in party regulations to extend the period of political office, this statement was, to say the least, somewhat disingenuous. It was questionable, too, whether committee members were accurately described as cadres, while with regard to full-time party officials (who clearly were cadres) the General had little to say.

In fact, the conferences had little influence on the staffing of the provincial secretariats. The rate of turnover of provincial first secretaries was stepped up in 1986, but most changes were made in the early part of the year or during the summer. Personnel changes, therefore, were generally made before the provincial conferences where the role

Table 8.4 *KW first secretaries (1975–80, 1981, 1983–86): main non-apparatus experience*

	1975–80		1981		1983–86	
	N	%	N	%	N	%
Industry	2	9	8	32	6	23.5
Agriculture	1	5	7	28	4	15
Government	10	45	3	12	6	23.5
Education	2	9	3	12	4	15
Youth organisations	5	22	2	8	4	15
Military	–	–	1	4	–	–
Parapolitical	1	5	1	4	1	4
Law	–	–	–	–	1	4
No non-apparatus experience	1	5	–	–	–	–
Total	22	100	25	100	26	100

of the elections was to confirm previous secretarial appointments rather than, as it was in 1981, to play a significant part in the selection of leading individuals.[62] Turnover of provincial first secretaries had been quite limited following the ten changes in that position made in 1982 under the State of War. Only four provincial first secretaries were changed in 1983, and five each in 1984 and 1985. Sixteen first secretaries, however, were changed in 1986. Despite this increased rotation, by the end of 1986 sixteen first secretaries, whose period of tenure dated from early 1981, remained in post, and in all nineteen first secretaries had exceeded their second term of office. Had the party regulations not been changed at the X Congress, then, their continuing tenure would have placed them in conflict with the party rules. As it was, their continued occupation of the leading provincial post clearly ran counter to the intentions that lay behind the decisions taken in 1981. All in all, thirty first secretaries were appointed in the three-year period 1983–86, the period of continuing political normalisation following the suspension of the State of War at the end of 1982.

The average age of those appointed between 1983 and 1986 was forty-seven, rather older than those appointed in the 1975–80 period (forty-five) and in 1981 (forty-three). The oldest first secretaries, however, were those appointed during the State of War and the subsequent period. The average age of those appointed from the December coup to the end of 1983 was forty-nine. Those appointed in

Table 8.5 *KW first secretaries (1975–80, 1981, 1983–86): time from first party appointment*

Years	1975–80		1981		1983–86	
	N	%	N	%	N	%
0	–	–	4	16	4	17
Up to 5	3	13	5	20	4	17
6–10	5	23	7	28	2	8
11–15	6	27	6	24	2	8
16–20	5	23	1	4	8	33
Over 20	3	14	2	8	4	17
Total	22	100	25	100	24	100

the 1983–86 period still represented a slightly older generation than those elected during the reform period and 19% had been born before 1934 in contrast to 16% of the 1981 cohort. Nevertheless, the age distribution is broadly similar to that of the 1981 cohort, and in that sense the end of the Gierek regime also marked an end to the dominance of an older generation from whom provincial first secretaries had up to that date been chosen. Nevertheless, the post-1982 appointments show the relative importance of an older political generation: 30% had joined the party during the Stalin period, 1944–55, in contrast to only 12% of those elected in 1981. None of those appointed after 1982 had joined the party in its more reformist phase, the years immediately following 1956, and there was a jump to the greater representation of a more recent political generation, those who joined the PZPR after 1959. Thus, the 1983–86 appointments show a significant generational shift away from the pool of candidates favoured under Gierek, but a qualification of the sharp change represented by the 1981 elections in which a distinct turn away from the generation of party members whose record extended back to the Stalin period was recorded.

The return to political 'normality', that is, the more conventional mode of centralised party rule, is also reflected in the educational background of the provincial secretaries appointed in post-State of War Poland. These elected in 1981 had been far less likely to have qualifications in 'economics' – qualifications which, we have suggested, were likely to have been gained through in-service or party training. The return to the dominance of this kind of conventional party-trained official was signalled by the frequency with which first

Table 8.6 *KW first secretaries (1975–80, 1981, 1983–86): previous apparatus experience*

	1975–80		1981		1983–86	
	N	%	N	%	N	%
Provincial committee secretary	15	68	10	40	16	62
First secretary of other committee	12	55	12	48	12	46
Either provincial committee secretaryship or other first secretaryship, or both	19	86	16	64	19	73
CC employment	1	5	–	–	3	12

secretaries with economics qualifications were appointed from 1983 to 1986. Accordingly, there were exactly half as many of those with more strictly technical qualifications relevant to industrial or agricultural activity appointed during this period than in 1981. Nevertheless, the proportion was not as low as in the 1975–80 period, when party-acquired economics qualifications and degrees in the less technical subjects were very much in the majority.

A similar pattern is detectable in terms of career experience outside the party apparatus. Compared with 1981, considerably fewer in the 1983–86 cohort had direct industrial or agricultural experience, and more had worked in government bodies. More, too, came from the established channels through which many had come to work in the party apparatus in the past, notably education and the youth organisations.

Appointments made during the 1983–86 period showed a marked shift in favour of the official with a lengthy record of party service. Exactly half of the appointees had received their first party posting at least fifteen years prior to appointment as provincial first secretary, in contrast to only 12% of those elected in 1981. Significantly, this was also a higher level of party experience than that characterising the appointments made between 1975 and 1980. On the other hand, there was also significant representation of those with little or no party record at all, the proportion of those appointed in 1983–86 with less than six years having elapsed since their first party appointment being roughly equivalent to that occurring amongst those elected in 1981. 'Normalised' cadres procedures as practised in the mid-eighties, therefore, appear to have combined a willingness to extend the careers of some with long records of party appointment, while also mobilising into service some with little or no prior party experience. Accordingly, this gave far less representation in 1983–86 to the apparatchik who had received his first party posting from six to fifteen years earlier. This, in turn, suggested that the provincial secretarial post was no longer seen as the prize of the established party official, gained after some considerable service in the party hierarchy but also a likely stepping stone to more elevated posts during subsequent career promotions. Experience between 1983 and 1986 showed a more diverse pattern of appointment.

The party experience of those appointed in the recent period nevertheless showed that new first secretaries had had more service in responsible posts than had their predecessors in 1981. Nearly threequarters had served already as a secretary of a provincial committee or as first secretary of another committee, not such a high level of experience as that shown in the 1975–80 appointments. However, more had served in the CC apparatus, an interesting sign of the closer links between the party centre and the provincial committees that had been maintained since the State of War. The changes made in the provincial leadership after the suspension of the State of War indicated a clear departure from the preferences evident among the electors of the first secretaries during the 1981 provincial conferences. The 'normalising' leadership was less inclined to appoint secretaries directly from work in industry and agriculture and placed greater weight on the experienced party official. Nevertheless, this did not mean a return to the cadres practices of the Gierek era and it was clear that attempts were being made to draw some lessons from the experiences of the party reform period and the pressures for change that had surfaced in 1981.

9   Conclusion

The role of the provincial committee: aspects of structure and function

We began this study by setting down a number of proposals about the nature of recent Polish politics and, to a certain extent, communist politics in general:
- that Polish politics has been characterised by a chronic authority deficit rather than a failure of party–state power;
- that this authority deficit was closely related to the form and capacity of party leadership embodied particularly in the operations of its intermediate organs;
- that the structurally determined capacity and quality of staff, and role of the provincial committees and their secretariats were critically affected by Gierek's 1975 administrative reorganisation and his subsequent political strategy.

Historical analysis and post-Gierek developments have generally substantiated these observations. The crisis of the party that lasted through 1980 and 1981 was deepened and perpetuated by the resistance of much of the party establishment to Solidarity and to rank-and-file demands for greater party democracy. Many were unwilling to follow the leadership's commitment to political renewal while, even amongst those of the central party authorities who had launched this policy, there was considerable ambiguity about the extensiveness of renewal and some doubt about the seriousness of their commitment. Resistance was, it was generally agreed, particularly strong amongst middle-rank officials and in the 'higher organs' of the party. This indicated the crucial position of party cadres superior to local secretaries but below the top level of national leaders and the CC secretaries – some 3,500 people, of whom 85% were based on the provincial apparatus. In this sense, resistance to political change and the problems

284

surrounding the rebuilding of party authority were also centred on the provincial committees and the outlook and actions of their staff.

Considerable numbers of party secretaries were changed after the fall of Gierek and many more swept away at the provincial elections that preceded the Extraordinary Congress of July 1981. The non-elected parts of the apparatus were less vulnerable to such democratic pressures, and turnover was more limited amongst those employees. The situation was similar after the Congress with the newly elected Central Committee. It rapidly became evident that, as a national organisation, the party could not operate according to both the conventions of 'democratic centralism' (or, more accurately, bureaucratic centralism) applied traditionally in the communist system and embodied in the practice of much of the apparatus, and those of parliamentary democracy (rule by freely elected representatives) reflected in the party electoral conferences of 1981 and the source of the authority of the new leadership. In terms of political rule, the critical position was held by the executive apparatus, without which the formal leadership was unable to act and which, in any case, had strong representation in the new leadership. Party leadership, in this formal sense, was effectively neutralised and the direction of political developments was set by an ambiguous coalition of apparatus forces, central party leaders, and military and security operatives. After October 1981 Jaruzelski could be claimed as leader by all three groups, a source of confusion that nevertheless helped strengthen the coalition and facilitated the transition to the State of War.

The contradictions between these forces necessarily continued under the political 'solution' of the State of War. Some measures were taken to restrict the influence of the established apparatus, particularly by removing some of its key representatives from central positions and developing military conceptions of administrative verification and cadres policy. But in general terms, developments in the party and outside it ran along lines that accorded with the interests and views of the apparatus conservatives. There were, nevertheless, continuing divisions within the party and its Central Committee about the implications of these actions for future political developments. The more explicit reliance on the power resources of the communist party–state to preserve its rule could not fail to have the effect of highlighting the party's lack of authority. Significantly, in accordance with our suggestion that the exercise of party authority is critically associated with the activities of the provincial committee, it was the provincial secretaries who, at least in the party centre, were most prominent in expressing doubts about the implications of the State of War for party leadership and the further difficulties it produced for the restoration of party authority.

Following these developments and with the continuing problems faced by the leadership in improving, let alone restoring, the economic position of the country, in the continuing stress on central control within the party, and in the regime's general lack of popular support, the outlook for the party in terms of establishing its authority was a bleak one. The regime has, instead, applied itself to the task of ruling without authority but has developed greater flexibility in dealing with some its pressing problems. This has necessarily involved it in perpetuating some of the ambiguities implicit in the State of War and the political order that developed out of it. Not the least of these have concerned the status of the party itself as a national organisation and the position of the provincial secretaries. In post-State of War, 'normalised' Poland, the PZPR is again claiming to be performing a leading role, even if in a more consultative and 'coalitional' fashion. As we have seen, though, the position of the party has remained very weak and it certainly appears to have lost some of the functions it performed earlier. It is notable that while General Jaruzelski passed on to colleagues his positions as Minister of Defence and as Prime Minister, he retained that of PZPR first secretary. Other military representatives continued to hold a number of major party positions following the X Congress. The anomalous status of a militarised party was thus perpetuated and the position of the PZPR has necessarily had to remain open to question.

This ambiguity has been reflected in academic analysis. Poland's relative political stability following the lifting of the State of War has been interpreted as reflecting a degree of normalisation that showed a return to conventional party leadership. Jaruzelski has been described as ruling largely through traditional communist institutions and operating in traditional Soviet-Leninist ways through the party apparatus. Other analysts have maintained that after 1981 the new military elite became a permanent component in the country's political structure and that subsequent developments served only to confirm this development.[1] Certainly there was no sign at the X Congress (June–July 1986) of any diminution of the military presence within the party's ruling body. On the contrary, the level of military representation in the Politburo established in the run-up to the State of War and during its early months was raised: the compromised General Milewski was replaced by General Baryła, already a CC secretary and previously head of the army's Main Political Administration, while Generals

Kiszczak and Siwicki were promoted from candidate to full membership.

In comparison with the pre-State of War Politburo, that elected in 1986 showed a decisive shift to the dominance of those drawn from the centres of power. In July 1981, two members of the central party organisation had been elected to the Politburo, in 1986, six; in 1981, three people occupying central government positions or posts of state were elected, in 1986, six. Two workers were elected in 1986 (three in 1981) and no academics (two in 1981), although one of those chosen in 1981 remained in the Politburo as Prime Minister. But while four representatives of the sub-national party organisation had made it to the Politburo in 1981 (three provincial first secretaries and one factory secretary), none were included in 1986. The Gdańsk and Katowice secretaries were, however, admitted as candidate members. The post-X Congress Politburo, therefore, showed increased military representation but the elimination of all sub-national party representation, a situation strongly in contrast with that in 1981. Roughly half the provincial first secretaries (twenty-seven) were elected to the 1986 Central Committee, more than in 1981. But this was still a marked change from the pre-1981 situation, when all first secretaries had been included as either full or candidate members.

The changes made in central party bodies in 1986, then, would not seem to suggest that the conventional relationship between the civilian party and the military had been restored, nor that the party organisation throughout the country played the same role or enjoyed the same status as it had in earlier years. The picture was probably different, as we have noted, throughout the country, a fact which in itself pointed to a departure from conventional practice. There were still some indications of the provincial first secretary's generalised leadership role. Gorzów secretary Kinecki thus reaffirmed that the 'secretary is responsible for the product of an enterprise's work regardless of who it is run by. He should be brought to account if he and the provincial committee he directs do not do anything, if the plan is threatened.'[2] Other accounts suggested not inconsiderable changes. In Bydgoszcz province, a decline of roughly a quarter was noted since 1983 in the number of posts appointment to which required the judgment of a party organ – a process significantly described as that which 'earlier used to be called *nomenklatura*.' This clearly reduced the powers of control and patronage exercised by local party organs. The provincial committee itself was described as having responsibility for slightly more than 1,000 posts, of which over a third lay within the party apparatus itself.[3]

The position of the provincial secretary had in fact changed rather more than Kinecki was willing to admit. It was precisely in his province that a conflict broke out over a newspaper report of the circumstances under which an old woman had frozen to death. There was considerable KW displeasure about this publicity, which led to an attempt to tighten up control over the local press by intensifying party discipline – which itself only caused further friction and broader publicity. Times had changed, it was pointed out, and that was not the way provincial party committees were now expected to act. The lesson was clearly one of importance to the party leadership, and it was noted in the party journal that not so long ago 'the first secretary was untouchable'. While former secretaries might well be the object of considerable criticism this was, it appears, the first time an incumbent secretary had been exposed to public criticism.[4] There were clearly some differences between the views taken of the role of the provincial committee and the nature of the influence legitimately exerted by its secretaries.

Some dissatisfaction with the role of the provincial committee derived from continuing doubts about the viability of the existing administrative division of country, the unfortunate inheritance of Gierek's ill-thought-out project from 1975. Some expert opinion still recommended a return to the three-tier structure that had previously been in operation. Most, however, were in favour of the existing system – though with significant amendments. Most striking was the continuing widespread recognition that the 1975 reform had had strongly negative consequences and that some further change was still on the agenda. One result of this was claimed to be an imbalance in the sub-national party structure. The local committees of the party, who were actually in everyday contact with the working people, were relatively small while provincial committees were well equipped and overstaffed – though their style of work was criticised for being superficial and bureaucratic in style.[5] There was, presumably, nothing new about this defect, but it had perhaps become more telling as the party leadership had again turned its attention to enhancing its standing in the eyes of the population and reversing the decline in membership numbers. This concern was underwritten by a Politburo decision in April 1987 to shift 10% of provincial committee employees to the local committees and to make the structure and size of the provincial apparatus more flexible. Others decried the abundance of organisation men in the party and the neglect of an instructors' cadre which now, it was thought, was the time to revive and develop with the regional centres of party work (ROPP), now (after the X Congress) directly subordinate to the provincial committees.[6]

What amounted to virtual admissions of the alienation of the provincial apparatus from the local population, their bureaucratic isolation and inability to exercise local leadership, were strangely reminiscent of the late Gierek period, as was growing evidence of the failure to conduct proper 'control' in the province.[7] Further echoes of the Gierek period were evident at the III CC Plenum (December 1986) when the state of the economy and the issue of economic reform were discussed. Real economic change would not occur, said provincial secretary Miller (Skierniewice), until decentralisation had been carried out; another first secretary, Zieliński (Chełm) described the reform as being threatened by bureaucracy and swamped by the 'nonsense of centralisation'.[8] The structural imbalance between the economic administration and the provincial party leadership that had emerged after 1975 and had been the source of much complaint by the local party secretaries, was not without parallel in post-State of War Poland. The composition of the Politburo elected at the X Congress reflected, as we have seen, the strengthening of central power and a greater role assigned to the state administration. At the end of 1986 the state administration and central management of the economy were probably considerably stronger than they had been ten years previously – the lessons of the late Gierek period, moreover, would be unlikely to prompt decision-makers to change that state of affairs with undue haste. The position of the provincial secretaries was in this sense not greatly different. It was, indeed, likely to be rather weaker, as the party organisation (itself considerably depleted in number) remained under close military surveillance, the role of the provincial party organisation in determining *nomenklatura* appointments was reduced, and stricter central control was exercised (again, by another general) over cadres policy and party staffing.

Cadres policy and the provincial party secretaries

Accompanying the growing emphasis in the leadership on issues of cadres policy, 1986 saw considerable change, as we have noted, in the provincial party secretariats, mostly during the period of preparation for the X Congress. Party records published after this process showed that the number of provincial secretaries had remained virtually the same since the mid-term conferences of late 1983 and early 1984.[9] Despite the reduced role of the provincial committee in the political system the number of provincial secretaries had seen no decline and, indeed, had steadily increased over the years. There had

Table 9.1 *KW secretaries (1975, 1986): age*

| | First secretaries | | | | Other secretaries | | | |
| | 1975 | | 1986 | | 1975 | | 1986 | |
Years	N	%	N	%	N	%	N	%
Under 40	6	14	6	12	55	43	29	23
41–45	12	27	14	29	44	35	49	39
46–50	18	41	14	29	17	13	29	23
51–55	8	18	10	20	11	9	15	12
over 55	–	–	5	10	–	–	4	3
Total	44	100	49	100	127	100	126	100
Average age	46		47		42		45	

been 210 KW secretaries in 1975, while 244 were reported to be in post in September 1981. By the end of the provincial conferences in 1986 there were 265. The increase in the number of KW secretaries since 1981 had, therefore, been small and the enlargement of the provincial secretariat implied by the adoption of new party election regulations at the 1984 Conference (see chapter 8) did not materialise. Apart from the first secretary, each provincial committee had four other secretaries with larger provinces (Gdańsk, Katowice, Warsaw) having six. The declining level of party membership throughout the eighties, though, meant that the provincial apparatus had greater numerical weight in the national party organisation. In the 1970s the rate of apparatus enlargement had kept pace broadly with the rise in party membership levels. In 1975 each of the 210 KW secretaries could be said to represent 116,000 party members, while in 1981 there was one KW secretary for 114,000 members. In 1986, due to the shrinkage of the party, there was one for each 83,000 members.

The accompanying tables show changes in the characteristics of the provincial secretaries between 1975 and 1986. Note that, in contrast with the tables in earlier chapters (which showed the characteristics of secretaries actually appointed in the different periods), these tables refer to all secretaries in post immediately after Gierek's 1975 reform and after the 1986 provincial conferences. They provide a reasonably

Table 9.2 *KW secretaries (1975, 1986): date of joining party*

| | First secretaries | | | | Other secretaries | | | |
| | 1975 | | 1986 | | 1975 | | 1986 | |
	N	%	N	%	N	%	N	%
before 1946	6	13	–	–	4	3	–	–
1946–48	10	23	1	2	9	7		1
1949–53	13	29	8	19	21	17	3	2
1954–56	10	23	1	2	27	21	8	6
1957–59	2	5	3	7	15	12	8	6
1960–63	2	5	12	29	32	25	28	22
1964–67	1	2	13	31	15	12	34	27
1968–70	–	–	4	10	4	3	27	22
after 1970	–	–	–	–	–	–	17	14
Total	44	100	42	100	127	100	126	100

full picture of the forty-nine first secretaries and one that includes well over half of the other secretaries. The 127 other secretaries whose profile is delineated for 1975, and the 126 shown for 1986 in tables 9.1 and 9.2, for example, refer to 79% and 61% respectively of the secretarial body. In general (table 9.1), the KW secretaries became slightly older as a body between 1975 and 1986, the average age of the first secretary rising from 46 to 47, and that of other provincial secretaries from 42 to 45 (although, in fact, the average age of the first secretaries had been higher in 1980 with the continuing tenure of some of the older, long-established provincial leaders). Thus, while the average first secretary in 1975 had been ten at the outbreak of the Second World War and twenty-four at the time of Stalin's death, he had in 1986 been only fourteen years old in 1953 and had reached adulthood under Gomułka.

In 1975 a majority of first secretaries (65%) had joined the party before the end of 1953 and a decisive majority (88%) had joined before the end of 1956, when Gomułka returned to power. By 1986 there were few who had joined the party by the time of Stalin's death and the great majority (77%) had joined under Gomułka's leadership after 1956. Similar tendencies are noticeable in the case of the other secretaries and, by 1986, some of them had not joined the party until the time

Table 9.3 *KW secretaries (1975, 1986): higher education qualifications*

| | First secretaries | | | | Other secretaries | | | |
| | 1975 | | 1986 | | 1975 | | 1986 | |
	N	%	N	%	N	%	N	%
Economics	22	49	11	24	32	25	21	17
Industrial	8	18	5	11	15	11	22	18
Agricultural	3	7	7	16	19	15	30	24
History/teaching	6	13	8	18	21	16	19	15
Law/political science	3	7	7	16	13	10	15	12
Other	2	4	5	11	21	16	11	9
None	1	2	2	4	9	7	6	5
Total	45	100	45	100	130	100	124	100

Table 9.4 *KW secretaries (1975, 1986): main non-apparatus experience*

| | First secretaries | | | | Other secretaries | |
| | 1975 | | 1986 | | 1986 | |
	N	%	N	%	N	%
Industry	11	25	12	26	33	27
Agriculture	3	7	7	15	26	20
Government	11	25	6	13	19	15
Youth organisations	12	27	11	24	13	11
Education	3	7	6	13	27	22
Other	3	7	4	9	6	5
None	1	2	–	–	–	–
Total	44	100	46	100	124	100

when Gierek occupied the leading position. In terms of education, the number of first secretaries with qualifications in 'economics', whose value, we have suggested in earlier chapters, was open to much doubt, fell considerably and a greater diversity became evident in higher educational background. In 1986 a quarter of first secretaries had gained their qualification exclusively through study at party higher

Table 9.5 *KW secretaries (1975, 1986): time from first party appointment*

| | First secretaries | | | | Other secretaries | |
| | 1975 | | 1986 | | 1986 | |
Years	N	%	N	%	N	%
up to 5	5	11	9	20	36	28
6–10	2	4	4	9	21	17
11–15	11	25	9	20	44	35
16–20	13	30	14	31	11	9
21–25	6	14	6	13	11	9
over 25	7	16	3	7	3	2
Total	44	100	45	100	126	100

Table 9.6 *KW secretaries (1975, 1986): previous apparatus experience*

| | 1975 | | 1986 | |
	N	%	N	%
Provincial secretary	35	80	18	39
First secretary of other committee	4	9	10	22
Central committee post	3	7	6	13
Other apparatus appointment	–	–	4	9
No apparatus experience	2	4	8	17
Total	44	100	46	100

school – although 90% had taken some training at party schools either in Poland or in the Soviet Union.[10] Amongst provincial governors, the first secretaries' counterparts in the state administration, who were on average four years older, only two had received their higher education exclusively in party schools.[11] Interestingly, comparison of the situation in 1986 with that in 1975 showed little increase in the number of first secretaries with qualifications of direct relevance to industrial and agricultural production or to technology, although development had occurred in this direction among the other secretaries. It had been the 1981 cohort, chosen more freely by the work-force and the party rank and file, which was most distinguished by its qualifications in terms of technical expertise. Subsequent appointments showed a reversion to the less technically qualified secretary and a greater reliance on the arts-type graduate in the process of political normalisation.

Following this observation, comparison of the first secretaries in 1975 and 1986 shows little major difference in terms of career background. Rather more had been associated with agriculture and education, and fewer with government organisations. More again amongst the other secretaries had some greater experience in production activities. Employment in organisations of the youth movement continued to be a major channel of access for those working in the party apparatus, and other accounts suggest that as many as seventeen first secretaries had been employed in this area amongst those in post in 1986. Only four first secretaries had moved directly into their post from work in the state administration, although conversely twenty-five state governors in early 1987 had come from work in the political apparatus.[12]

First secretaries in 1986 had entered party employment more recently than their predecessors in 1975. Fewer had taken up work in the apparatus over twenty years prior to 1986, and more had gained their first party post in the preceding ten years. Nevertheless, the number of new arrivals in the provincial leadership was certainly less than it had been in 1981, when 45% of first secretaries had first found apparatus employment during the preceding ten years. This reflected both the higher rate of turnover in 1981 and the election of unconventional leaders at the provincial conferences. Political normalisation after the State of War meant, therefore, considerable modification of the changes introduced during the Solidarity period and the greater influence of the party rank and file.

More marked changes are evident in the apparatus experience of the first secretaries and in the promotion of provincial secretaries to the position of first secretary. In 1986 only 39% of first secretaries, in contrast to 80% eleven years earlier, had served previously as members of the provincial secretariat. This was a process that had got under way during 1980 and 1981 and, rather than being reversed, had intensified in the 1980s. More had come with experience from other parts of the apparatus, including the CC organisation, although it was pointed out that those appointed first secretary would also have personal affiliations with the relevant province. Considerably more first secretaries in 1986 came straight to the provincial leadership without any previous apparatus experience. This, too, was a feature that had initially developed in 1981 and which had received greater emphasis after 1981. A third of those in post in 1986 had not moved from an existing posting in the apparatus. Considerably reduced, it was reported, was the movement of cadres between the party apparatus and the economic administration, an observation that obviously had relevance to the relatively low proportion of secretaries with technical qualifications or experience of industrial work.[13]

Such developments suggested that a stronger line in cadres policy had been taken against automatic promotion within the apparatus (concerning, for example, the drift from provincial secretary to first secretary) and against the interpenetration of the party apparatus and the economic administration, a factor clearly involved in the drive for economic recovery and efficiency. The declining length of time spent by the secretary in the apparatus prior to appointment as first secretary, evident in the greater number of those without previous apparatus experience and date of first appointment, indicated closer links between party employment and experience in the other major institutions of rule. The question of a continuing 'carousel of cadres' had certainly not disappeared, and the frequency of exchanges between the provincial secretariats and the diplomatic service was noted in the press.[14]

Doubts about the consistency of current cadres policy and, by implication, its relation to the Party Statute and election regulations also arose about the rotation of cadres and limitations on tenure in party office. As we have noted (chapter 8) many provincial secretaries were due for replacement by the time of the X Congress if the decisions made at the IX Congress concerning limited tenure in party office were to be observed. The level of staff change did not meet these requirements and after the round of provincial conferences there were nineteen first secretaries who were beginning a third term of office in breach of this principle. Over a quarter of the other secretaries (59 of the 207 elected) were also beginning a third term of office.[15] Two of those in post at the end of 1986, indeed, had been first appointed provincial secretaries in 1975, at the time of Gierek's reorganisation of the party network. It was rather ironic, as one observer pointed out, that more success was achieved with provincial governors in moving them in and out of their job than with the first secretaries – although there was no official restriction on the length of service in post in the case of the governors.[16]

There were, then, continuing questions arising from the effectiveness of cadres policy in this area despite the emphasis placed on it by the leadership, particularly since 1983 and the XIII CC Plenum. Some reports gave a good impression of recent developments in this area, and emphasised the steady flow of candidates for work in the provincial apparatus and the demise of the permanent apparatchik, who moved from one local organisation to another but never left the organisation.[17] Other views of cadres policy took a different line, and it was asked whether the new principles employed had really had any effect at all. The greatest obstacles to achieving real change were, it was concluded, 'weak party cadres'.[18]

Political authority and party leadership

The relative stability of Poland in political terms since the lifting of the State of War was not due to any genuine reestablishment of political authority or of its reformulation to meet the demands of the 1980s. It was due, rather, to the continuing power of the party–state complex, its judicious exercise when necessary, and the continuing presence in core political institutions of leading military figures. The major conditions that had prevented the survival or reinvigoration of political authority in the Gierek period continued to operate during the subsequent decade. The recovery of the economy was very limited and the leadership was unable to boast of any great success in this area or to claim any particular competence in terms of its economic performance. Neither had the fortunes of the party greatly changed. The conflicts of 1980–81 and its eclipse in 1982–83 had left it in a poor state from which it showed few signs of recovering in terms of social popularity, level of membership or degree of activeness. Party leadership, the major form that political authority has taken in communist systems, was barely evident in any real sense and in the post-X Congress period it continued to be associated with qualities of military command and sustained by the influence of politically active generals.

To the extent that political authority was, as we have suggested, critically determined by the function and role of the provincial committee organisation and its capacity to exercise party leadership at the sub-national level, the prospects for its renewal were even less positive. Cadres policy and the characteristics of provincial secretaries had changed significantly, although the effects of these changes were open to some question and there was little evidence that they had brought about any improvement in the standing of the provincial party organisation. The role of the party at province level remained more limited than it had been in earlier periods by the character of the economic

administration, the emphasis placed on external checking and verification activity (*kontrola*), and the more formal specification of the role
of the party organisation and its apparatus. Its role was not the dominant one it had been in the past and 'party leadership' was no longer
identified with the personal prominence of the provincial first secretary. Alternative sources of political authority, however, were yet to be
discovered and the problems of economic stagnation and political
stalemate remained as pressing as ever in the post-X Congress period.
The major initiatives of the Jaruzelski leadership taken to stabilise the
political system, notably the successive waves of economic reform and
the diverse attempts to encourage a rapprochement between PZPR
and Polish society, had little positive effect and the leadership
remained caught between conflicting domestic pressures.

Any conclusion reached in terms of domestic Polish developments
must, nevertheless, be regarded as tentative in a broader context and
should be qualified by consideration of the situation within the Soviet
bloc as a whole. The major change in the broader context has been the
accession to power in the Soviet Union of Gorbachev and his increasingly radical programme of change. By early 1987 it was becoming
clear that this involved new conceptions of party democracy and a
reappraisal of the role and performance of the party apparatus. While
consideration of these developments, even in terms of their relevance
to Polish events, goes somewhat beyond our remit in this concluding
chapter, a brief reference to them will be made to point up the con-
ditional nature of any judgment made on the Polish political situation
in 1986 and to indicate the line of development these changes may
open up for the Polish leadership. Signs of change in this respect were
clearly evident at the IV CC Plenum of the PZPR (May 1987), devoted
to consideration of the state of the party and its local organisations. It
was precisely in the sphere of relations with the Soviet Union that
Jaruzelski was able to report 'the most extensive and rapid progress'.[19]

Elsewhere the situation was far less positive. The problems surrounding the Polish economy had an 'enormous influence' on the
position of the party – but the state of the economy depended 'in large
part' on the quality of party work. There was in this area, in Jaruzelski's
words, an organic interdependence; 'the results are obvious'. A new
phase of 'economic reform' had begun, but hopes of major success
were obviously qualified and earlier results of the reform process had
not been promising. Polish national income stopped falling after 1982,
but recovery was unsteady and only partial – the rate of growth of
national income fell in both 1984 and 1985. By the end of 1986, the level

of national income was around that achieved in 1976. The IV Plenum also received far from encouraging details of the current state of the party organisation. Overall membership stood at 2.133 million, only 7,000 more than immediately prior to the X Congress nearly one year earlier. Increasing numbers of new members were being accepted (35,000 in 1984, 63,000 in 1985, 74,000 in 1986), but they made little impact on the overall membership level which was 53,000 down on the situation at the end of 1983.

In early 1987, then, party members represented 8.1% of the adult population and 16.2% of those employed in the socialised economy. The position with respect to strategic groups was not good. Workers officially made up to 38% of the party membership, but only 11% of workers were party members. Young people (those under thirty) now made up only 6.9% of party members, a group that had provided around a quarter of all members during the 1970s. Neither were qualitative indices any more encouraging. Internal research showed that 15% of members did not perform even the basic organisational duties, while 60% reached at least this minimum by paying their dues and attending party meetings but were still characterised as essentially passive. Only 25% were counted as active members. Of primary party organisations, 40% had not recruited any new members during the preceding two years, an average surpassed by party cells located in industrial enterprises, 55% of which had shown such inactivity. Taking both economic performance and the party record into account and, in particular, their crucial interdependence, Jaruzelski's gloomy assessment was not difficult to understand. Time was running out and in key respects the clock stood at 'five to midnight'.[20]

Persistent economic and political stagnation put more radical solutions on the agenda, a development clearly facilitated by the new current in the Kremlin. Reduction in the staffing levels of the Central Committee and the provincial committees had already been announced. The number of political workers in the party apparatus was stated to stand currently at 13,000, rather more than in 1981 when party membership had been considerably higher. Reorganisation was to be introduced at the party centre: several CC departments would disappear as separate entities and the number of departments would be reduced to twelve. A process of 'attestation' was to be implemented throughout the party apparatus – the checking and verification of party posts, staff and work practices. It had been carried out in the Central Control and Auditing Commission (established at the X Congress by merging the two existing commissions) and would be extended throughout the apparatus.

At province level, following an initial transfer of 10% of the staff to local work, greater flexibility was to be introduced into the organisational structure and staffing levels from the beginning of 1988. Provincial leaders were to have greater discretion in terms of the kind of staff employed in the provincial apparatus and their level of pay. This was to take place within a general framework of spending cuts and a reduction in administrative costs within the apparatus. According to CC secretary Cypryniak, there was no reason for this to affect the quality of work in CC and provincial committee departments. This was a response both to the gathering pace of change in Soviet political life as well as to growing dissatisfaction in Poland with developments in the party and with the effects of cadres policy concerning its apparatus. The top-heavy character of the provincial party organisation and the problems encountered in reducing the party establishment within the province were continuing themes.[21] All in all, these measures were designed to stimulate party leadership and encourage the development of the party as a social movement rather than an administrative structure. At local level the party organisation was only one among several groups, and was generally not the most active or influential. Active competition might be offered by PRON, the trade unions, employees' self-government, etc. Such group conflict was not necessarily to be discouraged but, as CC secretary General Baryła remarked, it was important that overall it should have positive consequences.[22]

Political changes in the Soviet Union, therefore, brought an additional factor to the stalemate that had developed in the Polish situation by 1986. The results of Gorbachev's leadership and his new policy had, of course, to remain open to many questions both domestically and internationally. But it was clear that the approach outlined at the CPSU CC Plenum in early 1987 was taken by the Polish leadership with sufficient seriousness to encourage the Poles to draw up a new set of plans involving closer scrutiny of the position of the party apparatus and the activities of its staff, particularly those based on the 'higher organs' of the party. The role of the apparatus and the status of its cadres had, of course, been very much a major item on the political agenda in 1981. The challenge to its position was, we have argued, relatively successfully countered at that time and the top party leadership steered towards the installation of the State of War. Subsequent attempts by the militarised leadership to modify the position of the apparatus, notably by evolving a more rigorous cadres policy, appeared to have little practical effect. The changes in the Soviet Union, however, opened up new perspectives and provided the Polish leadership with the opportunity to take more effective action. While there were still doubts about the security of Gorbachev's position and the significance of his 'new course', it appeared by early 1987 that major groups, both in the official and the unofficial spheres, were becoming convinced of the consolidation of the new line in the Soviet Union and of its importance for Polish developments.[23]

In the Polish context the consolidation and articulation of Gorbachev's new policy introduced a major new factor into the constellation of political forces – it deprived the conservative establishment of one of their major arguments in resisting change. It removed the Soviet alibi, the argument that change had to be resisted and that reform was impossible because the Soviet leadership would not tolerate it. The initiation of political change from the Soviet side was indeed a novelty for the Polish leadership and it promised major new opportunities. Reform-minded forces in Poland were understandably enthusiastic about the Gorbachev initiative, although it was recognised that there were major differences between the two countries with respect to political change and the process of reform.[24] Pressures for reform in Poland, for example, had generally originated from below, while those in the Soviet Union had come from above. It was proposed, however, that the two currents of change were likely in any case to merge and that the forces pressing in that direction were essentially indivisible.

Such a development was indeed possible, but inconsistencies and contradictions within the process of change could also be foreseen. Of primary significance was the fact that the Jaruzelski leadership owed its position to the defeat of forces in 1981 who had been pressing vigorously from below for change both within the party and in the communist system as a whole. To the extent that the characteristic 'reform mode' in Poland was one that originated from below, the Jaruzelski leadership clearly had to be somewhat cautious about the process of political change. It was unlikely to approach the issue without considerable ambivalence. In recognition of this background the leadership had, indeed, been cautious in its approach to the party and had, it appeared, to a large extent acquiesced in the low level of party activity and its poor showing in the public arena. The leadership had placed greater emphasis on other channels of communication and on bridges to Polish society apart from the party, which had hardly distinguished itself in this respect and which historically suffered from a lack of political authority. In contrast with Gorbachev, then, who was trying to mobilise party forces and enhance its strength, Jaruzelski had been attempting some devolution of power, 'to tempt non-party people and the moderate opposition into sharing responsibility for society with his Government'.[25] It was possible, then, to see major inconsistencies between the Polish and Soviet approaches to change and to perceive certain problems in the adoption of Gorbachev's strategy in the Polish context. The political stalemate that had emerged in Poland, in conjunction with the noted lack of social support for the party and the continuing economic crisis, meant that the political changes in the Soviet Union were likely to have been met with considerable enthusiasm as a means of finding a way out of the impasse and beginning the process of restoring political authority in Poland.

Notes

1 Communist power and party authority in Poland

1 R. Rose, 'Dynamic tendencies in the authority of regimes', *World Politics*, vol. 21, 4 (1969), p. 619.

2 J. Pakulski, 'Legitimacy and mass compliance: reflections on Max Weber and Soviet-type societies', *British Journal of Political Science*, vol. 16, 1 (1986), p. 455.

3 A. G. Meyer, 'Authority in communist political systems', in *Political Leadership in Industrialized Societies*, ed. L. J. Edinger, New York: John Wiley, 1967, p. 100. It has been easy, too, to exaggerate the degree of what S. Lukes ('Power and authority', in *A History of Sociological Analysis*, ed. T. Bottomore and R. Nisbet, London: Heinemann, 1978, p. 649) has called authority over belief in the East European systems which 'have, of course, been ruled on the unquestionable assumption that the Party is the authoritative interpreter and inculcator of the truths that Marxist-Leninist theory has discovered'. Formally and publicly unquestionable, perhaps, though by no means unquestioned in practice.

4 J. Tarkowski, 'Poland: patrons and clients in a planned economy', in *Political Clientilism, Patronage and Development*, ed. S. N. Eisenstadt and R. Lemarchand, Beverly Hills: Sage, 1981, p. 186.

5 See R. J. Hill, 'Party–state relations and Soviet political development', *British Journal of Political Science*, vol. 10, 2 (1980), p. 150.

6 Z. Bauman, 'Officialdom and class: bases of inequality in socialist society', in *The Social Analysis of Class Structure*, ed. F. Parkin, London: Tavistock Publications, 1974, p. 142.

7 B. Moore, *Soviet Politics – The Dilemma of Power*, White Plains: International Arts and Sciences, 1950, p. 286. This aspect of the communist political system is highlighted by M. E. Urban, ('Conceptualizing political power in the USSR: patterns of binding and bonding', *Studies in Comparative Communism*, vol. 18, 4 (1985), pp. 220–21) who writes of 'jerry-built authority relations' and indicates the importance to them of the *nomenklatura* system and the fact that appointment powers are staggered throughout the party and state hierarchies.

8 D. W. Benn, 'Problems of authority in the Soviet Union', *The World Today*, March, pp. 108, 113.

9 Z. Gitelman, 'Power and authority in Eastern Europe', in *Change in Communist Systems*, ed. C. Johnson, Stanford: Stanford University Press, 1970, p. 236.

10 Report of the Central Committee, *XXVI Congress of the CPSU: Documents and Resolutions*, Moscow: Novosti, 1981, p. 54.

11 D. N. Nelson, 'Charisma, control and coercion: the dilemma of communist leadership', *Comparative Politics*, vol. 17, 1 (1984), p. 12.

12 G. W. Breslauer, *Khruschev and Brezhnev as Leaders: Building Authority in Soviet Politics*, London: Allen and Unwin, 1982, pp. 4–7.

13 T. H. Rigby, 'A conceptual approach to authority, power and policy in the Soviet Union', in *Authority, Power and Policy in the USSR*, ed. T. H. Rigby, A. Brown and P. Reddaway, London: Macmillan, 1980, p. 10.

14 J. Hoffman, 'The coercion/consent analysis of the state under socialism', in *The State in Socialist Society*, ed. N. Harding, London: Macmillan, 1984, p. 139.

15 Pakulski, 'Legitimacy', p. 457.

16 M. E. Spencer, 'Weber on legitimate norms and authority', *British Journal of Sociology*, vol. 21, 1 (1970), p. 125; L. Schapiro, *The Communist Party of the Soviet Union*, London: Methuen, 1970, p. 623.

17 Bauman, 'Officialdom', p. 136.

18 C. J. Friedrich, *Man and His Government*, New York: McGraw-Hill, 1963, p. 219; E. D. Watt, *Authority*, London: Croom Helm, 1982, p. 105.

19 H. Arendt, *Between Past and Future*, London: Faber and Faber, 1961, p. 106. It is important, though, not to exaggerate the amount of consensus that is required for a viable practice of authority: 'every known practice of authority has maintained and regularly used an apparatus of coercion' while even long-lasting systems of authority have been accompanied by 'widespread and intense disagreement' (R. E. Flathman, *The Practice of Political Authority*, Chicago: University of Chicago Press, 1980, p. 29).

20 Meyer, 'Authority', p. 100.

21 B. Moore, *Injustice: the Social Bases of Obedience and Revolt*, London: Macmillan, 1978, pp. 458–59.

22 J. Staniszkis, 'On some contradictions of socialist society: the case of Poland', *Soviet Studies*, vol. 31, 2 (1979), p. 167.

23 Nelson, 'Charisma', p. 6.

24 A. L. Stinchcombe, *Theoretical Methods in Social History*, New York: Academic Press, 1978, p. 35.

25 R. L. Peabody, 'Authority', in *International Encyclopaedia of the Social Sciences*, New York: Macmillan, 1968, p. 474.

26 Z. Radłowski, 'Prestiż Polski i Polaków, *Nowe Drogi*, July 1985, pp. 63, 65.

27 *Nowe Drogi*, November 1981, p. 24. As happens not infrequently in Polish political life, this development carried strong historical overtones. Before World War II, under Piłsudski, there arose a 'cult of the state' which

J. Rothschild (*East Central Europe Between the Two World Wars*, Seattle: University of Washington Press, 1974, p. 60) describes as 'both intellectually and politically dubious' – 'The concept of "interest of state" was, under certain circumstances, an adequate guide to foreign policy, but it was not sufficiently refined to be serviceable for the resolution of serious domestic socioeconomic policy problems.'

28 K. Wolicki, 'Polska: 1980 i potem', *Krytyka*, 8 (1981), p. 14; *Polityka*, 1980, 37. By no means the least important function of these statements was influence over those occupying positions of responsibility within the party who might have held different views. There appears to have been a strongly established conviction within the party, whose bases were laid down by early PZPR leaders, that any significant split would provoke Soviet military intervention (J. Bujnowski, 'W oczach komunistów – słowo wstępne', introduction to T. Torańska, *Oni*, London: Aneks, 1985, p. 20).

29 F. Anderson, *Lineages of the Absolutist State*, London: Verso, 1979, pp. 282, 285.

30 R. Szporluk, 'Poland', in *Crises of Political Development in Europe and the United States*, ed. R. Grew, Princeton: Princeton University Press, 1978, p. 395.

31 N. Ascherson, *The Polish August*, Harmondsworth: Penguin Books, 1981, p. 87. In independent Poland, between the wars, the Church had been accorded under the constitution a preeminent position among the other faiths in Poland and it succeeded in 'maintaining a privileged position in Polish society' (C. Cviic, 'The Church', in *Poland: Genesis of a Revolution*, ed. A. Brumberg, New York: Vintage Books, 1983, pp. 93, 307).

32 I. Deutscher, *Marxism in Our Time*, London: Jonathan Cape, 1972, pp. 117–18.

33 C. Baryka, 'Polish communists, 1937–1944', *Survey*, vol. 26, 4 (1982), p. 129.

34 Deutscher, *Marxism*, p. 152.

35 C. Gati, 'The Soviet stake in Eastern Europe', in *Russia at the Crossroads*, ed. S. Bialer and T. Gustafson, London: Allen and Unwin, 1982, p. 186; H. Carrère d'Encausse, *Le grand frère*, Paris: Flammarion, 1983, pp. 29, 40–41.

36 C. E. Cochran, 'Authority and community: the contribution of Carl Friederich, Yves R. Simon and Michael Polanyi', *American Political Science Review*, vol. 71, 2 (1977), pp. 546, 549. J. Raz ('Authority and justification', *Philosophy and Public Affairs*, vol. 14, 1 [1985], p. 20) has argued that acceptance of the authority of an institution is 'a way of defining one's own identity as a member of a national or some other group'; in the Polish context the converse may also be suggested, as rejection of party authority has been felt to be an expression of Polish character.

37 Gati, 'Soviet stake', p. 186

38 R. Luza, 'Czechoslovakia between democracy and communism', in *A History of the Czechoslovak Republic*, ed. V. S. Mamatey and R. Luza, Princeton: Princeton University Press, 1973, p. 389.

39 J. Karpiński, *Countdown*, New York: Karz-Cohl, 1982, pp. 5–8.

40 Ł. Socha, 'Poland: must history repeat itself?', *Dissent*, Spring, 1983, p. 214.

41 A. Korbonski, 'The Polish army', in *Communist Armies in Politics*, ed. J. Adelman, Boulder: Westview Press, 1982, p. 112.

42 Ł. Socha, 'Skazani na śmierć i ich sędziowie (1944–1946)', *Krytyka*, 13–14 (1983), p. 134.

43 M. Checinski, *Poland: Communism, Nationalism, Antisemitism*, New York: Karz-Cohl, 1982, p. 50.

44 Checinski, *Poland*, p. 31; J. J. Lipski, 'Examen de conscience', *Esprit*, 63 (1982), p. 30.

45 Ascherson, *Polish August*, p. 43; *Polityka* 1982, 28.

46 Z. Brzezinski, *The Soviet Bloc*, Cambridge, Mass.: Harvard University Press, 1967, p. 96; W. Wąsowicz and Ł. Socha, 'Z archiwum Bolesława Bieruta', *Krytyka*, 8 (1981).

47 G. Sakwa, 'The Polish October', *Polish Review*, vol. 23 (1978), p. 76.

48 Z. Kozik, *PZPR w latach 1954–1957*, Warsaw: Państwowe Wydawnictwo Naukowe, 1982, p. 287.

49 R. Zambrowski, 'Dziennik', *Krytyka*, 6 (1980), p. 80.

50 Z. Korybutowicz, *Grudzień 1970*, Paris: Instytut Literacki, 1983, p. 35.

51 D. Pienkos, 'Party elites and society', *Polish Review*, vol. 20 (1975), p. 37.

52 C. Beck, 'Leadership attributes in Eastern Europe', in *Comparative Communist Political Leadership*, ed. C. Beck *et al.*, New York: David McKay, 1973, p. 98; Ascherson, *Polish August*, pp. 62–66.

53 Gitelman, 'Power and authority', p. 225.

54 A. Bromke, 'Poland under Gierek: a new political style', *Problems of Communism*, vol. 21, 5 (1972), pp. 6–7.

55 A. Bromke, 'La nouvelle élite politique en Pologne', *Revue de l'est*; July 1974, p. 17; S. Tellenback, 'The logic of development in Poland', *Social Forces*, vol. 57, 2 (1978), pp. 447–54.

56 R. Dean, 'Gierek's three years', *Survey*, vol. 20 (1974), pp. 60–61.

57 M. Dziewanowski, *The Communist Party of Poland*, Cambridge, Mass.: Harvard University Press, 1977, p. 319.

58 W. Brus, 'Aims, methods and political determinants of the economic policy of Poland 1970–1980', in *The East European Economies in the 1970's*, ed. A. Nove, H.-H. Höhmann and G. Seidenstecher, London: Butterworths, 1982, p. 93.

59 *Rocznik Statystyczny* (Statistical Yearbook), 1979, p. 77.

60 Brus, 'Aims, pp. 113, 135; L. Schapiro, 'The fiscal crisis of the Polish state', *Theory and Society*, vol. 10, 4 (1981), p. 489.

61 P. T. Wanless, 'Economic reform in Poland 1973–79', *Soviet Studies*, vol. 32, 1 (1980), p. 51.

62 A. Chawluk, 'Economic policy and economic reform', *Soviet Studies*, vol. 26, 1 (1974), p. 113.

63 See G. Blażyca, 'The degeneration of central planning in Poland',

pp. 116–17, and P. G. Lewis, 'Political consequences of the changes in party-state structures under Gierek', in *Policy and Politics in Contemporary Poland*, ed. J. Woodall, London: Frances Pinter, 1982, pp. 84–87.

64 A. Smolar, 'The rich and the powerful', in *Poland: Genesis of a Revolution*, ed. A. Bromberg, New York: Vintage Books, 1983, p. 51.

65 P. G. Lewis, 'Legitimation and political crises: East European developments in the post-Stalin period', in *Eastern Europe: Legitimation and Political Crisis*, London: Croom Helm, 1984, pp. 30–33.

66 See Lewis, 'Political consequences', p. 81.

67 S. Gebethner, 'Political and institutional changes in the management of the socialist economy: the Polish case', in *East–West Relations and the Future of Eastern Europe*, ed. M. Bornstein, Z. Gitelman, and W. Zimmerman, London: Allen and Unwin, 1981, pp. 268–69.

68 J. de Weydenthal, *The Communists of Poland*, Stanford: Hoover Institution, 1986, pp. 139–44, 153.

69 A. Korbonski, 'Poland', in *Communism in Eastern Europe*, ed. T. Rakowska-Harmstone and A. Gyorgy, Bloomington: University of Indiana Press, 1979, pp. 53, 63.

70 T. Szafar, 'Contemporary political opposition in Poland', *Survey*, vol. 24, 4 (1979), p. 42.

71 See P. G. Lewis 'Institutionalisation and political change in Poland', in Harding, *State*, pp. 229–32.

72 Karpiński, *Countdown*, pp. 174–75.

73 S. Starski, *Class Struggle in Classless Poland*, Boston: South End Press, 1982, p. 51; G. Schöpflin, 'The political structure of Eastern Europe as a factor in intra-bloc relations', in *Soviet–East European Dilemmas*, ed. K. Dawisha and P. Hanson, London: Heinemann, 1981, pp. 80–81.

74 W. Bieńkowski, *Rachunek partyjnego sumienia*, Chicago: Polonia, 1982, p. 15.

75 'Uwagi o sytuacji gospodarczej kraju', *Aneks*, 20 (1979), pp. 21, 28; J. Drewnowski (ed.), *Crisis in the East European Economy*, London: Croom Helm, 1982, p. 11.

76 Konwersatorium 'Doświadczenie i Przyszłość', *Raport o stanie narodu i PRL*, Paris: Instytut Literacki, 1980, p. 138.

77 Gebethner, 'Political and institutional', p. 273.

78 *Ibid*, p. 279.

79 J. Kowalski, 'Urzeczywistnienie demokracji socjalistycznej', *Nowe Drogi*, February 1980, p. 154.

80 J. Bartecki, *Gospodarka na manowcach*, Paris: Instytut Literacki, 1979, p. 69.

81 J. Reykowski, 'Rozum i serce', *Polityka*, 1981, 46.

82 Wolicki, 'Polska', p. 14.

83 R. F. Leslie (ed.), *The History of Poland Since 1863*, Cambridge: Cambridge University Press, 1980, p. 416.

84 Lewis, 'Political consequences, pp. 84–94, and 'Institutionalisation', pp. 225–38.

2 Provincial party secretaries

1 Lewis, 'Institutionalisation', pp. 227–42.

2 M. F. Rakowski, 'Ważne ogniwo', *Polityka*, 1973, 42.

3 'Nomenklatura', *Aneks*, 26 (1981). It is also at this level, suggests Tarniewski, that major decision-makers can be counted as part of the Polish power elite (M. Tarniewski, *Ewolucja czy rewolucja*, Paris: Instytut Literacki, 1975, p. 95).

4 P. Frank, 'Political succession in the Soviet Union', *University of Essex Russian and Soviet Studies Centre*, Discussion Paper no. 2 (1984), p. 2.

5 T. H. Rigby, 'The Soviet regional leadership: the Brezhnev generation', *Slavic Review*, vol. 37, 1 (1978), p. 1.

6 P. Frank, 'The CPSU obkom first secretary: a profile', *British Journal of Political Science*, vol. 1, 2 (1971), p. 173.

7 R. J. Hill and P. Frank, *The Soviet Communist Party*, London: Allen and Unwin, 1981, p. 120.

8 J. F. Hough, *The Soviet Prefects*, Cambridge, Mass.: Harvard University Press, 1969, pp. 3 and 5.

9 R. E. Blackwell, 'The Soviet political elite – alternative recruitment policies at the obkom level', *Comparative Politics*, vol. 6, 1 (1973), pp. 100, 101.

10 G. Fischer, *The Soviet System and Modern Society*, New York: Atherton Press, 1968, p. 136.

11 F. J. Fleron, 'Towards a reconceptualisation of political change in the Soviet Union', *Comparative Politics*, vol. 1, 2 (1969), pp. 238–44; 'Cooptation as a mechanism of adaption to change: the Soviet leadership system', in *The Behavioral Revolution and Communist Studies*, ed. R. E. Kanet, New York: Free Press, 1971, pp. 125–39; 'System attributes and career attributes: the Soviet leadership system, 1952 to 1965' in *Comparative Communist Political Leadership*, C. Beck *et al.*, New York: David McKay, 1973, pp. 47–51.

12 Fleron, 'Cooptation', p. 176.

13 G. Hodnett, 'The *obkom* first secretaries', *Slavic Review*, vol. 24 (1965), pp. 645, 648, 652.

14 Frank, 'CPSU obkom', p. 176; J. F. Hough, 'The party apparatchiki', in *Interest Groups in Soviet Politics*, ed. H. G. Skilling and F. Griffiths, Princeton: Princeton University Press, 1971, pp. 56–57; P. D. Stewart, *Political Power in the Soviet Union*, Indianapolis: Bobbs-Merrill, 1968, pp. 154–55.

15 B. Harasymiw, *Political Elite Recruitment in the Soviet Union*, London: Macmillan, 1984, p. 46.

16 R. E. Blackwell, 'Elite recruitment and functional change', *Journal of Politics*, vol. 34, 1 (1972), pp. 135–39, 151.

17 R. E. Blackwell, 'Career development in the Soviet obkom elite', *Soviet Studies*, vol. 24, 1 (1972), pp. 33–39.

18 J. F. Hough, 'The Soviet system: petrification or pluralism', *Problems of Communism*, vol. 21, 2 (1972), p. 34.

19 J. C. Moses, *Regional Party Leadership and Policy-Making in the USSR*, New York: Praeger, 1974, p. 251.

20 Hough, 'System', pp. 40–41.
21 Rigby, 'Regional leadership', p. 13.
22 J. H. Miller, 'Cadres policy in nationality areas – recruitment of CPSU first and second secretaries in non-Russian republics of the USSR', *Soviet Studies*, vol. 29, 1 (1977), p. 19.
23 Rigby, 'Regional leadership', p. 17.
24 *Ibid.*, p. 18. More recent evidence still suggests some conflict about conclusions concerning career specialisation among Soviet apparatchiki. See R. J. Hill, 'Soviet political development and the culture of the apparatchiki', *Studies in Comparative Communism*, vol. 19, 1 (1986), pp. 27–28.
25 Rigby, 'Regional leadership', pp. 21–22.
26 S. Bialer, *Stalin's Successors*, Cambridge: Cambridge University Press, 1980, pp. 118–19.
27 Rigby, 'Regional leadership', p. 12; J. F. Hough, 'Andropov's first year', *Problems of Communism*, vol. 32, 6 (1983), p. 55.
28 Bialer, *Successors*, p. 85.
29 Frank, 'Political succession', p. 5.
30 T. Gustafson and D. Mann, 'Gorbachev's first year: building power and authority', *Problems of Communism*, vol. 35, 3 (1986), p. 2.
31 J. Armstrong, *The Soviet Bureaucratic Elite*, New York: Praeger, 1959, p. 47.
32 Rigby, 'Regional leadership', p. 13.
33 J. C. Moses, 'Functional career specialisation in Soviet regional elite recruitment', in *Leadership Selection and Patron–Client Relations in the USSR and Yugoslavia*, ed. T. H. Rigby and B. Harasymiw, London: Allen and Unwin, 1983, pp. 21, 23–24.
34 Stewart, *Political Power*, pp. 159–60; J. Miller, '*Nomenklatura*: check on localism?', in *Leadership Selection*, p. 71.
35 G. Hodnett, *Leadership in the Soviet National Republics*, Ontario: Mosaic Press, 1978, p. 119.
36 Gustafson and Mann, 'Gorbachev's first', p. 8.
37 Bialer, *Successors*, pp. 99–112; J. F. Hough, *Soviet Leadership in Transition*, Washington: Brookings Institution (1980), pp. 65–78.
38 G. W. Breslauer, 'Is there a generation gap in the Soviet political establishment?: demand articulation by RSFSR provincial party first secretaries', *Soviet Studies*, vol. 36, 1 (1984), p. 1.
39 L. Cohen, 'Regional elites in socialist Yugoslavia', in *Leadership Selection*, pp. 118–22.
40 D. S. Goodman, 'The provincial first party secretary in the People's Republic of China, 1949–78: a profile', *British Journal of Political Science*, vol. 10 (1980), p. 62.
41 W. de B. Mills, 'Leadership change in China's provinces', *Problems of Communism*, vol. 34, 3 (1985), p. 28.
42 L. A. Dellin, 'The communist party of Bulgaria', in *The Communist Parties of Eastern Europe*, ed. S. Fischer-Galati, New York: Columbia University Press, 1979, pp. 61–62.
43 J. de Weydenthal, *The Communists of Poland*, Stanford: Hoover Institution, 1986, p. 151.

44 T. Gilberg, 'The Communist Party of Romania', in *Communist Parties*, p. 290.

45 R. R. King, *A History of the Romanian Communist Party*, Stanford: Hoover Institution, 1980, pp. 95, 105.

46 G.-J. Glaessner, *Herrschaft durch Kader, Leitung der Gesselschaft und Kaderpolitik in der DDR am Beispiel des Staatsapparates*, Opladen: Westdeutscher Verlag, 1977, pp. 223, 242–43. The superior training for party cadres in the GDR compared with Poland is also noted by J. Lovenduski and J. Woodall, in *Politics and Society in Eastern Europe*, London: Macmillan, 1987, pp. 226–27.

47 'Polityka kadrowa partii', *Nowe Drogi*, April 1986, p. 69.

48 Weydenthal, *Communists*, pp. 149–50.

49 J. B. Weydenthal, 'Party development in contemporary Poland', *East European Quarterly*, vol. 11, 3 (1977), p. 351; J. Cave, 'Local officials of the Polish United Workers' Party, 1956–75', *Soviet Studies*, vol. 33, 1 (1981), pp. 133–38.

50 J. M. Montias, 'Poland: roots of the economic crisis', *Bulletin of the Association for Comparative Economic Studies*, vol. 24 (1982), p. 14.

51 A. Szczypiorski, *The Polish Ordeal*, London: Croom Helm, 1982, p. 92.

52 M. Hirszowicz, *The Bureaucratic Leviathan*, Oxford: Martin Robertson, 1980, pp. 111–12.

53 *Nowe Drogi*, October–November, 1980, p. 256.

54 'Siedem głosów o Gomułce', *Polityka*, 1984, 8.

55 T. Ito, 'Controversy over nomenklatura in Poland', *Acta Slavica Japonica*, vol. 1 (1983), p. 62.

56 M. Tarniewski, *Płonie komitet*, Paris: Kultura, 1982, p. 103.

57 A. Smolar, 'The rich', p. 48.

58 Armstrong, *Soviet Bureaucratic*, p. 52.

59 Tarniewski, *Płonie*, p. 97.

60 K. Czabanski, 'Przywileje', *Tygodnik Solidarność*, 1981, 34.

61 J. Biernat, 'Z zagadnień polityki kadrowej', *Nowe Drogi*, May 1979, p. 130.

62 E. Erazmus, 'Klasowe treści polityki kadrowej', *Nowe Drogi*, September 1984, pp. 41, 50.

63 *Nowe Drogi*, August 1981, p. 60.

64 I. Caban, *Zapis trzech dziesięcioleci PZPR*, Lublin: Wydawnictwo Lubelskie, 1978, pp. 599–680.

65 P. G. Lewis, 'The Polish party apparatus: changes in provincial first secretaries, 1975–84', *Soviet Studies*, vol. 38, 3 (1986), p. 373.

66 Frank, 'CPSU obkom', p. 178; Rigby, 'Regional leadership', p. 16.

67 Frank, 'CPSU obkom', p. 186.

68 Frank, 'CPSU obkom', p. 183; Rigby, 'Regional leadership', p. 17. A later study has also shown CPSU *obkom* first secretaries to have education backgrounds 'overwhelmingly from amongst the production disciplines' (P. Frank, 'The CPSU local apparat', in *The Soviet State: the Domestic Roots of Soviet Foreign Policy*, ed. C. Keeble, Aldershot: Gower, 1985, p. 165).

69 Hodnett, '*Obkom* first', p. 644; Rigby, 'Regional leadership', p. 18.

70 A. Brown, 'Gorbachev: new man in the Kremlin', *Problems of Communism*, vol. 34, 3 (1985), p. 6; V. Zaslavsky, 'The problem of legitimation in Soviet society', in *Conflict and Control*, ed. A. J. Vidich and R. Glassman, Beverly Hills: Sage, 1979, p. 199.

71 W. Raczkowski, *Rozwój organizacyjny PZPR w regionie krakowskim w latach 1948–1959*, Warsaw/Cracow: Państwowe Wydawnictwo Naukowe, 1981, pp. 151, 158.

72 Cave, 'Local officials', pp. 128–31, 135–36.

73 A. Banaszak, 'System pracy z kadrą partyjną', *Życie Partii*, December 1978, p. 25.

74 D. Mason, 'Elite Change and Policy Change in Communist Poland', unpublished Ph. D. thesis, Indiana University, 1978, p. 204.

75 F. Bafoil *et al.*, *Le pouvoir nu*, Paris: Syros, 1984, p. 156.

76 Z. Żandarowski, 'Rola kadr i polityka kadrowa PZPR', *Życie Partii*, June 1980, p. 3.

77 Rigby, 'Regional leadership', pp. 21–22.

78 Cave, 'Local officials', pp. 135–36.

79 Banaszak, 'System pracy', p. 25.

80 Blackwell, 'Career development', p. 35; Rigby, 'Regional leadership', p. 20.

81 R. Siemienska, 'Local party leaders in Poland', *International Political Science Review*, vol. 4, 1 (1983), p. 130.

82 W. Grochoła, 'Wszędzie jest u nas', *Polityka*, 1975, 26.

83 P. Li, *Quand les journalistes polonais parlaient*, Paris: Mégrelis, 1982, p. 254.

84 Rigby, 'Regional leadership', p. 13.

3 Provincial party committees in Poland, 1975–80

1 W. Grochoła, 'Partia bliżej ludzi', *Polityka*, 1973, 38.

2 M. F. Rakowski, 'Ważne ogniwo', *Polityka*, 1973, 42.

3 M. F. Rakowski, 'Czynnik decydujący', *Polityka*, 1975, 20.

4 C. Staszczak, 'Aparat partyjny', *Życie Partii*, April 1977, p. 6.

5 M. Wesełowska, 'Wielki ruch', *Polityka*, 1975, 23.

6 W. Kinecki, 'Programujemy, inspirujemy, kontrolujemy', *Życie Partii*, October 1977, p. 35.

7 *Czarna Księga Cenzury PRL*, London: Aneks, 1977, I, pp. 23, 104.

8 W. Michalski, 'Państwo prawa', *Nowe Drogi*, March 1981, p. 165.

9 S. Rapa, 'Czujemy się normalnie', *Polityka*, 1984, 23.

10 Wesełowska, 'Wielki'.

11 J. de Weydenthal, 'Party development in contemporary Poland', *East European Quarterly*, vol. 11, 3 (1977), pp. 351, 354.

12 M. Wesełowska, 'Przejść na ty', *Polityka*, 1976, 18.

13 Staszczak, 'Aparat', p. 6.

14 M. Wesełowska, 'Filtr', *Polityka*, 1977, 23.

15 *XIII Plenum KC PZPR*, Warsaw: Książka i Wiedza, 1978, p. 49.

16 E. Skalski, 'Zasady kierowania ruchem', *Polityka*, 1979, 48.

17 J. Piekalkiewicz, 'Polish local politics in flux', in *Local Politics in Communist Countries*, ed. D. N. Nelson, Lexington: University Press of Kentucky, 1980, p. 183.

18 A. Zarajczyk, 'W terenowych ogniwach administracji', *Życie Partii*, May 1977, p. 35.

19 R. R. King and J. F. Brown (eds.), *Eastern Europe's Uncertain Future*, New York: Praeger, 1977, p. 241.

20 J. Staniszkis, *Poland's Self-Limiting Revolution*, Princeton: Princeton University Press, 1984, p. 107.

21 *XVII Plenum KC PZPR*, Warsaw: Książka i Wiedza, 1975, p. 65; E. Makowski, *Ruch robotniczy w Wielkopolsce*, Poznań: Wydawnictwo Naukowe UAM, 1984, p. 273.

22 'Twarzą w twarz z robotnikami', *Polityka*, 1981, 5.

23 Bafoil, *Le pouvoir*, p. 41.

24 M. F. Rakowski, 'Wybierać najpilniejsze', *Polityka*, 1975, 48.

25 A. Przeworski, '"The Man of Iron" and men of power in Poland', *PS*, vol. 15, 1 (1982), p. 25.

26 J. Maziarski, 'Czas na dialog', *Polityka*, 1975, 44.

27 Wesełowska, 'Filtr'.

28 B. Olszewska, 'Wizytówka', *Polityka*, 1979, 49.

29 E. Szymański, 'Stawianie się województwem', *Nowe Drogi*, January 1979, pp. 77–79.

30 A. Kulicka, 'Najlepiej napisać do partii. . . ', *Polityka*, 1978, 42.

31 Wesełowska, 'Przejść'.

32 Staszczak, 'Aparat', p. 6.

33 *Ibid.*, p. 7.

34 B. Olszewska, 'Rozmawiać i słuchać', *Polityka*, 1975, 44.

35 R. Szpakowska, 'Wybrani przez powiatową organizację', *Życie Partii*, January 1975, p. 9.

36 W. Wodecki, 'Kto jest aktywistą?' *Życie Partii*, August 1977, p. 8.

37 J. F. Hough, 'Political participation in the Soviet Union', *Soviet Studies*, vol. 28, 1 (1976), pp. 11–12.

38 J. Doliński, 'Rozmyślania o partii', *Nowe Drogi*, October 1981, pp. 87, 90.

39 W. Gielczynski, 'Echa z Polski zielonej', *Polityka*, 1975, 42.

40 A. Onych, 'Co daje kontakt z POP', *Życie Partii*, December 1977, p. 5.

41 Maziarski, 'Czas'.

42 A. Strońska, 'Bierny aktyw', *Polityka*, 1980, 50.

43 J. Maziarski, 'Krytyka krytyki', *Polityka*, 1975, 13.

44 H. Rot, 'Władza widoczna – czy sprawna'. *Polityka*, 1975, 20.

45 D. V. Schwartz, 'Decision making, administrative decentralization and feedback mechanisms', *Studies in Comparative Communism*, vol. 7, 1/2 (1974), p. 154.

46 J. Woodall, *The Socialist Corporation and Technocratic Power*, Cambridge: Cambridge University Press, 1982, p. 88.

47 W. Madurowicz, 'Funkcja organów szczebla regionalnego w kierowaniu gospodarką', *Nowe Drogi*, April 1979, p. 103.

48 M. F. Rakowski, 'Granice centralizacji', *Polityka*, 1977, 45.

49 *Ibid.*; *Polityka*, 1977, 47.

50 *IX Plenum KC PZPR*, Warsaw: Książka i Wiedza, 1977, p. 57.

51 M. F. Rakowski, 'Skutki centralizacji', *Polityka* 1980, 47.

52 Piekalkiewicz, 'Polish', p. 187.

53 *XIII Plenum*, pp. 33–53. First secretary Kinecki, replaced as KW leader in Siedlce during December 1978, linked criticism of the current situation with an appeal at a CC Plenum for more inner-party democracy, but was now allowed to speak at the meeting. See W. Kinecki, 'Dwuzawodowiec', *Polityka*, 1987, 15.

54 Rapa, 'Czujemy'; J. Loch 'Dezyczja Albina Terki', *Polityka*, 1980, 40.

55 Makowski, *Ruch*, pp. 278–80.

56 *XVII Plenum*, p. 65.

57 D. Christian, 'The supervisory function in Russian and Soviet history', *Slavic Review*, vol. 40, 1 (1982), pp. 73–80.

58 Hough, *Soviet Prefects*, p. 87.

59 Schwartz, 'Decision making', p. 147.

60 T. Remington, 'Institution building in Bolshevik Russia: the case of "state kontrol"', *Slavic Review*, vol. 40, 1 (1982), p. 95. J. S. Adams also notes the persistence of ambiguities in both conception and practice of the Soviet experience of *kontrol*'. Early Leninist views of workers' control have continued to recur, while the supervisory role of citizen inspectors has been difficult to distinguish in practice from the managerial role exercised in decision making (see *Citizen Inspectors in the Soviet Union: the People's Control Committee*, New York: Praeger, 1977, pp. 3–4).

61 T. Dunmore, 'Local party organs in industrial administration: the case of the ob''edinenie reform', *Soviet Studies*, vol. 32, 2 (1980), pp. 196–98.

62 See, for example, J. Gluza, 'Efekty działania aktywu i aparatu partyjnego w gminach', *Życie Partii*, March 1977, p. 5.

63 L. Krasucki, 'O kontroli wykonania', *Nowe Drogi*, September 1977, p. 64.

64 *IX Plenum*, pp. 36, 70. Grabski later linked the ineffectiveness of the economic manoeuvre with the sabotaging by Prime Minister Jaroszewicz of proposals worked out by the central and local party *aktiv*. There was clearly strong opposition to Jaroszewicz among the leading provincial secretaries and steps had been taken by some of them in 1976 to eject him from the leadership. See G. Pomian (ed.), *Protokoly tzw, komisji Grabskiego*, Paris: Instytut Literacki, 1986, pp. 129, 155.

65 W. Wodecki, 'Szczerze, rzeczowo, życzliwie', *Życie Partii*, May 1978, p. 7.

66 'O dalsze umocnienie przewodniej roli partii', *Życie Partii*, February 1978, p. 12.

67 *IX Plenum*, p. 42.

68 B. Glinski, 'Kierunki rozwoju nauk organizacji i zarządzania', *Nowe Drogi*, October 1977, p. 66.

69 H. Krall, 'Spostrzegawczość, pomysłowość, dobra wola', *Polityka*, 1976, 22.

70 J. Maziarski, 'Sedno', *Polityka*, 1977, 48.

71 M. F. Rakowski, 'Swiadomi odpowiedzialności', *Polityka*, 1978, 3.
72 Z. Machowski, 'Przeciw stępianiu wrażliwości społecznej', *Życie Partii*, May 1977, p. 13.
73 W. Staniszewski, 'Niełatwo być współgospodarzem', *Życie Partii*, August 1977, p. 31.
74 L. Winiarski, 'Budzić wrażliwość – zapobiegać', *Życie Partii*, March 1977, p. 15.
75 J. Fasztyn, 'Porządni ludzi', *Życie Partii*, December 1977, p. 8.
76 J. Fasztyn, 'Partyjna kontrola w terenie', *Życie Partii*, February 1978, p. 34; 'Dyplomacja . . .', *Życie Partii*, May 1978, p. 10.
77 M. Wesełowska, 'Sumienie', *Polityka*, 1978, 18.
78 Bafoil, *Le pouvoir*, p. 45.
79 Christian, 'Supervisory function', p. 84.
80 Lewis, 'Institutionalisation', pp. 227–31.
81 J. Fasztyn, 'Zawiódł', *Życie Partii*, March 1978, p. 17; see also 'Wierzyć i. . . kontrolować', *Życie Partii*, May 1980, p. 4.
82 Dunmore, 'Local party', pp. 202–3.
83 E. Wojcik, 'Cel: umacnianie partii', *Życie Partii*, April 1978, p. 15.
84 T. Kołodziejczyk, 'Skreślenia – problem niepokojący', *Życie Partii*, August 1979, p. 7.
85 Wesełowska, 'Sumienie'.
86 S. Pawlak, 'Kontrola warunkiem sprawnego kierowania', *Życie Partii*, March 1979, p. 2.
87 *Ibid.*
88 Skalski, 'Zasady'.
89 Fasztyn, 'Partyjna kontrola', p. 34.
90 G. Kolankiewicz, 'Bureacratised political participation and its consequence in Poland', *Politics*, vol. 1, 1 (1981), p. 37.
91 Fasztyn, 'Partyjna kontrola'.
92 A. Barzyk, 'Gdy odchodzi kandydat . . .', *Życie Partii*, September 1979, p. 16.
93 Wesełowska, 'Sumienie'.
94 J. Grochmalicki 'Umacnianie małych POP – ważnym zadaniem', *Życie Partii*, November 1978, p. 35.
95 *XIII Plenum*, pp. 35, 49.
96 J. Buziński, 'Skuteczność inspiracji i kontroli', *Życie Partii*, April 1979, p. 1.
97 K. Cypryniak, 'Kontrolne działania instancji', *Życie Partii*, January 1979, p. 10.
98 E. Szymański, 'Kształtowanie partyjnej i obywatelskiej odpowiedzialności', *Nowe Drogi*, December 1979, p. 33.
99 L. Winiarski, 'Partyjna ocena administracji gminnej', *Życie Partii*, February 1979, pp. 28–29.
100 Christian, 'Supervisory function', p. 83.
101 Z. Grudzień, 'Droga wytyzcaną przez partię', *Życie Partii*, July 1979, pp. 5–6.
102 A. Orchowski, 'Klimat', *Polityka*, 1979, 51–52.

103 J. Kowalski, 'Urzeczywistnianie demokracji socjalistycznej', *Nowe Drogi*, February 1980, p. 154.

104 W. Kruczek, 'Na straży norm partyjności i zasad socjalizmu', *Nowe Drogi*, May 1980, p. 41.

105 Dunmore, 'Local party', p. 199.

106 E. Charkiewicz, 'Dobosz bez tchu', *Polityka*, 1985, 10.

107 Z. Żandarowski, 'Rola kadr i polityka kadrowa PZPR', *Życie Partii*, June 1980, p. 3.

108 W. Wodecki, 'Rozmowy – elementem polityki kadrowej', *Życie Partii*, September 1980, p. 11.

109 Lewis, 'Legitimation', pp. 16–17; also, M. E. Urban, 'Conceptualizing political power in the USSR: patterns of binding and bonding', *Studies in Comparative Communism*, vol. 18, 4 (1985), pp. 211–19.

110 Z. Falinski, 'Agitator powinien być działaczem', *Życie Partii*, January 1979, p. 28.

111 P. Musiewicz, 'O produkcji – łatwiej', *Życie Partii*, February 1979, p. 31.

112 Szymański, 'Kształtowanie', p. 34.

113 Doliński, 'Rozmyślania', p. 87.

114 J. Kusiak, 'Rozbudowa partii działaniem planowym', *Życie Partii*, June 1978, p. 6.

115 *XVI Plenum KC PZPR*, Warsaw: Książka i Wiedza, 1979, p. 35.

116 Orchowski, 'Klimat'.

117 G. Blażynski, *Flashpoint Poland*, New York: Pergamon Press, 1979, p. 333.

118 P. Raina, *Political Opposition in Poland 1954–1977*, London: Poets and Painters Press, 1978, p. 447.

119 J. Bielasiak, 'The party: permanent crisis', in Bromberg, *Poland*, pp. 21–22.

120 G. C. Malcher, *Poland's Politicized Army*, New York: Praeger, 1984, pp. 93–98.

121 *Życie Partii*, March 1980, p. 16.

122 J. de Weydenthal, 'Workers and party in Poland', *Problems of Communism*, vol. 29, 6 (1980), pp. 4, 6.

123 *Nowe Drogi*, September 1980, p. 21.

124 W. F. Robinson (ed.), *August 1980: the Strikes in Poland*, Munich: RFE Research, 1980, pp. 100, 343.

125 *Kultura* (Paris), October 1980, p. 145.

126 *Nowe Drogi*, September 1980, p. 21.

127 *Ibid.* pp. 35, 45, 57.

128 Robinson, *August*, pp. 368–69.

129 *Nowe Drogi*, September 1980, pp. 30, 47.

130 B. Toruńczyk, *Gdańsk 1980 oczyma świadków*, London: Polonia Book Fund, 1980, pp. 44–45, 50.

131 *L'Alternative*, no. 7 (1980), pp. 34–35.

132 T. Garton Ash, *The Polish Revolution*, London: Cape, 1983, p. 62; Ascherson, *Polish August*, p. 162.

133 Ascherson, *Polish August*, p. 184; see also *Kultura* (Paris), October 1980,

p. 142; A. Kemp-Welch (ed.), *The Birth of Solidarity*, London: Macmillan, 1983, p. 195.

134 K. Pomian, *Pologne: défi à l'impossible*, Paris: Editions Ouvrières, 1982, p. 30.

135 D. Passent, 'Rzecz naprawdę pospolita', *Polityka*, 1980, 38.

136 *Życie Partii*, October 1980, p. 15.

137 *Nowe Drogi*, October/November 1980, pp. 64, 75, 233, 256, 262.

138 *Ibid*, pp. 313, 337, 345.

139 Staniszkis, *Self-Limiting*, p. 190.

140 P. Moszyński, 'Budujemy nowy dom', *Polityka*, 1980, 42; A. Grodzki, 'Dżungla wśród lasów i jezior', in *Glos*, Paris: Instytut Literacki, 1980, pp. 123–27.

141 'Korupcja polskiej "nomenklatury"', *Zeszty historyczne* no. 64, Paris: Instytut Literacki, 1983.

142 Robinson, *August*, p. 223.

143 M. Wesełowska, 'Trzeba patrzeć na ręce', *Polityka*, 1980, 41.

144 'Plan rozmowy układamy wspólnie', *Polityka*, 1980, 44.

145 B. Misztal, 'Apathy-participation-apathy: the vicious circle of collective behaviour in contemporary Poland', in *Poland After Solidarity*, ed. B. Misztal, New Brunswick: Transaction Books, 1985, p. 10.

146 W. Pawłowski, 'Weryfikacja', *Polityka*, 1980, 45.

147 Strońska, 'Bierny'.

148 K. Ruane, *The Polish Challenge*, London: British Broadcasting Corporation, 1982, p. 83.

149 J. Kołodziejski, 'W Gdańsku zaczęło się 14 sierpnia', *Polityka*, 1983, 34.

150 Ascherson, *Polish August*, p. 185.

151 G. Sanford, *Polish Communism in Crisis*, London: Croom Helm, 1983, p. 65.

152 Loch, 'Decyzja'.

153 J. Porębski, 'Ważny jest każdy signał', *Życie Partii*, November 1980, p. 33.

154 *Polityka*, 1980, 44.

155 Pawłowski, 'Weryfikacja'.

156 Loch, 'Decyzja'.

157 T. Kowalik, 'Experts and the working group', in Kemp-Welch, *Birth*, pp. 157, 166–67.

158 J. J. Wiatr, 'Sprostać nowym oczekiwaniom', *Życie Partii*, December 1980, p. 19.

4 Indecision and *odnowa*

1 *Nowe Drogi*, January/February, 1981, p. 40.

2 *Nowe Drogi*, December 1980, p. 10, 14–16, 18, 42.

3 B. Holub, 'Oddział zakaźny', *Polityka*, 1981, 7.

4 *Nowe Drogi*, January/February 1981, pp. 13, 117, 127–28, 138–39.

5 J. Holzer, *'Solidarność' 1980–1981*, Paris: Instytut Literacki, 1984, p. 160.

6 *Nowe Drogi*, January/February 1981, pp. 41, 80, 102–4.

7 *Życie Partii*, March 1981, p. 10.
8 A. Wiśniewski, 'Busola', *Życie Partii*, 1981, 9.
9 *Nowe Drogi*, January/February 1981, p. 143.
10 *Ibid.*, pp. 140–41.
11 *Ibid.*, pp. 333–34.
12 *Nowe Drogi*, December 1980, p. 174.
13 *Ibid.*
14 *Nowe Drogi*, January 1981, p. 371.
15 *Ibid.*, pp. 112, 331.
16 *Ibid.*, p. 355.
17 W. Pawłowski, 'Bez upojenia', *Polityka*, 1981, 12.
18 D. Fikus, *Foksal 81*, London: Aneks, 1984, p. 160.
19 'Sezon rządu', *Polityka*, 1981, 8.
20 E. Skalski, 'Kto przeciw ?' *Polityka*, 1981, 8.
21 M. Hirszowicz, *Coercion and Control in Communist Society*, Brighton: Wheatsheaf, 1986, p. 92.
22 See *Nowe Drogi*, January/February 1981, March, April.
23 *Nowe Drogi*, January/February 1981, p. 76.
24 Kozik, *PZPR*; pp. 280–81.
25 Konwersatorium 'Doświadczenie i przyszłość', 'Raport trzeci: Społeczeństwo wobec kryszysu', *Kultura*, May 1981, p. 134.
26 'Dyskusja w Krakowie', *Polityka*, 1981, 4.
27 M. Szulc, 'Lekcja sądecka', *Polityka*, 1981, 5.
28 *Polityka*, 1981, 2.
29 M. F. Rakowski, 'Szanować partnera', *Polityka*, 1981, 3.
30 W. Wodecki, 'Mieć prawo do własnego zdania', *Życie Partii*, January 1981, p. 20.
31 *Polityka*, 1981, 6.
32 P. Moszyński, 'Potrzeba gwarancji', *Polityka*, 1981, 4.
33 *Życie Partii*, January 1981, pp. 5, 29.
34 E. Erazmus, 'Kierownicza rola PZPR', *Życie Partii*, January 1981, p. 8.
35 E. Erazmus, 'Rola aparatu partyjnego', *Życie Partii*, February 1981, p. 5.
36 M. Wasio, 'Filozowie i robotnicy', *Życie Partii*, February 1981, p. 17.
37 W. Wodecki, 'Polityka kadrowa – propozycje', *Życie Partii*, February 1981, p. 21.
38 P. Green, 'The anti-apparatus movement', *Labour Focus on Eastern Europe*, vol. 4, 4–6 (1981), p. 51.
39 L. Witkowski, 'Partia: zjednoczenie w działaniu', *Polityka*, 1981, 6.
40 'Interrogations Polonaises', *La Documentation Française*, 417 (1981), p. 34.
41 Witkowski, 'Partia'.
42 Green, 'Anti-apparatus', pp. 50–51; Makowski, *Ruch robotniczy*, p. 295.
43 *Życie Partii*, February 1981, p. 8.
44 P. Moszyński, 'Sprawa wyborów, *Polityka*, 1981, 10.
45 *Polityka*, 1981, 6.
46 A. Dobieszewski, 'Centralizm i demokracja w partii', *Życie Partii*, February 1981, p. 2.

47 *Nowe Drogi*, March 1981, p. 26.
48 *Nowe Drogi*, May/June 1981, p. 122.
49 *Nowe Drogi*, March 1981, pp. 7, 8.
50 *Ibid.*, pp. 26, 44–47.
51 *Ibid.*, pp. 68, 88–89, 101.
52 'Od-nowa członka Biura Politycznego', *Aneks*, 24–25 (1981), 57–61.
53 *Nowe Drogi*, March 1981, pp. 78–79, 82.
54 Ascherson, *Polish August*, p. 263.
55 'Partia odnowiona – czyli jaka', *Polityka*, 1981, 11.
56 E. Erazmus, 'System wyborczy jako mechanism przekazywania władzy w partii', *Życie Partii*, March 1981, p. 7.
57 S. Brodzki, '". . . Obywatele cementują państwo . . ."', *Polityka*, 1981, 13.
58 W. Lebiedziński, 'Refleksje o demokracji wewnątrzpartyjnej', *Nowe Drogi*, January/February 1981, pp. 271–73.
59 *Polityka*, 1981, 8; S. Sołtysiński, 'Bezpartyjni a partia', *Polityka*, 1981, 9.
60 J. Czuła, 'Bez pobłazania', *Życie Partii*, January 1981, pp. 14–15.
61 *Ibid.*; I. Bak, 'Działanie szybkie i rozważne', *Życie Partii*, February 1981, p. 28.
62 *Polityka*, 1981, 7; 1981, 11.
63 *Nowe Drogi*, March 1981, p. 33.
64 *Polityka*, 1981, 11.
65 J. Czuła, 'Niepokój'; B. Hołda 'Oczyszczanie atmosfery', *Życie Partii*, March 1981, pp. 23, 26.
66 Pawłowski, 'Bez upojenia'.
67 *Polityka*, 1981, 13.
68 *Communist Affairs*, vol. 1, (1982), p. 262.
69 Staniszkis, *Self-Limiting*, p. 202; W. Kuczyński 'Kwestia krwi', *Aneks*, 37 (1985), p. 122.
70 K. Gerner, *The Soviet Union and Central Europe in the Post-War Era*, Aldershot: Gower (1985), p. 75; J. Kuśmierek, *Stan Polski*, Paris: Instytut Literacki, 1982, p. 68.
71 N. G. Andrews, *Poland 1980–81*, Washington: National Defense University Press, (1985), p. 20. The importance of these links has been strengthened by the revelations of Colonel Kukliński, member of the Polish General Staff up to 8 November 1981 and a major internal source of information concerning military planning in Poland during 1980–81. He has confirmed the existence of plans for military action in the spring of 1981 and the central part taken in this by the Ministry of Internal Affairs and its head, General Milewski, whose formal political career came to a conclusion for undetermined reasons following the death of Father Popiełuszko in 1984. See *Kultura* (Paris), 4 (1987), p. 25. Further details of his account will be examined in chapter 6.
72 *Documentation Française*, p. 8; J. Powiórski, 'Powtórka z rozgrywki', *Krytyka*, 17 (1984), p. 236.

73 Holzer, 'Solidarność', p. 199.
74 Fikus, *Foksal*, p. 88.
75 Powiórski, 'Powtórka', p. 234.
76 M. Szejnert and T. Zalewski, *Szczecin: Grudzień–Sierpień–Grudzień*, London: Aneks, 1986, p. 309.
77 *Polityka*, 1983, 9.
78 *Nowe Drogi*, April 1981, pp. 17–19.
79 *Nowe Drogi*, August 1987, p. 60.
80 *Nowe Drogi*, April 1981, pp. 64, 88, 101, 150.
81 *Ibid.*, pp. 87, 122–23, 139–40.
82 *Ibid.*, pp. 51–54, 69, 72–74, 91, 110, 155–57.
83 *Ibid.*, pp. 114–15.
84 G. Pomian (ed.), *Protokoly tzw. komisji Grabskiego*, Paris: Instytut Literacki, 1986, p. 8.
85 E. Skalski, 'Notatki z Gdańska', *Polityka*, 1981, 15.
86 *Nowe Drogi*, May/June 1981, p. 116.
87 *Polityka*, 1981, 18.
88 M. Wesełowska and P. Moszyński, 'Żyć własnym życiem', *Polityka*, 1981, 17.
89 J. Loch, 'W trybie nadzwyczajnym', *Polityka*, 1981, 16.
90 E. Kotas, 'Potrzebny jest stały przegląd sił', *Życie Partii* 8, 1981, 12.
91 P. Moszyński, 'Zanim mnie zweryfikyją', *Polityka*, 1981, 14.
92 *Polityka*, 1981, 19; M. Wesełowska, 'Możecie się oprzeć', *Polityka*, 1981, 15. The conditions for such a development were certainly not facilitated or encouraged by the provincial party committee. The Warsaw organisation was distinguished by the strict provincial control of the party press and the concentration of its efforts on attacking 'enemies of socialism' rather than on informing members of current developments in the organisation. See Z. Simbierowicz, 'Poszukiwanie nowego ładu', *Kultura* (Warsaw), 22 March, 1981.
93 B. Olszewska, 'Dyskusja', *Polityka*, 1981, 14.
94 Holzer, 'Solidarność', p. 145.
95 D. S. Mason, *Public Opinion and Political Change in Poland, 1980–1982*, Cambridge: Cambridge University Press, 1985, p. 151.
96 J. de Weydenthal, B. Porter and K. Devlin, *The Polish Drama: 1980–1982*, Lexington: Lexington Books, 1983, p. 122.
97 Skalski, 'Notatki'.
98 *Nowe Drogi*, May/June 1981, pp. 42, 92, 116, 171, 192.
99 *Nowe Drogi*, March 1983, p. 137.
100 Sanford, *Polish Communism*, p. 176.

5 Renewal and party authority

1 *Nowe Drogi*, May/June 1981, pp. 16, 41, 85.
2 'U schyłka kadencji', *Polityka*, 1981, 19.
3 *Nowe Drogi*, May/June 1981, pp. 163–64; *Communist Affairs*, vol. 1, 1 (1982), p. 278.

4 *Nowe Drogi*, May/June 1981, p. 118; *Życie Partii*, April 1981, p. 9.

5 *Nowe Drogi*, May/June 1981, pp. 80, 102, 144–45, 189.

6 *Polityka*, 1981, 21; *Nowe Drogi*, July 1981, p. 99; A. Stroński, 'Front rozsądku', *Polityka*, 1981, 25; *Nowe Drogi*, August 1981, p. 173.

7 *Życie Partii*, June 1981, p. 25; B. Pietkiewicz, 'Ludzie chcą mieć nadzieję', *Polityka*, 1981, 20.

8 P. Moszyński, 'Co zrobić z apartem ?', *Polityka*, 1981, 22.

9 A. Adamus, 'Temat otwarty', *Polityka*, 1981, 26.

10 Pietkiewicz, 'Ludzie'. The practice spread and, at the provincial conferences, 37 of the 49 elections for first secretary were contested. See W. Hahn, 'Electoral choice in the Soviet bloc', *Problems of Communism*, vol. 36, 2 (1987), p. 33.

11 'Barcikowski delegatem na zjazd', *Polityka*, 1981, 23.

12 M. Szejnert and T. Zalewski, *Szczecin*, p. 297.

13 T. Gutkowski, 'Demokracja i odpowiedzialność, *Życie Partii*, July 1981, p. 14.

14 Szejnert and Zalewski, *Szczecin*, p. 298.

15 T.Ito, 'Nomenklatura and free election: a Polish experiment, 1980–81', Paper presented at the Third World Congress for Soviet and East European Studies (1985), p. 9.

16 Gutkowski, 'Demokracja'.

17 L. Winiarski, 'Nowa "dziecięca choroba"?', *Życie Partii*, July 1981, p. 11.

18 Pomian, *Protokoły*, p. 8.

19 J. Czuła, 'Oczyszczanie partii trwa', *Życie Partii*, June 1981, p. 17.

20 Winiarski, 'Nowa'.

21 M. Wesełowska, 'Podejrzliwość, *Polityka*, 1981, 23.

22 *Ibid*.

23 E. Michaluk, 'Plecami do wielkich haseł', *Życie Partii*, July 1981, p. 13.

24 *Nowe Drogi*, July 1981, p. 69.

25 G. Pomian, *Polska 'Solidarności'*, Paris: Instytut Literacki, 1982, p. 342.

26 Wesełowska, 'Podejrzliwość'.

27 G. Kolankiewicz, 'The politics of "socialist renewal"', in *Policy and Politics*, ed. Woodall, p. 71.

28 Ito, 'Nomenklatura', p. 6.

29 J. Czuła, 'Sprawa Iwanówa czyli równia pochyła', *Życie Partii*, July 1981, pp. 27–28.

30 *Polityka*, 181, 23.

31 W. Pawłowski, 'Junior', *Polityka*, 1981, 24.

32 W. Wodecki, 'Nie spełnione oczekiwanie', *Życie Partii*, July 1981, pp. 8–9.

33 M. Heller, *Sous le regard de Moscou*, Paris: Calmann–Lévy, 1982, p. 116.

34 Sanford, *Polish Communism*, p. 87.

35 *Nowe Drogi*, July 1981, pp. 30–31.

36 Makowski, *Ruch robotniczy*, p. 36.

37 Ruane, *Polish Challenge*, p. 194.

38 *Nowe Drogi*, July 1981, pp. 33, 35, 46, 51, 118–19.

39 *Polityka* 1981, 25.

40 *Nowe Drogi*, July 1981, pp. 60, 65, 94, 124.

41 *Ibid.*, pp. 8, 25.

42 F. S. Larrabee, 'Soviet crisis management in Eastern Europe', in *The Warsaw Pact: Alliance in Transition?*, ed. D. Holloway and J. Sharp, London: Macmillan, 1984, p. 132.

43 Przeworski, 'Man of Iron', p. 28.

44 E. Moreton, 'The Soviet Union and Poland's struggle for self-control', *International Security*, vol. 7, 1 (1982), p. 93; O. MacDonald, 'The Polish vortex: Solidarity and socialism', *New Left Review*, 193 (1983), p. 39.

45 Holzer, *Solidarność*, p. 235.

46 M. F. Rakowski 'Czasy nadzei i rozczarowań, *Polityka*, 1985, 31; Andrews, *Poland*, p. 167.

47 Fikus, *Foksal*, p. 105.

48 *Nowe Drogi*, July 1981, pp. 77, 129.

49 T. Kołodziejczyk, 'Nad przemianami w aparacie', *Życie Partii*, 1981, 9.

50 B. A. Misztal and B. Misztal, 'The transformation of political elites', in *Polish Politics: Edge of the Abyss*, ed. J. Bielasiak and M. D. Simon, New York: Praeger, 1984, p. 176.

51 J. Pakulski, 'Leaders of the Solidarity movement: a sociological portrait', *Sociology*, vol. 20, 1 (1986), p. 71.

52 Kołodziejczyk, 'Nad przemianami'.

53 Lewis, 'Institutionalisation', pp. 239–41.

54 D. Kędzierska *et al.*, 'Smarem jest zaufanie', *Polityka*, 1986, 42.

55 *Nowe Drogi*, August 1981, p. 173.

56 Malcher, *Politicized Army*, p. 143.

57 *Nowe Drogi*, April 1981, pp. 155–56.

58 R. Łukasiewicz, 'Partia odradza się w działaniu', *Życie Partii*, 1982, 1.

59 'Delegaci', *Polityka*, 1981, 26.

60 'Członkowie i delegaci', *Polityka*, 1986, 27.

61 *Nowe Drogi*, August 1981, pp. 28–29, 121; 'Jak rodził się statut', *Życie Partii*, August 1981, p. 25.

62 J. Wiatr, 'Poland's party politics: the Extraordinary Congress of 1981', *Canadian Journal of Political Science*, vol. 14, 4 (1981), p. 822.

63 *Nowe Drogi*, August 1981, p. 164.

64 G. Kolankiewicz, 'Renewal, reform or retreat: the Polish Communist Party after the Extraordinary Ninth Congress', *The World Today*, October 1981, p. 370; Ito, 'Nomenklatura', p. 14.

65 W. Wodecki, 'Spotkania w gminie', *Życie Partii*, August 1981, p. 29.

66 Staniszkis, *Self-Limiting*, pp. 134, 205.

67 Z. A. Kruszewski, 'The communist party during the 1980–81 democratisation of Poland', in *Polish Politics*, ed. Bielasiak and Simon, p. 257.

68 N. Davies, *Heart of Europe: a Short History of Poland*. Oxford: Oxford University Press, 1986, p. 21.

69 J. Bielasiak, 'Solidarity and the state: strategies of social reconstruction', in *Poland After Solidarity*, ed. Misztal, pp. 19–38; Mason, *Public Opinion*, p. 159.

70 A. Arato, 'Empire vs. civil society: Poland 1981–82', *Telos*, 50 (1981–82), p. 74.
71 J. Kowalski, 'Rozkład partii i Państwa', *Kultura*, October 1981, p. 78.
72 *Nowe Drogi*, September 1981, p. 8.
73 *Życie Partii*, 1981, 9.
74 Powiórski, 'Powtórka', p. 237.
75 *Nowe Drogi*, September 1981, pp. 21, 29, 32.
76 Mason, *Public Opinion*, pp. 145–46. By no means all Poles were even aware of the Extraordinary Party Congress. In early July 20% were reported not to know that the Congress was due to open in the immediate future (*New Statesman*, 31 July, 1981).
77 B. Lesiewicz, 'Zmienić – tylko jak?', *Życie Partii*, 1981, 9.
78 E. Kotas, 'Potrzebny jest stały przegląd sił', *Życie Partii*, 1981, 12.
79 'Rozmyślenia o partii', *Nowe Drogi*, October 1981, pp. 89–90.
80 L. Bogusławski, 'Bez podziałów branżowych', *Życie Partii*, 1981, 9.
81 E. Skrzypczak, 'Rozmowa', *Krytyka*, 18 (1987), pp. 156–58; M. Jagiełło, 'Kilka refleksji o aparacie partyjnym 1980–1981', *Krytyka*, 18 (1987), p. 138; Kolankiewicz, 'Renewal', p. 375.
82 W. Wodecki, 'Myślenie o przyszłości', *Życie Partii*, 1981, 12.
83 T. Wojewódzki, 'Czego nie lubi aparat', *Polityka*, 1981, 37.
84 J. Giermek, 'Jeszcze kilka słów o aparacie partyjnym', *Polityka*, 1981, 42.
85 Kołodziejczyk, 'Nad przemianami'.
86 W. Wodecki, 'Odejścia ze smakiem piołunu', *Życie Partii*, 1981, 9.
87 Bafoil, *Le pouvoir*, p. 90.
88 T. Warczak, 'Niełatwy powrót do czołówki', *Życie Partii*, 1981, 11.
89 Ash, *Polish Revolution*, p. 198; Holzer, *'Solidarność'*, p. 258.
90 Fikus, *Foksal*, p. 168.
91 Ruane, *Polish Challenge*, p. 236.
92 G. Sanford, 'Poland', in *Leadership and Succession in the Soviet Union, Eastern Europe and China*, ed. M. McCauley and S. Carter, New York: M. E. Sharpe, 1986, p. 48.
93 D. M. Nuti, 'Poland: economic collapse and socialist renewal', *New Left Review*, 130 (1981), p. 29.
94 Carrère d'Encausse, *Grand frère*, p. 238.
95 *Życie Partii*, 1981, 11.
96 *Nowe Drogi*, October 1981, p. 31.
97 *Ibid.*, p. 32.
98 A. Touraine *et al.*, *Solidarité: analyse d'un mouvement*, Paris: Fayard, 1982, p. 226.
99 *Nowe Drogi*, October 1981, p. 31; *Nowe Drogi*, November 1981, pp. 12, 16, 17, 40.

6 The advance of the military

1 W. Honkisz, 'Zrodzone z ideii partii', *Życie Partii*, 1981, 12.
2 *Nowe Drogi*, November 1981, pp. 28, 115, 155–56.

3 *Nowe Drogi*, October 1981, p. 31.
4 *Nowe Drogi*, November 1981, pp. 56, 74–75, 128, 131, 159, 168.
5 *Ibid.*, pp. 56, 85, 129, 159.
6 *Ibid.*, pp. 184, 207, 69–70; *Nowe Drogi*, July 1981, p. 98.
7 *Uncensored Poland News Bulletin*, (London), 1984, 5.
8 *Nowe Drogi*, November 1981, pp. 56, 171, 201.
9 *Ibid.*, p. 168, 179, 194.
10 *Ibid.*, pp. 63–65, 95, 171, 173.
11 *Ibid.*, p. 141; *Polityka*, 1981, 15 and 24.
12 *Polityka*, 1981, 41.
13 *Nowe Drogi*, November 1981, pp. 16–17, 87, 97, 159, 165; *Polityka*, 1981, 44 and 46.
14 *Nowe Drogi*, December 1981, pp. 99–104.
15 Fikus, *Foksal*, p. 136; *Polityka*, 1981, 45.
16 *Nowe Drogi*, November 1981, p. 17.
17 O. MacDonald, 'The Polish vortex: Solidarity and socialism', *New Left Review*, 139 (1983), p. 39.
18 *The Observer*, 27 September, 1981.
19 S. I. Ploss, *Moscow and the Polish Crisis: an interpretation of Soviet policies and intentions*, Boulder: Westview, 1986, p. 125; D. K. Simes, 'Clash over Poland', *Foreign Policy*, 46 (1982), p. 54.
20 K. S. Karol, 'Les saboteurs de la "quatrième force"', *Le Nouvel Observateur*, 3 October 1981.
21 Holzer, *Solidarność*, pp. 310–11; Powiórski, 'Powtórka', p. 238.
22 *Nowe Drogi*, November 1981, p. 178.
23 K. S. Karol, 'Chacun son general', *Le Nouvel Observateur*, 24 October 1981.
24 Larrabee, 'Soviet crisis management', pp. 132–33; Moreton, 'Soviet Union', p. 102.
25 A. Korbonski, 'The dilemmas of civil–military relations in contemporary Poland', *Armed Forces and Society*, vol. 8, 1 (1981), p. 15; Ploss, *Moscow*, p. 16.
26 *Soviet Weekly*, 20–27 December 1980, 10 January 1981.
27 *Nowe Drogi*, November 1981, p. 7.
28 *Ibid.*, pp. 52, 54, 108, 118, 209, 227.
29 A. Krzeminski, 'Wojsko i cywile', *Polityka*, 1981, 47.
30 Kruszewski, 'Communist party', p. 261.
31 *The Observer*, 1 November 1981, 22 November 1981.
32 Touraine, *Solidarité*, p. 226; J. de Weydenthal *et al.*, *The Polish Drama: 1980–1982*, Lexington, Mass./Toronto: Lexington Books, 1983, p. 50.
33 'Jest o czym pomyśleć', *Życie Partii*, 1981, 16.
34 *Ibid.*
35 *Polityka*, 1981, 50.
36 *Życie Partii*, 1981, 16; *Sunday Times*, 6 December 1981.
37 I. Wajszczuk, 'Poszukiwanie tożsamości', *Nowe Drogi*, February 1983, p. 67.

38 F. Dubet *et al.*, 'Un mouvement social', *Esprit*, 63 (1982), p. 11; Powiórski, 'Powtórka', p. 56.

39 Touraine, *Solidarité*, p. 244; 'Widziane z dołu, *Tygodnik Solidarność* 1981, 34.

40 Powiórski, 'Powtórka', pp. 44–45; K. Mrela and J. Zielonka, *The Crisis – Problems in Poland, Part II* (Crises in Soviet-Type Systems Research Project), Cologne: 1986, p. 25.

41 'Widziane', *Tygodnik Solidarności*.

42 A. Smolar, 'Między ugodą a powstaniem', *Aneks*, (1982), p. 15.

43 K. Kostrzewa, 'Ostatni akord, Reportaż z przeszłości', *Nowe Drogi*, August 1983, pp. 58, 66.

44 *Agencja Prasowa Solidarność*, 55, 23–25 November 1981; J. Sobolewski, 'Na taczkach', *Polityka*, 1984, 41.

45 Weydenthal, *Polish Drama*, p. 53.

46 A. K. Wróblewski 'Za ciasno w jednej Polsce', *Polityka*, 1981, 50.

47 *Nowe Drogi*, December 1981, p. 22; 'W stronę więzi trwałych', *Życie Partii*, 1982, 1.

48 *Nowe Drogi*, December 1981, pp. 55, 89, 112.

49 *Ibid.*, pp. 27–28.

50 *Survey*, vol. 26, 3 (1982), p. 7.

51 R. Spielman, 'The eighteenth brumaire of general Wojciech Jaruzelski', *World Politics*, vol. 37, 4 (1985), p. 572.

52 E. Podolska and Z. Imielnicki, 'Spisek przeciwko prawdzie czyli techniki przemocy propagandowej', *Krytyka*, 12 (1983), pp. 86, 89.

53 *Who Pushed Poland to the Brink?*, Moscow: Novosti Press Agency, 1982.

54 *Polityka*, 1982, 1.

55 E. Rozłubirski, 'Strzelałem . . . i do mnie strzelano', *Polityka*, 1986, 17.

56 P. G. Lewis, 'Institutionalisation of the party–state regime in Poland', in *Poland After Solidarity*, ed. Misztal, pp. 51–53.

57 Z. Bauman, 'Bez precedensu', *Aneks*, 32 (1983), p. 38.

58 A. Michnik, 'We are all hostages', *Telos*, 51 (1982), p. 174.

59 *Polityka*, 1983, 12.

60 T. J. Colton, 'The impact of the military on Soviet society', in *The Domestic Context of Soviet Foreign Policy*, ed. S. Bialer, Boulder: Westview Press, 1981, p. 120.

61 A. Perlmutter and W. M. Leogrande, 'The party in uniform: toward a theory of civil–military relations in communist political systems', *American Political Science Review*, vol. 76, 4 (1982), pp. 787–88; *Nowe Drogi*, July 1981, p. 6.

62 J. Rupnik, 'The Polish army and the crisis of the party–state', *Communist Affairs*, vol. 1, 3 (1982), p. 703.

63 R. Spielman, 'Crisis in Poland', *Foreign Policy*, 49 (1982–83), p. 23.

64 D. K. Simes, 'The military and militarism in Soviet society', *International Security*, vol. 6, 3 (1981–82), p. 133.

65 Colton, 'Impact', p. 133; D. Holloway, *The Soviet Union and the Arms Race*, New Haven: Yale University Press, 1984, p. 167.

66 *Polityka*, 1982, 1.

67 R. Łukasiewicz, 'Partia odradza się w działaniu', *Życie Partii*, 1982, 1.

68 H. Mamok, 'Droga do równowagi', *Życie Partii*, 1982, 10; Weydenthal et al, p. 289.

69 E. Jarecki, 'Trzy trudne lata w organizacji partyjnej Stoczni Gdańskiej im. Lenina (1980–1983)', *Nowe Drogi*, September 1983, pp. 64, 70.

70 E. Kijek, 'Idzie nam o spójność ideologiczną', *Życie Partii*, 1983, 21; *Nowe Drogi*, March 1983, p. 196.

71 K. Kostrzewa, 'Po burzy. Trzy podróże do wrocławskiego "Elwro"', *Nowe Drogi*, March 1984, pp. 69, 72.

72 Malcher, *Politicized Army*, pp. 195–96.

73 Łukasiewicz, 'Partia odradza'; *Mały Rocznik Statystyczny*, (Warsaw: Główny Urząd Statystyczny, 1984, p. 18.

74 Łukasiewicz, 'Partia odradza'; *Życie Partii*, 1982, 3.

75 *Uncensored Poland News Bulletin*, 1982, 4.

76 *Nowe Drogi*, March 1982, pp. 7, 61, 110, 143, 184.

77 'Nie zmieniłem poglądów', *Polityka*, 1982, 7.

78 *Polityka*, 1982, 44.

79 *Nowe Drogi*, March 1982, pp. 82, 92, 107, 146; 'From the prisons of Poland', *Dissent*, Winter 1983, p. 62.

80 *Nowe Drogi*, March 1982, pp. 237, 239, 242, 245.

81 Krajowa Konferencja Delegatów PZPR, *Nowe Drogi* 1984 Suplement 2 cz. II, p. 83.

82 *The Guardian*, 18 December 1981; *Kontakt* (Paris), 1 (1982), p. 32.

83 B. Szajkowski, *Next to God . . . Poland*, London: Frances Pinter, 1983, pp. 159–60.

84 Staniszkis, *Self-Limiting*, pp. 320–24.

85 Spielman, 'Crisis', pp. 28, 32; D. S. Mason, 'The Polish party in crisis, 1980–82', *Slavic Review*, vol. 43, 1 (1984), p. 43.

86 Malcher, *Politicized Army*, p. xvi.

87 Michnik, 'We are', p. 181.

88 Davies, *Heart*, pp. 369–70.

89 W. Honkisz, 'Nasze ludowe', *Życie Partii*, 1983, 21.

90 J. Staniszkis, 'Martial law in Poland', *Telos*, 54 (1982/3), p. 95; A. Płatek, 'Wypadek', *Krytyka*, 12 (1983), p. 17.

91 C. D. Jones, 'Soviet hegemony in Eastern Europe', *World Politics*, vol. 29, 2 (1977), p. 226.

92 Ruane, *Polish Challenge*, p. 98; D. A. Andelman, 'Contempt and crisis in Poland', *International Security*, vol. 6, 3 (1981/82), p. 97.

93 Andrews, *Poland*, p. 93; C. Gati, 'The Soviet empire: alive but not well', *Problems of Communism*, vol. 34, 2 (1985), p. 85.

94 Ploss, *Moscow*, p. 41; J. Valenta, 'Revolutionary change, Soviet intervention, and "normalization" in East-Central Europe', *Comparative Politics*, vol. 16, 2 (1984), p. 138.

95 J. Steele, *The Limits of Soviet Power*, Harmondsworth: Penguin, 1985, p. 110.

96 R. D. Anderson, 'Soviet decision-making and Poland', *Problems of Communism*, vol. 31, 2 (1982), p. 30.

97 S. Bratkowski, introduction to *Foksal*, p. 8. Brzezinski has been described as having come 'perilously close to exceeding prudence in personal actions' when he arranged for Solidarity leaders to be briefed in December 1980 and personally contacted the Pope to appraise him of current developments (R. L. Garthoff, 'Eastern Europe in the context of US–Soviet relations', in *Soviet Policy in Eastern Europe*, ed. S. M. Terry, New Haven: Yale University Press, 1984, p. 327).

98 Rupnik, 'Polish army', pp. 701–4; Davies, *Heart*, p. 22.

99 Ash, *Polish Revolution*, p. 95.

100 *Kontakt* (Paris) no. 1 (1982), p. 53; *Sunday Times*, 20 December 1981.

101 C. Barker and K. Weber, *Solidarność: From Gdańsk to Repression*, London: International Socialism, 1982, p. 79; Staniszkis, *Self-Limiting*, p. 321.

102 Ploss, *Moscow*, p. 151.

103 M. Pollack and J. Bugajski, 'Report on Poland', *Encounter*, vol. 58, 1 (1982), pp. 69–70; *Observer* 27 September 1981.

104 R. J. Kukliński, 'Wojna z narodem widziana od środka', *Kultura* (Paris), April 1987, pp. 4–47; C. Kiszczak, 'Bédé rozmawiał z każdym . . .', *Polityka*, 1986, 24.

105 Simes, 'Clash', p. 51.

106 *Nowe Drogi*, March 1982, pp. 128, 143, 159–60; J. Cegła, 'Grudzień, lutej i dalej . . .', *Polityka*, 1982, 3.

107 *Nowe Drogi*, March 1982, pp. 107, 232.

108 *Ibid.*, pp. 245–46; R. Łukasiewicz, 'Sprostać potrzebom ludzi pracy', *Życie Partii*, 1982, 2.

109 *Nowe Drogi*, March 1982, pp. 37, 174–76, 222; M. Skubisz, 'Pierwsze doświadczenia ROPP', *Życie Partii*, 1982, 2.

110 Skubisz, 'Pierwsze'; *Nowe Drogi*, March 1982, p. 150.

111 *Nowe Drogi*, March 1982, pp. 20, 24, 26, 28–29, 54.

112 J. Czuła, 'Kontrola orzecznictwa KKP', *Życie Partii*, 1982, 13.

113 *Polityka*, 1982, 19 and 7.

114 J. Kraszewski, 'Wokół sporów o charakter partii', *Nowe Drogi*, July–August 1982, p. 52.

115 'Kontrola znaczy pomoc', *Życie Partii*, 1982, 10; J. Tittenbrun, 'Klasa, partia, socjalizm', *Nowe Drogi*, July–August 1982, p. 108.

116 A. Wajda, 'Polityczne jutro PZPR', *Nowe Drogi*, July-August 1982, p. 28.

117 A. Walicki, 'The paradoxes of Jaruzelski's Poland', *Archives Européens de Sociologie*, vol. 26 (1985), p. 174.

118 E. Grzelak, 'Lektorat – żywe słowo', *Życie Partii*, 1982, 10; K. Marcinkowski 'Nie "nadsekretarze" . . .', *Życie Partii*, 1982, 5.

119 A. Gostomczyk, 'Organizacja i kierowanie w ROPP', *Życie Partii*, 1982, 6; J. Kubasiewicz, 'Jeden cel – wielość środków, *Życie Partii*, 1982, 8.

120 M. Machura, 'Najważniejsze, że jest potrzebny', *Życie Partii*, 1986, 3; A. Pawłowska and S. Kurcman, 'Inicjatywa wyszła od dołu', *Życie Partii*, 1982, 7.

121 W. Jurczak, 'Czym zamuje się ROPP', *Życie Partii*, 1982, 9; W. Wodecki, 'Łokieć sasiada', *Życie Partii*, 1982, 11.
122 Marcinkowski, 'Nie "nadsekretarze"'; Pawłowska and Kurcman, 'Inicjatywa'.
123 C. M. Hann, *A Village Without Solidarity: Polish Peasants in Years of Crisis*, New Haven: Yale University Press, 1985, p. 83.

7 Political normalisation and party authority

1 Malcher, *Politicized Army*, p. 188.
2 G. Sanford, *Military Rule in Poland*, London: Croom Helm, 1986, pp. 198, 201.
3 J.-Y. Touvais, 'Pologne: la guerre', *L'Alternative*, 19 (1982), p. 9; M. Hirszowicz, *Normalisation in Poland – Has It Progressed?*, Cologne: 'Crisis in Soviet-Type Systems Research Project', dir. Z. Mlynar, 1986, pp. 17–18. Other findings point to the diminished role of local party officials in relation to local government (R. Siemieńska, 'Popular demands and leadership responses in periods of economic retreat: a case study of Poland', in *Local Politics in Poland*: Twenty Years of Research, ed. J. J. Wiatr, Warsaw: University of Warsaw Institute of Sociology, 1984, p. 223) and to the loss by the party of its 'politically specific role' – the party had been suffering a loss of identity before the 1980–81 crisis but after 13 December 1981 was further deprived of its central role in the decision-making process (J. Staniszkis, 'The political articulation of property rights', in *Crisis and Transition: Polish Society in the 1980s*, ed. J. Koralewicz, I. Białecki, and M. Watson, Oxford: Berg, 1987, p. 59).
4 J. Morawski, 'System władzy: kryzys i reprodukcja struktur', *Krytyka*, 15 (1983), p. 68.
5 J. Kowalski and A. Malinowski, 'Pod wojskową dyktaturą: między "zamrożeniem" a "restauracją"', *Krytyka*, 12 (1982), pp. 39–40.
6 Konwersatorium 'Doświadczenie i przyszłość', 'Raport czwarty: Polska wobec stanu wojennego', *Kultura*, July/August 1982, pp. 176, 183.
7 Sanford, *Military Rule*, p. 200; T. Dziekan, 'Polityka kadrowa partii', *Życie Partii*, 1982, 21.
8 E. Lukasik, 'Trzeba mieć odwagé', *Polityka*, 1984, 33.
9 Morawski, 'System władzy', pp. 68–71.
10 Zawodziński, 'Nie zmieniłem'.
11 E. Grzelak, 'Na co czekamy ?', *Życie Partii*, 1982, 7.
12 E. Grzelak, 'W sprawie pilskiej rekontroli', *Życie Partii*, 1982, 13.
13 *Polityka*, 1982, 29.
14 J. Urbański, 'Odzyskiwanie społecznego zaufania', *Nowe Drogi*, November 1982, p. 27.
15 Malcher, *Politicized Army*, p. 189.
16 Misztal and Misztal, 'Transformation', p. 180.
17 K. Turowski, 'Czy narodowi polskiemu grozi upadek?', *Kultura*, December 1982, p. 84.

18 L. Winiarski, 'Rezygnację przyjęto . . .', *Życie Partii*, 1982, 17.
19 K. Morawski, 'Styl funkcjonowania partii', *Życie Partii*, 1982, 19.
20 J. R. Nowak, 'Jak węgry wychodziły z kryzysu', *Polityka*, 1982, 10.
21 T. Szaciło, 'Partia a ruch odrodzenia narodowego', *Życie Partii*, 1982, 8.
    The political implications and significance of these allusions and dis-
    cussion of Hungarian experiences in relation to the Polish context have
    been examined by Z. Gitelman in 'Is Hungary the future of Poland?', *East
    European Politics and Societies*, vol. 1, 1 (1987), pp. 155–59.
22 G. Blazyca, 'Poland's economy under military management', *The World
    Today*, February 1984, p. 59; *Polityka*, 1982, 40.
23 'Dlaczego nie ma samorząd?', *Polityka*, 1982, 19.
24 Konwersatorium 'Doświadczenie i przyszłość', 'Raport czwarty', p.
    157.
25 Bafoil, *Le pouvoir*, pp. 216–217.
26 J. Skir, 'Reforma gospodarcza po roku – kilka refleksji', *Krytyka*, 15 (1983),
    p. 84.
27 K. T. Toeplitz, 'Od sloganów do konkretów', *Polityka*, 1982, 39.
28 A. Halimarski, 'Armia i partia', *Polityka*, 1982, 27.
29 E. Joffe, 'Party and military in China: professionalism in command?',
    Problems of Communism, vol. 32, 5 (1983), pp. 56–58.
30 *Uncensored Poland News Bulletin*, 1982, 8.
31 Szaciło, 'Partia'; Z. Krenz, 'Zdecyduje aktywność POP', *Życie Partii*,
    1982, 10.
32 *Polityka* 1982, 44.
33 *Polityka* 1982, 40.
34 K. Jasiewicz, 'Przemiany świadomości społecznej Polaków 1979–1983',
    Aneks, 32 (1983), p. 137.
35 J. Działłowicki, 'Sondaż', *Krytyka*, 16 (1983), pp. 99–100.
36 K. Mrela, *System's Identity Crisis: Revolt and Normalization in Poland*, Co-
    logne: 'Crisis in Soviet-Type Systems Research Project', dir. Z. Mlyna,
    1986, p. 53.
37 Sanford, *Military Rule*, p. 189.
38 *Polityka* 1983, 31; *Rocznik Statystyczny*, Warsaw: Główny Urząd Statys-
    tyczny Statystyczny, 1985, p. 31.
39 K. Barcikowski, 'Odzyskiwać siły w działaniu', *Życie Partii*, 1982, 14.
40 J. Brożek, 'Nowy sposób myślenia', *Życie Partii*, 1982, 20.
41 E. Grzelak, 'Trzeba wyjść naprzeciw tej większości', *Życie Partii*, 1982, 20.
42 W. Wodecki, 'Prawda przeciw plotce', *Życie Partii*, 1982, 14.
43 'Działać szybko i stanowczo', *Życie Partii*, 1982, 18.
44 G. Pomian, 'Jest taka partia: PZPR', *Kultura*, March 1985, p. 51.
45 Weydenthal, *Polish Drama*, p. 292.
46 E. Grzelak, 'Szybciej iść drogą odrodzenia', *Życie Partii*, 1982, 18.
47 Grzelak, 'Trzeba wyjść'.
48 J. Czuła, 'W trosce o wnioski pokontrolne', *Życie Partii*, 1982, 22.
49 Wodecki, 'Prawda'.
50 *Uncensored Poland News Bulletin*, 1983, 15.

51 *Uncensored Poland News Bulletin*, 1982, 20; Sanford, *Military Rule*, p. 164.
52 *Polityka*, 1982, 39; 'Jedyny sprawiedliwy w Sodomie?', *Życie Partii*, 1982, 22.
53 *Polityka*, 1982, 44.
54 J. Łabęcki, 'Gdybym tak nie postąpił', *Polityka*, 1984, 19.
55 R. Taras, *Ideology in a Socialist State: Poland 1956–1983*, Cambridge: Cambridge University Press, 1984, p. 219.
56 Weydenthal, *Polish Drama*, pp. 292–93.
57 As of July 1983, see *Rocznik Polityczny i Gospodarczy, 1981–1983*, Warsaw: Państwowe Wydawnictwo Ekonomiczne, 1984.
58 Z. Czech, 'W jakim miejscu jesteśmy', *Nowe Drogi*, October 1984, p. 61.
59 *Życie Partii*, 1983, p. 3.
60 *Życie Partii*, 1983, p. 6.
61 *Ibid*; *Polityka*, 1983, 9.
62 *Polityka*, 1983, 9.
63 S. Miśkiewicz, 'Partia i robotnicy', *Życie Partii*, 1983, 5.
64 E. Łukasik 'Można więcej i lepiej', *Życie Partii*, 1983, 15; S. Bejger, 'Zespalanie sił społecznych', *Nowe Drogi*, May 1983, p. 69.
65 E. Mróz, 'Nikt nas nie hołubi', *Życie Partii*, 1983, 3.
66 W. Skrzydło, 'Złapaliśmy oddech', *Życie Partii*, 1983, 7.
67 S. Opałko, 'Zgodnie z linią historycznego zjazdu', *Nowe Drogi*, November/December 1983, pp. 6–7.
68 J. Bijak, 'Nie intencje lecz fakty', *Polityka*, 1983, 36.
69 *Polityka*, 1983, 12.
70 'Na cenzurowanym nie tylko słupskie', *Życie Partii*, 1983, 1.
71 S. Lewicki, 'Z podniewionym czołem', *Życie Partii*, 1983, 2.
72 A. Czarnecki, 'Nie jesteśmy żandarmerią w partii', *Polityka*, 1983, 5.
73 J. Czuła, 'Walka polityczna nie została zawieszona', *Życie Partii*, 1983, 4; 'Orzecznictwo partyjne w ocenie CKKP', *Życie Partii*, 1983, 21.
74 L. Winiarski, 'Krytyczne oczy partii', *Życie Partii*, 1983, 4; *Polityka*, 1983, 36.
75 M. F. Rakowski, 'Zjazd walki i porozumienia,' *Polityka*, 1983, 30.
76 Winiarski, 'Krytyczne oczy'; 'Wnioskowano w kampanii . . .', *Życie Partii*, 1983, 10.
77 W. Cymbała, 'Mniej luzu', *Polityka*, 1983, 9; A. Stasiak, 'Mapa i życie', *Polityka*, 1983, 25.
78 Czuła, 'Walka'; *Polityka*, 1983, 9.
79 G. Mink, 'Poland: double-faced normalisation', Paper delivered to the III World Congress for Soviet and East European Studies, Washington DC, 1985, p. 3; *Polityka* 1983, 22; *Uncensored Poland News Bulletin*, 1983, 10 and 15.
80 *XII Plenum KC PZPR: Podstawowe dokumenty i materiały*, Warsaw: Książka i Wiedza, pp. 31–32, 67; J. Rupnik, 'Soviet adaption to change in Eastern Europe', *Journal of Communist Studies*, vol. 2, 3 (1986), p. 254.
81 D. A. MacGregor, 'Uncertain allies? Eastern European forces in the Warsaw Pact', *Soviet Studies*, vol. 38, 2 (1986), p. 244; C. Rice, *The Soviet*

Union and the Czechoslovak Army, 1948–83, Princeton: Princeton University Press, 1984, p. 221.

82 Taras, *Ideology*, p. 257; J. Staniszkis, 'W trzy lata po Sierpniu', *Krytyka*, 16 (1983), pp. 34, 38.

83 E. Kux, 'Contradictions in Soviet socialism', *Problems of Communism*, vol. 33, 6 (1984), pp. 21, 25.

84 L. Krasucki, 'Nie taka sama', *Polityka*, 1983, 15.

85 M. Szyszko, 'Płaszczyzny jedności w partii', *Nowe Drogi*, May 1983, p. 76; Zey, 'O przyszłości', *Krytyka*, 16 (1983), p. 320.

86 *Polityka*, 1983, 31; M. Karwat and W. Milanowski, 'Dylematy budowy siły partii', *Nowe Drogi*, May 1983, pp. 90–91.

87 M. Mżyk, 'Ożywienie', *Życie Partii*, 1983, 11; L. Jucewicz, 'Co by było, gdyby . . .', *Życie Partii*, 1983, 11; E. Grzelak, 'Co by było, gdyby . . .', *Życie Partii*, 1983, 11.

88 L. Winiarski, 'Ożywienie z minusami', *Życie Partii*, 1983, 16; *XII Plenum*, pp. 63, 66.

89 P. Tymofiejski, 'Instruktor komitetu w działaniu', *Życie Partii*, 1983, 19; Kędzierska *et al.*, 'Smarem'.

90 E. Grzelak, 'Integrować działania', *Życie Partii*, 1983, 19; 'Ignorancja i arogancja często chodzą w parze', *Życie Partii*, 1983, 21.

91 *XIII Plenum KC PZPR: Podstawowe dokumenty i materialy*, Warsaw: Książka i Wiedza, 1983, pp. 21, 62, 68; T. Dziekan, 'Kadry bez tajemnic', *Polityka*, 1983, 47.

92 Z. Szeliga, 'Jest spokój, pora na niespokój', *Polityka*, 1983, 48; W. Wiśniewski, 'Czym jest związek pracowników aparatu', *Życie Partii*, 1984, 1.

93 T. Kołodziejczyk, 'W sprawie aparatu partyjnego', *Życie Partii*, 1983, 20. For the Congress decisions, see *IX Nadzwyczajny Zjazd PZPR: podstawowe dokumenty i materialy*, Warsaw: Książka i Wiedza, 1981, p. 185.

94 Opałko, 'Zgodnie z linią', p. 11; Mróz, 'Nikt nie'.

95 A. Michnik, 'List z Mokotowa – Grudniowe rekolekcje', *Krytyka*, 16 (1983), pp. 16–17.

96 *Polityka* 1984, 3; W. Budziło, 'Walka o jedność partii trwa', *Nowe Drogi*, March 1984, p. 30.

97 *XIII Plenum MC PZPR*, pp. 59, 105; 'Zasadnicze funkcje kampanii', *Życie Partii*, 1983, 23.

98 H. Bednarski, 'Będzie w tym co powiem optymizm', *Polityka*, 1983, 43; *Polityka* 1984, 4.

99 'Wniosków – ciąg dalszy', *Życie Partii*, 1984, 1; *Polityka*, 1984, 8.

100 T. Kołodziejczyk, 'Kilka myśli pod rozwagę', *Życie Partii*, 1984, 4.

101 Lewis, 'Polish party apparatus', pp. 382–83.

102 *Życie Partii*, 1984, 5; *Życie Partii*, 1984, 4.

103 A. Wiśniewski, 'Co partia może załatwić', *Życie Partii*, 1983, 22.

104 F. Ratajczyk, 'Musimy być wszędzie obecni', *Życie Partii*, 1983, 24; M. Wóżniak, 'Niczym nie zastąpi się pracy', *Życie Partii*, 1984, 2.

105 K. Barcikowksi, 'Stan umysłów, stan partii, stan państwa', *Polityka*, 1984, 9.

8 The Polish road to political stability

1 J. Bijak, 'Tworzyć fakty', *Polityka*, 1984, 12; 'Idziemy trudną drogą', *Życie Partii*, 1984, 6.

2 'W pół drogi', *Polityka*, 1984, 11; *Uncensored Poland*, 1984, 6. There did, indeed, seem to be some resistance to these procedures and CC secretary Mokryzyszczak identified some dissatisfaction with the convention of Politburo recommendation to the leading provincial committee post (Hahn, 'Electoral choice', p. 34).

3 *Krajowa Konferencja Delegatów PZPR: podstawowe documenty i materiały*, Warsaw: Książka i Wiedza, 1984, pp. 5, 7, 14–15, 18, 20, 30; *Uncensored Poland*, 1984, 5.

4 *Krajowa Konferencja Delegatów PZPR, Nowe Drogi*, 1984, Suplement 2, cz. 2, pp. 10, 68, 77, 175; H. Jąderko, 'ROPP sprawdziły się w działaniu', *Życie Partii*, 1984, 10; M. Marcinkowski, 'Tam sobie chwalą', *Życie Partii*, 1984, 17.

5 'Idziemy'; *Konferencja*, Suplement 2, pp. 28, 75–76; *IX Nadzwyczajny Zjazd*, p. 184.

6 'Regulamin a konsultacje', *Życie Partii*, 1984, 3; *Konferencja*, p. 107; *Życie Partii*, 1984, 4.

7 Kołodziejczyk, 'Kilka myśli'; *Konferencja*, Suplement 2, pp. 10, 76.

8 'Jak zwiększać skuteczność kontroli', *Życie Partii*, 1984, 1; *Konferencja*, Suplement 2, pp. 99–105.

9 'Partia i demokracja', *Nowe Drogi*, February 1984, p. 19; 'Uwagi o stylu działaniu partii', *Nowe Drogi*, March 1984, p. 47; K. Mżyk, *Centralizm demokratyczny w partii*, Warsaw: Książka i Wiedza, 1984, p. 32.

10 L. Jucewicz, 'A teraz to, co najtrudniejsze', *Życie Partii*, 1984, 8; W. Mokryzyszczak, 'Chcemy mieć partię silną i ofensywną', *Życie Partii*, 1984, 26.

11 A. Wajda and Z. Malak, 'Dlaczego wstępują do PZPR', *Nowe Drogi*, May 1984, p. 76.

12 L. Krasucki, 'Obszar stosunków specjalnych', *Polityka*, 1984, 17.

13 *XVI Plenum KC PZPR, Nowe Drogi* 1984, Suplement 3, pp. 15–16, 72, 75, 99, 136, 219, 369.

14 Pomian, 'Jest taka partia', p. 53; C. Schmidt-Haüer, *Gorbachev: the Path to Power*, London: Pan, 1986, p. 102.

15 *Le Nouvel Observateur*, 9 September 1983; P. Michel and G. Mink, *Mort d'un prêtre, l'affaire Popieluszko*, Mesnil: Fayard, 1985, p. 38; J. Morawski, 'Zabijanie nadziei i wiary', *Krytyka*, 17 (1984), p. 25.

16 P. G. Lewis, 'Turbulent priest – political implications of the Popiełuszko affair', *Politics*, vol. 5, 2 (1985), pp. 34–37.

17 T. Kołodziejczyk, 'Robotnicze opinie kształtują działania partii', *Życie Partii*, 1984, 17.

18 E. Lukasik, 'Trzeba mieć odwagę', *Polityka*, 1984, 33; *Polityka*, 1984, 38.

19 *Życie Partii* 1984, 18; L. Winiarski 'Robotniczym aspiracjom naprzeciw', *Życie Partii*, 1984, 24.

20 *Polityka*, 1984, 42.

21 'Inspekcja robotniczo-chłopska', *Życie Partii*, 1984, 19; J. Oleksy, 'W poszukiwaniu modelu', *Życie Partii*, 1984, 20.

22 M. Wieczorkiewicz, 'W obronie interesów ludzi pracy', *Życie Partii*, 1984, 12.

23 J. Sikorski, 'O wadze inspekcji robotniczo–chłopskiej', *Nowe Drogi*, December 1984, p. 85.

24 'Pierwsze doświadczenia kontroli', *Życie Partii*, 1984, 26; B. Lesiewicz, 'Nadzieje i oczekiwania', *Życie Partii*, 1985, 5.

25 K. Osmólski, 'Aktywność w skali kraju', *Życie Partii*, 1985, 17; E. Grzelak, 'Partia na czele opozycji wobec zła', *Życie Partii*, 1986, 22.

26 Grzelak, 'Partia'; J. Urbański, 'Najbardziej przekonuje osobisty przykład', *Życie Partii*, 1984, 18; *Polityka*, 1984, 41. A little later it was admitted that such forms of 'control' were too dispersed and not effective enough. The workers' and peasants' inspectorates were just not able, it was stated, to satisfy the excessive hopes attached to them (J. Kuciński, 'Doskonalenie systemu politycznego potrzebą casu', *Nowe Drogi*, 1987, September, p. 19).

27 E. Grzelak, 'Postęp nie może przesłaniać braków', *Życie Partii*, 1984, 24; J. Oleksy, 'Instancje bliżej POP', *Życie Partii*, 1985, 22.

28 W. Ossowski, 'Od czego kontrola musi być wolna', *Życie Partii*, 1985, 22.

29 S. Bejger, 'Województwo frontowe', *Polityka*, 1985, 30; *Polityka*, 1985, 13; Staniszkis, 'W trzy lata', p. 34.

30 *Uncensored Poland*, 1985, 15.

31 E. Michaluk, 'Nie ma granic dla wrażliwość,' *Życie Partii*, 1985, 14; 'Reagować szybko na ludzkie skargi', *Życie Partii*, 1985, 16.

32 S. White, 'Political communications in the USSR: letters to party, state and press', *Political Studies*, vol. 31, 1 (1983), pp. 57–60.

33 'Gdy dzieje się krzywda, gdy coś niepokoi', *Życie Partii*, 1986, 8; *Życie Partii*, 1985, 9. Letters sent and appeals made to party bodies in 1986 appeared to be at a lower level, a total of 401,600 being reported, of which 113,000 were made to the provincial committees (A. Przeczek, 'Krytyczna ścieżka listów i skarg', *Życie Partii*, 1987, 8). The address to which letters were sent was also subject to change – the number sent to the Council of State rose by half when Jaruzelski resigned the premiership and moved to head that body. The growing number of appeals made to central bodies was also reported to be interpreted by General Jaruzelski to reflect a lack of popular confidence in the local and intermediate levels of the power apparatus (M. Henzler, 'Osobiste, obywatelskie', *Polityka*, 1987, 20).

34 S. Kwiatkowski, 'Pesymizm – optimizm', *Polityka*, 1985, 32; J. Bijak, 'Spotkanie na największym placy', *Polityka*, 1986, 26.

35 A. Czyż, 'Program w codziennej działalności partii', *Życie Partii*, 1986, 21; M. Henzler, 'Najlepsi czy lojalni', *Polityka*, 1986, 23.

36 T. Czechowicz, 'Polityk odpowiada za skutki', *Polityka*, 1985, 51–52.

37 *Życie Partii*, 1985, 13; 'Musimy służyć ludziom', *Życie Partii*, 1985, 26; *Polityka*, 1986, 5; *Mały Rocznik Statystyczny*, 1987, p. 23.

38 *Życie Partii*, 1986, 7 and 14; 'Członkowie i delegaty', *Polityka*, 1986, 27. Doubt was soon cast on the value of this apparent improvement when it was pointed out that much of the inflow to the party between 1982 and 1986 was attributable to 'campaigning' and that party bodies (particularly

provincial committees) had artificially solicited the applications (W. Milanowski, 'Podstawowe ogniwa partii', *Nowe Drogi*, July 1987, p. 49).

39 *Życie Partii*, 1986, 14; 'Słowa uszą, przykłady przyciągają', *Życie Partii*, 1985, 15; 'Partyjna pryncypialność', *Życie Partii*, 1986, 6.

40 'Reagować szybko i skutecznie', *Życie Partii*, 1985, 20.

41 'Dwoistość aparatu partyjnego', *Nowe Drogi*, June 1985, pp. 125, 130; 'ROPP zdały egzamin', *Życie Partii*, 1985, 3.

42 K. Marcinkowski, '"Do sekretarza rejonowego . . ."', *Życie Partii*, 1985, 15; *Polityka*, 1986, 13.

43 'Drogą IX Zjazdu', *Polityka*, 1986, E. Erazmus, 'Czym jest leninowski styl pracy partyjnej', *Życie Partii*, 1986, 3.

44 *Życie Partii*, 1985, 14; 'Partia wysokich wymagań', *Nowe Drogi*, June 1986, pp. 43–44.

45 *Polityka*, 1986, 8; Z. Rykowski, 'Reguły gry', *Polityka*, 1986, 10.

46 *Życie Partii*, 1986, 1; P. G. Lewis, 'X Congress of the Polish United Workers' Party', *Journal of Communist Studies*, vol. 2, 4 (1986), pp. 432–33.

47 Czechowicz, '*Polityka*; C. Zwara, 'Więcej demokracji – więcej dysypliny', *Życie Partii*, 1986, 18.

48 *Trybuna Ludu*, 29 November 1984; W. Honkisz, 'W dwa lata po przyjęciu "Głównych   założeń polityki kadrowej PZPR"', *Życie Partii*, 1985, 23.

49 'Polityka kadrowa partii', *Nowe Drogi*, 1986 April, pp. 92, 112; E. Mróz 'Kadry – troska, obowiązek, odpowiedzialność, *Życie Partii*, 1986, 18.

50 'Partia wysokich wymagań', p. 34; Malcher, *Politicized Army*, p. 208; 'Polityka kadrowa partii', pp. 104–8.

51 E. Erazmus, 'Klasowe treści polityki kadrowej', *Nowe Drogi*, September 1984, pp. 50–51; Erazmus, 'Dwoistość, p. 131.

52 'Polityka kadrowa partii', pp. 90, 103; J. Gałęba, 'Partyjna powinność', *Nowe Drogi*, March 1985, p. 52.

53 J. Nowak, 'Czas nie leczy', *Polityka*, 1984, 22; *Życie Partii*, 1985, 13.

54 Honkisz, 'W dwa lata'; Kędzierska, 'Smarem'; 'Czas herosów już minął', *Polityka*, 1986, 25.

55 Z. Niemiński, 'Przewodzić, kierować, służyć', *Nowe Drogi*, October 1986, p. 48; J. Baryła, 'Decydująca faza', *Życie Partii*, 1986, 23.

56 H. Bednarski, 'Przewodnia, kierownicza i służebna rola partii', *Życie Partii*, 1987, 1.

57 'Dyskusja nad perspektywicznym programem PZPR', *Nowe Drogi*, May 1985, pp. 47, 54, 58, 62.

58 Walicki, 'Paradoxes', p. 191; J. Milewski *et al.*, 'Poland: four years after', *Foreign Affairs*, vol. 64, 2 (1985/86), p. 343.

59 J. Janicki, 'Ranga i najważniejsze zadania edukacji politycznej w partii', *Nowe Drogi*, October 1985, p. 29.

60 'W sprawie sojuszniczego sposobu sprawowania władzy', *Nowe Drogi*, January 1986, pp. 149–50.

61 M. Machura, 'Nie dawać się unosic dowolnym nurtom', *Życie Partii*, 1986, 12.

62 Lewis, 'X Congress'; *Polityka* 1986, 46; J. Baryła, 'Decydująca faza', *Życie*

Partii, 1986, 23. Nevertheless, of the 265 secretaries proposed for election during the autumn 1986 provincial conferences 9 were not confirmed by the delegates and further elections had to be arranged (*Polityka*, 1986, 45).

9 Conclusion

1 Sanford, 'Poland', pp. 59–60; J. Kowalski and A. Malinowski, 'Normalizacja, przetrwanie i kilka innych uwagi', *Krytyka*, 17 (1984), p. 16.
2 W. Kinecki, 'Dwuzawodowiec', *Polityka*, 1987, 15.
3 Kędzierska *et al.*, 'Smarem'. In Skierniewice, newly appointed first KW secretary L. Miller announced that the executive was proposing a 40% reduction in the *nomenklatura* of the provincial committee. This meant the withdrawal of KW responsibility for posts which did not have significance for the whole province or which were already under the supervision of the provincial governor (L. Miller, 'Partia czasu reform', *Polityka*, 1987, 34).
4 W. Markiewicz, 'Też mam kaca', *Polityka*, 1987, 16; J. Fasztyn, 'Szok', *Nowe Drogi*, March 1987, p. 127.
5 M. Henzler, 'Układanka', *Polityka*, 1986, 44; 'Nie bronimy naszych stołków', *Polityka*, 1987, 5.
6 *Rzeczpospolita*, 16 April 1987; S. Szczerba, 'Powinności aparatu partyjnego', *Życie Partii*, 1987, 8.
7 Z. Rola, 'Parawany', *Polityka*, 1987, 19.
8 *Życie Partii*, 1986, 27.
9 *Życie Partii*, 1986, 24. The overall staffing level of the party apparatus had nevertheless continued to rise slightly above the totals announced in 1981. By 1987 it stood at the level of 13 thousand political workers (*Życie Partii*, 1987, 11).
10 M. Henzler, 'Fotografia sekretarzy', *Polityka*, 1986, 45. Not all KW first secretaries had degrees at the time of their appointment, but in late 1986 48 of the 49 provincial leaders had completed some course of higher education while one was still in the process of completing his.
11 M. Henzler, 'Fotografia wojewodów', *Polityka*, 1987, 7.
12 Henzler, 'Fotografia sekretarzy', 'Fotografia wojewodów'.
13 Henzler, 'Fotografia sekretarzy'.
14 Kinecki, 'Dwuzawodowiec'.
15 Henzler, 'Fotografia sekretaryzy'.
16 Henzler, 'Fotografia wojewodów'.
17 Kędzierska *et al.*, 'Smarem'.
18 Rola, 'Parawany'.
19 *Życie Partii*, 1987, 11.
20 Ibid.; M. Henzler, 'Wyżej niż siódme', *Polityka*, 1987, 22.
21 *Polityka*, 1987, 22.
22 Henzler, 'Wyżej'; *Życie Partii*, 1987, 11.
23 *Uncensored Poland*, 1987, 10.
24 D. Passent, 'Program na żywo', *Polityka*, 1987, 11.
25 *The Observer*, 1 March 1987.

The following series titles are now out of print: